The Development of Expressive Behavior

BIOLOGY–ENVIRONMENT INTERACTIONS

COMMUNICATION AND BEHAVIOR

AN INTERDISCIPLINARY SERIES

Under the Editorship of **Duane M. Rumbaugh**

**Georgia State University and Yerkes Regional
Primate Research Center of Emory University**

DUANE M. RUMBAUGH (ED.), LANGUAGE LEARNING BY A CHIMPANZEE: THE LANA PROJECT. 1977

ROBERTA L. HALL AND HENRY S. SHARP (EDS.), WOLF AND MAN: EVOLUTION IN PARALLEL. 1978

HORST D. STEKLIS AND MICHAEL J. RALEIGH (EDS.), NEUROBIOLOGY OF SOCIAL COMMUNICATION IN PRIMATES: AN EVOLUTIONARY PERSPECTIVE. 1979

P. CHARLES-DOMINQUE, H. M. COOPER, A. HLADIK, C. M. HLADIK, E. PAGES, G. F. PARIENTE, A. PETTER-ROUSSEAUZ, J. J. PETTER, AND A. SCHILLING (EDS.), NOCTURNAL MALAGASY PRIMATES: ECOLOGY, PHYSIOLOGY, AND BEHAVIOR. 1980

JAMES L. FORBES AND JAMES E. KING (EDS.), PRIMATE BEHAVIOR. 1982

DONALD E. KROODSMA AND EDWARD H. MILLER (EDS.), ACOUSTIC COMMUNICATION IN BIRDS, VOLUME 1: PRODUCTION, PERCEPTION, AND DESIGN FEATURES OF SOUNDS. 1983. VOLUME 2: SONG LEARNING AND ITS CONSEQUENCES. 1983

GAIL ZIVIN (ED.), THE DEVELOPMENT OF EXPRESSIVE BEHAVIOR: BIOLOGY-ENVIRONMENT INTERACTIONS. 1985

The Development of Expressive Behavior

BIOLOGY–ENVIRONMENT INTERACTIONS

Edited by
Gail Zivin

Department of Psychiatry and Human Behavior
Jefferson Medical College of Thomas Jefferson University
Philadelphia, Pennsylvania

1985

ACADEMIC PRESS, INC.

(Harcourt Brace Jovanovich, Publishers)

Orlando San Diego New York London
Toronto Montreal Sydney Tokyo

ACADEMIC PRESS, INC.
Orlando, Florida 32887

United Kingdom Edition published by
ACADEMIC PRESS INC. (LONDON) LTD.
24/28 Oval Road, London NW1   7DX

Library of Congress Cataloging in Publication Data

Main entry under title:

The Development of expressive behavior.

  (Communication and behavior)
  Includes index.
  1. Expression. 2. Expression--Genetic aspects.
3. Expression in children. 4. Infant psychology.
I. Zivin, Gail, Date   . II. Series.
BF588.D48 1984   156'.36   84-12397
ISBN 0-12-781780-8 (alk. paper)

PRINTED IN THE UNITED STATES OF AMERICA

85 86 87 88   9 8 7 6 5 4 3 2 1

*For my parents
who indicated the road
and for Craig
who leveled the bumps*

Contents

9. Expression as Action: A Motor Perspective of the Transition
   from Spontaneous to Instrumental Behaviors
   Esther Thelen

10. Coordinative Structures in the Development of Expressive Behavior
    in Early Infancy
    Alan Fogel

Contributors

Numbers in parentheses indicate the pages on which the authors' contributions begin.

Margarita Azmitia (319), Institute of Child Development, University of Minnesota, Minneapolis, Minnesota 55455

Pamela M. Cole (269), Department of Psychology, University of Houston, Houston, Texas 77004

Kim G. Dolgin (319), Institute of Child Development, University of Minnesota, Minneapolis, Minnesota 55455

Saul Feinman (291), Department of Sociology, University of Wyoming, Laramie, Wyoming 82071

Alan Fogel (249), Department of Child Development and Family Studies, Purdue University, West Lafayette, Indiana 47907

Harold Gouzoules[1] (77), Field Research Center for Ecology and Ethology, Rockefeller University, Millbrook, New York 12545

Sarah Gouzoules[2] (77), Field Research Center for Ecology and Ethology, Rockefeller University, Millbrook, New York 12545

Robert A. Hinde (103), M.R.C. Unit on the Development and Integration of Behaviour, Madingley, Cambridge CB3 8AA, England

Michael Lewis (153), Department of Pediatrics, University of Medicine and Dentistry of New Jersey, Rutgers Medical School, New Brunswick, New Jersey 08903

Carol Zander Malatesta (183), The Graduate Faculty, New School for Social Research, New York, New York 10011

[1]Present address: Department of Psychology, Emory University, Atlanta, Georgia 30322.
[2]Present address: Yerkes Regional Primate Research Center, Lawrenceville, Georgia 30245.

Peter Marler (77), Field Research Center for Ecology and Ethology, Rockefeller University, Millbrook, New York 12545

William A. Mason (117), Department of Psychology, University of California at Davis, Davis, California 95616

Linda Michalson (153), Department of Pediatrics, University of Medicine and Dentistry of New Jersey, Rutgers Medical School, New Brunswick, New Jersey 08903

William Montgomery[3] (27), Library of the American Philosophical Society, Philadelphia, Pennsylvania 19106

W. John Smith (51), Department of Biology, Leidy Laboratory, University of Pennsylvania, Philadelphia, Pennsylvania 19104

Esther Thelen (221), Department of Psychology, University of Missouri at Columbia, Columbia, Missouri 65211

Gail Zivin (3), Department of Psychiatry and Human Behavior, Jefferson Medical College, Thomas Jefferson University, Philadelphia, Pennsylvania 19107

---

[3]Present address: School-Within-the-School, State University College of Arts and Science, Potsdam, New York 13676.

Preface

This volume brings together categories that traditionally have subdivided, rather than enriched, the understanding of expressive behavior and its development. Chief among these distinctions are human and nonhuman, emotion and behavior, emotion and cognition, innate and socialized. This book grew out of the challenge to each contributor to articulate at least one aspect of how biology and environment interact in the development of expressive behavior. Across their diverse disciplines of developmental psychology, ethology, primatology, history, and sociology, the contributors share the convictions that expression, expressive behavior, and other communicative behaviors have been treated too simply and that we now know enough to clarify the surrounding issues and to delineate specific features of biology–environment coaction in the development of expressive behavior. The contributors are also consistent in applying these issues and features, with differing emphases, to both humans and nonhumans. This reflects their reasoned attribution of increased cognitive functioning, social learning, and protocultural performance to nonhuman animals and human infants. The authors further concur on many features of the general form that biology–environment interactions take over the course of an organism's development. In proposing their approximations to this form, the chapters coincide in noting confluences of elements that are traditionally opposed to one another.

The unifying ideas that this book presents are not so developed or explicitly integrated as to be one theory of expressive behavior development. Rather, these unities are hypotheses and starting assumptions:

agreement on the old issues and metaphors that must be left behind; a reconceptualization of the purposive, instrumental, and cognitively loaded nature of behaviors that had previously been considered "merely" expressive in humans and nonhumans; a general approach to biology–environment interaction in expressive behavior development; a general view of the course of expressive behavior development in humans; and a set of processes that contribute to the socialization of human expressive behavior. In the organization of the book, the reader finds detailed focus on the first two points in the chapters in Part I, explication of the last two points in Part II, and agreement on the general shape of biology–environment interaction throughout.

In constructing this volume, it has been of major importance to make explicit and easily available the concurrences and contacts across the chapters. The aim has been a coherent work that consistently and evenly illuminates each chapter's contribution to a more unified and complex understanding of expressive behavior development. The chapter authors were selected to present their areas of concern. Those areas, as uniquely approached by their authors, combine to form a new, rich picture of expressive behavior development. The coherence across chapters is emphasized for the reader in two ways: (1) through an initial framing chapter, which outlines the old issues that the chapters challenge, and which suggests the newer views to which they subscribe; and (2) through brief introductions that relate each chapter to the larger issues in the field, to the specific issues noted in the framing chapter, to the view of biology–environment interaction that the chapter exemplifies, and to important similarities and contrasts with other chapters. Although the seed for this work grew from a symposium presented jointly by the Ninth International Congress of Primatology and the International Meeting of the International Society for Human Ethology, and although the core of four chapters started there, particular care has been taken to avoid the variability and lack of cumulative coherence found in many current scholarly anthologies. The chapters were preconceived and specifically written and rewritten for this book, guided by a unified view of the issues that needed to be raised and by the specific developmental processes that needed to be explicated.

This work does not emphasize theories of emotion, although most chapters consider the relationship of emotional state to expressive behavior. It is nevertheless interesting to note that this book unites the approaches to emotion that Averill asserted (*American Psychologist*, December, 1983) as the two new—and mutually resistant—viewpoints on emotion in the 1980s: the "biologically based theories with an emphasis on expressive reactions" and those with a more social orientation (pp.

1145–1146). It is the uniting, the crossing of old boundaries to present empirically justified conceptions of a more complex phenomenon, that is the goal of this work.

Much of the thinking that resulted in this book took place when I was supported by a grant from the Harry Frank Guggenheim Foundation. I am grateful to the colleagues whose conversation and critiques helped shape my thinking for this work. I wish to thank those friends here, while assuming myself responsibility for any errors that may have occurred in the structuring of this book. My sincere appreciation is extended to Herbert M. Adler, Klaus E. Grossmann, Robert A. Hinde, Carol Z. Malatesta, W. John Smith, and Laurence J. Stettner.

PART I

Issues in Biology-Environment Interactions in Expressive Development

Chapter 1

Separating the Issues in the Study of Expressive Development: A Framing Chapter

Gail Zivin

Relationship to Other Chapters and to the Field

Relationship to the Field

This chapter provides a frame of major issues in the field of expressive behavior development, through which the other chapters in this volume may be viewed with consistency. Two very general issues that encompass other major ones are selected to structure this frame: (1) difficulties in defining the characteristics of expressive behavior due to assumed consequences of its innate features, and (2) conceptions of biology-environment interaction that look beyond previous dualistic thinking on expression and its development. The more specific issues (such as the degree and breadth of linkage between states and expressive behaviors, the theoretical and empirical specification of the referent of an expressive behavior, and the methodological choices in studying the phenomenon) that are subsumed under these broader topics are indicated in the framing chapter.

Besides presenting these framing issues, this first chapter specifies terminology for the volume, pointing out its commonality and variance with language use in the field. It also compares the other chapters' views on these issues and points out the general model of expressive behavior development they suggest.

Brief chapter introductions, parallel in form to this one, precede each chapter. The particular relationships of a chapter to the important issues in the field are indicated in this first section of the chapter introduction.

THE DEVELOPMENT OF EXPRESSIVE BEHAVIOR:
BIOLOGY-ENVIRONMENT INTERACTIONS

3

Relationship to Other Chapters

This section of the chapter introductions specifically compares and contrasts the chapters—the positions they take and the data they present. These include the several issues noted in the framing chapter but usually go beyond them to particular specialized issues that two or more chapters jointly address. These comparisons and contrasts are not in the framing chapter.

For Consistent Terminology

This last section of the chapter introductions clarifies meanings if a chapter uses terms in ways that vary from generally applicable definitions or from common uses of other terms.

This framing chapter presents the definitions of the key terms that are used throughout this volume and that often cause confusion: expression, expressive behavior, signal, index, sign, icon, symbol, referent, epigenesis, genetic assimilation, Baldwin effect, and so forth.—ED.

Introduction

How do I let you know how I feel? Is it what I truly feel? By what course have I come to be able to show feelings that we both think reflect my reaction to an event? How are you able to interpret signals of my true state? Of my deception? What does our relationship contribute to this interplay of signaling and interpreting, and how does this interplay influence our relationship?

These are questions of expressive-behavior development. They are also questions of mutual interpretation, of relationship building, and even of mind–body dualism. This book stays within the first realm, using psychological and biological approaches to emphasize the first three questions. It is organized around the third question and thoroughly examines innate and experimental influences on the development of expressive-behavior production. It often considers but does not emphasize the related processes of emotional development and interpersonal relationship.

The aim of this chapter is to frame the entire volume. It does this by clarifying issues within the limited perspective just described and by indicating how the chapters that follow illuminate them. The present chapter focuses these issues through two broad areas: (1) characteristics from innateness confusingly attributed to expressive behavior, and (2) broadened conceptions of biology-environment interactions in expressive-behavior development.

Let us first specify what we mean by expressive behavior. *Expressive behavior* is the behavior component of what is commonly called expression. *Expression* involves behaviors emitted by an individual that are interpreted—inferentially or automatically, rightly or wrongly—to convey information about the internal state of that individual. Expression therefore assumes some relationship between an inner state and the behavior that accompanies it. Because the assumption of state is controversial, the term *expressive behavior* is used to refer to behavior that is often interpreted as expressive of state without implying that it is indeed state related. The assumption of a state is not universal, however. Since the 1960s (Schacter & Singer, 1962), a more social–psychological view has asserted that the central fact of emotion is appraisal of one's circumstances such that one attributes an emotion to oneself, usually in conjunction with a condition of nonspecific physiological arousal. Specific emotional states have no place in this view except, perhaps, as secondary effects of arousal-plus-emotion attribution. Recent work, however, supplies serious evidence for autonomic differentiation between basic emotions in adults (Ekman, Levenson & Friesen, 1983). When the behavioral aspect need not be so carefully emphasized, the terms *expression* and *expressive behavior* are interchangeable.

It was a nineteenth-century commonplace accepted by Darwin that a person's demeanor expressed his or her moods, motivations, and emotions, and also indicated the person's moral character. Current researchers of expressive behavior agree that some behaviors do convey an individual's emotion, mood, and immediate motivational tendency. Most also agree that some intricate combination of processes combines biological propensity with social learning to yield an adult who is capable generally of inhibiting, modifying, or feigning expressive behavior in culturally appropriate circumstances. They may disagree, however, on the degree of biological inheritance or learning and on the nature of the processes that influence expressive behavior—its eliciting conditions, its consonance with the state it supposedly expresses, and an observer's interpretation of it. And they might disagree on the specific processes by which these biological propensities interact with social-learning phenomena to produce an expressively sophisticated adult. This last is still rare, as researchers are only beginning to consider the details of the interaction of biology and environment in expressive development.

Despite some disagreements on the roles of specific variables and on how relatively active or pervasive biological and environmental factors might be, the contributions to this volume that describe human behavior can be encompassed by one general model of expressive-behavior development. This model sees the infant's expressive states and behaviors as initially—if briefly—determined by biological factors, which progressively loosen their influence as the infant, by maturational schedule, becomes increasingly influenced by environmental factors, which become pervasive by adolescence. The hereditary opens to the experiential, as variables from each source run in parallel and dovetail at key points. This description specifies, for expressive-behavior development, the model of general biology–environment interaction in individual development that the last section of this chapter cites as most frequently assumed by current developmental theorists. The goal of this volume is to illuminate this general model and to fill it in with specific processes and variables.

Characteristics of Expressive Behavior Associated with Innateness

The Problematic Dichotomies

Most researchers in the field of expressive development assume some genetic contribution to at least some expressive behaviors. This link to innateness creates several hidden issues in expressive-behavior development: the assumed characteristics of expression itself. Western culture is laden with old and pervasive assumptions about the duality of innate versus learned behavior, particularly expressive behavior. This is a primary dichotomy in received Western thinking, and as shown below, it generates related dichotomies of thought. The existence of the dichotomies in themselves is not the only problem for clear thinking on expressive behavior. Another is the tradition—now only beginning to be broken by such researchers as those noted in this chapter—that assumes that all human and nonhuman expressive behavior can be characterized only by one side of these polarities. As these assumptions are often vague, in the manner of received tradition, they do not easily present themselves to researchers' awareness for explicit examination or report: several were explicated by Buck as recently as 1982. He incorporated the dichotomies that were asserted (Osgood & Sebeok, 1954, p. 76) and that were then extensively qualified by Sebeok (1963). Old polarized thinking resists change, and therefore deserves further exposure.

The treatments of interactions that contributors to this book present here represent their current resolutions of such dichotomies. Hinde's (Chapter 5, this volume) continuum from expression to negotiation is a seminal reconceptualization toward such a resolution. However, Mason (Chapter 6, this volume), Feinman (Chapter 12, this volume), perhaps Lewis and Michalson (Chapter 7, this volume), and also Smith (Chapter 3, this volume) hold views that circumvent these dichotomies. The first four share the social–psychological view that sees a socially learned interpretation of circumstance and of attribution to self, rather than a biologically based state, as central to the experience of emotion. Smith's view is more biological, but he sees the internal condition of a *signaler* as, by definition, a physiological–motivational correlate of the signaling action, rather than as an isolatable emotional state. Several contributors have also found Ekman's neurocultural model of emotion and expressive behavior (Ekman, 1977) useful in formulating interactive conceptions that minimize dualistic thinking.

Obstacles to clarifying one's assumptions about the characteristics of expressive behavior arise because many supposed features of expressive behavior are best analyzed through the concepts of other disciplines: questions of the origins, consequences, and variabilities of innateness require the study of animal behaviorists, ethologists, and evolutionary biologists; questions of how expressive signal systems can work require the technical concepts of semioticians; questions of the variability and fit of such systems in social structures require the knowledge of anthropologists, sociologists, and comparative animal behaviorists. Each of these specialties works from its own perspective, hindering cross-discipline clarification and accumulation of knowledge.

Because of all these problems, it is worthwhile to specify the features that may be unquestioningly attributed to expressive behavior. The ease with which simple antitheses are assumed reflects the degree to which our thinking is influenced by the global duality in late nineteenth-century ideas about innateness and naturalness. Darwin argued, in 1872, that (many) human expressive behaviors arise through evolution, are genetically inherited, and are innately linked to internal states. This has often been interpreted by contemporary theorists to suggest that all expressive behaviors are either fundamentally innate or fundamentally learned. As we see in this chapter and throughout this volume, the newest understanding of animal communication and infant interactions should prevent simple attribution of either extreme to all expressive behaviors. Some innate features apply to some expressive behaviors or to some points in development, and the same complexity is true for learned features.

The duality between innate- and learned-expressive behaviors suggests antitheses between other features associated with them. Innate-expressive behaviors are assumed to be more reliable, or more *veridical*, indicators of state than the potentially *nonveridical* ones that are learned. Furthermore, by analogy with the older view of involuntary instinctive behavior, innate behaviors are thought to be unintentional, or *spontaneous*—the opposite of intentional, *instrumental* action. Only one or the other side of these dichotomies is usually assumed as fundamental to all expressive behaviors: innate versus learned, spontaneous versus instrumental, and veridical versus nonveridical.

Two other pairs of polar characteristics become associated with naive human-expressive behavior when it is analyzed as a form of innate animal communication. Although with newer animal studies (e.g. Griffin, 1981; de Waal, 1978), it is becoming clear that not even untrained animal communication can always be characterized by only one side of these oppositions. Once again, however, there is a tradition of one-sided attribution to expressive behavior that requires that each side be clarified.

The first of these two polar pairs is most apparent to those interested in the phylogenetic origins of expressive behavior. It is important here because nonbiologists tend to characterize expressive behavior by one pole without, perhaps, intending its evolutionary implications. The distinction between the sides of this first pair reflects the differences between traditional ethology's conception of the evolutionary origins of expressive behaviors and Darwin's conception. Ethologists since Huxley (1923) and Tinbergen (1951) have termed animal communication behavior as *display behavior* when that communication behavior is believed to have become specialized through evolutionary natural selection for its communication properties. Such specialization occurs when natural selection repeatedly selects only those forms that best facilitate particular communication functions, as when a behavior is exaggeratedly noticeable. This specialization is called *ritualization* (Huxley, 1923). Darwin, however, saw even exaggeratedly noticeable expressive behavior as often inherited for noncommunicative functions (for example, blushing as a by-product of inherited thermoregulation) and not as inherited because of its communication function. (See Montgomery, Chapter 2, this volume, for a thorough treatment of Darwin's interpretation of the inheritance of expressive behaviors and of how this differs from his natural selection view of the evolution of other behaviors and of morphological structures.) Although most of the spectacular forms of animal signals do seem to be displays in this evolutionary sense, other unspecialized animal behaviors are recently being shown to be communicative (see Menzel & Halpern, 1975) and perhaps even expressive (see Mason,

Chapter 6, this volume). Thus, not all animal expression is by evolutionarily specialized display behavior, and not all human expression should be assumed to be.

For developmentalists there are two implications of this distinction between display and nondisplay behaviors. First, the term *display* has come to be used so generally in the discussion of interpersonal signals that it is useful to recall that it means more than a genetically inherited communication behavior. Its original meaning is based on an evolutionary criterion that cannot be assessed by observing current behavior patterns. Second, display behavior, selected as it is by evolution, implies a fairly high degree of evolutionary specialization of the observer's interpretation of the display. To call a behavior a display is to make claims about the conspecifics' interpretation capacities. For both these reasons, display versus nondisplay is another antithesis worth noting when characterizing expressive behavior.

The second dichotomy made notable by the assumed identity of human expression and animal communication involves the referent of the communicative behavior. By *referent* is meant the traditional semiotic concept of that to which a signal points. *Signal* is used here and throughout this volume as a completely unspecified type of indicator. It is synonymous with *cue* when the signal is produced in interpersonal interaction. Specified types of signals are *index*, which occurs when the signal is attached in some natural way to its referent—as a higher pitch in voice is attached to emotional arousal; *icon* or *sign*, which occurs when the signal resembles its referent—as motions of eating refer to eating or food; and *symbol*, which occurs when the relationship between signal and referent is arbitrary and created by the consensus of the community that assigns this relationship—as words refer only by the community's agreement on their meaning. These traditional semiotic terms, in slight variation on Peirce's founding definitions (Gallie, 1966, pp. 116–117), are used with these meanings throughout this book.[1] Smith, Chapter 3

[1]Some expansion of these meanings appears in this book. Smith (see Chapter 3, this volume) means exactly this traditional definition of *referent* but employs the potentially different-seeming defining phrase, "that information which a signal makes available." In order to emphasize that the features of the honeybee dance have external reference to the pollen source and physically bear little simple iconic relationship to it, Gouzoules, Gouzoules, and Marler (Chapter 4, this volume) describe the dance as a symbol type of signal. This use of *symbol*, now common in discussing the complex signal process of the honeybee's dance, relies on Morris's semiotic definition of a symbol: "a sign of another sign," in which *sign* is a generically unspecified signal type and not an icon (e.g., Griffin, 1976, p. 24). Others argue that the similarities of dance features (e.g., the direction and length of the flight path to the pollen) indicate a complex set of icons and not true symbols; still

in this volume, reviews in detail the semiotic distinctions that are necessary for clear thinking on these and other problems of animal and human nonverbal communication.

The determination of the referent of an animal signal was for a long time rather uncontroversial. Since the 1960s, Sebeok (e.g., 1962) has been an influential codifier of features that distinguish between verbal (human linguistic) and nonverbal (animal and human bodily) signals. Building on and qualifying Kroeber's distinction (1952) that nonhuman signs convey emotion and human speech conveys cognitive information, Sebeok put forth (1962) what was believed by most theorists of animal and human communication at the time: that innate animal signals—and by extension, human nonverbal ones—usually refer to internal states of the signaling organism. These signaled states were either emotions or motivational action tendencies. (Ethology's current emphasis [Smith, 1977, and Chapter 3, this volume] on motivations rather than on emotions as signal referents allows sharper behavioral measurement of animal reference.) Whereas traditional ethology since the 1920s has included the possibility of an animal signal referring to an external referent, as in the case of the honeybee dance, it did not have a well-analyzed stance on the possibilities and criteria of reference. The idea that signals are naturally attached to the organism's states coincides with the Darwinian view of the matter: expressive behaviors are inherited as behavioral accompaniments to internal motivational and emotional conditions. It also corresponds to the widely held Western view articulated by Freud (1924, pp. 36–44), who asserted that our true feelings are revealed in unguarded expressive behaviors that refer to them and to the emotion-producing thought behind them. A large and influential body of received ideas, then, suggests that the referent of innate signals must be some concurrent state of the signaler. In the face of arguments, presented subsequently, that there may be times when there is no state to which an expression may refer and that some animals may be geneti-

---

others argue that there can be no symbol unless its meaning can be arbitrarily changed by the community. Lewis and Michalson (see Chapter 7, this volume) broaden the use of *sign* and *symbol*. They use *sign* for both *index* and *icon*, as do other analysts who define iconicity to include a physical link (Sebeok, 1967), or who contrast *sign*, used for emotional referents, with *symbol*, used for more cognitive referents (Kroeber, 1952). Lewis and Michalson emphasize by using the term *symbol*, that the form or use of an emotional expression can be learned and thus can be a false indication of state; by this, they point to the nonnecessary, arbitrary link of a signal and a state. They ignore the origin of the expressive behavior as possibly having been an index before it became unattached from an accompanying state and then used as a socially controlled signal.

cally programmed to refer dishonestly to their motivational state, and in light of new evidence that external reference by animals may be much more common than previously thought, it becomes of some interest to note the dichotomy, *self-reference versus external reference*. This is almost synonymous with the traditional distinction of *emotional versus cognitive*.

Table 1 collects these dichotomies in an attempt to summarize the two columns of extreme features that have been erroneously, when exclusively and undiscriminatingly, attributed to expressive behaviors. The table thus points up the features that, it is argued in the next section, should no longer be assumed globally to characterize expressive behavior, whether human or nonhuman. Each behavior must be explicitly characterized on (either pole of) these dichotomies, and that characterization may have to change with age.

Collapsing the Dichotomies

The error in the use of these dichotomies is the exclusive and global attribution of one side, usually the innate, left-hand pole, to naive human-expressive behavior and to animal communication as its assumed analogue. To show that these terms do not characterize all of animal communication is also to argue that they may not characterize all naive human-expressive communication. A few persuasive examples of animal communication that do not fit these features suffice to explode this package attribution to both animal and human nonverbal communicative behaviors.

Since the mid-1970s, examples of animal communication that possess elements of the noninnate side of these dichotomies have been mounting. Extremely telling are observations by Menzel (Menzel, 1974; Menzel & Halpern, 1975), who found that chimpanzees that know the location

TABLE 1

Problematic Dichotomies Associated with Expressive Behavior

Expressive behavior feature	Dichotomies	
Origin of signal	Innate	Learned
Motivation for signal	Spontaneous	Instrumental
Indication of state by signal	Veridical	Nonveridical
Specialization for communication	Display	Nondisplay
Relationship of referent to signaler	Self-reference	External reference
Category of reference	Emotional	Cognitive

of a desired object in the open field will inhibit giving behavioral cues of its location—for example, by not glancing toward the object—and will later sneak back to retrieve it. This is an example of an experientally *learned instrumental* inhibition of the *nondisplay* but is a communicative and potentially expressive act of glancing. The nonglance conveys no veridical information about the chimpanzee's state of knowledge or desire about the object, and its looking in other directions could provide *nonveridical* information in reference to the *external* environment. Many other examples of similarly complex, nonstereotypic social communications in animals are accumulating. (See de Waal [1978] for clever affiliation strategies and Dawkins and Krebs [1978] for animal deception.) In this volume, Mason (see Chapter 6) reviews evidence that monkeys learn to produce and to interpret cues as the result of experience; Hinde (see Chapter 5, this volume) analyzes animal interactions as blending spontaneous and instrumental signal productions in negotiations rather than in set display exchanges; and Gouzoules, Gouzoules, and Marler (see Chapter 4, this volume) review evidence for animals' external reference, indicating that *both emotional and cognitive* elements occur in mammals' external reference.

Although it would strengthen the argument against assigning only one side of the dichotomies to nonverbal-communicative behaviors, it hardly seems necessary to review other violations of the common oppositions: that animals can learn symbols and that human expressive behavior comes under the control of learning. The Rumbaughs have demonstrated that chimpanzees can nontrivially use computer-generated symbols (Savage-Rumbaugh, Rumbaugh, & Boysen, 1978) and incidentally observed symbols (Savage-Rumbaugh, 1983). The Premacks have convincingly analyzed the abstract-cognitive capacities that chimpanzees can display in carefully constructed logical tasks using plastic chips as learned symbols: reading (Premack, 1976), abstract problem solving (Premack & Woodruff, 1978), and achieving primitive mathematical concepts (Woodruff & Premack, 1981). Conversely, it is well-known—but only clearly documented in the 1980s—that humans modify their production of possibly innate-expressive behaviors through reinforcement contingencies (examples are in Malatesta, Chapter 8, this volume, Lewis & Michalson, 1983), by learning display rules (Cole, Chapter 11, this volume), in learned deception (DePaulo & Jordan, 1982), and in learned interpretation of them (Dolgin & Azmitia, Chapter 13, this volume). Clearly, neither human-expressive behaviors nor the innate capacities of animals for communication and communicative cognition can be adequately characterized by the terms on only one side of the associated dichotomies.

Appearance of the Dichotomies in Research Questions

Much of the research on expressive behavior and its development is motivated by these problematic dichotomies. Many studies attempt to document the existence of innate-expressive components and to understand their contribution to enculturated human life. Examples are work to identify the innate facial patterns of infants (Izard, 1977; Oster, 1978) or to establish their universal identifiability with states or circumstances likely to elicit states (Ekman, 1973). Ekman further presents evidence of correspondence between differentiated physiological states and voluntarily or involuntarily made facial gestures of four of the "basic" emotions (Ekman, Levenson & Friesen, 1983). On the other hand, there are arguments that behavior-state correspondences may not be so simply innate in young humans: Oster (1978) notes that the infant's rate of producing facial features usually associated with different emotions is so rapid that it is questionable whether each associated state actually accompanies each facial behavior; Lewis and Michalson (1983, and Chapter 7, this volume) suggest that, as opposed to innate packaging, much learning may be necessary before the toddler can align states with expressive behaviors. The large methodological problems (Mead, 1975) of how one documents a state's presence or its innate correlation with unguarded behavior are methodological corollaries to the substantive problem of whether patterns, states, and their correspondences are innate. For example, some descriptive instruments have been designed for noninferential behavior description (Ekman & Friesen, 1978; Scherer & Ekman, 1982), while others (Izard, 1979; Izard & Dougherty, 1980) assume behavior-state correspondences. Work on voluntary human deception (Ekman & Friesen, 1974), as well as on the location of cultural differences in prescribed public show of emotion (Eibl-Eibesfeldt, 1972) and on the display rules that dictate them (Saarni, 1979) all speak of the question of how such behavioral variabilities arise if patterns and states are innately given. Searches for gender differences in emotion tendency and socialization (Haviland & Malatesta, 1981) are attempts to separate the genetic and the socialization components of expressive development. Examinations of adult responses to innate infant-expressive patterns (Stettner & Loigman, 1983). Work on animal deception (Dawkins & Krebs, 1978; Redican, 1982, pp. 268–273) cuts the dichotomies somewhat differently; it examines, among other things, whether sets of specific states must innately accompany communicative animal-behavior patterns.

Another set of widely researched questions looks at the other side of the dichotomies. These seek the specific learning conditions and proc-

esses by which expressive behavior becomes socialized to follow culturally prescribed expectations. Although several of these may assume
little or no innate potentiation of the expressive behaviors whose modification by learning they study, each provides clues to how environmental forces may interact with the biological potentiation that is
possible for some expressive behavior. Such studies of expression socialization are summarized at the end of the section on biology-
environment interaction. Their full range is detailed in the chapters of
the second part of this book.

Research and theoretical writing on every current question about nonverbal or expressive development exhibit the tension between the poles
of these dichotomies. In the next section we examine ways to circumvent dichotomous thinking through conceptions that highlight the constant and thorough interaction of biology and environment.

Planes of Biology–Environment Interaction

Developmentalists' views of biology–environmental interactions usually take the following form. Inheritance provides many morphological
and biochemical patterns, some few behavioral patterns, and schedules
of changes for these patterns and for unfolding capacities within the
individual's lifetime; experiences feed necessary information to these
innate processes, sometimes providing too little and thus limiting potential, and sometimes providing more than the genetic program was
set for and thus pushing it beyond its usual potential. This interaction
occurs during the life of the individual, and variation of the interaction
process is conceived as difference among individuals or between an individual and a norm. This is biology–environment interaction on the
ontogenetic or *individual* plane. It is easy to become trapped in these
rather small steps of interaction and to forget that other biology-
environment interactions occur simultaneously over hundreds and
thousands of generations. These lengthier interactions can only be noticed by differences, over generational time, in the distribution of characteristics in a population. This is biology–environment interaction on
the phylogenetic or *population* plane. Finally, there is interaction between planes that yields the multiplane realm of evolution. When
viewed from that multiplane perspective, biology–environment interactions in ontogeny are cast in a new light, particularly when the continuous interactive steps, in and between planes, are emphasized.

That new light is partially the result of emergence. *Emergence* is a property of the principles that govern a system (Popper, 1972). Principles

emerge from each unique level of organization of a system, and they do not appear on, and thus do not apply to, the logically lower levels of organization of the system. In our examples, lower levels include biological inheritance and environmental forces seen in isolation from each other as they interact to create either the individual or the population plane. The individual plane is a lower level, as it contributes to the functioning of the population plane, and both planes are lower levels that contribute to the realm of evolution.

In a richly interactive conception of a system, the component levels, or subsystems, differ from each other due to the different emergent principles that they follow. Further, when viewed from higher levels, the subsystems of the lower levels appear in interaction to yield the higher levels. The next sections attempt to convey such a view of expressive-behavior development.

The Individual Plane

A sophisticated view of biology–environment interaction (Bateson, 1979) asserts on the individual level that (1) inheritance and experience interact in the individual to offer variation for and limitation to each other and (2) the product of this interaction is input to the population plane. In individual development, the original variation and limitation come from genetic change, by mutation or reassortment, which is limited by the necessity of a rough match between chromosomes and by the organism's early general viability. Simultaneously, inheritance provides the possibilities for, and sets the limits on, the organism's range of capabilities and responses to the environment. With birth, the external environment presents a wide variety of possibilities to which the organism may respond. The possibilities of environmental experiences can be too much or too little in quantity or can be different experiences that the genetic programs can use. Thus, the environment limits as well as provides possibilities for phenotypes in ontogeny, whereas genetic programs offer opportunities and limitations for uses made of environmental exposures. This set of cumulative interactions over otogeny has been called *epigenesis* or *ontogenetic probabilistic epigenesis* (Fuller, 1976).

The Population Plane

Just as the individual plane has as its basic time unit the length of an individual's life, the population plane has as its time unit the length of time required for a trait to spread through or be removed from a population. Both planes are seen to be composed of stop-motion time units. This contrasts with the structure of evolution as composed of patterns encompassing unit changes on both planes.

Interactions on the individual plane produce packages of genotype, of phenotype, and of each one's fit with the environment. These units are input to natural selection on the population level. As interactions occur in the life of the individual, natural selection has the opportunities to act on the variations provided by these packages. It favors the bulk of those individuals who adaptively use the environmental opportunities that their genes allow them to use—or do not prevent them from using. Adaptation, it should be noted, is technically measured by biologists as the probability of transmitting or of protecting the transmission of one's genes in the next generation. The terms *adaptation* and *survival* and *reproduction* are shorthand for this technical notion of evolutionary adaptation. On this plane, adaptive variations proposed at the individual level become stabilized and predominate as traits in the population; maladaptive variations do not. This is the most commonly suggested form of biology–environment interaction for populations.

Evolution's Realm across Planes

Evolution traces the flow of variations across the units on the individual and the population planes. Evolution absorbs both time frames and the interactions between planes. It sees both individual and population units as elements in larger continuous patterns of species change, with genetic elements and environmental elements simultaneously offering variation and limitation to each other's processes.

There are two particularly interesting types of evolutionary interaction across planes whose actual frequency in evolution is unknown. They are exciting because they are ways in which environment at Time 1 affects inheritance at Time 2. One process was empirically modeled with fruit flies by Waddington (1957), who called it *genetic assimilation*. It has been approached in current developmental psychological literature as "Waddington's canalization" (Scarr, 1983), and similar processes have been cited by biologists who note their importance (Bateson, 1979; Wilson, 1975). We use Bateson's method to describe one.

Envision genetic inheritance as setting the ranges for the possible values, not the absolute values, of the millions of variables that describe an organism. Under usual conditions, midrange values are the values most frequently shown in the phenotypes. In some new environment, however, perhaps as the result of somatic acclimation to new conditions, several of these variables may show range-end values that would be realized very infrequently in the older environment. If facilitation of threshold-biased values is important for survival and reproduction, and if the population stays long enough in the new environment, natural selection may increase greatly the proportion of the population that has a shift in range toward the threshold values. With selection lowering the threshold needed for actualization of the lower-end values, these values may become much closer to the new midrange values, no longer requiring special conditions for their actualization.

Bateson illustrates how this interaction could occur, by the hypothetical example of selection acting upon the range of somatic acclimation of persons moving to live for long periods at altitudes over 17,000 feet. At this altitude, many slowly developing and long-lasting somatic changes occur in the person: heart function changes, blood contains more hemoglobin, rib cage changes, and respiratory habits shift. This is actualization of threshold-biased values from the range of values for which the person inherited the genetic potential. Easier adaptation is plausible for persons whose midrange values shift, even slightly, toward this threshold, increasing the proportion of the population with lower midrange values. Such selection would be possible because the acclimatized somatic changes made available a large number of acclimatized persons to select while blocking from selection all nonacclimatized persons.

The second process, envisioned by Baldwin (1896), is importantly different from genetic assimilation in that it does not require a specific genetic potential at Time 1. Learning is what is crucial to the *Baldwin effect*. Through learning, a population may acquire a new response that is highly adaptive. The learning of this new response by some individuals effectively changes the heredity–environment relationship for all: those individuals who more easily learn to have this response will be favored by natural selection. Thus, any genetic propensity to acquire this response will be selected for, and the genotypes related to this propensity will increase in the population. Learning has propelled the population into a new set of values for genetic–environmental fit and into a new distribution of genotypes. From the simple pair of assumptions that the human infant's propensity to acquire the 4-month social smile was once entirely learned and that this smile aids survival by endearing caregivers, one can easily build a plausible example of how the Baldwin effect may have affected the stabilization of inherited propensities for human smiling and for related interpersonal alertness. In Chapter 3 in this volume, Smith notes the relevance of the Baldwin effect for phylogenetic change and for stability of expressive behaviors.

It seems unnecessary to point out that the processes noted on both planes combine to form a logically higher, multiplane system of evolution. From the perspective of this unified multiplane system, however, the processes on each plane appear quite different than when viewed upon each plane alone. Within this system, the interactions within and between planes are easy to conceptualize—and are even obvious. Guided by a sense of their emergence, the processes of individual and of population variation and limitation can be seen as interacting elements that hold equivalent roles in the system as a whole. Furthermore, the question of whether the sources are more genetic or environmental becomes emotionally and theoretically indifferent: both provide variation and limitation in continuous interplay. To view biology–environment interactions from this perspective is to be aware of the warp and woof in one fabric. It is to see no sense in the question of the priority of inheritance or experience. The interesting theoretical questions from this perspective take the form, ''What are the (emergent) properties, the elements and processes, by which the system functions?''

Studying Biology–Environment Interactions
on the Individual Plane

Unsurprisingly, the few studies of human-expressive development that make clear the evolutionary interaction of biology and environment come out of strongly ethological orientations. This is provided in the pioneering work of Charlesworth (included in Charlesworth, 1982) and summarized by Camras (1982). It is also part of Bakeman's sensitive methodology (e.g., Adamson & Bakeman, 1982) for observation of interpersonal interaction.

A representative sample of individual-plane approaches to biology–environment interactions in expressive development appears in this volume. Their range is described in this section. The approaches vary, among other ways, in how broad or minute the steps in the interaction are and in how mutually active the biological and environmental forces are seen to be. It is more difficult to be aware of interactions in the views using broader steps, in those seeing one or the other set of forces as more continually active, and in those using language traditionally associated with only one set of forces. All of these following views do, however, employ interactions, at least implicitly, just as specific forms of learning become obvious as emergents when it is noted that they would not exist without the biological potential for them.

Documentation of Unexpected Interactions

From the history of assumed stereotypes of expressive behavior described in the first section of this chapter, it is apparent that one approach to biology–environment interactions is to document unexpected
examples of them. Such examples are found in this volume's chapters
by Mason (Chapter 6), Hinde (Chapter 5), and Smith (Chapter 3), and
by Gouzoules, Gouzoules, and Marler (Chapter 4). They show important roles for the environment in influencing patterns of animal communication that had been seen on the innate poles of the aforementioned
dichotomies as resistant to environmental influence. Mason meticu-
lously provides evidence for the pervasive effect of general experience
upon the course of the rhesus monkey's expressive development. Most
unexpected is his suggestion that these effects are mediated by quite
sophisticated cognitive–social interpretations that accrue with social experience. Hinde analyzes how, even in birds, survival-related communicative interactions are accurately seen not as patterns of automatically
run action but as step-by-step negotiations of next-likely actions that are
influenced by expectations of the other's response. Marler and the Gouzouleses attack a tenacious feature of the problematic dichotomies by
demonstrating mammals' external-reference signaling that contains all
the referent information in the signal, regardless of context; they move
animal cognition closer to traditional definitions of symbol use. These
analyses all suggest a continually responsive, mutually adjusting view
of expressive interaction. Smith augments them by showing how such
changes fall within the range of continued intelligibility.

Searches for Specific Interactions in Human
Expressive Development

The majority of interactive approaches to human expressive-behavior
development study a few related processes by which biological givens
are linked to environmental influences. Of these, the most frequent are
studies of specific types, contexts, or contingencies of learning that modify early innate tendencies. The most studied of these specific learning
processes are examined in this volume. Cole (see Chapter 11, this volume) reviews children's learning of display rules for emotions. Feinman
(see Chapter 12, this volume) examines infant learning of the emotional
evaluation of situations through the process of social referencing. Malatesta (see Chapter 8, this volume) and Lewis and Michalson (see Chapter 7, this volume) review expressive-learning phenomena occurring

within adult–infant interaction. Dolgin and Azmitia (see Chapter 13, this volume) summarize what little is known of the early learning of expressive-signal interpretation and its facilitation by innate sensitivities. These thinkers seem to see learning factors as being more active than the biologically given patterns they harness and transform. Thus, they tend not to emphasize explicitly the constant role of heredity's provision of raw materials. Those who cite the roles of innate sensitivities to particular stimuli or of the adaptive values of particular learning interactions make biology proportionally more continuously active in their formulations.

In work not emphasized in this volume, Saarni (1983) adds an interesting loop in this social-learning approach to biology–environment interaction. She cites the work of Laird (1974), Hochschild (1979), and Bauermeister and Cooper (1981), to suggest that once display rules of expressive behavior become extremely automatic, the expressive behavior changes or determines the feeling state. Thus, learning of behavior is seen emergently to change the direction of its influence in coming to determine the presence of emotional states.

Although not directly studying expressive-behavior development, approaches similar in form to those of the preceding social-learning interactionalists are made by researchers who examine the social cognition that contributes to it. Again, Feinman (see Chapter 12) in this volume exemplifies such work, as do, for example, Sroufe (1979), Kagan (1978), and the large body of social-cognitive work reviewed by Shantz (1975). In these conceptualizations, the biology–environment interactions occur in the building of cognitive structures that interpret the environment about which the child expresses (or edits) his or her reaction and through which he or she uses expressive behaviors for social goals. Those cognitive theorists who emphasize more heavily the stage- or experience-graded biological limits on, or the innate potentials for, cognitive change attribute more explicit action to biological factors in these interactions.

More infrequent are approaches that emphasize the active role of biological schedules in allowing the individual to be open to environmental influences. Two powerful examples for infancy and for early childhood appear in this book. Thelen (see Chapter 9, this volume) details how at the level of the innate-action program there occur points open to voluntary control, and how increased application of control at these points transforms the entire action structure. Fogel (see Chapter 10, this volume) enlarges this insight to suggest that the coordinative structures that are basic to this innate action transformation provide the maturationally timed internal coordination for the many dimensions of emotional experience and expression. Work reported elsewhere (Zivin, 1982) traced over the years the opening to social influence and to cognition of the rigid form and context of preschoolers' seemingly innate agonistic gesture of the plus face: from 7 years through adulthood it came to be used for subtle management of one's social image.

Alternations in activity between biological and environmental forces are much more evident in the broad steps of the course of expressive development suggested by Lewis and Michalson (see Chapter 7) in this volume. They see biology as providing uncoordinated pieces of behavior and internal-state physiology in a first stage, learning acting to coordinate these pieces in a second stage, and, in a third stage, more traditional social-learning processes working to disconnect the behavior pieces from state physiology and to integrate them into culturally prescribed communication patterns. Similar alternation between the activity of these forces is also seen in Malatesta and Haviland's (in press) analysis of the last two stages.

The most minute and continuous alternations between biological and environmental activity are seen in the work of researchers who focus on the development of adult–infant social interaction and who see expressive development as only one thread in this growth. At least two anthologies (Field & Fogel, 1982; Tronick, 1982) have collected the work of such sensitive observers, and summaries of long series of observations, such as Kaye's (1982) have appeared. Malatesta (see Chapter 8) represents this approach in the present book. The minute attention of these observers to steps in interpersonal interactions and to systems of mutual regulation seems to generate fine-grained conceptions of biology–environment interactions. Among these observers, too, are the most noticeable emergent conceptions of factors in these interactions. One example is the notion from Bruner (1982) and Kaye (1982) that parental expectations about, and unwitting assistance toward, infant skills start to function as though they were part of the infant's innate endowment, thus *scaffolding* the infant on the climb to these skills. Similarly, in the present volume, Malatesta's mother–infant observations have led to her conception of mutual imitation as emerging from their interpersonal interaction and incorporating expressive teaching within itself.

From this summary of biology–environment conceptualizations, it appears that we are still in the early part of the transformation from nineteenth-century dichotomies to multileveled systems: most theorists of human expressive-behavior development with an interactive view of genetics and experience see these interactions on the individual plane only. And most theorists tend to focus on one active side in the interaction. The movement to higher logical levels that incorporate old dichotomies is slow (Manicas & Secord, 1983). But from such levels we

shall be better able to characterize the steps and the flow of the interactions that transform inherited fragments of infantile-expressive communication into the integrated and subtle signal system that has eluded
complex study.

Summary

This chapter examines issues that block cumulative knowledge in the
study of expressive-behavior development. It points out hidden dichotomies concerning innateness that still haunt us from nineteenth-
century conceptions of expression. This requires some clarification of
ideas about animal communication and of some semiotic concepts. The
chapter describes current conceptualizations of biology–environment interactions on the planes of the individual and the population and in the
joint realm of evolution. Finally, it examines current conceptions of
biology–environment interactions in the ontogeny of human-expressive
behavior. It indicates how the volume chapters illuminate these issues
and accord with a multi-layered, systemic model of expressive behavior
development.

References

Adamson, L., & Bakeman, R. Affectivity and reference: Concepts, methods, and tech-
    niques in the study of communication development of 6- to 18-month-old infants.
    In T. Field & A. Fogel (Eds.), *Emotion and early interaction*. Hillsdale, NJ: Erlbaum,
    1982.
Baldwin, J. M. A new factor in evolution. *American Naturalist*, 1896, *30*, 441–451, 536–553.
Bauermeister, R., & Cooper, J. Can the public expectation of emotion cause that emotion?
    Journal of Personality, 1981, *49*, 49–59.
Bateson, G. *Mind and nature*. New York: Dutton, 1979.
Bruner, J. S. The organization of action and the nature of the adult–infant transaction. In
    E. Z. Tronick (Ed.), *Social interchange in infancy: Affect, cognition, and communication*.
    Baltimore: University Park Press, 1982.
Buck, R. Spontaneous and symbolic nonverbal behavior and the ontogeny of communi-
    cation. In R. S. Feldman (Ed.), *Development of nonverbal behavior in children*. New York:
    Springer-Verlag, 1982.
Camras, L. A. Ethological approaches to nonverbal communication. In R. S. Feldman
    (Ed.), *Development of nonverbal behavior in children*. New York: Springer-Verlag, 1982.
Charlesworth, W. R. An ethological approach to research on facial expressions. In C. E.
    Izard (Ed.), *Measuring emotions in infants and children*. New York: Cambridge Uni-
    versity Press, 1982.
Darwin, C. R. *The expression of the emotions in man and animals*. London: John Murray, 1872.
Dawkins, R., & Krebs, J. R. Animal signals: Information or manipulation? In J. R. Krebs

& N. B. Davies (Eds.), *Behavioral ecology: An evolutionary approach.* Oxford: Blackwell Scientific Publications, 1978.

DePaulo, B. M., & Jordan, A. Age changes in deceiving and detecting deceit. In R. S. Feldman (Ed.), *Development of nonverbal behavior in children.* New York: Springer-Verlag, 1982.

de Waal, F. B. M. Exploitative and familiarity-dependent support strategies in a colony of semi-free-living chimpanzees. *Behaviour,* 1978, *66,* 268–312.

Eibl-Eibesfeldt, I. Similarities and differences between cultures in expressive movements. In R. A. Hinde (Ed.), *Nonverbal communication.* Cambridge: Cambridge University Press, 1972.

Ekman, P. Cross cultural studies of facial expression. In P. Ekman (Ed.), *Darwin and facial expression: A century of research in review.* New York: Academic Press, 1973.

Ekman, P. Biological and cultural contributions to body and facial movement. In J. Blacking, (Ed.), *The anthropology of the body.* London: Academic Press, 1977.

Ekman, P., & Friesen, W. V. Detecting deception from the body or face. *Journal of Personality and Social Psychology,* 1974, *29,* 288–298.

Eckman, P., & Friesen, W. V. *Facial Action Coding System (FACS): A technique for the measurement of facial action.* Palo Alto, CA: Consulting Psychologists Press, 1978.

Ekman, P., Friesen, W. V., & Ellsworth, P. Conceptual ambiguities. In P. Ekman (Ed.), *Emotion in the human face* (2nd ed.). Cambridge: Cambridge University Press, 1982.

Ekman, P., Levenson, R. W. & Friesen, W. V. Autonomic nervous system activity distinguishes among emotions, *Science,* 1983, *221*(4616), 1208–1210.

Field, T., & Fogel, A. (Eds.), *Emotion and early interaction.* Hillsdale, NJ: Erlbaum, 1982.

Freud, S. *A general introduction to psychoanalysis.* New York: Washington Square, 1924.

Fuller, J. L. Genetics and communication. In M. E. Hahn & E. C. Simmel (Eds.), *Communicative behavior and evolution.* New York: Academic Press, 1976.

Gallie, W. B. *Peirce and pragmatism.* New York: Dover, 1966.

Griffin, D. R. *The question of animal awareness* (rev. ed.). New York: Rockefeller University Press, 1981.

Harre, R., & Secord, P. *The explanation of social behaviour.* Totowa, NJ: Littlefield, Adams, 1973.

Haviland, J. M., & Malatesta, C. Z. A description of the development of sex differences in non-verbal signals. In C. Mayo & N. Henley (Eds.), *Gender and non-verbal behavior.* New York: Springer-Verlag, 1981.

Hochschild, A. R. Emotion work, feeling rules and social structure, *American Journal of Sociology,* 1979, *85,* 551–575.

Huxley, J. Courtship activities in the red-throated diver (*Colymbus stellatus* Pontopp.); together with a discussion of the evolution of courtship in birds, *Journal of the Linnean Society of London, Zoology,* 1923, *53,* 253–292.

Izard, C. E. *Human emotions.* New York: Plenum, 1977.

Izard, C. E. *The maximally discriminative facial movement coding system (Max).* Newark, DE: Instructional Resources Center, 1979.

Izard, C. E., & Dougherty, L. M. *A system for identifying affect expressions by wholistic judgments.* Newark, DE: Instructional Resources Center, 1980.

Kagan, J. On emotion and its development: A working paper. In M. Lewis & L. A. Rosenblum (Eds.), *The development of affect.* New York: Plenum, 1978.

Kaye, K. *The mental and social life of babies.* Chicago: University of Chicago Press, 1982.

Kroeber, A. L. Sign and symbol in bee communications, *Proceedings of the National Academy of Science,* 1952, *38,* 753–757.

Laird, J. D. Self-attribution of emotion: The effects of expressive behavior on the quality of emotional experience, *Journal of Personality and Social Psychology,* 1974, *29,* 475–486.

Lewis, M., & Michalson, L. *Children's emotions and moods.* New York: Plenum, 1983.

Malatesta, C. Z., & Haviland, J. M. Signals, symbols and socialization: The modification of emotional expression in human development. In M. Lewis & C. Saarni (Eds.), *The socialization of affect.* New York: Plenum, in press.

Manicas, P. T., & Secord, P. F. Implications for psychology of the new philosophy of science. *American Psychologist,* 1983, *38,* 399–413.

Mead, M. Review of Darwin and facial expression: A century of research in review, *Journal of Communication,* 1975, *25,* 209–213.

Menzel, E. W. A group of young chimpanzees in a one-acre field. In A. M. Schrier & F. Stollnitz (Eds.), *Behavior of nonhuman primates.* (Vol. 5). New York: Academic Press, 1974.

Menzel, E. W., & Halpern, S. Purposive behavior as a basis for objective communication between chimpanzees. *Science,* 1975, *189,* 652–654.

Osgood, C. E., & Sebeok, T. A. *Psycholinguistics—a survey of theory and research problems.* Baltimore: Waverley, 1954.

Oster, H. Facial expression and affect development. In M. Lewis & L. A. Rosenblum (Eds.), *The development of affect.* New York: Plenum, 1978.

Premack, A. J. *Why chimps can read.* New York: Harper Colophon, 1976.

Premack, D., & Woodruff, G. Chimpanzee problem-solving: A test for comprehension, *Science,* 1978, *202,* 532–535.

Popper, K. R. *Objective knowledge: An evolutionary approach.* London: Oxford University Press, 1972.

Redican, W. K. An evolutionary perspective on human facial displays. In P. Ekman (Ed.), *Emotion in the human face* (2nd ed.). New York: Cambridge University Press, 1982.

Saarni, C. Children's understanding of display rules for expressive behavior, *Developmental Psychology,* 1979, *15,* 424–429.

Saarni, C. *Suggestions and expectancy in emotional socialization.* Paper presented at the Biennial Meeting of the Society for Research in Child Development, Detroit, April 1983.

Savage-Rumbaugh, E. S. *Primate communication: From action to gesture to symbol.* Plenary address at the Annual Animal Behavior Society Meeting, Lewisburg, PA, June 1983.

Savage-Rumbaugh, E. S., Rumbaugh, D. M., & Boysen, S. Symbolic communication between two chimpanzees (*Pan troglodytes*), *Science,* 1978, *201*(4356), 641–644.

Scarr, S. S. An evolutionary perspective on infant intelligence. In M. Lewis (Ed.), *Origins of intelligence: Infancy and early childhood.* New York: Plenum, 1983.

Schacter, S., & Singer, J. E. Cognitive, social, and physiological determinants of emotional state. *Psychological Review,* 1962, *69,* 379–399.

Scherer, K. R., & Ekman, P. (Eds.), *Handbook of methods in nonverbal behavior research.* Cambridge: Cambridge University Press, 1982.

Sebeok, T. A. Coding in the evolution of signalling behavior, *Behavioral Science,* 1962, *7*(4), 430–442. (Bobbs-Merrill reprint A-252)

Sebeok, T. A. On chemical signs. In *To honor Roman Jakobson: Essays on the occasion of his 70th birthday.* The Hague: Mouton, 1967.

Shantz, C. U. The development of social cognition. In E. M. Hetherington (Ed.), *Review of child development research.* Chicago: University of Chicago Press, 1975.

Smith, W. J. *The behavior of communicating: An ethological approach.* Cambridge, MA: Harvard University Press, 1977.

Sroufe, L. A. Socioemotional development. In J. D. Osofsky (Ed.), *Handbook of infant development.* New York: Wiley, 1979.

Stettner, L. J., & Loigman, G. *Emotion cues in baby faces as elicitors of functional reaction choices.* Paper presented at the Biennial Meeting of the Society for Research in Child Development, Detroit, April 1983.

Tinbergen, N. *The study of instinct*. Oxford: Oxford University Press, 1951.

Tronick, E. Z. *Social interchange in infancy: Affect, cognition and communication*. Baltimore: University Park Press, 1982.

Waddington, C. H. *The strategy of the genes: A discussion of some aspects of theoretical biology*. London: George Allen & Unwin, 1957.

Wilson, E. O. *Sociobiology: The new synthesis*. Cambridge, MA: Harvard University Press, 1975.

Woodruff, G., & Premack, D. Primitive numerical concepts in the chimpanzee: proportionality and numerosity, *Nature*, 1981, *293*, (5833), 568–570.

Zivin, G. Watching the sands shift: Conceptualizing development of nonverbal mastery. In R. S. Feldman (Ed.), *Development of nonverbal behavior in children*. New York: Springer-Verlag, 1982.

Chapter 2

Charles Darwin's Thought on Expressive Mechanisms in Evolution

William Montgomery

Relationship to Other Chapters and to the Field

Relationship to the Field

As a historian specializing in Darwin studies, Montgomery gives psychological and biological students of expressive behavior surprising information on the origins and details of Darwin's thought on expressive mechanisms. This chapter raises three issues for researchers of expressive behavior: (1) does Darwin always see state as accompanying expressive behavior? (2) what are the contemporary implications of Darwin's emphasis on the inheritance of acquired characteristics in the origin of expression? (3) what are the contemporary implications of Darwin's rarely ascribing natural selection mechanisms to expressive behaviors? From Montgomery's analysis, it does appear that, consistent with all current interpretations of Darwin as the father of the scientific concept of state-generated expression, Darwin always did ascribe a state as the condition for expressive behaviors. However, the mere fact that the second two questions are raised is inconsistent with the pervasive assumption that Darwin asserted that the inheritance of emotional expression is (always) the result of natural selection for expressive behaviors.

Montgomery's chapter points out and explains why Darwin's different books, On the Origin of Species (referred to herein as Origin) and The Expression of the Emotions in Man and Animals (hereafter referred to as Expression of Emotions), used predominantly different mechanisms to explain the origin *of a trait for inheritance: natural selection in the* Origin *and inheritance of acquired characteristics in* Expression. *This is curious to contemporary non-biologists, who assume that natural selection is necessarily implied by genetic evolution, whereas, in fact, Darwin and early evolutionary biologists employed several mechanisms of evolution. Montgomery notes that Darwin tended to use inheritance of acquired characteristics for inherited behaviors and natural selection for more morphological traits.*

The contemporary impact of Darwin's acceptance of expression as arising through the inheritance of acquired characteristics is minimal, as contemporary evolutionary theory has eliminated considerations of genetic transmission changes that are not made in genetic material. However, new attention to the intricate interaction of genetic and environmental interactions in the course of evolution—described in the framing chapter as genetic assimilation *and as the* Baldwin effect, *reflect a new understanding of environmental effect upon later inheritance. One implication of Darwin's inattention to the natural selection of expression is to urge upon current researchers a more critical use of language and empirical evidence, in reference to expressive behavior actually having been specialized through natural selection for communication. The popular ethological term* display *technically denotes inherited behavior patterns that indeed have been evolved through natural selection to be specialized for particularly effective communication. Though we may be surprised that Darwin greatly emphasized the origins of expression both in habitual association (his first principle) and in physiologic ties of behavior to features subjected to natural selection for nonexpressive adaptive functions (his third principle), it may remind us that expressive behaviors are not necessarily specialized in evolution for a communicative function.*

The prevalence before Darwin of ideas that influenced his thinking on expression shows how deeply many Western assumptions about expressive behaviors are ingrained in our culture. Darwin conveyed his scholarly contemporaries' beliefs that many types of inner conditions were ''expressed'' through visible behavior. And the psychological thinking which he comfortably blended with evolutionary ideas about expression were adopted from the writings of his physician grandfather, Erasmus Darwin.

Relationship to Other Chapters

Darwin's authority as originator of the scientific study of expression is cited in most chapters in this book Thereby the authors usually invoke the assumption of the inherited correlation of state and expressive behavior and go on to assert revised theory of a state's relationship to expressive behavior, usually emphasizing the separation of state and behavior through socialization. Some

*chapters strongly modify the old correlation: Mason (see Chapter 6) and Fein-
man (see Chapter 12) subsume* state *under the effects of central cognitive appraisal. Smith (see Chapter 3) and Hinde (see Chapter 5), plus Gouzoules,
Gouzoules, and Marler (see Chapter 4), demote* state *to a partial contribution,
along with cognition, to signaling. And one chapter by Lewis and Michalson
(see Chapter 7) explicitly questions the original correlation.*—ED.

Introduction

Most students of emotional expression and nonverbal communication
regard Charles Darwin as the founder of the field. His book, *The Expression of the Emotions in Man and Animals* (1872), is frequently cited in research publications and has received extended attention in the light of
modern work (Ekman, 1973). The scientist of today owes to Darwin the
insight that expression is an evolutionary product, heavily influenced
by hereditary factors. Darwin was the first to demonstrate that the
expressions of humans and animals have arisen by the same evolutionary mechanisms and that human expression often resembles that of
closely related animals. Furthermore, he introduced research strategies
that have remained useful in the evolutionary interpretation of expression. He made comparative studies of humans and animals, he studied
human infants and children, he conducted experiments to test the
response of observers to different expressions, he carried out cross-
cultural investigations of expression, and he inquired into the expressions of the blind and the insane. In addition to his imaginative observations, Darwin also introduced theoretical mechanisms designed to
account for the evolutionary origin of expressions. These mechanisms
deserve close attention because they differ from the mechanisms of evolution laid out in the *Origin of Species* (1859). In *Origin*, Darwin had
explained evolution primarily as an adaptive process guided by natural
selection. In *Expression of Emotions*, Darwin argued that expression arose
chiefly through nonadaptive processes in which the inheritance of acquired characteristics frequently played a role.

The striking contrast between the two books demands investigation,
and this chapter is intended to explain the unusual features of Darwin's
theories of expression. Four topics are discussed: Darwin's immediate
predecessors, his own theories of expression, the early sources of his
thinking, and the application of his theories in *Expression of Emotions*
(1872). To understand Darwin's own position, one needs a knowledge
of his chief predecessors. These were medical writers whose special in-

terests were very important in shaping the study of expression before Darwin. After their views are explained, Darwin's theories of expression are outlined. Next, attention is devoted to Darwin's earliest speculations about expression and to his debt to the psychological theories of his grandfather, Erasmus Darwin. Although Darwin (1872) did not mention his grandfather's influence in the *Expression of Emotions,* it is not possible to explain the distinctive character of Darwin's theories without taking this early influence into account. Finally, the more general features of Darwin's book are described, and its relationship to the wider body of his evolutionary thought is presented. The evidence indicates that Darwin's nonadaptive approach to expression derived from his strong belief that psychological mechanisms played an independent role in evolution, supplementing the adaptive influence of natural selection. Darwin made two general claims in the *Expression of Emotion:* expression is an evolutionary product, and it has evolved in large part through distinctive processes.

The Medical Approach to Expression

In writing his book on expression, Darwin was able to draw on the work of several predecessors. Psychologists sometimes touched on the subject briefly (Bain, 1855, 1859; Spencer, 1855, 1860), but most of the literature was written by doctors. The subject was then considered a medical problem, one requiring the special expertise of the trained physician. During the 1860s three significant works appeared, all by physician authors. In France the neurologist Duchenne produced a major study (1862/1876), and the posthumous lectures of the anatomist Gratiolet were published (1865). An obscure German physician, Piderit, also contributed an interesting book (1867). Darwin also relied heavily on two older British authors: Bell (1806) and Burgess (1839). Of these works, Bell's *Essays on the Anatomy of Expression in Painting* set the standard for nineteenth-century research on the subject. Later retitled *The Anatomy and Philosophy of Expression as Connected with the Fine Arts* (1844), it enjoyed lasting influence, appearing in a sixth edition in 1872, the year of Darwin's own publication.

Bell's most important contribution to the study of expression may have been his emphasis on emotion. Emotion is not the only point of reference one might choose in studying expression, and, indeed, most of Bell's contemporaries took a different view of the matter. In the early nineteenth century, the study of expression—or *physiognomy* as it was usually called—was primarily devoted to an elucidation of human *character*. From Aristotle onward, physiognomy had attempted to devise methods for analyzing human character from facial expression. In the late eighteenth century the writings of J. C. Lavater gave the subject an enormous revival. In spite of the criticism of G. C. Lichtenberg and others, Lavater's works were quickly translated and repeatedly republished in most European countries, where they found favor with quite a number of scientists and physicians (Graham, 1961). Bell was not the first to investigate the relationship between expression and emotion, but the quality of his work and its timing were of considerable importance. He deserves considerable credit for directing attention away from the nebulous question of character and toward the more manageable one of emotion and thus rescuing expression as a subject for effective scientific study. Of course, the interest in emotion did not exclude an interest in character too. Piderit (1867) had hopes that the reformed study of expression might still create a genuine scientific basis for the otherwise inept pursuit of physiognomy. As he saw it, the habitual repetition of certain emotions in the face would produce an habitual expression related to character type. But even Piderit recognized that the study of character could only be carried out as a secondary goal based on the study of emotion.

Bell and his followers did not agree about all aspects of their work; nevertheless, they were close enough to one another in outlook to allow some rough generalizations. Perhaps the most obvious common feature among them was their interest in the anatomical mechanisms underlying expressions. With the exception of Burgess (1839), who wrote only about blushing, this meant the action of the facial muscles. The study of human anatomy is, of course, a preeminently medical topic, and the importance of muscular action for expressiveness helps to explain why the subject of expression was, for the most part, left to the medically trained. At the same time, expression created few problems for doctors beyond the anatomical issue. One had no need to perform experiments or undertake any elaborate scientific procedures; a simple knowledge of facial musculature was sufficient. This was particularly important for Bell, who had strong religious objections to vivisection (Geison, 1978, pp. 22–23). Expression offered an interesting subject for research, which required none of the unpleasant procedures customarily necessary in investigating bodily functions. Nevertheless, Duchenne (1876) managed to go beyond Bell's observational approach in an interesting way—by stimulating the muscles of the face electrically. Duchenne had employed electrical stimulation of muscles to study a variety of neurological problems with considerable success. Working with a volunteer subject who

suffered from a disorder that made his face insensitive to pain, Duchenne was able to simulate various emotional expressions merely by
applying electrodes to the man's face.

   In analyzing the action of facial muscles, the doctors were particularly
interested in the practical implications of their work for sculptors and
painters. Through the study of facial anatomy and its role in expression,
they hoped to provide a scientific basis for the display of emotion in
works of art. Given the developing academic tradition in nineteenth-
century painting and sculpture, with its emphasis on natural realism,
medical students of emotion felt, quite reasonably, that they had something constructive to offer the artists. Bell was especially well qualified
to undertake such a program. A gifted amateur artist, he filled his book
with numerous fine drawings of his own, designed to illustrate the cases
of expression he had studied. He considered not only human but also
animal expression. Dissatisfied by many representations of animals he
had seen, Bell demonstrated that human musculature is far better
equipped to produce nuances of expression than the facial muscles of
most animals, and he warned against anthropomorphic representations
of such animals as lions and horses in the painter's work. No doubt the
artistic quality of Bell's book had much to do with its long-standing pop-
ularity.

   Piderit (1867), no less than Bell, concerned himself with the esthetic
goals of the research. He clearly wanted to provide artists with a guide
for understanding expression. However, in order to make this guide as
objective as possible, Piderit had his illustrations reduced to simple line
drawings, each carefully designed to portray expressions as bare ab-
stractions. Duchenne (1862), the technological sophisticate, carried this
trend toward objectivity one step further: he employed photography.
His text was accompanied by an atlas of numerous large photographs,
handsomely reproduced, that have made it a classic in the history of
medical illustration. As in the case of Bell and Piderit, Duchenne also
hoped to influence practice in the fine arts, and he included a lengthy
discussion of famous works of art and the adequacy of their presentation
of emotion. It seems clear, then, that the search for accurate illustration
was directly related to the interest of physicians in influencing artists.

   Bell successfully encouraged scientists to concentrate on anatomy,
emotion, and artistic applications in studying expression. But in one regard the investigators of the 1860s were unwilling to follow him. Bell
made a point of insisting that some facial muscles exist only for the purpose of creating expressions (1806, p. 85). Writing in the third edition
of his text—the one used by Darwin—Bell remarked,

> In the lower creatures there is no expression, but what may be referred, more or less plainly, to their acts of volition, or necessary instincts; while in man there seems to be a special apparatus, for the purpose of enabling him to communicate with his fellow-creatures, by that natural language, which is read in the changes of his countenance. There exist in his face not only all those parts, which by their action produce expression in the several classes of quadrupeds, but there is added a peculiar set of muscles to which no other office can be assigned than to serve for expression. (1844, p. 121).

Bell may have proposed this curious breach between man and animals because it seemed to support his religious views; he believed strongly in natural theology, the faith that God had designed living beings with all their functional needs in mind and that man occupied a special place in God's creation (Bell, 1833).

By the 1860s, such theologically motivated special pleading no longer impressed anatomists. Even Gratiolet, a conservative French Catholic (Coleman, 1972), rejected it out of hand: "There is not a single muscle, a single organ created uniquely for the needs of expression" (Gratiolet, 1865, p. 12). Gratiolet agreed that expression constituted a "language"; and he frequently employed the term in his discussion. However, for him the language did not depend on any special apparatus; he understood it rather as "metaphor," a symbolic extension of meaning derived from the nonexpressive uses of facial muscles. Thus, the expression of relaxed, easy breathing becomes the expression of happiness (pp. 23–24); the expression of vomiting becomes the expression of extreme disgust and horror (p. 26). Expression requires no special muscles because it derives its meaning precisely from those muscular activities with more specific functions. Piderit (1867) agreed very closely with this interpretation. Piderit (1867) explained expression as "mimicry," and he argued that expression derived from the action of muscles that served to support the sense organs. Thus, the squinting that people do, say in the presence of a very bright light, is mimicked to produce the expression for any unpleasant impression, visual or mental (p. 45). Or the expression produced by efforts to avoid the sensation of a bad-tasting object in the mouth is mimicked by the expression signifying objectionable sensations generally (pp. 72–73).

Darwin's Theories

In turning to Darwin's work on expression, one finds many reminders of the work of the physicians. Darwin followed their example in stressing emotion as the central topic and paying close attention to the anatomical basis of expression. However, Darwin paid much less attention to artistic matters. He quoted Shakespeare occasionally, and he mentioned looking at a few paintings, but in his later years he had little interest in art and certainly no ambition to instruct artists. Darwin took up expression primarily because he wanted to relate the subject to evolution. His evolutionary assumptions led him to investigate expression in ways that had not occurred to the physicians. It also led him to react against the natural theology of Bell and Bell's belief that some muscles of the human face were created solely for the purpose of expression. Bell's theory created an unbridgable gap between animals and humans that directly contradicted evolution. Darwin simply could not agree that human facial musculature presented unique features related solely to expression, and he argued bluntly against such a view:

> The simple fact that the anthropoid apes possess the same facial muscles as we do, renders it very improbable that these muscles in our case serve exclusively for expression; for no one, I presume, would be inclined to admit that monkeys have been endowed with special muscles solely for exhibiting their hideous grimaces. Distinct uses, independently of expression, can indeed be assigned with much probability for almost all the facial muscles. (Darwin, 1872, p. 10).

In making his case against Bell, Darwin (1872) argued that an organ can be adapted to perform tasks quite different from those it may once have performed. The human face does express emotion but not necessarily because its muscles were expressly designed for this purpose. To contradict this view Darwin proposed three principles in order to account for expression as an indirect result of evolutionary developments that had occurred for quite different reasons. He called them the principle of "serviceable associated habits," the principle of "antithesis," and the principle of "actions due to the constitution of the nervous system." These principles were designed to dispense with any need to refer to design in dealing with expression. They reflected Darwin's conviction that neither man's bodily form nor his behavior had been uniquely created but that both had been gradually modified to the state in which they now exist.

According to the principle of serviceable associated habits,

> Certain complex actions are of direct or indirect service under certain states of the mind, in order to relieve or gratify certain sensations, desires, &c; and whenever the same state of mind is induced, however feebly, there is a tendency through the force of habit and association for the same movements to be performed, though they may not then be of the least use. (Darwin, 1872, p. 28)

Darwin cited Gratiolet's observation that a man

> who vehemently rejects a proposition, will almost certainly shut his eyes or turn away his face; but if he accepts the proposition, he will nod his head in affirmation and open his eyes widely. The man acts in this latter case as if he clearly saw the thing, and in the former case as if he did not or would not see it. (1872, p. 32).

Furthermore, when repeated over many generations, associated habits may become reflex actions through the inheritance of acquired characteristics. Thus,

> Dogs, when they wish to go to sleep on a carpet or other hard surface, generally turn round and round and scratch the ground with their fore-paws in a senseless manner, as if they intended to trample down the grass and scoop out a hollow, as no doubt their wild parents did, when they lived on open grassy plains or in the woods. (Darwin, 1872, p. 42).

According to the principle of antithesis,

> Certain states of the mind lead to certain habitual actions, which are of service, as under our first principle. Now when a directly opposite state of mind is induced, there is a strong and involuntary tendency to the performance of movements of a directly opposite nature, though these are of no use; and such movements are in some cases highly expressive. (Darwin, 1872, p. 28).

By way of example, Darwin cited the contrasting behavior of an aggressive dog and a friendly one:

> When a dog approaches a strange dog or man in a savage or hostile frame of mind, he walks upright and very stiffly; his head is slightly raised, or not much lowered; the tail is held erect and quite rigid; the hairs bristle, especially along the neck and back; the pricked ears are directed forwards, and the eyes have a fixed stare . . . These actions, as will hereafter be explained, follow from the dog's intention to attack his enemy. (Darwin, 1872, pp. 50–51).

Now Darwin continued by describing the same dog approaching his master:

> Instead of walking upright, the body sinks downwards or even crouches, and is thrown into flexuous movements; his tail, instead of being held stiff and upright, is lowered and wagged from side to side; his hair instantly becomes smooth; his ears are depressed and drawn backwards, but not closely to the head; and his lips hang loosely. From the drawing back of the ears, the eyelids become elongated, and the eyes no longer appear round and staring. (1872, p. 51).

Darwin then went on to explain how such contrasts might have come about:

> As the power of intercommunication is certainly of high service to many animals, there is no *à priori* improbability in the supposition, that gestures manifestly of an opposite nature to those by which certain feelings are already expressed, should at first have been voluntarily employed under the influence of an opposite state of feeling. The fact of the gestures being now innate, would be no valid objection to the belief that they were at first intentional; for if practised during many generations, they would probably at last be inherited. (1872, p. 61).

Finally, Darwin introduced a "principle of actions due to the constitution of the Nervous System, independently from the force of the Will, and independently to a certain extent of Habit." As he explained, "When the sensorium is strongly excited, nerve-force is generated in excess, and is transmitted in certain definite directions, depending on the connection of the nerve-cells, and partly on habit: or the supply of nerve-force may, as it appears, be interrupted" (1872, pp. 28–29). Darwin had in mind a number of physiological responses commonly associated with strong feeling, such as trembling of the muscles, rapid heartbeat, perspiration, blushing, or reddening of the face. He believed that they frequently had no practical value; thus, like expressions arising according to his first two principles, they could not be the result of design.

These principles accounted for emotional expression as an evolutionary product. Thus, the principles integrated expression into the broader scheme of Darwin's biological thinking. However, in treating expression, Darwin made use of some rather specialized evolutionary mechanisms. In the *Origin* (1859), Darwin maintained that natural selection outweighed all other agents of evolutionary change. It is true that in later editions of the book he accorded greater recognition to the inheritance of acquired characteristics; however, even in the final, sixth edition, he clearly expressed confidence in the primacy of selection (1872a, p. 421). This emphasis on selection in the *Origin* contrasts sharply with the principles advanced by Darwin in *Expression of Emotions* (1872) in which he made little direct use of natural selection and instead relied heavily on the inheritance of acquired characteristics. Furthermore, in *Expression*, Darwin seemed to lose interest in the concept of adaptation that interested him so much in the *Origin*. He indicated that expressions might have evolved for adaptive reasons, as in the preceding discussion of antithesis, but he made it clear that they had not necessarily done so. Most strikingly, his explanation of antithesis shows that he sometimes considered *use-inheritance* (i.e., the inheritance of acquired characteristics) an adequate explanation for expressions even if they were adaptive.

In some ways Darwin's theories of expression bear interesting resemblances to his more familiar concepts. Lorenz (1965) has suggested that expressions are conservative phenomena that have outlived their original functions, much in the manner of vestigial organs. Expressions, like vestigial organs, are entities with no particular functions that have evolved from other functional states, but the parallel is by no means complete. In the case of vestigial organs, the original organ has lost its function and withered over the course of evolution. In the case of expressions, the original function continues to be exercised, and the muscles that made it possible are as well developed as ever. Expressions are not vestiges of a now-lost ability; rather they are an adventitiously acquired "bonus" that has come to the organism for other reasons.

Ghiselin (1969, pp. 205–206) has suggested a better parallel, one between Darwin's theories of expression and his notion of correlated growth. Even in the *Origin* (1859), Darwin did not insist that all evolutionary developments must be adaptive with respect to the external environment. He observed that the growth of an organism is correlated in such a way that modifications in one part tend to produce modifications in other parts as well, a phenomenon frequently observed in malformations. As a result of this correlation of growth, natural selection may effect changes in an indirect manner for reasons that have nothing to do with adaptation (pp. 143–146). Ghiselin (1969) notes that Darwin's principles of expression operate in much the same way because marginally adaptive or even nonadaptive expressions may be acquired along with more immediately practical abilities. This seems particularly evident in the case of Darwin's (1872) third principle of actions due to the constitution of the nervous system. In this case, as in the case of correlation, the inner constitution of the animal produces modifications in a character for reasons quite unrelated to adaptation. Darwin's first two principles also display a similarity to correlation, but one must bear in mind a distinction. According to these principles of expression, new modifications are introduced not by an inner mechanism of growth but rather by a psychological response: the association of ideas and experiences passed on to the next generation through Lamarckian use-inheritance.

The nonadaptive aspects of expression proved especially useful for Darwin's campaign against the natural theology of Charles Bell. Bell (1844) had stressed the functional character of human expression and the unique design of human facial musculature required to produce it. He further denied that animals shared in this human gift. None of the anatomists of the 1860s followed Bell in this respect, and Gratiolet (1865) and Piderit (1867) anticipated Darwin in proposing an indirect explanation for human expression. Of course, neither of them incorporated this explanation into an evolutionary framework. As an evolutionist, Darwin could not accept Bell's opinion that human expression differed fundamentally from that of animals. Given a theory of serviceable associated habits, he found Bell's belief in uniquely designed muscles of expression unnecessary. Indeed, in Darwin's philosophy of science such teleological mechanisms were misleading and undesirable. However, these points do not clearly establish why Darwin chose to account for nonadaptive expressions through the inheritance of acquired characteristics.

Fortunately, Darwin's early manuscripts (Barrett, 1980) on the species question shed some light on the question. They indicate that Darwin tended to view behavioral questions differently from morphological ones. Richards (1981) has shown that Darwin continued to explain animal instincts as the result of Lamarckian use-inheritance for a number of years after he became a selectionist; the problem of accounting for the instincts of social insects led him to adopt selection only in the 1850s. Darwin's attitude toward expression was evidently similar, but in the case of expression, Darwin encountered no special difficulties; his Lamarckian account even proved convenient in opposing Bell's natural theology. He had worked out at least two principles of expression to his satisfaction before he developed the theory of natural selection. These principles survived intact because they served a useful purpose in his case against Bell and because he faced no serious counterarguments. However, they survived above all because Darwin believed psychological mechanisms contributed to evolution.

Erasmus Darwin's Psychology

The evidence for this interpretation appears in the evolutionary notebooks that Charles Darwin began keeping after he returned from the *Beagle* voyage. It is now well established that Darwin was converted to evolution in March 1837 primarily by the anatomical and taxonomic studies that Richard Owen and John Gould conducted on Darwin's South American and Galápagos collections (Sulloway, 1982). In June of that year he began keeping a series of notebooks on various aspects of the species question, most of them devoted to geological, zoological, and botanical topics (De Beer, 1960; De Beer & Rowlands, 1961; De Beer,

Rowlands & Skramovsky, 1967). Two other notebooks, the so-called M and N Notebooks, dealt directly with human behavior and expression. Darwin began the M Notebook on July 15, 1838 and completed it on October 2, 1838. The N Notebook began on October 2, 1838 and was completed some time the following year. Both notebooks contain numerous remarks about expression, anticipating in brief form much that Darwin was later to include in his book; however, the M Notebook is of special interest because it was completed on October 2, 1838, only a few days after Darwin's celebrated reading of Robert Malthus's *Principles of Population* inspired his theory of natural selection on September 28 (Barrett, 1980 & Kohn, 1980).

A reader of the M and N Notebooks soon discovers what a reader of *Expression* (1872) might not guess, namely that the most important medical text for the young Darwin was his grandfather Erasmus's (1794–1796) celebrated *Zoonomia; or, the laws of Organic Life* (hereafter cited as *Zoonomia*). Charles mentioned the book explicitly several times in the notebooks, and his theories of expression obviously drew heavily on his grandfather's discussion. Erasmus Darwin was an outstanding representative of the English Enlightenment, a man quite secular and anti-traditional in his thinking. He had been a founding member of the Lunar Club of Birmingham, a stronghold of radical political, religious, and social ideas (King-Hele, 1977). His text *Zoonomia* was designed to replace the age-old humoral physiology in medicine with a mechanistic concept of fibrous motions more in keeping with the scientific outlook of the eighteenth century. In this respect the work was hardly novel, and Erasmus Darwin's speculative mechanism was due to be swept away by the rise of a more exacting scientific medicine that began to appear after his death. Nevertheless, the book exhibited considerable practical wisdom, and it also contained a number of very suggestive ideas, among them a theory of evolution.

So far as expression was concerned, much of Erasmus Darwin's thinking grew out of the sensationalist tradition of the eighteenth century. David Hume, E. B. de Condillac, and other representatives of this tradition had embraced a theory of reason and learning that emphasized the effect of related events on the mind. Erasmus Darwin followed this line of theorizing with his notion of association: "All the fibrous motions, whether muscular or sensual, which are frequently brought into action together, either in combined tribes, or in successive trains, become so connected by habit, that when one of them is reproduced the others have a tendency to succeed or accompany it" (1794, Vol. 1, p. 49). He continued: "In learning any mechanic art, as music, dancing, or the use of the sword we teach many of our muscles to act together or in succession by repeated voluntary efforts; which by habit become formed into tribes or trains of association" (1794, Vol. 1, p. 51). These tribes and trains of association applied to learning and to behavior of any kind in both humans and animals. Robert Richards has demonstrated that this theory of learning was critical for breaking down the Cartesian distinction between animals presumed to be unthinking automatons and reasoning human beings. By putting people and animals on essentially the same footing when it came to learning processes, the sensationalists paved the way for evolutionary speculation by Erasmus Darwin, by J. B. Lamarck, and by Charles Darwin (Richards, 1979).

The theory of associations also played a key role in Erasmus Darwin's account of expression. He devoted several pages to expression in his chapter on instinct, treating such familiar expressions as fear, grief, pleasure, anger, and attention. Here was Erasmus Darwin's explanation for the expression of attention:

> The eye takes in at once but half our horizon, and that only in the day, and our smell informs us of no very distant objects, hence we confide principally in the organ of hearing to apprize us of danger: when we hear [even] the smallest sound, that we cannot immediately account for, our fears are alarmed, we suspend our steps, hold every muscle still, open our mouths a little, erect our ears, and listen to gain further information: and this by habit becomes the general language of attention to objects of sight, as well as hearing; and even to the successive trains of our ideas. (1794, Vol. 1, pp. 152–53).

Erasmus Darwin had similar accounts for each of the other expressions he treated, all based on his principle of association. He explained the characteristic expression of fear, for example, from the response of the infant during the birth process. Not all of these ideas were attractive to Charles Darwin, but the general principle seems to have convinced him thoroughly. A likely example is his comment on attention in the M Notebook: "Fear probably is connected with *habitual* stopping of breath to hear any sound—attitude of attention" (M Notebook, p. 131e, Barrett, 1980, p. 31). This was very close to Erasmus's account, and one can surmise that Charles was recalling it.

Whatever Charles's response to individual cases, his enthusiasm for the general principles of *Zoonomia* (1794–1796) was obvious: "Expression is an hereditary habitual movement consequent on some action, which the progenitor did when excited or disturbed by the same cause, which/now/[1] excites the expression" (M Notebook, p. 107, Barrett, 1980,

---

[1]The diagonal marks that appear in Barrett's transcription of the M Notebook indicate corrections inserted into the text by Charles Darwin.

2. Darwin's Thought on Expressive Mechanisms

p. 26). Furthermore, Darwin had also arrived at his insight that expressions derived by association need not be adaptive. In a case involving horses he remarked: ''good instance of useless muscular tricks accompanying emotion—when horses fighting, they put down ears, when kicking/turning round to kick/they do the same, although it is then quite useless'' (M Notebook, p. 146e; Barrett, 1980, p. 34). In another passage, Darwin notes, ''With respect to sneering, the very essence of an habitual movement is continuing it when useless,—therefore it is here continued when the uncovering the canine useless'' (M Notebook, p. 96, in Barrett, 1980, p. 23). Uncovering the canine teeth when sneering is one of the most visible links between human behavior and that of animals. The fact that the behavior is also purposeless made it all the more interesting to Darwin.

Charles's second major principle of explanation, that of antithesis, seems to have been his own invention. There is nothing comparable to it in Erasmus's book. But it too was already spelled out in the M Notebook:

> Why does dog put down ears when pleased—is it opposite movement to drawing them close on head, when going to fight, in which case expression resembles a |[2] fox—I can conceive the opposite muscles would act, when in a passion.—dog tail curled when angry & very stiff. back arched. just contrary. when pleased tail loose & wagging. (M Notebook, pp. 146e–147, in Barrett, 1980, p. 34).

From the evidence of the M Notebook, it seems that Charles Darwin had already formed the main outline of this theory of expression by October 2, 1838 when he completed the M Notebook. The date is important because it helps explain the character of his theory: at that time Darwin had just begun to develop his theory of natural selection. Evidence from his other notebooks shows that during the late summer of 1838 he still held a Lamarckian view of evolution (Kohn, 1980). It was only after he read Malthus's *Principles of Population* in September, 1838 that he came to his idea of natural selection. Furthermore, there is little indication in either the M or N Notebook that Darwin was concerned to refute the views of Bell. To be sure, Darwin was already employing a theory of nonadaptive expression that was inconsistent with Bell's views, but the M Notebook contains no mention of Bell, and the N Notebook makes only one vague allusion to matters discussed in Bell's work on expression (N Notebook, p. 41; in Barrett, 1980, p. 78). We have

[2]Horizontal bar was Barrett's symbol to indicate a page break in Darwin's manuscript.

every reason to believe that Darwin was attracted to his grandfather's associationist psychology on its own merits, quite apart from its specific utility in combating Bell's position. Converting this psychology to evolutionary ends required a belief in Lamarckian use-inheritance, which caused Darwin no difficulty because this was his evolutionary belief already. After Darwin became a selectionist he continued to employ selection and use-inheritance side by side to solve various evolutionary problems (Richards, 1981). Use-inheritance provided him with a weapon against Bell's natural theology by allowing him to employ the psychological approach that he had preferred from the beginning.

The story of Charles Darwin's theory of expression is in one respect very characteristic of Darwin's intellectual style. In keeping with his strong theoretical interests, Darwin usually developed the rudiments of a theory first and then spent years collecting evidence and working out the implications of the idea (Rudwick, 1982). The intellectual roots of much of his later work can be traced to the notebooks he was keeping in the late 1830s. His theory of expression illustrates the usual pattern very nicely; important parts of the theory were in place early, though the final book did not appear until decades later. Of course, Darwin did not work steadily on the problem of expression during most of this period. His study of expression represented a subordinate aspect of his evolutionary program as a whole, and serious work on the problem had to wait until he had, in turn, taken up the issues of natural selection, variation, human evolution, and sexual selection in his major evolutionary books. Indeed, Darwin also paused to initiate a new program in his study of flower forms and plant movement before he finally completed the cycle of his evolutionary books. However, in the late 1860s, he finally turned serious attention to the subject of expression and began the reading and observation that led to his book. By this time the works of Duchenne, Gratiolet, and Piderit had appeared, and Darwin was in a far better position to attack the subject than he had been previously. He had originally intended to include a discussion of expression as part of his book, *Descent of Man* (1871); however, when that study began to grow ominously long, he deferred expression for a separate publication. In this way his initially minor interest in expression came to demand an independent publication of its own.

The Evolution of Expression

As a result of Darwin's research he was able to illustrate his theoretical ideas. The book on expression, *Expression of Emotions* (1872), contains two chapters of observational findings on animal expression and several

more chapters on human expression. However, these chapters were designed to go beyond Darwin's three principles of expression and demonstrate further important points. In the chapters on animals Darwin
especially argued against Bell's view that animal expression is a restricted phenomenon, serving only to exhibit a narrow range of violent
emotions. In the chapters on human expression, Darwin emphasized
the common hereditary basis of expression in all human races. Both sections of the book contributed to his overall argument that expression is
an evolutionary product that both humans and animals share in common. However, in spite of this unified approach to expression in both
animals and humans, Darwin did allow a slightly different emphasis to
creep into the two sections. In the chapters on animals, he somewhat
relaxed the interpretation of his three principles and allowed a degree
of direct adaptationism: he sometimes explained expression in terms of
its utility for coping with the external environment. In the chapters on
humans no such relaxation took place, and the three principles are
maintained throughout the discussion. Darwin nowhere acknowledges
or explains this contrasting treatment, yet it serves to quietly underline
his opposition to teleological explanations.

In the chapters on animal expression Darwin's concern was to over-
turn Bell's view that animal expression was a restricted phenomenon,
capable only of displaying such strong feelings as rage and fear. As an
evolutionist, Darwin naturally opposed this bestial view of animal
expression and sought to counter it by pointing to the broad range of
expressions that animals routinely display. In part, Bell's disparagement
of animal expression resulted from his esthetic interest. He had wanted
to point up the absurdity of anthropomorphism in the artistic representation of animal faces. As a result, he concerned himself only with the
facial expressions of animals. Darwin hastened to undermine Bell's approach by describing the wide variety of nonfacial expressions that animals employ, noting especially vocal sounds, ruffling of fur and
feathers, the puffing up of reptiles and amphibians, and the drawing
back or erection of ears. However, when he came to the behavior of
apes and monkeys, he was able to point out a considerable number of
facial expressions too—some of them comparable to equivalent human
expressions. In doing so he laid a firm groundwork for the evolutionary
interpretation of human expression.

Darwin's chapters on animals are particularly interesting because of
his frequent attention to the adaptive consequences of animal expression. He points out the obvious utility of ruffling fur or feathers in a
frightened or aggressive animal, and he also notes the contrasting behavior of frightened birds that press their feathers together to appear
smaller: "The habit is intelligible in these birds from their being accus-

tomed, when in danger, either to squat on the ground or to sit motionless on a branch so as to escape detection" (1872, p. 100). In another interesting comparison, Darwin observes that animals that bite, like dogs and horses, draw back their ears when fighting, whereas nonbiting animals, like cattle, sheep, and goats, do not (pp. 111–114). Darwin even goes so far as to explain ruffling behavior as due partly to natural selection:

> for the males which succeeded in making themselves appear the most terrible to their rivals, or to their other enemies, if not of overwhelming power, will on an average have left more offspring to inherit their characteristic qualities, whatever these may be and however first acquired, than have other males. (p. 104).

This is the only expression in the book explicitly attributed to natural selection. Apparently, in dealing with nonfacial expression Darwin felt free to employ an adaptive viewpoint that he avoided when discussing facial expressions. Because Bell had neglected nonfacial expressions, Darwin did not confront any teleological interpretations of adaptation in this area. Darwin could introduce his own adaptive approach and even relate it to natural selection.

In investigating human expression Darwin was concerned to find natural subjects whose behavior reflected a minimum of social conventions. He believed that children and the mentally ill would make especially good subjects because they were less inclined to restrain their expressions than are healthy adults. Observing children was not difficult, for he had many of his own, but he had no opportunities to see the mentally ill. His problem was solved, though, when he made contact with James Crichton-Browne, director of the West Riding Lunatic Asylum. Crichton-Browne was an innovative physician who had developed an interest in photographing patients. He mailed Darwin a large number of photographs of patients, depicting many expressions (Gilman, 1979). The grateful Darwin wrote Crichton-Brown, "Sometime ago I went into several shops in London to try to buy photographs of the insane, but failed; so you may believe with how much interest I have carefully looked at your excellent ones" (June 8, 1869).[3]

In his effort to get beyond the effects of social convention, Darwin employed some of his most innovative strategies. One of these was to

---

[3]Please see "Unpublished Source," following "Acknowledgments" and preceding "References."

check the response of observers to various expressions. As he wrote to Crichton-Browne, "In order to test Duchenne's plates I have shown the most characteristic (hiding any indication of what they were meant to express) to between 20 and 30 persons of all kinds, and have recorded their answers: when all or nearly all agree in their answers, I trust him" (June 8, 1870). This use of photographs was entirely novel on Darwin's part, but his most ambitious experiment did not employ photographs. Darwin surmised that if he could show that the same expressions appeared around the world in many different cultures, he would have useful evidence for their common ancestry. This was not a demonstration he could carry out personally, but through the large network of his correspondents he was able to gather information about a surprising number of the world's peoples. Missionaries, merchants, and ordinary travelers contributed to his stock of evidence, most of it supporting his position. Things did not always turn out as expected: he was fascinated, for example, to learn that shaking the head for negation and nodding it for affirmation were by no means universal human gestures (1872, pp. 274–277). However, he was usually gratified to learn that most expressions seemed universal. As a special support for this position he was able to cite the case of Laura Bridgeman, an American woman who was both blind and deaf. The information that Laura Bridgeman shrugged her shoulders or stood with raised hands and open mouth in surprise seemed to Darwin evidence that these behaviors were innate (p. 267). Finally, there was evidence of similar expressions in man and some animals. The baring of eye teeth while snarling seemed a strong evolutionary indication as did the pouting behavior of small children and chimpanzees.

The information collected by Darwin made a powerful case for explaining expression in evolutionary terms, but he remained faithful to his original conviction that the evolutionary mechanism at work was only indirectly adaptive. In summing up his conclusions he remarked,

> The power of communication between the members of the same tribe by means of language has been of paramount importance in the development of man; and the force of language is much aided by the expressive movements of the face and body. We perceive this at once when we converse on an important subject with any person whose face is concealed. Nevertheless there are no grounds, as far as I can discover, for believing that any muscle has been developed or even modified exclusively for the sake of expression. The vocal and other sound-producing organs, by which various expressive noises are produced, seem to form a partial exception; but I have elsewhere attempted to show that these organs were first developed for sexual purposes, in order that one sex might call or charm the other. (1872, p. 355).

Darwin did see that expression had value for purposes of communication. Almost as a final statement he remarked,

> The movements of expression in the face and body, whatever their origin may have been, are in themselves of much importance for our welfare. They serve as the first means of communication between the mother and her infant; she smiles approval, and thus encourages her child on the right path, or frowns disapproval. We readily perceive sympathy in others by their expression; our sufferings are thus mitigated and our pleasures increased; and mutual good feeling is thus strengthened. (1872, pp. 365–366).

In this statement Darwin came very close to the kind of adaptive thinking that appears so prominently in his other evolutionary writings. Yet the statement occurs at the end of his book, almost as an afterthought. Against the weight of the argument he constructed for the three principles, it makes very little impression.

Conclusion

Darwin's *Expression of Emotions* (1872) sometimes makes difficult reading today, not because its ideas are especially complex, but rather because they bear a deceptive resemblance to more familiar ideas. One finds oneself almost at home in the book, and it is easy to read into it a set of assumptions about Darwin and Darwinism that may not really be there. Our Darwin is the scientist who wrote the *Origin of Species* (1859) and based evolutionary theory primarily on the adaptive mechanism of natural selection, but the historical Darwin had other concerns as well. To be sure, his text on expression is thoroughly evolutionary, and it exhibits the same opposition to teleological thinking that one finds in the *Origin*. Darwin's work on expression followed a medical tradition in concentrating on emotion, emphasizing anatomy, and seeking out good illustrations. He managed to extend this approach by tying the subject to evolution and by introducing new research methods designed to distinguish between cultural and innate influences. His success in testing the evolutionary hypothesis against a broad range of evidence is one of the triumphs of the book. Yet in retrospect the book raises problems with its heavy emphasis on use-inheritance and its peculiar concentration on nonadaptive evolution. There is no longer any danger that Darwin's contributions will be overlooked because of their connection with unfamiliar or rejected ideas. The difficulty is rather that we will misinterpret Darwin's intentions in an effort to extract our own preferred ideas.

In developing his nonadaptive approach to expression, Darwin came into direct conflict with the natural theology of Charles Bell (1844) with its notions of a uniquely functional musculature of expression reserved solely for the human species. To judge by the evidence of the M and N Notebooks (Barrett, 1980) Darwin was not thinking primarily of Bell when he developed his initial views. Darwin's belief in the origin of expression through mental associations that lacked a specifically adaptive function was derived from his broader desire to push the sensationalist position as far as he could. Bell's theories offered the most important concrete opposition to Darwin's program, and Darwin was certainly pleased to turn the associationist argument against Bell. It is noteworthy that natural selection appears in *Expression of Emotions* (1872) chiefly in connection with the nonfacial expression of animals, a matter that Bell did not address. Nevertheless, it would be a mistake to view Darwin's interest in nonadaptive evolution simply as a reaction against the specific arguments of Bell. At the very least, one must recognize that Darwin employed nonadaptive theories in other areas of evolution; they are not unique to his treatment of expression.

Darwin's heavy reliance on the inheritance of acquired characteristics poses a second problem. The sophisticated reader sagely overlooks Darwin's use of this outdated conception, explaining it as a consequence of the times. Yet the sophisticated reader may be missing something. Darwin did make concessions to his contemporaries' belief in use-inheritance, but he always retained his basic faith in natural selection. The place of use-inheritance in *Expressions of Emotions* (1872) is of an entirely different order. In this book, use-inheritance is closely related to the sensationalist psychology that lies at the core of Darwin's theories. Darwin wanted to show not only that behavior has an evolutionary basis but also that behavior plays a role in evolution. He believed this from his earliest days as an evolutionist, even before he adopted natural selection. This belief explains both the nonadaptive and Lamarckian aspects of his theories. Indeed, it does a great deal to explain why he wrote a book on expression at all. Conceptually we may wish to edit Darwin's sensationalist convictions; historically we need to recognize their central position in his achievement. Scientists may see further by standing on the shoulders of giants, but it is well to remember that every giant had a distinctive vision of his own.

Summary

Charles Darwin's work, *The Expression of the Emotions in Man and Animals* (1872), hardly employs the concept of natural selection to explain the inheritance of expressive behaviors. This striking theoretical contrast with *The Origin of Species* and its implications for how he did conceive of expressive behavior can be illuminated by a combination of factors in his intellectual history: he believed that the evolution of behavior, as contrasted with the evolution of morphology, can be accounted for by the inheritance of acquired characteristics; he applied his grandfather Erasmus Darwin's theory of associationist psychology to the acquisition of expressive habits; and he had an interest in arguing that human facial musculature is not specially adapted for expressive functions. He aimed this last argument against Charles Bell's natural theology, which, by claiming the special design of this musculature for expression, separated man from animals and denied the evolution of man. To explicate Charles Darwin's views of the inheritance, evolution, and psychological functioning of expression, this chapter puts forth the preceding points in a context that reviews Erasmus Darwin's theories of evolution and psychology and the thinking of other nineteenth-century theorists of expression. The latter reveals assumptions about expression whose original formulations might be erroneously attributed to Charles Darwin alone.

Acknowledgments

An earlier version of this chapter was delivered as a lecture cosponsored by the Historical Division of the Cleveland Health Sciences Library and the History of Science and Technology Program of Case Western Reserve University. I further wish to thank Professors Mark B. Adams and Russell C. Maulitz for their comments and criticism. Quotations from Darwin's letters to Crichton-Browne are printed with permission of the Syndics of the University of Cambridge Library. Quotations from the M Notebook (as transcribed in Barrett, 1980) are printed with the permission of the Syndics of the University of Cambridge Library, Professor Paul H. Barrett, and Georges Borchardt, Inc.

Unpublished Source

The M Notebook is preserved in the Darwin Collection at University Library, Cambridge, Volume 125. Copies of Darwin's letters to Crichton-Browne are preserved in Volume 143. I wish to thank the Syndics of Cambridge University Library for permission to quote from these sources.

References

Bain, A. *The senses and the intellect.* London: Parker, 1855.
Bain, A. *The emotions and the will.* London: Parker, 1859.
Barrett, P. H. (Ed.). *Metaphysics, materialism, and the evolution of mind: Early writings of*

Charles Darwin. With a commentary by Howard E. Gruber. Chicago: University of Chicago Press, 1980.

Bell, C. *Essays on the anatomy of expression in painting.* London: Longman, Hurst, Rees, & Orme, 1806.

Bell, C. *The anatomy and philosophy of expression as connected with the fine arts* (3rd. ed./6th ed.). London: Bohn, 1844/1872)

Bell, C. *The hand, its mechanism and vital endowments, as evincing design.* London: Pickering, 1833.

Burgess, T. *The physiology or mechanism of blushing.* London: Churchill, 1839.

Coleman, W. Louis Pierre Gratiolet. In C. C. Gillispie (Ed.), *Dictionary of scientific biography* (Vol. 5). New York: Scribner's, 1972.

Darwin, C. *On the origin of species by means of natural selection, or the preservation of favoured races in the struggle for life* (1st ed./6th ed.). London: Muray, 1859/1872a.

Darwin, C. *The descent of man, and selection in relation to sex* (2 vols.). London: Murray, 1871.

Darwin C. *The expression of the emotions in man and animals.* London: Murray, 1872.

Darwin, E. *Zoonomia; or, the laws of organic life* (2 vols.). London: Johnson, 1794–96.

De Beer, G. Darwin's notebooks on transmutation of species. *Bulletin of the British Museum (Natural History), Historical Series.* London, 1960, 2,(2–5).

De Beer, G., & Rowlands, M. J. Darwin's notebooks on transmutation of species: Addenda and corrigenda. *Bulletin of the British Museum (Natural History), Historical Series,* 1961, 2(6).

De Beer, G., Rowlands, M. J., & Skramovsky, B. M. Darwin's notebooks on transmutation of species, VI: Pages excised by Darwin. *Bulletin of the British Museum (Natural History), Historical Series,* 1967, 3(5).

Duchenne, G. B. *Mecanisme de la physionomie humaine ou analyse electrophysiologique de l'expression des passions* (2nd ed.). [*The mechanism of human physiognomy; or, electrophysiological analysis of the expression of passions*] Paris: Balliere, 1876. (Originally published 1862)

Ekman, P. *Darwin and facial expression: A century of research in review.* New York: Academic Press, 1973.

Geison, G. L. *Michael Foster and the Cambridge school of physiology.* Princeton: Princeton University Press, 1978.

Ghiselin, M. T. *The triumph of the Darwinian method.* Berkeley: University of California Press, 1969.

Gilman, S. L. Darwin sees the insane. *Journal of the History of Behavioral Sciences,* 1979, *15,* 253–262.

Graham, J. Lavater's physiognomy in England. *Journal of the History of Ideas,* 1961, 22, 561–72.

Gratiolet, P. *De la physionomie et des mouvements d'expression.* [*On physiognomy and expressive movements*]. Paris: Hetzel, 1865.

King-Hele, D. *Doctor of revolution: The life and genius of Erasmus Darwin.* London: Faber & Faber, 1977.

Kohn, D. Theories to work by: Rejected theories, reproduction, and Darwin's path to natural selection. In W. Coleman and C. Limoges (Eds.), *Studies in History of Biology* (Vol. 4). Baltimore: Johns Hopkins University Press, 1980. pp. 67–170.

Lorenz, K. Preface. In C. Darwin, *The expression of the emotions in man and animals.* Chicago: University of Chicago Press, 1965.

Piderit, T. *Wissenschaftliches system der mimik und physiognomik.* [*Scientific system of mimicry and physiognomy*] Detmold: Kingenberg, 1867.

Richards, R. J. Influence of sensationalist tradition on early theories of evolution of behavior. *Journal of the History of Ideas,* 1979, 40, 85–105.

Richards, R. J. Instinct and intelligence in British natural theology: Some contributions to Darwin's theory of the evolution of behavior. *Journal of the History of Biology*, 1981, *14*, 193–230.

Rudwick, M. J. S. Charles Darwin in London: The interpretation of public and private science. *Isis*, 1982, *73*, 186–206.

Spencer, H. *The principles of psychology*. London, 1855.

Spencer, H. The physiology of laughter. *Macmillan's Magazine*, 1860, *1*, 395–402. Reprinted in *Essays: Scientific, political, speculative* (Vol. 2). London: 1863.

Sulloway, F. J. Darwin's conversion: The Beagle voyage and its aftermath. *Journal of the History of Biology*, 1982, *15*, 325–96.

Chapter 3

Consistency and Change in Communication

W. John Smith

Relationship to Other Chapters and to the Field

Relevant Issues in the Field

Although Smith's emphasis in this chapter is on how change in signals can take place without losing intelligibility, his chapter teaches an issue of even more fundamental importance for the field of expressive-behavior development—a broad view of what information may be made available by expressive behavior. He expands semiotic analyses for identifying referents by asserting that a referent of a signal can be anything with which the signal systematically correlates— internal state, external event, and/or the next behavior of the signaler. This goes far beyond the usual analysis of human expression as referring only to an internal state, usually emotional. And Smith notes that the "state" that accompanies a signal is probably not a full emotional condition, but a physiological-motivational fraction of the condition that accompanies the signaling. His is an animal behaviorist, ethological view that emphasizes the prediction of the signaler's behavior as usually the most adaptively important information that a recipient can get from a signal; he asserts that we do not know what type of information, whether about a state, an external event or both, best leads to such predictions. Smith focuses on the interpretative response capacity of the recipient more than on the condition of the signaler. He contends that recipients always respond not just to the information made available by signals but also to information contextual to them. It is the orderliness of the contextual infor-

51

mation that allows a signal to change form, over age or generations, without losing intelligibility.

Smith contributes to an understanding of biology–environment interactions in expressive development by explicating the complex role of the recipient's learning about the environment, which makes increasingly flexible and adaptive use of the information provided by even prewired signals. In this he holds a position very much like other animal behaviorists in this volume: Marler and the Gouzouleses (see Chapter 4), Hinde (see Chapter 5), and most clearly, Mason (see Chapter 6). He further points out the environment-dependent course of some evolutionary developments in his explication of the Baldwin effect *and in his analysis that the signaler and the recipient are necessary environmental influences on each other such that there must be coevolution of conspecifics' signal and interpretation capacities, which continue to confer on average positive benefits on both roles.*

Relationship to Other Chapters

With context-dependent interpretation of signal information, Smith touches important concerns of Hinde (Chapter 5), Mason (Chapter 6), and Gouzoules, Gouzoules, and Marler (Chapter 4). Smith suggests the orderliness of the use of contextual information as an explanation for the continued intelligibility of the ambiguous information exchanged in Hinde's conception of negotiation between signalers. Smith and Marler and the Gouzouleses share the particular methodological interest in accurately apportioning the sources of a message's information to signal and to context. To make their argument of similarity between human and nonhuman cognition, Marler and the Gouzouleses need to locate a signal that could, in principle, refer to an external event without the use of contextual information. However, they do acknowledge that its contextless use might be rare. Smith would assert that contextless interpretation never occurs. Both Smith and Mason imply the importance of the unexamined processes by which signalers and recipients select relevant contextual information. Mason emphasizes the signaler's experiential learning of the environment that leads to appraisal, emotional reaction, and signal, whereas Smith (and Marler and the Gouzouleses) emphasize the recipient's analysis of the context. Smith claims, in principle, that change in signal form is one major way of evolving new semantic units, but this appears to conflict with Mason's conclusion that, at least in rhesus monkeys, signal form appears not to change as the result of experience in facial movements, although it does change in vocalizations. However, Smith and Mason are examining different ranges of change and of species: Smith considers all species, in principle, and emphasizes phylogenetic change; Mason examines rhesus monkeys for only ontogenetic change. Resolution here will rest on examining similar ranges of species over similar periods and mechanisms of change. Thelen (see Chapter 9), as well as Mason, raises the question that Smith here primarily addresses—the limits on signal-form change while preserving intelligibility—although she does not propose an analysis of it.

Smith explicitly criticizes the assumption that most (human) expressive behaviors reveal a concurrent emotional state, but he does assert that some aspect of the physiological state must correlate with the signal and hence be in some sense one of its referents. He thus suggests the importance of Montgomery's Chapter 2 which clarifies the assumptions that Darwin did and did not make about the necessary correlation of emotional state and expressive behavior. Smith thereby questions a major assumption of most of the chapters in the second secton of this book—that emotional states are the internal conditions that accompany expressive behaviors in naive signaling.

For Consistent Terminology

The semiotic terms signal *and* referent *are explicated in the framing chapter. Smith uses both in ways that are more precise than, but consistent with, those definitions. He states that* signal, *standardly a term for unspecified type of indicator, specifically indicates a* formalized signal *(one that is evolutionarily specialized for communication effect); however, his use of* signal *is not specialized according to the signal types of index, icon, or symbol, and thus is consistent with the rest of this volume. Smith uses interchangeably* referent, *the information that a signal makes available, and* message. *In the study of expressive behavior, it is unusual to use* referent *to mean contextual information that may be indicated by a signal but not somehow specified within the signal itself. However, Smith's work emphasizes that, in natural signaling situations, the recipient of a signal goes beyond the referent to contextual information to extract the* meaning *of the entire situation—*ED.

Introduction

Communication involves provision of information and selection of responses to that information by its recipients. When communication incorporates specialized signaling, subsequently defined, numerous distinctions are possible both in providing and in responding to the information. Considerable consistency is required in the relationships between the signals and the information they make available. If these relationships change, recipients of the signals must be able to track the shifts. Otherwise the ways they are predisposed to respond to the signals will become obsolete.

But communication must change, at least in animals adapted to deal with complex life styles and changing worlds. In ontogenetic development in particular, there can be gross changes in the situations with which an individual must deal and in the ways in which the individual copes. Much behavior, communication included, changes during ontogeny. This raises the question of how communication continues to work. The key is in the orderliness and detectability of change. Patterns of change can themselves be consistent and can enrich instead of interfere with communication. In addition to changing during individual lifetimes, communication changes over evolutionary time; again, detectability is a key issue.

This chapter is concerned with the reconciliation of change and consistency. It begins by defining communication and the concept of formalized signaling, then discusses referents—the information made available by signaling—and the conditional and probabilistic nature of predictions that are engendered by signaling. The next section surveys repertoires of signaling behavior and the procedures employed by individuals responding to signaling. This sets the stage for consideration of changes in signaling and of how these changes are marked to facilitate changes in responding.

Communication and Formalized Signaling

To communicate is to share information. *Information* is a property of all things and events that enhances their predictability. It thus enables its possessors to make more appropriate choices than can individuals with less information (discussed by Smith, 1977, Chapter 1, 8).

To respond actively to their surroundings, animals need information continuously. During evolution they have acquired the capacity to obtain and evaluate information from many sources. Among the most pertinent sources from which all animals seek information are other animals, particularly members of their own species.

Animals are thus selected to be attentive to, and to benefit by getting information from one another. But there is an additional evolutionary effect: animals are also selected to provide certain kinds of information to each other. In social interactions, each participant has information that is not, or not readily, available to other participants. It is essentially private. When the information is made publically available, it can enable other participants to predict a signaler's behavior better and perhaps to predict some other aspects of an event. If appropriately informed, recipients should respond in ways useful to those who signal—although they will do so only if their responses are, on the average, to their own advantage too.

Evolutionary pressures thus shape predispositions both to respond to other animals and to share some kinds of information with them by signaling. The latter effects yield a dichotomy among the sources of information available to each individual. Because anything that can be sensed can be informative, sources are plentiful. However, most stimuli are not *specialized* to be informative: rocks, streams, an individual's height, and many observed activities such as sleeping and eating. In contrast, other activities and structures are specialized in form or performance to make available certain information: smiling, laughing and talking of people, grimacing and lipsmacking of other primates, "singing" of birds, whales, and crickets, flashing of fireflies, adornments such as crests or color patches on the body surface, and so on. Behavior patterns and structures that are specialized to be informative can be termed *formalized* (Smith, 1977, pp. 326–330, a term embracing products of both genetic and nongenetic evolution).

Formalization entails an established relationship between special activities or structures and the information they make available (i.e., their referents, see next section). Because this relationship must be public (i.e., a code specifying it must be held by more than one individual), the relationship and the form of the signaling specializations must be fixed. Formalized signals need not be invariant, but the form of the free variation must be sufficiently minor so as not to confuse recipients and the form of the remainder must be rule-bound. In rule-bound variations, the ways in which the form of signaling can be varied are themselves formalized or otherwise linked to public constraints. I return to this later in considering how such variation contributes to the distinctions that can be made by signaling.

Formalized sources of information can be especially relevant to interacting individuals because these sources reduce the ambiguity inherent in so many other actions (Smith 1977, p. 9). One individual who approaches another, for instance, may soon stop short, veer off, join and simply associate with the approached individual, or instead make contact in any of numerous ways that include such different extremes as copulating and attacking. The act of approaching is informative but by itself highly ambiguous. If an approaching rhesus monkey grimaces or lipsmacks (see Mason, Chapter 6, this volume), however, or an approaching human smiles or adopts the raised brows, the steady stare, and the elevated chin of the *plus face* (Zivin, 1977), highly pertinent additional information is provided. These formalized arrangements and movements of facial features, gaze, and head angles enable conditional prediction of behavior the signaler may perform after approaching. Ambiguity is not eliminated but it is reduced in ways important to the orderly development of interactions. These formalized signals thus render the costs and risks of making choices more acceptable to each participant. In the context of information from other sources (e.g., from approach behavior), the information made available by formalized sources can make the difference between faltering, ineffective, or dangerous interactions and orderly, well-managed, functional ones of relatively low-risk.

The terms *formalized signal* and *signal* are used interchangeably in this chapter, although the latter is sometimes used by ethologists to denote any source of information, formalized or not. Despite its imprecision, signal is a word in common usage and can be a convenient relief from jargon such as the ethological term *display* or *expression*, a term more common in psychology. Further, expression sometimes has connotations that are too narrow. In its broadest sense (e.g., Brown, 1968, p. 307), expression is used to mean that signaling provides information about characteristics of the signaler—any characteristics. Unfortunately, the term is commonly used to imply that the referents of signaling are emotional states. As is argued in the next section, this view omits much. It also is based on insufficient evidence. As a further problem, Darwin (1872) and others have held that emotional expressions are simply obligate epiphenomena of physiological states that leak information about those states without being specialized to do so (see Darwin's third principle or explanation of involuntary expressions, for instance). Nonetheless, conspicuousness, elaboration, details of underlying muscle actions (H. Oster, June 2, 1983, personal communication,), timing of performance, and the like all suggest considerable formalization of most of the acts called expressions: for example, laughing, smiling, blushing, or medially furrowing the eyebrows.

The Referents of Formalized Signals

A *referent* is anything that becomes knowable or predictable through the performance of a signal (Smith, 1981), exclusive of information from sources contextual to that performance. For instance, a limited range of other behavior typically correlates, either concurrently or (conditionally) afterward, with the performance of those signals ethologists term displays. Each behavioral correlate of a display is a referent. Particular sig-

nals are also correlated with particular signalers, thus providing information about who the signaler is. Its species, its dialect group, and often
even its individual identity are then referents. Performance of some signals is also correlated with definable external stimuli to which the signaler is responding (e.g., predators, or particular kinds of predators)
and so has those things as referents. (See Gouzoules, Gouzoules & Marler, Chapter 4, this volume, for treatment of external reference.)

Some physiological mechanism is necessary for the production of any
kind of behavior, and thus signals that correlate with particular kinds
of behavior must also be correlated with the signaler's internal states—
not the whole states at any moment, but some consistent features that
are, in principle, definable. As with any correlates, these features could
be referents. Until we understand the cognitive processing of signaled
information we will not know if recipients use information about behavior, internal states, or both as they respond. Behavior, however, is
often what recipients must predict from moment to moment as they
work to manage interactions.

The relationships of internal states to signals has led signals to be
called *expressions of the emotions* in much work on human signaling, especially facial signaling. There is no obvious reason why relevant
internal states should be just emotional, however.

The assumption that what is expressed is information about emotions
remains untested. It is not sufficient to give subjects a list of emotions
and a set of pictures of facial configurations to see if they can match
any. They can match some, but the technique does not necessarily show
how the configurations contribute to communication in real events.
When subjects have to assign anger, fear, or happiness to a smiling face,
for instance, they will choose the last—but do they usually assume smiling people are happy? Probably not, granted that people who are sad,
anxious, bewildered, and so on will smile, often without intent to deceive. A study that directly addresses this issue found that happiness
correlates much less well with smiling than does engaging in social interaction, even in diverse emotional states (Kraut & Johnston, 1979).
Frijda (1969) showed that people will match photographs of facial
expressions with listed emotions if asked to, but if allowed "free" interpretation, they much more often describe situations (e.g., she looks as
if she is watching a small child play) or anticipated behavior. Useful as
it is to know about emotional states of individuals with whom we interact, it is not clear that we get more than clues to these from formalized
signals. We may usually infer emotions only from information gleaned
from multiple sources and accumulated over more than just momentary
intervals.

The only facial signal of humans I have studied is a formalized showing of the tongue (Smith, Chase, & Lieblich, 1974). Darwin (1872) interpreted this signal as an expression of disgust or contempt. We found it abundant in natural events and rarely saw disgusted or contemptuous signalers. Rather, they appeared reluctant to interact socially, either at all or in some way pertinent to a particular event. Our prediction that recipients would be more reluctant to begin interacting with a tongue-showing person than with one who is not has been experimentally confirmed (Dolgin & Sabini, 1982). Thus, although people who are disgusted may show their tongue and subjects might match pictures of it with "disgust" in a limited list of emotions, its usual value seems tied to behavioral referents. In real events, an interpretation of disgust probably requires information not just from the tongue-showing signal but also from sources contextual to it, for example, the sight of a signaler avoiding or rejecting some noxious stimulus.

To summarize, formalized signals appear to make available information about who the signaler is, where the signaler is, and what the signaler is doing or may do. They may also provide information about the signaler's internal states, although the extent of such information and its relevance in communicating is not well understood as yet. Some signals also make information available about external stimuli to which the signaler is responding.

The Conditionality of Predictions
Fostered by Signaling

Although a signal may identify a signaler precisely, it does not provide information about just one class of that individual's behavior. Rather, it informs about alternatives that may be selected. For example, displays functionally classifiable as "threat" (on which Professor Hinde focuses Chapter 5 in this volume) commonly enable the relative probabilities of at least attack and escape behavior to be predicted, plus a class of activities such as vacillating shifts in orientation, intention movements, or even frozen immobility—a class I have described as *indecisive* behavior (Smith, 1977, p. 106–108). As an individual threatens, it usually performs indecisive acts and, in at least the short term, is usually more likely to continue such actions than to switch to attack or to escape. The average probability that the individual will select either of those alternatives can also be ranked for each form of signal. However, what it actually proceeds to do is *always* conditional on the nature and development of the event. That is, probabilistic predictions based on its signaling are accurate only at the instant of the signaling act, are conditional on the circumstance of the moment, and are changeable, subject to changing circumstances (Smith, 1977, p. 127–133).

The ephemerality of predictions is especially evident when attack is predicted because attack is so very often obviated by an opponent that flees or cowers. Further, if the opponent threatens back, attack may be forestalled. An opponent's response to signaling can render obsolete the predictions of that signaling. Yet there is no convincing basis for the claim (Caryl, 1979) that formal signaling predicts attack less accurately than it predicts escape behavior. We cannot hope to measure the accuracy of predictions when the act of signaling itself radically changes an event.

Even in less dramatic situations, in which signals are not threats and the information made available is about gentler activities such as associating with a companion, signaling does not commit a signaler to follow through in spite of changing circumstances. Recipient individuals must make do with conditional predictions. Even these, however, are usually a considerable improvement over the predictions that are possible in otherwise comparable events in which there is no signaling.

Making Distinctions in Signaling and Responding to Signals

As circumstances change and events progress, individuals who are in communication must make numerous distinctions. These distinctions come both as they signal and as they respond to signals.

Signaling

A signaler contributes an array of signaling specializations, both behavioral and nonbehavioral. Among the latter are color patterns and other features of its appearance, chemicals it can release or deposit, and in some species even artifacts it constructs. The behavioral specializations comprise several repertoires of signaling procedures. The repertoires each have different properties, and each operates within its own set of constraints.

The more signaling specializations that are available, the more closely appropriate can be the information provided in any event. And the combined performance of signaling from different repertoires can inform with considerable precision. In addition, the signaler inevitably provides information by means not specialized to do so, for example, by its size, by where it is, and by aspects of its demeanor that reveal its degree of relaxation or alertness. (Features can be specialized to provide such information or to conceal it; the point is that any characteristic or behavior of an organism is informative although most are specialized for other functions.)

The several repertoires of signaling procedures outlined next are more fully described and discussed by Smith (in press-a).

Signal Acts

Fundamental to the communicating of any species is a repertoire of signal acts. These can be vocal or other sounds (e.g., a dog's barks, growls, or whines), postures or movements (e.g., the dog's head thrust forward and teeth bared or its wagging tail), special ways of depositing scents (e.g., leg-raised urinating on communal scent posts), special touching patterns (e.g., a dog nuzzling another dog's jawline), and so on. Each such act is a unit of the repertoire of signal acts, a basic information-carrying vehicle.

No species seems to have a very large number of such units, about 40 to 45 by conservative criteria (Moynihan, 1970; Smith, 1969) and perhaps no more than twice that by more generous criteria. This has apparently been a factor in the evolution both of context-dependent communication and of a trend toward broadly defined referents (Smith, 1969, 1977).

Variations of Signal Form

A second repertoire is made up of reversible ways of modifying the form of acts in the first repertoire. Sounds may be altered in peak frequency, duration, amplitude, harshness, inflection, or more complex ways. Visible signals can be varied in speed, extent and angle of movement, and so forth. Each such procedure appears either to alter the information made available by the basic acts (e.g., shifting the relative probabilities of behavioral referents or changing information about their intensity of performance) or to add information of its own (quavering a sound, for instance, appears to indicate that the vocalizing individual is likely to break off whatever it is doing and adds this information to whatever predictions are facilitated by the basic vocalization that is being quavered). Form variations have also been implicated in providing information about stimuli to which the signaler is responding (e.g., different classes of predators or other agents that cause fleeing behavior—see Owings & Leger, 1980).

These immediate and reversible shifts in the physical characteristics of other acts are signals that appear to have evolved largely independently of the signal acts they modify. Many (e.g., prolonging, quavering, or inflecting a sound) can be applied to more than one act in the basic signal repertoire of a species and even appear to have comparable employment and significance across diverse species. Although the number of such classes of variation available in the repertoire of any individual is apparently limited, they are different in an important way from the units of the previous repertoire. Each variational procedure may encompass a continuum of forms.

Patterned Combinations of Signals

Many simultaneous and sequential combinations of signals occur fortuitously, evoked by characteristics of unfolding events. However, other combinations are specialized to operate as units in their own right. We know little as yet about repertoires of formalized simultaneous combinations, but some repertoires of formalized sequences are becoming understood. These sequential formalizations can be defined by regularities in the intervals between successive acts, or by grammars that give special order to the sequences in which different acts are combined. Grammars have been found in the singing of some species of birds, for instance, and appear to operate by making clearly evident the proportional contribution of each different component act to a continuing signal performance.

In all formalized combinations a signaler performs two or more signal acts as components of the combined pattern, each act providing context for the others. Thus the combinations give signalers some control over sources of information available contextually to each of the component acts. Because other individuals' responses to their signals are always context-dependent (see the section "Responding"), this control can be very important in communicating.

A final significant feature of repertoires of formalized sequential combinations is their potential size. The number of sequential patterns that can be generated by even a few sequencing rules and basic signal acts can be quite large.

Formalized Interactions

There are also repertoires of cooperative performances: units of signaling that, like a human handshake, cannot be performed by a single individual. Some of these cooperative units are extended and elaborate, with many choice points and subroutines: greetings and courtship sequences, for instance. Although each species may again have only a limited number in its repertoire, the complexity and variability that is possible in the more extensive formalized interactions can add greatly to the elaboration of communication.

In sum, there are at least four repertoires of different kinds of signaling specializations available to individuals of many species. Although the number of units in each repertoire appears to be limited, each repertoire extends signaling capacities in special ways, and their combined effects greatly extend the scope of communicating.

Responding

In different circumstances, recipients of signals respond differently. They make many distinctions even if the signaling performances have been identical. This is done by taking into account information from both the signaling and the pertinent sources contextual to it. By never responding just to the information made available by a signal itself, they distinguish among and adjust to the conditions of each event.

Some important sources of information that are available contextually to performances of a signal are not readily evident to an outside observer. Most crucially, the experience of individual recipients with events in which a signal has been performed becomes a source of information stored in memory and can be used contextually to any subsequent performance of that signal. Memories give responders expectations of the stimuli that elicit signaling. Thus adult vervets probably expect to see an eagle on hearing another adult vervet utter an eagle alarm call because they have learned that association (Seyfarth, Cheney, & Marler, 1980). Their expectations are probably much less precise when they hear an infant vervet call. In responding, they should take into account both information from current sources about the age of the signaler and from past sources in their memories of stimuli associated with events in which they have heard the call uttered or have uttered it themselves. Hinde (see Chapter 5, this volume) uses fundamentally the same reasoning in interpreting seasonal shifts in responses to formalized signals of blue tits *Parus caeruleus* from a study by Stokes (1962). Indeed, reliance on information from contextual sources is one of the main ways of dealing with changes in the behavior of communicating. The next portion of the chapter discusses changes and their assimilation.

Marked Changes in Signaling Behavior

Changes during an Individual's Lifetime

Changes that occur in an individual's use of signaling are commonly *marked*, that is, made evident. The indicators are often changes in the form of the signals. Vocalizations may become lower pitched, for instance, as an individual grows. The form of the signaler also changes, at least during ontogeny, providing a set of clues contextual to the signals themselves.

Two sorts of differences in signaling are marked in these ways. The referents of a changing signal may change or the stimuli eliciting the signaling may change—even if the referents of that signaling do not.

Signal Form

First, changes in signal form can occur. Changes in fatty deposits and musculature make a human infant's facial movements different from those of older children (Oster & Rosenstein, in press). Changes in the size and shape of the vocal apparatus alter the sounds produced. As the forms of the signals change with age, some change in information about physical capacities and the level of experience of the signaling individuals is provided. To this extent at least, there are predictable changes in the referents of the signaling.

If referents regularly change in other ways during ontogeny, for example, incorporating different behavior, this too is marked by the changed signal forms. That is, because a lower-pitched vocalization of an older signaler can be distinguished from the vocalizations of a younger one, no confusion need result if members of the two age-classes perform differently in correlation with their vocalizations. Even if otherwise comparable in form, the signals of different pitches are not the same. This sort of change, unlike that described earlier in the chapter as classes of reversible form variation, is long term. Maturational examples are irreversible; others may be more nearly reversible but not on a momentary basis.

These signaling changes are important. When both the needs and capacities of an individual change progressively over more than momentary time, as they do in ontogeny, then signaling must keep pace. As developing individuals pass through successive phases of interacting with caregivers and peers, many of the functions they obtain from communication change. They become experienced with different kinds of interactions, develop long-term relationships with other individuals, and learn to operate within the restrictions and opportunities of the structured groups and neighborhoods within which they live. They become more adept at complex and subtle interacting.

Some of the changing function of the communication requires the signaling of information different from that which they provided when younger. This is achieved through the development of new signal forms, either by adding to the repertoire or by changing existing signals. Possible additions may be limited in number, which makes form changes important. Some form change is inevitable during ontogeny, as already suggested. Many other changes, although not simply by-products of the growth of signaling structures, also occur. Signals of adults are thus often recognizably different from those of younger individuals.

Eliciting Stimuli

The second sort of change in communicative behavior is in the stimuli to which individuals respond by signaling (Barlow, 1977; Burghardt, 1977). During ontogeny, and with experience at all phases of life, the competence with which individuals seek and use information changes and the stimuli they accept as pertinent change. They learn to adjust signaling more discriminately to features of the eliciting stimuli, or to different features as their needs change, effectively gaining a finer or otherwise altered tuning of the information that is made available.

Changes in the stimuli-eliciting signaling can coincide with changes in signal form. They can also occur though signal form remains unchanged. In the latter case, changed cues for signaling probably do not involve changes in a signal's referents. The referents are often largely behavioral: the ways in which the signaler is responding or may respond to the stimuli rather than the stimuli themselves. For instance, as an individual matures it develops increasing numbers of needs that can be satisfied socially. It may solicit with "infantile" signals when receptive to many kinds of interactions, yet the information provided by its signaling (i.e., that it is receptive) is fundamentally the same at all stages. At no time does the signaling itself specify the kinds of interactions that are sought—distinctions among the possibilities depend on information from sources contextual to the signaling.

As a further example, many things and events can elicit fleeing. Many of these stimuli change as an individual grows, but the correlation of a signal with the escape behavior may remain unchanged. It is the probability of fleeing rather than the diverse frightening stimuli that serves as the signal's referent. (Sometimes both the stimuli and the escape behavior appear to be referents. Young vervet monkeys utter an eagle alarm to diverse objects flying or passing overhead and gradually learn to restrict it to appropriate aerial predators [Seyfarth & Cheney, 1980]. Whether there is age-dependent detectable form change in this call has not been reported.) Often the stimuli that elicit signaling are too diverse and too unpredictably changeable to be revealed by the signaling; they are thus not among its referents.

There is not yet much in the literature to help us to evaluate and separate the effects of changes either in the form of signaling or in the eliciting stimuli. There is evidence that the usual form in which signals are performed may be modified as new circumstances are encountered in ontogeny. For instance, the human plus face (predictive of a win) becomes briefer (Zivin, 1977), and two of its components (the staring at an opponent and the medially raised brows) tend to drop out as the circumstances shift from confrontations to more individualistic challenges. Simultaneously, the main function changes from simply threatening to more subtle managing of the impression of confidence conveyed to others. The vocalizations of most or all nonhuman primates become less variable in form during ontogeny (Newman & Symmes, 1983). Whether the form of the complex and variable "threat face" of rhesus monkeys (Mason, see Chapter 6, this volume) changes ontogenetically was not studied, but as Mason's rhesus monkeys learned about social relationships they developed more diverse and complex social maneuvers that depended on special orientations of their formal signaling behavior. These procedures altered the contributions of signals to the function he discussed: gaining access to a resource controlled by a dominant individual. Like developing humans, young rhesus monkeys became more able to adjust their signaling performances to intricate and relatively subtle social opportunities as they learned the consequences of new tactics. Zivin (1982) has expressed this as a distinction between "(primarily) spontaneously–expressively" performed signaling, governed largely by genetic programs, and subsequent "(primarily) voluntarily–instrumentally" performed signaling, much affected by learned social consequences.

Individual Differences and Calibration

Related to the issue of marked changes in signaling is that of differences among individuals in signaling. These provide changes from the standpoint of a recipient, who encounters shifts in signal forms and in referents on switching attention from one signaler to another. These shifts are marked to the extent that the signalers are individually recognizable (indeed, some of the differences between individuals are specializations with the function of marking individual identity).

Differences in the referents of a signal as it is performed by different individuals place a strain on communication. To select a response, the recipient of a signal needs to know what to predict, that is, what information this act makes available. This would be easiest if each individual assigned the same information to the same form of signaling. But completely identical use of a given signal by two individuals is unlikely. Nearly every vertebrate animal is unique genetically, and all are in personal ontogenetic histories. As humans, we know well that we differ slightly to considerably amongst ourselves in both nonverbal signaling and in speech, even if raised within the same cultural norms. It is easier to understand and to communicate with a longstanding friend or an acquaintance than with a stranger. Yet we do communicate with strangers. We share intelligibility to a considerable extent and can learn to understand idiosyncracies we do not share.

Individual differences are not insurmountable because we calibrate one another as signalers. There is even experimental evidence for this, for example, Ekman and Friesen's work on deception clues (1969). It is also highly likely that in many species of mammals and birds who live in close social groups for prolonged periods, individual calibration is a well-developed skill. I am not aware of experimental evidence for the latter, but there are promising observations (e.g., Tinbergen's, 1939, 1953, on responses of herring gulls *Larus argentatus* to neighbors' alarm calling). Such calibration is an instance of the context dependency of signals. That is, recipients base their responses partly on the information made available by the signal and partly on information from sources contextual to it: in this case, concurrent sources that identify the individual signaler and sources that are stored as memories of its consistent idiosyncracies. And when responses must be made to an uncalibrated signaler, the responding individual can compensate by treating the signals as relatively ambiguous.

Changes in Signaling Behavior during Evolutionary Time

The signaling behavior of whole populations changes over evolutionary time. This is especially evident in comparative studies: even the obviously homologous signaling patterns of closely related species differ somewhat in form and often diverge considerably in the information they make available and in the stimulus situations eliciting their performance.

The essential rudiments for evolutionary modification of communication are continuously present. As in all evolution, the basis for change is in differences among individuals that may give some an adaptive advantage: the inevitable individuality of signaling behavior. When not an overwhelming problem for intelligibility, some of these idiosyncracies contribute the raw materials of evolutionary change: altered forms and referents for signals that can improve communicating, and even create new opportunities.

No adaptive advantage would follow for an individual who chanced upon an improved way of signaling if this failed to elicit appropriate responses. But, as just discussed, the very inevitability of individualistic signaling has led to the evolution of procedures by which all recipients calibrate signalers (when possible, thereby deriving expectations based on real correlations) and also attend to sources of information contextual to signaling. That they can learn to respond appropriately makes it possible for innovative signaling changes to be adaptive for the first individuals who show them. As a result, individuals genetically predisposed to the altered signaling will become proportionately more and more numerous in successive generations.

With some lag, evolution will also affect predispositions to respond. Although initially achieved through learning, a change in responding can become genetically fixed through the *Baldwin effect*. There is a cost in time and errors for an individual to learn to make a particular response. Learning can be less adaptive than being genetically predisposed to that response. As shifted signalers become sufficiently common, natural selection should favor individuals who respond to them not only appropriately, but also relatively automatically—who need less time or fewer trials (see Baldwin, 1896, although he did not realize that the process is purely Darwinian and not an alternative kind of evolution). When these individuals eventually predominate in the population, both signaling and responding will have changed evolutionarily.

Unmarked Changes in Signaling Behavior

It is sometimes suggested that an individual could increase the informative scope of its basic signal acts, even without modifying their form, by altering the relationship between each signal and its referents on a momentary, reversible basis. That is, its signals would be semantically flexible, providing different information from event to event. This would violate the requirement of consistency, of course, and must always have the cost of endangering intelligibility. Why, then, does this suggestion come up?

One reason, now popular among some biologists, is because signalers and responders need not share the costs equally. The procedure of quickly shifting referents thus opens the possibility for selfish distortion of reliable communicating into misinforming. This is considered more fully later. Three other reasons, treated first, assume that semantic flexibility could function in reliable communicating.

Reason 1

Sometimes the proposal that it might be possible for a signaler to shift a signal's referents quickly arises from a failure to realize how fundamentally individuals responding to a signal depend on information from sources contextual to the signal. The same signaled information leads to very different response behavior in different events because recipients take into account differences in the circumstances, assessing and integrating information from various sources. Differences in responding are not good indications that the information provided by a signal differs among events, only that information from some sources differs. In analyzing communication, it is essential to apportion information to its appropriate sources, crediting neither formal signals nor sources contextual to them with more or less information than they make available.

Working experience with human speech may be a source of some confusion here. Take a common word such as *cup* for which we recognize many possible exemplars, from tea cups to sporting trophies (see Labov, 1973). Superficially, our experience might suggest that these exemplars are separate referents. Yet they do have features in common and features that (imperfectly, with overlap) enable them to be separated from other classes, such as *bowl*. Thus we could also propose that *cup* has a single, broadly inclusive referent, and that we recognize specific instances through information from other sources, for example, objects present when the word is uttered, or other words in its phrase: *tea* or *loving*, for instance.

It seems not to have been clarified how cognition operates in any particular event. One possibility is that we follow a two-step process when we hear a word with a broadly defined referent. First, we may assume the most commonly occurring exemplar of that referent within the circumstance as we see it, then we may adjust (refine, or reject, and replace) our interpretation as further contextual clues become apparent. While either step might seem to imply a choice of referents, and hence semantic flexibility, observations show consistency in the class of interpretations over many events. This reveals the set of features linking all the assumptions made in responding. That set of features is the only referent that can be known in the absence of information from sources contextual to the word.

Finally, metaphor is a technique with which we change referents without altering signal form. But interpreting metaphors demands special work and is based on information from sources contextual to the signal. The circumstances in which metaphors appear indicate that the customary referents of the words now apply only as clues to some kind of commonality with the novel information that the signaler is trying to convey. We leave communication by extensive creation of metaphors to poets, whose products are not always readily understood. And while there is no reason to assume that, at levels of difficulty far less than those risked by poets, members of other species may not have some access to the metaphor procedure, we as yet have no evidence for their use of it.

Reason 2

Short-term semantic flexibility is sometimes proposed because it is assumed that the stimuli eliciting signaling must be its referents. Thus, when a signal is performed in response to different stimuli, its referents appear to differ from event to event. But the assumption is weak, and again overlooks the crucial role of context. A better postulate is that the referents are either some common characteristics of the stimuli (e.g., they may all appear suddenly, and all move rapidly) or some behavior that the signaler may show in response to them (e.g., probably fleeing), or both behavior and stimulus commonalities.

Reason 3

Semantic flexibility may also be proposed because humans, exceptional in depending enormously on learning in the development of communicative skills (Moynihan, 1976), do learn referent shifts readily. Faced with new kinds of tools (which Moynihan stresses), events, and social and other environmental problems, we are able to change the lexical meanings of words or invent and disseminate new words, creating jargons. We let words drift over time (e.g., *presently* has shifted over decades from referring to *now*, then to *soon*, and once again to *now*). In slang and its nonverbal counterparts, words of other signals may be stable for at most only a few years and can even flip their referents in a matter of months, as *hot* and *cool* and *good* and *bad* have done recently. It has yet to be shown that other species make such rapid and dramatic changes in their natural communicating.

More important, it does not follow that because we humans alter signal-referent relationships over periods of months to years we make much use of moment-to-moment alterations. We can stipulate definitions for limited use, say during the presentation of a paper at a conference, but left undefined, personalized use of terms reduces intelligibility. Further, when we use undefined terms we often shift referents unknowingly, damaging or ruining both logic and intelligibility.

Momentary semantic flexibility can be creative as metaphor if recipients have clues to the new relationships, but it is confusing and costly if they do not. On the whole, I suspect that unmarked, moment-to-moment referential shifts are hard to detect and interfere with communicating.

Misinforming

Quickly altering a signal's referents could function for a signaler by misinforming recipients. Although neither full reliability nor misinforming can be presumed for signaling, the latter practice should influence only a part, and perhaps a small part, of intraspecific communication. Discovering how, and how frequently, referent shifts that misinform occur is a current challenge in ethology.

What we know about signaling that misinforms among nonhuman animals comes primarily from studies of life-and-death interactions between members of different species—predators and prey, for instance. This misinforming depends, as must *all* provision of information that is specialized to engender unreliable predictions, on mimicry. It is thus a secondary development, requiring the prior and continued existence of reliable predictors as models.

The extent to which intraspecific misinforming occurs is a matter of debate. Whether because cases are rare or hard to detect, or both, no well-documented evidence has been reported in the natural, formalized-signaling behavior of any vertebrate animal other than humans; very few cases have been reported for invertebrates (see Steger & Caldwell, 1983; Thornbill, 1979). Even in captive chimpanzees, misinforming seems to be based only on glances, orientations, and other nonformalized behavior (Menzel, 1971). Chimpanzees interacting with a human trainer have achieved limited invention: two out of four young chimpanzees learned to point in a misleading direction (Woodruff & Premack, 1979), but they could not generalize to any other circumstance or even to another location and never used the procedure to misinform one another (Premack & Premack, 1983).

Evolutionary dynamics suggest that specializations for misinforming must usually be severely limited in intraspecific behavior. A signaler and a responder usually share, although rarely equally, benefits from the response made to a signal. Their behavioral predispositions coevolve. The signaler performs because this elicits responses that are, on the average, useful to it; and recipients only evolve predispositions to respond that are, on the average, to their benefit. Natural selection produces social interdependence, each participant gaining from the other's actions.

(This coevolutionary process is unrelated to *group selection*, a hypothetical cause that has never had an important influence on ethological theory.) Social interdependence renders most misinforming innovations evolutionarily unstable.

Much recent theorizing about communication is gravely limited by failing to deal adequately or at all with evolutionary coadaptation in socially interdependent animals. Most proponents of "deception" theories offer one or both of two points. First, animals often should not signal information they have. This truism follows from basic evolutionary constraints on formal signaling, treated later. Second, individuals should often signal unreliably: they should misinform. This assumes they can often get away with it. However, conditions in which they should be able are restricted.

The conditions are set by coevolutionary pressures. Although an individual might sometimes benefit from misinforming another, costs to the latter lead to selection for skeptical responding. Counteradaptations to being misinformed arise. These include procedures for seeking confirmatory evidence by monitoring signalers, or even directly eliciting information that tests signalers (by making probing attacks, for instance). Social costs can be imposed on misinforming by devaluing unreliable signals or unreliable classes of signalers, by responding less to the signalers, and by punishing or even ostracizing unreliable members of a group.

In turn, these countermeasures create divergent selection pressures. One is for "improved" misinforming techniques, and thus, an escalation of adaptation and counteradaptation continues. This is necessary in the life-threatening interactions of predators and prey, but it is a socially divisive route intraspecifically. The other countermeasure leads to breaking out of the spiral by signaling reliably. To forestall skeptical responses, this route can lead to evolution of procedures by which signalers certify themselves, for example, by providing measures of their reliability (an idea first advanced by Zahavi, 1975). A threatening individual's signals might provide direct measures of its power, for instance.

Although ethological research on the topic is only recent, good examples exist of all the following: seeking and testing for confirmatory evidence, devaluing signals and signalers, and providing self-certification of reliability (Smith, in press-b). The implication is that the scope of intraspecific misinforming is severely constrained.

Conditions under which some misinforming might succeed can be suggested. For instance, misinforming should be more likely (but skeptical responding should also be favored) in relationships between individuals that are ephemeral and anonymous than in those that endure and involve learning of individual behavior patterns. In the latter, misinforming will work best if it is rare and unpredictable relative to reliable signaling, and if it is done in events in which checking and testing would not be worth the cost to the responding individual. Misinforming should be much more common in competitive situations than when individuals are more or less equally dependent on one another. Many kinds of interactions are not fundamentally competitive, however; no party to them can gain by misinforming others over the central issues. And even competitive interactions (e.g., the settlement of territorial boundaries by neighboring songbirds, or dominance relationships among male baboons as an immigrant meets troop residents) can in principle be negotiated to the profit of all participants with only reliable signaling.

Withholding information can sometimes function like misinforming when it is done unexpectedly. This would require that some withholding be under optional control because animals must evolve to expect the information made available by any signal to be selective: no animal ever informs about everything it might do, its entire internal state, or all the stimuli it perceives. To do so would bog down interacting. More to the point, natural selection can only favor providing information when this yields a net advantage to the signaler. Signals do not evolve to provide information that is better withheld. The information that signals do provide is thus a selected portion of the information that the signaler has.

Because selective informing is universal, natural selection cannot favor the evolution of predispositions for individuals to respond to formal signals as if these provided all the information they might need. This surely creates the sort of social encounters that favor the evolution of procedures for negotiating. Signaling individuals should generate Hinde's *optimal ambiguity* (1981) by revealing indecisiveness and enabling some conditional predictions, while withholding other information. Responding individuals should monitor, probe, and test, using any means of eliciting information that is not signaled.

The question is whether withholding information might be to some extent optional and shift unexpectedly from event to event. Might an individual elect not to signal, withholding information it could in principle make available? We do not know. There are cases in which the stimulus conditions for signaling are remarkably intricate. For example, a ground squirrel *Spermophilus beldingii* will not call after sighting a predator unless a sufficient number of its own close relatives are nearby (Sherman, 1977, 1980). But its predispositions to utter the call are preset by local demography; there is no indication of momentary, optional flexibility for withholding information in a way that would imply sudden shifts in the relationship between the call and the referent.

Deliberate withholding of information or misinforming, based on an individual's anticipation of how it could affect profitable responding by altering its signaling, would be the most obvious kind of evidence for unmarked changes in signaling. Unfortunately, it is not easy to find evidence for such conscious anticipation.

Summary

Individuals have repertoires of formalized signal acts, of classes of form variation that are applicable to these acts, of combinations of signal acts, and of performances done in cooperation with other participants. With these signaling tools they make available information that enables probabilistic and conditional prediction of their behavior, reflects aspects of their internal states, and sometimes reveals things or situations to which they are responding.

In responding to a signal, its recipients must know (in some sense) what can be predicted from the information it makes available. This requires considerable consistency on the part of signalers. It is hard to overemphasize the need for this consistency. It is the basis of the *shared code* so often referred to in explaining the mutual intelligibility of signals within a community of interacting individuals. Each individual must provide largely the same information as do other individuals when performing the same signal. The uniqueness of individuals of all living organisms precludes absolutely identical use of signals, but within limits this is manageable and can even be useful. Probably no better illustration exists of the consequences of failing to adhere to the shared code than Lewis Carroll's Humpty Dumpty; he was so idiosyncratic in his choice of words that his utterances had to be rephrased before Alice could understand him.

Consistent adherence to a shared code does not preclude change in the stimuli that elicit performance of a signal, provided the initial stimuli are not the referents of that signal. It also does not preclude changes in the relationship between signal and referents, provided that those changes are orderly and expectable, and are well marked.

Various changes in the forms of signaling specializations can occur during ontogeny. These modifications tune signaling to the changing needs and capacities of developing individuals. Further, even without alterations of signal form, development introduces change by making individuals responsive to new and usually more complex and subtle kinds of stimuli, so that the circumstances in which they signal change. Similarly, predispositions to respond to formalized signals, which are always context-dependent, change as developing individuals accumulate experience with signals and with other sources of information. They must develop increasingly detailed expectations not only of the information to be gleaned from various sources, but also of the kinds of information they cannot get from signals and must seek elsewhere.

The main sources of ontogenetic change in communicating thus appear to result on the one hand from changes in signal form, and on the other from the increasing experience of developing individuals as both signalers and responders. This is not the whole story, however. Ontogenetic changes in signaling and responding represent just one of three time frames within which communicative shifts occur. Within much shorter, momentary intervals there are shifts in signal form. Far from being changes in the basic organization of communication, however, these are coded, reversible shifts and simply represent performance of the repertoire of variational procedures (the second of the repertoires of signaling behavior mentioned above). On a much longer, intergenerational scale, there is evolutionary change in communicating. This has its roots in individual differences and in the capacity of responding individuals to calibrate these differences. Probably through a sequence of learned changes followed by genetic fixation (the Baldwin effect), both signaling and response predispositions are altered in whole populations.

Acknowledgments

I am deeply indebted to Gail Zivin for discussions of many of the issues considered in this chapter and to the following for discussions of particular topics: Robert Hinde, Bill Mason, Harriet Oster, John Newman, David Premack, Paul Rozin, Jon Schul, and Chuck Snowdon.

References

Baldwin, J. M. A new factor in evolution. *American Naturalist*, 1896, *30*, 441–451, 536–553.
Barlow, G. Modal action patterns. In T. A. Sebeok (Ed.), *How animals communicate*. Bloomington: Indiana University Press, 1977.
Brown, R. *Words and things. An introduction to language.* New York: Free Press, 1968.
Burghardt, G. M. Ontogeny of communication. In T. A. Sebeok (Ed.), *How animals communicate*. Bloomington: Indiana University Press, 1977.
Caryl, P. G. Communication by agonistic displays: What can games theory contribute to ethology? *Behaviour*, 1979, *68*, 136–169.
Darwin, C. *The expression of the emotions in man and animals.* London: Appleton, 1872.

Dolgin, K. G., & Sabini, J. Experimental manipulation of a human non-verbal display: The tongue-show affects an observer's willingness to interact. *Animal Behaviour,* 1982, *30,* 935–936.

Ekman, P., & Friesen, W. V. Nonverbal leakage and clues to deception. *Psychiatry,* 1969, *32,* 88–105.

Frijda, N. H. Recognition of emotion. In L. Berkowitz (Ed.), *Advances in experimental social psychology. IV.* New York: Academic, 1969.

Hinde, R. A. Animal signals: Ethological and games-theory approaches are not incompatible. *Animal Behaviour,* 1981, *29,* 535–542.

Kraut, R. E., & Johnston, R. E. *Social and emotional messages of smiling: An ethological approach.* Unpublished manuscript, 1979.

Labov. W. The boundaries of words and their meanings. In C. J. Bailey & R. Shuy (Eds.), *New ways of analyzing variation in English.* Washington, DC: Georgetown University Press, 1973.

Menzel, E. W., Jr. Communication about environment in a group of young chimpanzees. *Folia primatologica,* 1971, *15,* 220–232.

Moynihan, M. The control, suppression, decay, disappearance and replacement of displays. *Journal of Theoretical Biology,* 1970, *29,* 85–112.

Moynihan, M. *The New World primates.* Princeton: Princeton University Press, 1976.

Newman, J. D., & Symmes, D. Inheritance and experience in the acquisition of primate acoustic behavior. In C. T. Snowdon, C. H. Brown, & M. R. Petersen (Eds.), *Primate communication.* New York: Cambridge University Press, 1983.

Oster, H., & Rosenstein, D. Analysing facial movement in infants. In P. Ekman & W. V. Friesen (Eds.), *Analyzing facial action.* New York: Plenum, in press.

Owings, D. H., & Leger, D. W. Chatter vocalizations of California ground squirrels: Predator- and social-role specificity. *Zeitschrift für Tierpsychologie,* 1980, *54,* 163–184.

Premack, D., & Premack, A. J. *The mind of an ape.* New York: Norton, 1983.

Seyfarth, R. M., & Cheney, D. L. The ontogeny of vervet monkey alarm calling behavior: A preliminary report. *Zeitschrift für Tierpsychologie,* 1980, *54,* 37–56.

Seyfarth, R. M., Cheney, D. L., & Marler, P. Vervet monkey alarm calls: Semantic communication in a free-ranging primate. *Animal Behaviour,* 1980, *28,* 1070–1094.

Sherman, P. W. Nepotism and the evolution of alarm calls. *Science,* 1977, *197,* 1246–1253.

Sherman, P. W. The limits of ground squirrel nepotism. In G. W. Barlow & J. Silverberg (Eds.), *Sociobiology: Beyond nature/nurture?* Boulder, CO: Westview Press, 1980, 505–544.

Smith, W. John, Messages of vertebrate communication. *Science,* 1969, *165,* 145–150.

Smith, W. John. *The behavior of communicating. An ethological approach.* Cambridge: Harvard University Press, 1977.

Smith, W. John. Referents of animal communication. *Animal Behaviour,* 1981, *29,* 1273–1275.

Smith, W. John. Signaling behavior: Contributions of different repertoires. In R. Buhr, R. Schusterman, J. Thomas, & F. Wood (Eds.), *Dolphin cognition and behavior: A comparative approach.* Hillsdale, NJ: Erlbaum, in press (a).

Smith, W. John. An "informational" perspective on manipulation. In R. W. Mitchell & N. S. Thompson (Eds.), *Deception: Perspectives on human and non-human deceit.* State University of New York Press, in press (b).

Smith, W. John, Chase, J., & Lieblich, A. K. Tongue Showing: A facial display of humans and other primate species. *Semiotica,* 1974, *11,* 201–246.

Steger, R., & Caldwell, R. L. Intraspecific deception by bluffing: A defense strategy of newly molted stomatopods (Arthropoda: Crustacea). *Science,* 1983, *221,* 558–560.

Stokes, Allen W. Agonistic behaviour among Blue Tits at a winter feeding station. *Behaviour*, 1962, *19*, 118–138.

Thornbill, R. Adaptive female-mimicking behavior in a scorpionfly. *Science*, 1979, *205*, 412–414.

Tinbergen, N. On the analysis of social organization among vertebrates, with special reference to birds. *American Midland Naturalist*, 1939, *21*, 210–234.

Tinbergen, N. *The herring gull's world*. London: Collins, 1953.

Woodruff, G., & Premack, D. Intentional communication in chimpanzee: the development of deception. *Cognition*, 1979, *7*, 333–362.

Zahavi, A. Mate selection—a selection for a handicap. *Journal of Theoretical Biology*, 1975, *53*, 205–214.

Zivin, G. On becoming subtle: Age and social rank changes in the use of a facial gesture. *Child Development*, 1977, *48*, 1314–1321.

Zivin, G. Watching the sands shift: Conceptualizing development of nonverbal mastery. In R. S. Feldman (Ed.), *The development of nonverbal communication in children*. New York: Springer, 1982.

Chapter 4

External Reference and Affective Signaling in Mammalian Vocal Communication

Harold Gouzoules, Sarah Gouzoules, and Peter Marler*

Relationship to Other Chapters and to the Field

Relevant Issues in the Field

The specific goal of this chapter is to review sound empirical evidence that animal communication can, more commonly than in the isolated example of the honeybee dance, refer to objects outside the signaler and that, furthermore, there are instances of such external reference in which all the semantic information necessary to refer to the object is contained in the signal. Such a signal is independent of context, although context may be used by perceivers to enrich the decoded message beyond the information made available by the signal itself. Such signals share the denotative context-independence of human language symbols and thus bring animal signaling closer, in principle, to human verbal signaling. The authors also show that, even in the use of context-independent, externally referring signals, there is a mixture of affective and cognitive information. By demonstrating the existence of such signals and of the cognitive–affective blend of information for signals that might otherwise be considered more like human

*We thank Professor D. R. Griffin for comments on the manuscript. Research on rhesus monkey vocal communication was supported by NIMH postdoctoral fellowship F32-MH08533 to Harold Gouzoules, NIMH postdoctoral fellowship F32 MH08473 to Sarah Gouzoules, NSF grant BNS-8023423T to Peter Marler, and Biomedical Research Support Grant PHS-RR07065-15 to the Rockefeller University.

77

symbols, the authors present evidence at least consistent with a continuum between human and nonhuman cognition.

One inference about expressive behavior the authors draw is that some of the simple dichotomies between animal and human communication are now obsolete. As noted there, the tendency still exists to equate naive human-expressive behavior with rigid innateness of form, with involuntary elicitation, with veridical information about the individual's concurrent emotional state, and features that have been stereotypically attributed to animal signals, hitherto viewed as void of external reference or cognitive content.

This chapter exemplifies a form of biology–environment interaction in which learning to interpret the environment is integral to the use of signals, even when actual signal morphology is, so far as is known, innate.

Relationship to Other Chapters

For the understanding of many externally referring signals, the authors agree with Smith's formulation that the meaning a recipient interprets is a mixture of the information made available by the signal itself, plus the information provided by the context. They agree with Smith that a signal by itself can yield several meanings, depending upon context. While this is Smith's conception of how all signal situations typically function, Gouzoules, Gouzoules, and Marler seek to identify the existence of mammalian signals that can and do function independently of context. They assert further that the users of these signals have cognitive capacities more similar to human cognition than previously thought, and that such signals could function independently of context. Again in concurrence with Smith, at least in certain situations, the authors assign more cognitive complexity to the act of decoding a message—which, in the case of monkeys' agonistic recruitment signals, for example, they describe as being a decentered process—than to the act of encoding—which they describe as typically egocentric.

The evidence that Marler and the Gouzouleses bring to bear on the question of different signal forms creating different semantic units concurs with Mason's evidence in consideration of the same question. Mason notes that only for vocal signals, in the rhesus monkeys examined, does there seem to be evidence that new forms through experience can refer to new referents. While they do not discuss the origin of their signal forms, Marler and the Gouzouleses present only vocal signals as having sharply differentiated semantic functions.

For Consistent Terminology

Many of the semiotic concepts in this chapter are specified in the framing chapter. The framing chapter puts more emphasis on complete arbitrariness of reference for symbolic than does this chapter's use of symbolic in reference to *the honeybee dance. The degree of iconicity in the honeybee dance is still in question among biologists. The fact of different "dialects" of dance among different bees suggests another classic definitional element of symbols, the dependence for a symbol's meaning on the local interpretation of the community. For other interpretations of the semantic relations of the honeybee dance, see the Footnote 1. This chapter also uses several phrases interchangeably:* truly, completely, strictly, *or* purely representational; *these phrases refer, as defined in this chapter, to a signal's property of context-independent external reference.*

As do other theorists and several other chapters, this chapter uses emotion *and* affect *rather interchangeably, although* affect *is a slightly more inclusive term.* —ED.

Introduction

Human cognitive capacities and language skills are so intertwined that debates over their coevolution must inevitably be inconclusive. Lyons (1972, 1977), for one, argues that the question of the origin of language is a futile one because of the intimate interpenetration of the linguistic and nonlinguistic features of language. Most linguists (e.g., Chomsky, 1972) have not been swayed by biological reasoning that language must have evolved from some nonhuman communication system. As Lyons notes (1977, p. 85), the attitude tends to be one of agnosticism because there is no evidence from language itself of increased complexity in present day over past forms. Phylogenetic comparisons based on the design features of language have revealed no clear signs of an increasing approximation to language as one proceeds from primitive to advanced animal taxa (Hockett & Altmann 1968; Thorpe, 1972). On the contrary, such comparisons tend to highlight phylogenetic continuities in the basic substrates for language. A renewed interest in cognitive ethology (Griffin 1976, 1978, 1981, 1984; Shafton, 1976) has focused attention on animal communication, with the goal of investigating possible continuities in awareness, conceptual thinking, internal representation, and higher-cognitive abilities. While animal studies may not shed light directly on the evolution of language (e.g., Chalmers, 1980), they can tell us much about the cognitive prerequisites and correlates of language and its various design features.

Semanticity is a particularly important feature of language, intimately related to human cognition. As defined by Hockett and Altmann (1968) and employed by Thorpe (1972), *semanticity* is based on associative ties between signal elements and features of the outside world. As one of the three major distinctions or constructs of semiotic theory, the semantic level of analysis is of value in focusing attention on the kinds of information potentially provided by a signal (Smith, 1977). The signal itself becomes useful because of its associations with other behaviors, events, or objects, that stand as referents of the signal. Lyons (1977) prefers the neutral Latin term *significatum* for whatever it is that a sign stands for, but because of its prevalent use in the literature, Ogden and Richards's (1923) term *referent* will be retained in this chapter. The investigation of the semantic content of any signal is enormously complicated, but it is at least simplified if the signal has a clear, distinct external referent that the signal might symbolize (Marler, 1983).

The term *referent* has traditionally had limited application in studies of animal communication, primarily because early ethological work considered animal signals as largely stereotyped and innate. Referents of animal signals, the things and events about which the signals provide information, were thought to be the signaling animals themselves or attributes of the signaler, such as its current or expected behavior and associated motivational states (self-reference) (Smith, 1977). Until the 1980s, it was widely believed that the communication systems of even nonhuman primates could not, in contrast to human language, "exploit the auditory-vocal medium for purposes of symbolic expression" (Marin, Schwartz, & Saffran, 1979, p. 184). The vocal repertoires of nonhuman primates were, instead, thought to reflect affective, or emotional, rather than cognitive dimensions, with the signal conveying information solely about the internal state or motivation of the caller (e.g., Green, 1975a; Itani, 1963; Rowell & Hinde, 1962). As a corollary, nonhuman primate vocal signals, in and of themselves, were not viewed as constituting a complete signal, but were "only a part of a constellation of sound, posture, movement, and facial expression" (Lancaster, 1968, p. 442; see also Rowell & Hinde, 1962). However, views concerning animal communication have begun to shift from a focus on the probable behavior of the signaler or its arousal level as the primary information conveyed by all animal signals. Deceit and manipulation of receivers are now considered important topics (Caryl, 1979; Dawkins & Krebs, 1978), and new examples of animals apparently communicating about objects and events external to the signaler have come to light (Cheney & Seyfarth, 1982; Gouzoules, Gouzoules, & Marler, 1984; Seyfarth, Cheney, & Marler, 1980). These studies suggest a greater complexity in the communication systems of animals than was hitherto suspected and have been cited as arguments against adopting a dualistic view of human and nonhuman cognition (Seyfarth, 1982). In this Chapter we review some of the recent evidence concerning external referents of nonhuman mammalian vocal signals. We attempt to sort out the roles of affective and representational signals in communicating about external referents and to make some inferences about what cognitive correlates are implied by such behavior.

Cognitive ethologists have proposed that valuable insight into the thought processes and mental states of animals can be gained through careful analysis of their communication. Griffin (1978) notes that when animals signal one another or send messages of courtship, threat, or submission, it is possible that they are *thinking* something comparable to the message itself. A test of this hypothesis might be devised through the use of models or motion pictures of gestural communication and of playback of sounds from tape recordings, as illustrated in several studies described in this chapter. This latter technique has added much to our knowledge about the function of animal vocal signals under natural conditions. For example, studies of the external referents of animal signals have provided insight into the ways in which an animal views its world and categorizes or classifies objects and events (Cheney, 1982; Griffin, 1981; Marler, 1982). Furthermore, external referents themselves are in the public domain, lending themselves to such experimentation.

Confidence about specifying the referent of a call and using this information to gain insight into the nature of the animal's world should be tempered with caution, however. Smith (1981) has noted that ethologists have disagreed over the kinds of referents it is appropriate to invoke for animal signals. Broadly, a referent may be viewed as anything about which a signal communicates information. That the relatively narrow concept of *external reference* has been applied to referents in the environment of a signaler (Smith, 1977, p. 75) does not completely eliminate potential problems. Smith has emphasized that a signal may have several referents and that it is critical to distinguish among the different sources of information provided by a signal. For example, an animal's signal can have more than one referent. In the case of a vervet monkey alarm call, one referent may be external (e.g., a leopard), whereas another may be motivational (e.g., the monkey's internal state or pending behavior). Under these circumstances, to what extent can an assessment of the monkey's cognitive abilities be derived exclusively from studies of external reference?

In the remainder of this chapter we review examples of mammalian communication involving external referents. While selective pressures to communicate about objects and events external to the signaler have shaped the behavior of many species, it is clear that this capacity has been achieved through a variety of means. In each example we attempt to determine if information about an external referent is the primary information conveyed. Are terms such as *semantic* and *representational*, which have been applied to animal referential communication warranted in all cases of external reference? In other words, is the predominant function of the signal to provide information about an external referent? We also consider what the nature of the external referent and the behavior of the signaler and the receiver can reveal about the animal's abilities to classify objects in its world and, tangentially, its cognitive skills. Is there evidence that a signal with an external referent emitted by one animal encodes and evokes a symbolic concept in the receiver? Does the concept of a mental image have a role in the interpretation of such signaling behavior, or does the evidence, at best, indicate that a form of *associative indexing* is involved?

External Reference in Nonhuman Mammalian Communication

California Ground Squirrel Alarm Calls

California ground squirrels (*Spermophilus beecheyi*) are small diurnal rodents that inhabit colonial burrows in grassland and open, oak woodland. Males maintain home ranges, defending them from incursions from other males, whereas the females' home ranges overlap extensively (Owings, Borchert, & Virginia, 1977). The ground squirrels' rich repertoire of social signals includes an interesting set of alarm calls.

Two classes of calls (whistles and chatters) are given in widely varying circumstances (Leger, Owings, & Boal, 1979; Leger, Owings, & Gelfand, 1980; Owings & Virginia, 1978; Owings & Leger, 1980). Whistles tend to be given to hawks and chatters to foxes and other ground predators, although on occasion both are evoked by mammalian and avian predators. Whistles and chatters are also given by both chasers and chasees during conspecific aggression. Individuals giving and responding to calls during these varying circumstances behave differently (i.e., flee to a burrow when a predator is nearby, but stand vulnerably on top of a boulder to view a conspecific chase). Although the two call classes appear to form discrete signal categories, both vary along several acoustic dimensions, and initial published reports inferred that it is the arousal level of signalers that is primarily communicated by these vocalizations. The message about arousal level, along with accompanying contextual information, determines the meaning of the particular whistle or chatter to receiving animals (Leger *et al.*, 1979; Owings & Virginia, 1978). In this respect, as Leger *et al.* (1979) point out, the ground squirrel vocalizations function in a way that Smith (1965, 1977) has described as characteristic of most vertebrate signals; that is, they depend for their meaning upon the assessment of contextual information and the motivational information being conveyed about the signaler's likely behavior in the immediate future and do not represent external referents.

However, subsequent to these original reports, acoustic and multivariate statistical analyses of the fine structure of whistle and chatter vocalizations revealed that reliably different acoustic variants of the calls occur in different social contexts (Leger *et al.* 1980; Owings & Leger, 1980). This finding resembled that reported by Green (1975a) in his study of the patterns of usage of variants of the ''coo'' vocalization of Japanese monkeys (*Macaca fuscata*). Such predictably distinguishable vocal signals associated with different social contexts and situations are clearly a prerequisite for externally referential communication.

At the very least, these data suggest that ground squirrel vocalizations have multiple referents as Smith (1981) has proposed. For example, although acoustic variants of the calls are situation specific, they are also motivation specific, in the sense that the variants correspond consistently to different subsequent behaviors on the part of the signaler. Given covariation of subsequent signaler behavior and signal type, one cannot conclude that signalers are primarily referencing external objects.

Stated another way, it remains an open question whether or not the signal primarily encodes information about external objects. But what about receivers? Is the vocal signal itself sufficient to elicit a particular, referentially appropriate response from receivers? Can the signal, alone, function representationally? In the case of the ground squirrel calls, the answer is, probably not. In playbacks of the two major types of vocalizations, information other than the particular acoustic variant being played, was provided to receivers, and this additional information was apparently necessary in order to elicit differential responses. By varying information other than the acoustical features of the call, for example, the number of calls played, different responses were elicited. During whistle playbacks, contextual information about the number of individuals calling (indicated by the number of notes played) was varied (Leger *et al.* 1979). Arousal, or excitation-level information, (indexed by the number of notes and the noise content of calls) was varied in playbacks of chatter vocalizations (Leger & Owings, 1978).

While these results probably indicate that the ground squirrel vocalizations are not representational in the sense that the acoustical features of the call itself are sufficient to elicit an appropriate response, they do present an example of a sophisticated communication system that cannot be accounted for by a simple arousal or motivationally referential interpretation. For example, Leger and Owings (1978) speculate that, through assessment of a number of parameters both in the signal and contextual to it, an external referent can actually be specified or decoded, as can the arousal level of the signaler (Premack, 1975). Although the vocal signal itself is not employed in a completely representational manner, the communication system in which that signal is embedded is capable of providing rather precise information about an external object or event. Thus we may view some calls as functioning, concomitant with other information, to communicate about an external referent, even though the calls themselves are not strictly representational, because appropriate responses cannot be elicited by them in the absence of other information sources. Contextual or motivational information is not necessary for the interpretation of the meaning of a *truly representational* signal.

The California ground squirrel vocalization studies provide compelling evidence that the arousal information associated with much animal signaling is best viewed, not as conflicting with more complex cognitive functions, but instead as supplementing them (e.g., Marler, 1978). Signalers must themselves survive and reproduce, and a dissociation of signaling from other aspects of physiological and behavioral responding that contributes to individual fitness is likely to be dysgenic in most circumstances, (e.g., Seyfarth *et al.* 1980).

The particular constellation of relationships between reference, arousal, and signaler motivation manifest in much animal signaling, often affective in nature, should not be thought of as evidence that animals are incapable of pure representational signaling. Rather it suggests an adaptive compromise that, even in animals, can best be seen as a continuum of specificity depending on which particular evolved solution solves a given problem most efficiently. For example, in certain of the vocalizations of the highly social Old World monkeys, the balance between a primarily affective basis on the one hand, and externally referential representation on the other has apparently been shifted towards the latter, presumably in response to pressures imposed by complex social and natural environments.

Vervet Monkey Alarm Calls

The vervet monkeys (*Cercopithecus aethiops*) of Amboseli National Park, Kenya, have provided some of the most intriguing evidence about the potential of the natural communication systems of animals for conveying information about external objects and events. Vervets are highly social Old World monkeys. They are more terrestrial than other species within the genus and range from mangrove swamps, through rain forests, to the semiarid savannahs of Kenya. Among the dangers associated with combining arboreal and terrestrial habitats is an increased vulnerability to predators, different species of which employ a variety of hunting strategies. This increased predation pressure has had a strong influence on vervet monkey vocal communication.

Vervet monkeys employ acoustically distinct vocalizations when confronted with different types of predators, such as snakes, leopards, or eagles (Struhsaker, 1967; Seyfarth *et al.* 1980). The vervet alarms are discretely separate and are readily distinguishable to human ears. Responses of vervet monkeys to the presence of different types of predators, with contrasting hunting strategies, vary predictably and in an adaptive fashion. They run into tree tops in response to a call given because of the presence of leopards, which hunt primarily by lying in ambush on the ground in dense brush, and they run out of trees and into dense brush in response to a call triggered by eagles, which pluck young vervets from branches.

That the vervet alarm calls satisfy more of the criteria for representational functioning than those of the California ground squirrels is indicated by at least two lines of evidence. First, the behavior of monkeys following the utterance of different alarm calls does not always covary in predictable ways with calling, as would be expected if these vocalizations were inextricably associated with other groups of responses to the predators; that is, monkeys may give alarms while not exhibiting escape responses. Thus, as Seyfarth *et al.* (1980, p. 1091–1092) note, "the link between call and escape behaviour, while real, can be severed." Therefore, vervet alarm calls do not appear to depend upon multiple referents in the way the ground squirrel calls do; they may be given, and responded to, independently of the vocalizer's other behavioral responses to the referent.

A second line of evidence also supports the notion that vervet alarm calls function representationally. Field playbacks of alarm calls were conducted in order to test whether the vocal signal alone, in the absence of contextual information or visual signs of the signaler's arousal level, was sufficient to evoke appropriate responses from receivers; in other words, can the vocal signal alone function representationally? The results of these playback experiments (Seyfarth *et al.* 1980) strongly support the hypothesis that each alarm call represents a specific class of danger and that receivers, upon hearing the signal, assess the danger, their degree of vulnerability, and respond accordingly. The monkeys behave *as if* the vocal signal itself stands for or designates an external object.

It is yet another question whether the vervet alarms function by evoking in receivers an *internal representation* or mental image of a leopard or an eagle. Here we must appeal to the particular quality of the responses elicited by the playback of different calls. A serendipitous feature of the array of predators confronting vervets in nature is that they approach from different directions. Eagles, for example, stoop from the open sky above, whereas snakes are liable to strike from the ground close by. There is in fact a strong probability that vervets that are played an eagle alarm call will look up into the sky. A snake alarm, on the other hand, evokes bipedal standing and a visual search of the monkey's surroundings. This response dichotomy and the specific nature of the reactions to the calls is a strong indication that they do in fact elicit internal representations of these different predators—or equivalent primers of action and cognitive search. By comparison with the ground squirrel system, the vervet alarm-call behavior is clearly more complex, with signal meaning depending less upon affective information. It should be noted, however, that Seyfarth *et al.* (1980) conclude that affective information is capable of *enriching* the meaning of alarm calls but remains peripheral to the determination of their meaning. For example, in playback experiments of vervet monkey alarm calls, lengthening the string of calls in some cases increased responsiveness and yet had no influence on the qualitative distinctions among responses to the different alarm types. Marler (1984) has noted that the ideas and the feelings associated with a referent are closely related, perhaps inextricably so. Although it is clear that alarm calling is potentially dissociable from other behaviors associated with predator escape, it is also true that an exposed vervet monkey that did not itself flee upon seeing a leopard and calling would not survive long. It seems reasonable to propose that leopards engender fear in vervet monkeys in proportion to their vulnerability at the time of a sighting.

Toque Macaque Food Calls

The toque macaque (*Macaca sinica*) which inhabits the island of Sri Lanka is another species of Old World monkey. Like other macaques, it lives in social groups composed of males, females, and associated infants and juveniles. Also in common with other macaques, the toque macaque diet is remarkably eclectic. Dittus has studied a population of toque macaques at an archaeological sanctuary at Polonnaruwa, Sri Lanka, since the mid-1970s (Dittus, 1977, 1979, 1980). The habitat at this site is described as a natural semievergreen forest.

Dittus (1984) has recently suggested that food calls used by this population of toque macaques constitute another example of representational signaling. These calls are typically given by foraging individuals upon encountering food of high quality or in a large quantity. Individuals who perceive the calls run to the signaler's vicinity and begin to eat. Dittus suggests that these vocal signals are representations of the referent, food, although the information actually conveyed is the abundance or quality, rather than the specific type of food. Dittus concludes that the food call has evolved signal value, externally referential in nature, because it provides pertinent information about feeding conditions to other group members which are likely to be kin.

Smith (1977) has noted that signals with a resource-sharing function are extremely rare among vertebrates. While there are many examples in the ethological literature of displays by animals that possess food, resulting in the approach of conspecifics, this behavior per se is insufficient evidence that the referent of the signal is food (Marler, 1967). Some species of birds give particular calls upon finding abundant food resources (Green & Marler, 1979). Although these calls seem to attract other individuals, with very few exceptions (e.g., Stokes, 1967) such displays are generally performed more or less irrespectively of the state of the caller or of the presence or absence of an audience, and the message encoded may relate to a general readiness to interact (Smith, 1977, p. 148).

Macaque food calls have been traditionally viewed as clear manifestations of arousal. For example, they are frequently elicited in provisioned groups just before scheduled feeding times (Green, 1975b). However, Dittus (1984) rejects the arousal interpretation of the food call of the toque macaque under natural conditions. He cites, as one line of evidence, that the monkeys do not call early in the morning, when hunger levels might be expected to be highest, unless, of course, a rich food source is encountered. Furthermore, Dittus argues that the behavior of the caller subsequent to the signal is not qualitatively different from that preceding it. In other words, because a toque macaque's behavior is similar (foraging and eating) both before and after giving the call, it is unlikely that the caller's behavioral motivation is the primary message conveyed. It is debatable, however, whether the caller's behavior must change after calling in order for behavioral referents to be specified. Calling might conceivably signal the likelihood of continuation of a behavior, or a change in the rate of behavior, as opposed to change or termination of a behavioral state.

The description that Dittus provides of toque macaques' responses to food calls of group members indicates that the monkeys clearly associate the call with the location of food. But the critical question is, how is this association made? Are the food calls truly representational signals like the vervet alarm calls, capable of encoding sufficient information to specify a feeding response in the absence of any contextual or affective cues? Or, do they, like the ground squirrel alarm calls, depend upon other classes of information for their meaning. For several reasons we suspect the latter explanation is the more likely one for toque macaque food calls. First of all, vocalizations virtually indistinguishable from food calls are given also in other contexts that appear to be associated with pleasure or euphoria, for example, sudden appearance of a warm patch of sunlight on a cloudy day (Dittus, 1984; authors' personal observation). Secondly, there is, as yet, no evidence that the acoustic structure of the food call varies in any orderly, systematic way in association with food as opposed to warmth, or in relationship to different quantities or types of food. Thus, until fine-structure acoustic analyses establish that variants of the call are consistently evoked by particular stimuli and playbacks establish that the different responses of the receivers to the variants are context independent, these calls might best be interpreted as analogous to the ground squirrel alarm calls. That is, the food calls themselves are likely to be affective signals evoked by particular external stimuli, and other individuals (out-of-sight of the caller) can only respond appropriately by assessing the vocalization and the context in which it is given. Again, this is not to suggest that the communication event is not a complex one, requiring considerable cognitive involvement, merely that the meaning of the vocal signal has not achieved complete independence from other sources of information.

As Seyfarth et al. (1980, p. 1092) note, "It is entirely possible that, in evolutionary terms, alarms [or any other representational signal] with different acoustical features first appeared as manifestations of different emotional states." This clearly seems to be the case with the ground squirrel alarms. And as Marler (1984) has pointed out, "The intermingling of cognition and affect in signaling behavior, whenever it was achieved in the course of animal evolution, greatly enriches its communicative content." In fact Marler (1984) discusses at length the dual involvement of both affect and cognition in vertebrate signaling behavior. Again, the emphasis on cognitive or on affective contributions to signaling behavior probably varies, depending upon the particular situation. We suggest that the ground squirrel alarms and the toque macaque food calls are examples of signaling systems in which both affective and cognitive processes make joint contributions to the specification of external referents. We may then pose the question, are the representational alarm calls of the vervet monkeys unique in mammalian signaling?

Vervet Grunts

Research by Cheney and Seyfarth (1982) has revealed that a second class of vervet vocalizations (grunts) apparently functions in a representational manner. These calls are given by vervets in a variety of social circumstances, for example, as a monkey approaches a dominant or a subordinate individual, when a group moves into an open area of their range, or upon observing a neighboring vervet group. Like the within-class variants of ground squirrel whistles and chatters, acoustical variants of the vervet grunts are not readily distinguishable to human ears; grunts have traditionally been viewed "as a single, highly variable call which reflects the arousal state of the signaller" (Cheney & Seyfarth 1982, p. 739). However, playback experiments of recorded grunts originally uttered in different contexts consistently evoked differential responses from receivers, indicating that vervet monkeys probably perceive fine-structure acoustical differences between grunts given in the various social circumstances. For instance, when subjects were played the sound of a grunt-to-a-subordinate recording, they tended to move away from the hidden speaker, whereas a grunt-to-a-dominant recording elicited looking in the direction of the speaker. A move-into-the-open grunt often elicited looking in the direction the speaker was pointed.

During these field playbacks both context and acoustic variables that might have provided cues to the signaler's arousal, such as amplitude or duration, were controlled. Thus, certain of the grunt vocalizations, that is, those indicating another group or a move into the open, are apparently capable of transmitting specific information about external objects and events, and they can do so in a purely representational manner. Cheney and Seyfarth (1982) note that it is not immediately clear why natural selection would have favored the evolution of such representational signals in social contexts in which animals are always in visual contact with one another, but they suggest that the use of these situationally specific vocalizations may reduce uncertainty and ambiguity while increasing the information that can be conveyed.

Rhesus Macaque Screams

Our research (Gouzoules *et al.*, 1984) on the vocal signals of rhesus monkeys on Cayo Santiago, an island off Puerto Rico, has yielded a number of findings relevant to the present discussion of external referents in animal communication. The Cayo Santiago colony, founded in 1938, is unique among rhesus study sites because of the extensive documentation available on matrilineal genealogies of each free-ranging troop inhabiting the island. These long-term records can be employed, for example, to identify patterns of social behavior that are influenced by kin relationships.

One such behavioral system is that involving alliance formation during fights. In fact, patterns of agonistic behavior in this species suggest a context in which representational signaling might be highly advantageous. In macaques and baboons, combatants often solicit support from other group members against opponents, and scream vocalizations appear to play a major role in the recruitment of aid. One hypothesis about this behavior that we set out to test experimentally was that these calls function in a representational manner, conveying information about external features of an agonistic event to spatially distant allies. Such information would provide the basis for an ally's decision about whether or not to intervene. Other interpretations are possible. Recruitment might occur merely because of vocal recognition of the caller and of information about the nature and the intensity of the caller's emotional or internal state. Like vervet grunts, rhesus screams have been traditionally viewed as communicating nothing beyond the signaler's arousal level and identity. Of course, these two views are not necessarily mutually exclusive, but we sought to determine if one had a primary role in the recruitment process.

As a first step we performed an acoustical classification of over 500 rhesus monkey scream bouts recorded from Cayo Santiago's Group L. For 378 scream bouts information concerning the identity of the caller and its opponent as well as contextual information about the agonistic episode had been recorded. Analysis revealed that in an agonistic encounter rhesus monkeys generally used one of five acoustically distinct screams. Importantly, each scream type was significantly associated with a particular class of opponent, defined in terms of dominance rank and matrilineal relatedness to the signaler, as well as with the nature of the aggression, differentiated as to whether or not physical contact occurred (Figure 4.1). These results led us to conclude that the five acoustically discrete scream classes had the potential to function as designators for different types of opponents and agonistic situations. Earlier studies by Kaplan (1977, 1978) had shown that allies come to the aid of fighting monkeys with differing probabilities, depending upon the identity of opponents and the severity of aggression involved. For example, a female is more likely to aid her immature offspring if its opponent is a high-ranking unrelated individual than if the opponent is a relative, such

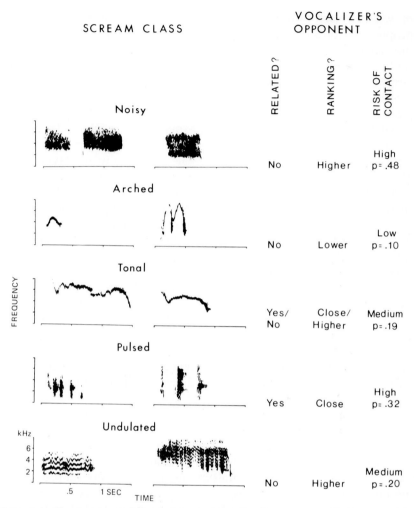

Figure 4.1. Spectrograms of five rhesus monkey calls. The relative dominance rank and relatedness of opponents typically associated with each scream class are presented, as are risks of contact aggression. The probability of contact aggression varies significantly with call type, but does not covary with response intensity to playbacks. Screams were recorded at 3¾ speed and are displayed at a wide band (300 Hz) setting. Y-axis shows frequency and X-axis time.

as a cousin. Do scream vocalizations convey specific information of this kind about opponents and about agonistic events or do they merely reflect the caller's fear in response to aggression?

One line of evidence for representational signaling comes from data on whether each of the five scream types signaled different behavioral propensities of the caller. It was clear from analysis of the behavior of the signaler subsequent to emitting a scream that there was no significant association between the caller's subsequent behavior and the different call types (Gouzoules *et al.*, 1984). We concluded that the different scream types did not primarily represent future signaler behavior as a motivational referent.

We next performed field-playback experiments in which, by playing recorded screams, we eliminated any contextual information originally available to potential allies. Adult female monkeys were played examples of the different scream classes recorded from their immature offspring. We controlled acoustic cues that might reflect signaler arousal such as the amplitude and duration of the short samples of scream calls used in the playback experiments. These experiments tested whether the different vocal signals alone were sufficient to elicit differential response.

We considered two sets of predictions about the mothers' responses. Our data on the agonistic contexts associated with different scream classes were used to assign each scream type a probability estimate reflecting the risk of potential injury, and the scream classes were rank ordered on this basis. If screams communicated the fear experienced by juveniles in different agonistic situations, mothers should respond in line with this rank ordering. We deemed this the *affect hypothesis*.

On the other hand, mothers might determine their support decisions on factors other than or in addition to the likelihood of physical aggression. Here further insight into the nature of dominance relationships in macaques is required. As juveniles mature, they attain a dominance rank in the adult hierarchy near that of their mothers and other matrilineal kin. The process by which this rank is attained is a dynamic one, in which challenges from individuals in the group, usually subordinate to the immature's adult relatives, are thwarted or diverted by aid from other monkeys, usually relatives or dominant unrelated individuals (e.g., Cheney 1977; Walters 1980). The provision of aid in such circumstances is important not only for the juvenile's eventual rank, but also for the ranking in the troop of the entire matrilineage of which the juvenile is a member. We found that rank-challenge encounters were typically associated with the class of calls labeled "arched screams". Importantly, this scream class was also associated with the lowest probability of physical contact of any of the scream classes. Thus, although rank-challenge encounters involving a juvenile are likely to be crucially important to the attainment of dominance rank, they are not associated with much risk of injury. Arched screams therefore play a pivotal role in assessing whether or not the arousal level of a juvenile caller, that is the fear experienced during an agonistic encounter, is the critical information determining an ally's decision to enter on the juvenile's behalf. A strong response from mothers to playback of arched screams recorded from their own offspring would demonstrate that the caller's arousal level is not the primary information conveyed. A more reasonable conclusion would then be that mothers assess the nature of the agonistic encounter, using the screams to infer features of the contest encoded in the signal in a representational manner, such as the relatedness and the rank of the opponent and the type of interaction. This is the *representational hypothesis*.

Our playback experiments indicated that mothers responded to their offspring's vocalizations as though the class of scream alone encoded differential information about external features of the agonistic event. Although the strongest maternal response elicited came from playback of *noisy screams* (those associated with encounters with higher-ranking opponents and the highest probability of physical contact), *arched screams* elicited the next greatest response, even though they had the weakest association with physical aggression of any of the call classes. Like the vervet monkey alarm calls, rhesus screams apparently function not only in an externally referential manner, but in a truly representational fashion.

Referential Specificity: Roles of Affective and Representational Signals

What do these examples of communication about external referents suggest about the roles of affect and representation in signaling behavior? On the one hand, some signal systems, such as the ground squirrel alarms and the toque macaque food calls, illustrate that both affective and cognitive dimensions are probably simultaneously involved to a large extent in communication events. Thus, while the signaler in these systems may encode primarily affective information (level of arousal) or motivational information (probable behavior), the receiver may still actually be able to decode information about an external referent, perhaps using more complex cognitive processes than are employed by the signaler, assessing fine-structure acoustic differences, and appraising the signaler's context. Clearly these signals, although not strictly representational, carry meaning beyond simply specifying the probable behavior of the signaler (see Premack, 1975).

On the other hand, even the unequivocally representational systems considered here, the vervet alarms and grunts and the rhesus screams, undoubtedly also incorporate some affective information. For example, Seyfarth *et al.* (1980) point out that "monkeys responding to alarms use such features as amplitude, length, rate of delivery, and the number of individuals alarming when assessing how close a predator is and whether or not it poses immediate danger" (p. 1092). Also, Cheney and Seyfarth (1982) note that "contextual variables (including the vocaliser's own behaviour) are [not] irrelevant to determining the 'meaning' of a grunt to other monkeys" (p. 750). Finally, in the case of the rhesus screams, variation in the duration of scream bouts or in the amplitude of screams probably conveys to receivers some information about the signaler's arousal level. However, in none of these cases is contextual, or motivational information *necessary* for the "proper" interpretation of the meaning of the signal, and this is what we proposed as a criterion for a truly representational signal system. As Cheney and Seyfarth (1982) have suggested, other sorts of information (contextual, behavioral) enrich the meaning of the signal in the same way it may enhance the meaning of human language. It would probably be incorrect to conclude that affect plays no role in any of these systems. We emphasize again that cognitive and affective elements are jointly involved in communication events, to greater or lesser degrees (see Marler 1978, 1984).

Cognitive Implications of Representational Signaling

To what extent do the examples of truly representational signal systems we have discussed differ in the cognitive implications of the communication event. For example, is the process of identifying and referencing a leopard or an eagle likely to involve the same cognitive processes as the categorizing and referencing of a dominant- or subordinate-group member? We shall take as an analogy Miller and Johnson-Laird's (1976) discussion of two fundamentally different frames of reference in human language, illustrated by the terms that all human languages employ in dealing with color and with kinship.

In essence, *color* terms refer to properties of objects, and the information they convey is always potentially accessible by perception. That is, an aspect of direct perceptual experience of the object is being conveyed by the color term. In contrast, terms which denote *kinship* refer, not to properties of objects, but the relationships among objects. Furthermore, the information signaled by them is given via memory. The relationship itself is the information conveyed, and previous knowledge of the relationship that involves the stimulus object is a necessary pre-requisite.

Color terms are determined primarily by the functional organization of the visual system. The tendency to divide the spectrum into percep-tual categories, with focal regions and relatively fixed boundaries, is ubiquitous among most humans (for example, see Marler, Zoloth, & Dooling, 1981). In other words, there is a shared or common perception of the stimulus. Kinship terms, on the other hand, when they are used as a form of address, refer to attributes of external stimulus objects that vary systematically depending on who utters the term. The person I refer to as *mother* is unlikely to be the identical person you refer to by the same term, unless you and I are members of the same family. In referring to the same person, you will use a different term, reflecting your relationship to them.

The vervet alarm calls and most of the grunts studied by Cheney and Seyfarth (1982; Seyfarth *et al.* 1980) can be viewed in the same manner as human color-terms. Insofar as they indicate properties of objects, they are elicited perceptually and, no matter which animal utters them, they consistently index an object defined by properties shared and perceived commonly by group members, such as a leopard, or other ground pre-dator, or another group of vervets. On the other hand, certain vervet grunts, such as those given by animals as they approach other individ-uals, vary in form depending on the dominance rank of the individuals relative to that of the signaler. For instance, a given animal, Animal A, may hear both Grunt Type 1 (from Animal B which is subordinate to Animal A) and Grunt Type 2 (from Animal C which is dominant to An-imal A). Both grunts mean roughly that you are being approached. In this particular instance it is not clear exactly what information is con-veyed by the grunts other than the approach of a particular class of in-dividuals defined by their relationship to the signaler, but the grunt type employed in a given situation clearly depends upon the prior knowl-edge of relationships between the individuals involved.

The vocal recruitment signaling of the rhesus monkeys illustrates an even more complex system, resembling the kinship referencing de-scribed by Miller and Johnson-Laird (1976). In fact, certain rhesus screams are primarily concerned with indexing kinship, whereas others indicate relative-dominance rank. Note that in the case of the domi-nance-related vervet grunts, however, the intended receiver or addres-see of the signal is also a subject of the relationship being signaled about. The case of the rhesus is even more abstract in that, as in human-kinship labeling, the receiver is not necessarily involved in the reference relationship. Thus as produced by one signaler, the array of scream types indicates a set of individuals that is different when the same scream types are produced by another signaler. The same opponent may be referenced as a higher-ranking, unrelated opponent by one signaler, and as a lower-ranking relative by another. The meaning of the signal, then, depends upon the receiver's knowledge not only of the identity of the signaler but also of the network of relationships in which the signaler is involved.

Miller and Johnson-Laird (1976) point out that there are two ways to "exploit the kinship concept" (p. 372). One is the egocentric way, involving naming your own relationships, the other is the decentered way, requiring the understanding of someone else's relationships. Our data suggest that the vocal recruitment signaling of the rhesus involves both processes. The caller signals in an egocentric way about its relationships to the opponent. The receiver decodes the signal in a decentered way. The cognitive processing involved in kinship referencing is thus complex—more so than in color naming as Miller and Johnson-Laird point out. The case of representational signaling illustrated by the rhesus recruitment screams appears to involve the highest degree of abstraction (without human tutoring) yet implicated in the process of internal representation in a nonhuman primate (see Premack, 1975; Ristau & Robbins 1982). Just as Hinde (1976) describes the network of relationships among individuals in social groups as being essentially patterned out of the interactions of group members, so the relationships represented by the rhesus screams also represent a higher level of organization than the underlying interactions. Cheney and Seyfarth (1980) have demonstrated that vervet monkeys in fact recognize the kinship networks that exist between mothers and juveniles in the group. What we have demonstrated with the rhesus scream vocalizations is that these animals not only recognize the different social relationships they have with other groups members, but also they can communicate about them by means of representational reference.

Associative Naming
versus Representational Symbolism

The remarkable symbol-using ability of captive apes in artificial language experiments goes well beyond anything so far discovered in the natural communication of animals (see review, Ristau & Robbins, 1982). This apparent discrepancy may lie partly in the difficulty of devising experiments using animals' natural signals that provide a direct test of what individuals mean when they signal. In field experiments, meaning can be assessed only indirectly—by inference from observable behavior. Chalmers (1980) has in fact argued that field studies of the communication skills of primates reveal considerable capabilities for associative learning but have yielded little evidence of linguistic capacities.

Savage-Rumbaugh, Rumbaugh, Smith & Lawson, (1980) even suggest that there is little evidence from most of the previous captive ape research for truly representational symbolic cognitive functioning. Instead, they conclude that most use of symbols by apes can be attributed to specific paired-associative responses developed during training. Savage-Rumbaugh *et al.* (1980) devised a complex series of experiments to test whether or not two young chimpanzees could achieve representational symbolic communication. They conclude that these experiments demonstrate for the first time that chimpanzees are capable of symbolically encoding an abstract relationship. The challenge for the ethologist is to design field experiments that test for the existence of such cognitive skills in more natural contexts.

Evolutionary Considerations

Lockard (1978) has remarked that many current discussions of the evidence for higher-cognitive abilities and higher consciousness in nonhuman animals, or the likelihood of their occurrence, display a neglect of evolutionary questions. What is the adaptive significance of cognition and consciousness in nonhuman species? Moreover, what ecological and social pressures have given rise to these traits and in what species are we most likely to discover them? Lockard suggests that complex cognitive processes will be most common in gregarious social species such as social carnivores, marine mammals and primates, in which recognition of individual conspecifics is important and in which there is evidence of cooperative behavior in the rearing of offspring, finding food, or in predator defense. We need only look to eusocial insects such as honeybees, however, in which cooperative behavior exceeds anything found among higher vertebrates and in which truly symbolic[1] com-

---

[1]*Symbolic* here, refers to the apparent arbitrariness of the waggle dance as a code to refer to objects distant in space and time. That this structure lacks an iconic relationship is supported by considerable evidence regarding dialects among different races of bees.

munication is employed, to conclude that cognition is not a necessary correlate of these behaviors (Gould & Gould, 1982).

Lockard (1978) also points to Mayr's (1974) distinction between open and closed genetic programs in order to account for the evolution of higher-cognitive abilities: when ecological and social contingencies, including complex events and situations that are critical to an animal's survival, are not always predictable, selection for cognitive skills would no doubt be great. For example, dominance in some social systems is determined, not by physical traits such as size but, instead, by the history of relationships among many individuals over extended periods of time. Communication about status in such a system requires both current understanding and memory of an extensive network of relationships. In species in which we can empirically document this degree of social complexity, we are also likely to find the most complex communication systems, including those involving not only affective expression but also external reference and representation.

Summary

Evidence suggests that external reference is more prevalent in animal communication than was previously believed. Here we review some examples of nonhuman, mammalian vocal signals that concern external referents, and we attempt to sort out the role representational signaling plays in the communication system. In order to communicate about external objects and events, some species employ discrete signals modified by affective components and/or contextual information that together form a composite signal that specifies the referent (e.g., California ground squirrels and toque macaques). Other species (e.g., vervet monkeys and rhesus monkeys) employ representational signals that can designate the external referent in the absence of affective input, although here too, affective cues may influence conspecific response.

Inferences are drawn about the cognitive and associative processes involved in the use of signals with external referents. Communication about certain objects and events depends on the properties of those objects (e.g., predators) and involves a shared or common perception of the stimulus. In contrast, other referents, namely those that index attributes of external-stimulus objects that vary systematically depending upon the identity and relationship to them of the signaler, demand more complex interpretation on the part of receivers. Monkey vocalizations that index kinship and relative-dominance rank are examples of signals whose meaning depends upon the receivers' knowledge, not only of the identity of the signaler, but also of the network of relationships in which the signaler is involved.

References

Caryl, P. Communication by agonistic displays: What can games theory contribute to ethology? *Behaviour*, 1979, *68*, 136-169.

Chalmers, N. Can a study of nonhuman primate social behavior contribute to a greater understanding of symbolism? In M. L. Foster & S. H. Brandes (Eds.), *Symbol as sense*. Academic Press: New York, 1980.

Cheney, D. L. and Seyfarth, R. M. Vocal recognition in free-ranging vervet monkeys. *Animal Behaviour*, 1980, *28*, 363-367.

Cheney, D. L. The acquisition of rank and the development of reciprocal alliances among free-ranging immature baboons. *Behavioral Ecology and Sociobiology*, 1977, *2*, 303-318.

Cheney, D. L. Category formation in vervet monkeys. In V. Reynolds & R. Harre (Eds.), *Meaning of primate signals*. Cambridge: Cambridge University Press, in press.

Cheney, D. L., & Seyfarth, R. M. How vervet monkeys perceive their grunts: Field playback experiments. *Animal Behaviour*, 1982, *30*, 739-751.

Chomsky, N. *Language and mind*. New York: Harcourt Brace Jovanovich, 1972.

Dawkins, R., & Krebs, J. R. Animal signals: Information or manipulation? In J. R. Krebs & N. B. Davies (Eds.), *Behavioural ecology*. Sunderland, MA: Sinauer, 1978.

Dittus, W. P. J. The socioecological basis for the conservation of the toque monkeys (*Macaca sinica*) of Sri Lanka (Ceylon). In H. S. H. Prince Ranier III of Monaco & G. H. Bourne (Eds.), *Primate conservation*. New York: Academic Press, 1977.

Dittus, W. P. J. The evolution of behaviors regulating density and age-specific sex ratios in a primate population. *Behaviour*, 1979, *69*, 265-203.

Dittus, W. P. J. The social regulation of primate populations. In D. G. Lindburg (Ed.), *The Macaques*. New York: Van Nostrand Rheinhold, 1980.

Dittus, W. P. G. Toque macaque food calls: semantic communication concerning food distribution in the environment. *Animal Behaviour*, 1984, *32*, 470-477.

Gould, J. L., & Gould, C. G. The insect mind: Physics or metaphysics? In D. R. Griffin (Ed.), *Animal mind–human mind*. Dahlem Konferenzen Life Sciences Research Report 21, 1982.

Gouzoules, S., Gouzoules, H., & Marler, P. Rhesus monkey (*Macaca mulatta*) screams: Representational signaling in the recruitment of agonistic aid. *Animal Behaviour*, 1984, *32*, 182-193.

Green, S. Communication by a graded system in Japanese monkeys. In L. Rosenblum (Ed.), *Primate Behavior*. New York: Academic Press, 1975a.

Green, S. Dialects in Japanese monkeys, vocal learning and cultural transmission of locale-specific behavior. *Zeitschrift für Tierpsychologie*, 1975, *38*, 304-314, b.

Green, S. & P. Marler. The analysis of animal communication. In P. Marler & J. G. Vandenbergh (Eds.), *Handbook of behavioral neurobiology: Social behavior and communication* (Vol. 3). New York: Plenum, 1979.

Griffin, D. R. *The question of animal awareness*. New York: The Rockefeller University Press, 1976.

Griffin, D. R. Prospect for a cognitive ethology. *Behavior and Brain Science*, 1978, *4*, 527-538.

Griffin, D. R. *The question of animal awareness* (2nd ed.). New York: The Rockefeller University Press, 1981.

Griffin, D. R. *Animal Thinking*. Cambridge: Harvard University Press, 1984.

Hinde, R. A. Interactions, relationships and social structure. *Man*, 1976, *11*, 1–17.

Hockett, C. F. & Altmann, S. A. A note on design features. In T. A. Sebeok (Ed.), *Animal communication*. Bloomington: Indiana University Press, 1968.

Itani, J. 1963. Vocal communication of the wild Japanese monkey. *Primates*, 1963, *4*, 11–66.

Kaplan, J. Patterns of fight interference in free-ranging rhesus monkeys. *American Journal of Physical Anthropology*, 1977, *47*, 279–288.

Kaplan, J. Fight interference and altriusm in rhesus monkeys. *American Journal of Physical Anthropology*, 1978, *49*, 241–250.

Lancaster, J. Primate communication systems and the emergence of human language. In P. Jay (Ed.), *Primates: Studies in adaptation and variability*. New York: Holt, 1968.

Leger, D. W., & Owings, D. H. Responses to alarm calls by California ground squirrels: Effects of call structure and maternal status. *Behavioral Ecology and Sociobiology*, 1978, *3*, 177–186.

Leger, D. W., Owings, C. H., & Boal, L. M. Contextual information and differential responses to alarm whistles in California ground squirrels. *Zeitschrift für Tierpsychologie*, 1979, *49*, 142–155.

Leger, D. W., Owings, D. H., & Gelfand, D. L. Single-note vocalizations of California ground squirrels: graded signals and situation-specificity of predator and socially evoked calls. *Zeitschrift für Tierpsychologie*, 1980, *52*, 227–246.

Lockard, J. S. Speculations on the adaptive significance of cognition and consciousness in nonhuman species. *Behavior and Brain Science*, 1978, *4*, 583–584.

Lyons, J. Human language. In R. A. Hinde (Ed.), *Non-verbal communication*. Cambridge: Cambridge University Press, 1972.

Lyons, J. *Semantics* (Vol. 1). Cambridge: Cambridge University Press, 1977.

Marin, O. S., Schwartz, M. F., & Saffran, E. M. Origins and distribution of language. In M. S. Gazzaniga (Ed.), *Handbook of behavioral neurobiology* (Vol. 2). New York: Plenum, 1979.

Marler, P. Animal communication signals. *Science*, 1967, *157*, 769–774.

Marler, P. Affective and symbolic meaning: Some Zoosemiotic speculations. In T. A. Sebeok (Ed.), *Sight, sound and sense*. Bloomington: Indiana University Press, 1978.

Marler, P. Avian and primate communication: The problem of natural categories. *Neuroscience & Biobehavior Review*, 1982, *6*, 87–94.

Marler, P. Monkey calls: How are they perceived and what do they mean? In J. F. Eisenberg & D. G. Kleiman (Eds.), *Advances in the study of mammalian behavior*. American Society of Mammalogists Special Publication No. 7, 1983.

Marler, P. Animal communication: Affect or cognition? In K. Scherer & P. Ekman (Eds.), *The nature and function of emotion*. Hillsdale, NJ: Erlbaum, 1984.

Marler, P., S. Zoloth & R. Dooling. Innate programs for perceptual development: An ethological view. In E. S. Gollin (Ed.), *Developmental plasticity*. New York: Academic Press, 1981.

Mayr, E. Behavior programs and evolutionary strategies. *American Scientist*, 1974, *62*, 650–659.

Miller, G. A. & Johnson-Laird, P. N. *Language and perception*. Cambridge, MA: Harvard Univ. Press, 1976.

Ogden, C. K. & Richards, I. A. *The meaning of meaning*. London: Routledge & Kegan Paul, 1923.

Owings, D. H., Borchert, M., & Virginia, R. The behaviour of California ground squirrels. *Animal Behaviour*, 1977, *25*, 221-230.

Owings, D. H. & Virginia, R. A. Alarm calls of California ground squirrels (*Spermophilus beecheyi*). *Zeitschrift für Tierpsychologie*, 1978, *46*, 58-70.

Owings, D. H. & Leger, D. W. Chatter vocalizations of California ground squirrels: Predator- and social-role specificity. *Zeitschrift für Tierpsychologie*, 1980, *54*, 150-163.

Premack, D. On the origins of language. In M. S. Gazzaniga & C. Blakemore (Eds.), *Handbook of Psychobiology*, New York: Academic Press, 1975.

Ristau, C. H. & D. Robbins. Language in the great apes: A critical review. *Advances in the Study of Behavior*, 1982, *12*, 141-255.

Rowell, T. E. & Hinde, R. A. Vocal communication in the rhesus monkey (*Macaca mulatta*). *Proceedings of the Zoological Society of London*, 1962, *138*, 279-294.

Savage-Rumbaugh, E. S., Rumbaugh, D. M., Smith, S. T., & Lawson, J. Reference: The linguistic essential. *Science*, 1980, *210*, 922-925.

Seyfarth, R. M. Communication as evidence of thinking—Group report. In D. R. Griffin (Ed.), *Animal mind—human mind*. Berlin: Dahlem Konferenzum, 1982.

Seyfarth, R. M., Cheney, D. L., & Marler, P. Vervet monkey alarm calls: Semantic communication in a free-ranging primate. *Animal Behaviour*, 1980, *28*, 1070-1094.

Shafton, A. *Conditions of Awareness*. Portland, OR: Riverstone Press, 1976.

Smith, W. J. Message, meaning, and context in ethology. *American Naturalist*, 1976, *99*, 405-409.

Smith, W. J. *The behavior of communicating*. Cambridge, MA: Harvard University Press, 1977.

Smith, W. J. Referents of animal communication. *Animal Behaviour*, 1981, *29*(4), 1273-1275.

Stokes, A. W. Behaviour of the bobwhite, *Colinus virginianus*. *Auk*, 1967, *84*, 1-33.

Struhsaker, T. T. Auditory communication among vervet monkeys (*Cercopithecus aethiops*). In S. A. Altmann (Ed.), *Social communication among primates*, Chicago: University of Chicago Press, 1967.

Thorpe, W. H. The comparison of vocal communication in animals and man. In R. A. Hinde (Ed.), *Non-verbal communication*. Cambridge, MA: Cambridge University Press, 1972.

Walters, J. Interventions and the development of dominance relationships in female baboons. *Folia primatologica*, 1980, *34*, 61-89.

Chapter 5
Expression and Negotiation

Robert A. Hinde

Relationship to Other Chapters and to the Field

Relevant Issues in the Field

The common view of human expression and animal behavior assumes that all nonverbal signals give information about the signaler's internal state or about the behavior he or she is likely to perform next. As noted in Chapter 1, this traditional view has recently been questioned by several authors. Hinde here contributes to this questioning by suggesting that it is profitable to think of signals as ranging from pure expressions of state, which are performed without regard for a recipient, to expressions involving negotiation, which are necessarily made in interaction with a recipient and are partly determined by the recipient's expected response. Most signals, Hinde asserts, lie between these two extremes. Hinde thus circumvents the troublesome dichotomy presented in the framing chapter as spontaneous versus instrumental signaling, with instrumental negotiation revealing probabilities about the signaler's intentions. Further supporting the idea of signals as negotiations, Hinde reviews data suggesting that an optimal ambiguity of threat signals is adaptive: ambiguity allows a safe compromise between too much rigidity in the signal-state relationship and too little consistency to allow communication.

Hinde notes that ethological analyses indicate that many (but not all) display movements depend on conflict between more than one state. He points out that in signals involving negotiation, the cognition of the signaler, in expectation of

*a response and other environmental considerations, is involved in the deter-
mination of the signal. Behavior after the signal is related to but not solely
determined by the internal state during signalling.*

Relationship to Other Chapters

In his analysis of the signal situation, Hinde shares elements in agreement
with Smith (see Chapter 3). He and Smith agree that an excellent way to understand the conditional probabilities of next behaviors is often as the prediction
of some disjunctive action, such as stay-or-attack, rather than as the simple
prediction of attack. They also agree that whatever behavior is predicted, the
prediction holds only very momentarily; within this, both agree that the situation changes through the recipient's responses and through the signaler's interpretations of the entire changing situation, all in systemic interaction. Smith's
analysis of contextual regularities when confronted with changing signals can
be invoked as an explanation of how Hinde's optimal ambiguity avoids unintel-
ligible communications. Hinde does not here explicitly discuss the role of contextual information and does not mention the place or the possibility of animal
signals having either of the forms of external reference described by Gouzoules,
Gouzoules, and Marler (see Chapter 4).

Concerning the development of signaling skill, Hinde does agree with Marler
and the Gouzouleses who emphasize the close connection in animal communication of emotion and cognition. But while Marler and the Gouzouleses and
Smith highlight the cognition of the recipient, Hinde is closer to Mason (see
Chapter 6) in emphasizing the cognition of the signaler in his or her interpretation of the situation. In indicating that the expected direction of signaling
development is from primarily expressive to primarily instrumental negotiative
signals, Hinde presents the developmental course that is an implicit commonality among the contributors to this volume who are human developmentalist.
This aspect of the course is most explicitly stated by Thelan (see Chapter 9).
Again in spirit with the socialization developmentalists, best exemplified by Lewis
and Michalson (Chapter 7), Malatesta (Chapter 8), and Feinman (Chapter 12)
is Hinde's novel suggestion that learning successful nonverbal negotiation may
be as or more crucial to nonverbal mastery as are the traditional forces of reward
and modeling.

Hinde and Smith (Chapter 3) alone in this volume consider the evolutionary
constraints on signaling and interpreting. They agree that there must be adaptive benefit to both roles in order for a signal to evolve among conspecifics, and
both question the generality of arguments made for evolved animal deception.—
ED.

Introduction

Some trends in the study of animal and human communication suggest that it is helpful to think of signals in terms of *negotiation* as well as, or instead of, *expression*. This chapter attempts to bring together some of the evidence on that point. For brevity, discussion is largely, though not entirely, limited to some analyses of animal threat signals on the one hand, and to Zivin's (e.g., 1982) penetrating analysis of the *plus face,* an expression predictive of a win in children's disputes, on the other. It will be necessary to refer not only to the causal bases of signal movements but also to their functions. Whilst biological function must ultimately be assessed in terms of the survival and reproduction of the individual (or perhaps more properly, in terms of the propagation of genes; see Hamilton, 1964; Dawkins, 1976), it will be sufficient here to refer only to more immediate costs and benefits.

Earlier studies of nonverbal signals have often implied two interrelated assumptions: (1) Each signal depends on a more or less specific state in the actor—an assumption embodied in the title of Darwin's (1872) book *The Expression of the Emotions in Man and Animals,* and (2) That state outlasts the signal and determines subsequent behaviour. While these assumptions are made primarily in studies of animal communication, they are present also, though sometimes somewhat diluted, in studies of human facial expressions and gestures. These assumptions provide a convenient starting point for discussion.

How Complex Are the Factors Affecting
the Final Common Path?

Whilst it is reasonable to assume a final common path whose state is linked closely to the nature of the signal emitted and determines the nature of the signal, the issue to be discussed concerns the complexity of the factors affecting that path. Although it is generally recognised that the control of signal movements can be complex, the simplifying assumption that they depend on one or two relatively simple motivational factors has often facilitated ethological analysis (e.g., Baerends, 1975). Yet this assumption may have biased our view about the nature of signal movements. In fact a number of lines of evidence suggest that the relation between a signal and the internal state is by no means so simple as was once supposed. For example:

1. Field studies have shown that the relations between signals and subsequent behaviour may change with time. For instance Stokes (1962), studying the behaviour of blue tits (*Parus caeruleus*) at a winter feeding station, found not only that the tolerance versus aggressiveness of the birds changed through the season but also that the probability that a particular postural element would lead to attack, escape, or stay changed. Stokes discussed a number of possible explanations, including changes in hunger and increases in tolerance towards known individuals. Another possibility, to which we return, is that the responsiveness of the threatened bird changes through the season.

Again, changes in the frequency with which threat postures are shown while dominance hierarchies are being established are well known to students of animal behaviour, although so far as I know changes in the relationship between signal and subsequent behaviour that occur in this context have not been documented. However, a reasonable explanation is that the nature of the signals given depends in part on expectations held by the actor about the behaviour of the reactor—a dominant animal does not need to threaten because he or she expects to get what is wanted without resistance. This incidentally implies that the relevant internal state is not merely emotional or affective but involves a strong cognitive component concerned with assessment of the probable behaviour of the reactor. Assessments of the desirability of the object of a dispute, or of the availability of alternatives, may also be important. More extensive evidence on this point is provided by Mason's (see Chapter 6) contribution to this volume.

2. Comparison between human cultures have revealed many examples of cultural differences in the extents to which signal movements have been elaborated and in their sequelae. Such differences imply that the relation between signal and internal state (as indicated by the sequelae) is determined during individual development. Ekman and Friesen (Ekman & Friesen, 1969; see also Ekman, 1977) have analysed the several points in the sequence of events from stimulus to response at which experiential influences may operate.

3. Two signal movements of human children, the *plus* and *minus* faces, are used in disputes and are associated respectively with high probabilities of winning and losing an encounter (Zivin, 1977). A number of lines of evidence indicate that the dependence of the signal on the internal state changes. For example, the plus face correlates with domi-

nance rank only up to about 10 years of age. Furthermore, the context in which the plus face is used shifts from overt conflict to nonhostile exhibitions of competence: thus the plus face, initially used in controlling discrete isolated conflicts, comes to be used in "generalized impression management and formation" (Zivin, 1982). A comparable shift occurs in the development of the Burmese red junglefowl, in which a signal occurring in a context of overt conflict later appears in contexts without other overt agonistic content (Kruijt, 1982, personal communication).

4. Some nonhuman primates (e.g., Menzel, 1971) and human beings are able to dissemble, feign, exaggerate, and conceal emotional states (Ekman & Friesen, 1975; Ekman, 1981).

These several lines of evidence indicate complexity in the relations between internal state and signal, present in some degree in nonhuman species, but increasing phylogenetically through nonhuman primates to man. This is in harmony with later views on the bases of emotional behaviour. In the 1940s, psychologists were prone to distinguish clearly between the emotions on the one hand and cognitive functioning on the other. Now the two are seen as closely interwoven (Hinde, in press). For instance Ekman (1977) has emphasized that cognition enters into emotional behaviour in (1) the appraisal of the situation which evokes the emotion in the first instance; (2) the learned attempts to modulate emotional expression to fit the requirements of the situation, including cultural demands; and (3) the learned attempts to cope with the source of emotion. Whilst other authors have emphasized the importance of cognition in emotion (e.g., Schachter & Singer, 1962), Ekman emphasizes that cognition plays an integral part in calling forth the physiological changes, whilst recognizing that the physiological bases as well as the behavioural concomitants of the several emotions may be differentiated (Ekman, 1983, personal communication). (In addition we must of course recognise not only the role of cognitions in emotion but also that of emotion in cognition).

Does the Internal State That Accompanies Signals Persist and Determine the Behaviour that Follows?

This has been a basic assumption in ethological analyses, where the principle evidence used to assess the motivational states accompanying signal movements has been the behaviour that follows them (e.g., Baerends, 1975; Moynihan, 1955; Tinbergen, 1959). Current discussion about this question, which concerns the causation of the sequelae of signal movements, stems from consideration of a functional question: do signals function to convey information about the internal state or probable behaviour of the actor?

This is a matter over which students of animal behaviour have not always been clearheaded. Some ethologists have written as though signals, by conveying information about the internal state of the actor, were of similar mutual benefit to actor and reactor (e.g., Marler, 1967). This implies the presupposition that natural selection acts to promote the behaviour of groups of individuals—a view unlikely to be correct except in certain rather special cases (Lack, 1954; Maynard Smith, 1976; Williams, 1966). Others, and probably the majority, have taken the view that signals have become elaborated by natural selection through the benefits they confer on the actor, whilst responsiveness to those signals has arisen through natural selection acting through benefits it confers to the reactor (e.g., Blest, 1961). The issue has been highlighted by two papers. One, by Dawkins and Krebs (1978), argued that it is at least usually in the interests of the actor to manipulate the behaviour of the reactor and thus not to reveal his or her internal state. The other, by Caryl (1979), whilst making the same point, focussed also on the empirical question of whether displays do actually convey information about the actor's subsequent behaviour. Whilst these papers misrepresented some of the earlier ethological work on animal signals (Hinde, 1981; see Caryl, 1982, for contrary view), they highlighted the important question of the precise nature of the selective forces involved in the elaboration of signal movements.

Both of these papers, and especially Caryl's, were concerned primarily with threat movements. Turning to causal questions, ethological analyses have shown that threat movements can be interpreted as depending on conflicting tendencies. The tendencies usually considered are those to approach or attack the rival and to withdraw or flee from the rival: some workers consider also a tendency to stay put (Baerends, 1975). Evidence as to the tendencies involved comes not only from the sequelae but also from the context, the form of the movement, and the behaviour accompanying it. For example, early in the breeding season the territorial boundaries of breeding birds are lines along which each is more or less equally prone to attack and flee from the other; it is along those boundaries that threat displays are most used. The postures often involve intention movements of attacking or fleeing and are accompanied by movements towards or away from the rival. Caryl (1979), reviewing data from earlier studies, pointed out that, whilst threat postures were sometimes reasonably accurate predictors of escape, they seldom predicted attack accurately. For instance Stokes's (1962) data on the aggressive behaviour of blue tits at a winter feeding station showed that two of the threat postures predicted escape with high accuracy (94 and 89% of all occasions), but the best predictors of attack were followed by attack on only 48, 44, and 43% of occasions. Thus whilst some postures seemed to carry reasonably accurate information about impending withdrawal, none carried accurate information about attack.

Given that threat postures could be followed by a number of different actions by the signaller, Hinde (1972, 1975) earlier suggested that displays were given when the bird was uncertain what to do and that which of the several possible responses it showed next depended on the behaviour of the rival. It seemed reasonable to suppose that an animal that was definitely going to attack or definitely going to flee would do best to do so immediately, without giving warning displays first. Whilst warning before an intended attack might be useful if it rendered an attack unnecessary by causing the opponent to flee, or deterred a preemptive attack by a rival, these are both situations in which the attacker is uncertain of what he or she should best do next. On this view, threat displays would be useful only in moments of indecision: if what the signaller A should do depended in part on the subsequent behaviour of B, threatening by A might elicit a response from B that would permit a decision by A. Such a view is in harmony with the protracted duels shown in some species, in which the eventual winner and the eventual loser show apparently identical behaviour in a gradually escalating encounter until more or less suddenly one becomes dominant (e.g., Simpson, 1968). It supposes that the displays do not predict *either* attack *or* stay, but that they predict either attack-or-stay or flee-or-stay; this is in harmony with Stokes's (1962) data, for the postures he studied predicted either the former with 79–90% probability or the latter with 93–100%.

Of course, as Caryl (1982; see also 1981) rightly points out, combining categories in this way inevitably enhances the accuracy of prediction. But he goes too far in his belief that a full understanding of the interactions between the combatants would lead to little improvement in our ability to predict the sequelae of signal movements: his only positive reason for this despairing suggestion is that games theory would predict otherwise. Ultimately, the issue must rest on empirical data, and an important and independent study by Bossema and Burgler (1980) has provided clear support for an interactionist position. Studying the behaviour of jays (*Garrulus glandarius*) when a dominant on a feeder was approached by another, they identified two signals—monocular and binocular fixation combined with particular postures—by the dominant bird. They showed that

1. Attack was more likely to follow binocular fixation than monocular fixation and was more likely to follow if the subordinate bird were near than if it were more distant.
2. The subordinate bird was more likely to hop away when the dominant bird gave a signal likely to be followed by attack (e.g., binocular threat at short distance) than one relatively unlikely to be followed by attack (e.g., monocular threat at long distance). Thus although these two signals are relatively unritualized, they do have regular (probabilistic) sequelae, and they do influence the behaviour of the other individual.
3. After signalling, the probability of attack by the actor was highest if the reactor showed behaviour indicating approach and lowest if it retreated. In general, the higher the apparent interest of the reactor in approaching the feeder, the greater the probability of attack.

Thus these data show that the two threat signals are associated with different probabilities of attack by the actor and that whether attack actually follows depends on the behaviour of the reactor. Whilst the signal can be regarded as dependent upon the actor's internal state, it gives only an approximate indication of the signal's sequelae. The data are in harmony with the view that the internal state associated with the signal does persist after its causation but that the actor's subsequent behaviour is influenced also by the response of the reactor.

This view readily accommodates the finding that escape is predicted better by threat signals than is attack. When the stay-or-probably-attack display is shown, the reactor can know that, although the probability of attack by the actor is low if he is not further provoked, it will be much higher if the reactor approaches. The latter may therefore act so as not to precipitate attack. But if the stay-or-probably-flee display is shown, the reactor may do well to go in and supplant the signalling individual.

These considerations point to the conclusion that although threat postures can be considered as expressive of an internal state, they can also be considered as signals in a process of negotiation between two individuals. Whilst some signals are nearer the expressive end of this continuum (e.g., the begging calls of a young bird), threat postures are farther along towards the negotiating end. At the extremes, expressive signals are broadcast independently of the presence of a receiver, whilst signals used in negotiation appear in intimate interactions and are directed with respect to the recipient, depending in part on his behaviour.

This distinction between expression and negotiation is similar to that between signals that are primarily expressions of the emotion and signals that are primarily conversational in character (Ekman, 1982, personal communication). It is also similar to that used by Zivin (1982) between expressive and instrumental behaviour. By comparing the behaviour of children in a dispute when they knew that their rival could and could not see their face, she was able to show that the frequency of occurrence of the plus face dropped significantly in the latter condition. This indicates that it has an instrumental function. However, its frequency did not drop to zero, indicating that it also has an expressive aspect. Interestingly, Zivin's (1982) data show that young children use the plus face predominantly in limited conflicts in which it is presumably primarily instrumental, and older children come to use it more and more outside conflict situations as an expression of competence. This might seem in some senses to be the opposite to the ontogenetic sequence that would be expected if the signals used by young children were to be regarded as primarily expressive, an instrumental application emerging gradually with age or experience. However, at both ages, both expressive and instrumental aspects are probably found in some degree.

Thus, to revert to our original question of whether the internal state accompanying a signal persists and determines the subsequent behaviour, we conclude that it may persist but is only one of the factors affecting the subsequent behaviour. Another and often more important factor is the behaviour of the rival. Such signals are thus to be seen as involving negotiation with the rival as well as expression of an internal state. The term *negotiation* does not necessarily imply *manipulation* (see Dawkins & Krebs, 1978) but emphasizes the continuous interaction between the two individuals involved.

Some Further Issues

Two kinds of information may be conveyed by a threat posture: (1) information about the actor's strength, size, ownership and so forth, collectively referred to as *Resource Holding Potential* or RHP (Parker, 1974), and (2) information about his or her intentions. Maynard Smith (1979) has argued that, during a contest between two individuals, information mainly about RHP should be transferred, because information about RHP affects the outcome of an escalated conflict, while intentions can be easily exaggerated. Whilst the distinction may not be so simple as Maynard Smith implied, it provides an important starting point for discussion. His view is in harmony with a number of examples of signals containing information about strength, which must be accurate because relevant parameters (pitch, duration, etc.) of the signal depend on the strength of the performer (Clutton-Brock & Albon 1979; Davies & Halliday, 1978). However Van Rhijn and Vodegel (1980) argue that a large proportion of conflicts occur between individuals who are already known to each other, and to whom any asymmetry in RHP would already be known. They argue, therefore, that communication about intentions should be conveyed. A dominant individual may signal, for instance, "I want to eat now, but if you do not go away I shall hit you," or as an alternative, "I am not hungry, do not worry." Such a view is of course entirely in accord with the view of signals as involving negotiation and with the data of Bossema and Burgler (1980). It is also in accord with the behaviour of groups of captive animals (e.g., monkeys) whose strengths are well known to each other but whose changing postures and use of signals reflect changes in their current motivation and assessments of each other's probable behaviour.

There is no necessary correspondence between this distinction between information about RHP and information about intentions, and that between expression and negotiation: both expression and negotiation can involve either type of information. The change in usage of the plus face with age could be described as a change from conveying information about intentions to conveying information about RHP.

Another issue concerns the use of graded signals. It is generally presumed that it is better to threaten before attacking because a threat involves less energy expenditure and less risk of injury than an attack. However, why should signallers use a graded series of signals, rather than a single unequivocal signal indicating, for example, "I am likely to attack you if you approach"? The view that the successive signals in a graded series are more energy consuming, though perhaps true, is unconvincing because the differences are so small. Van Rhijn (1980) offers the alternative explanation that graded signals may be useful in permitting individuals to evaluate their relative interests in a given resource. The individual with the greater interest would presumably invest more in a conflict, and would be identified by signalling at a higher intensity. He suggests that, in a group of individuals known to each other, conflicts might be settled by a process of heterogeneous summation of the strength differences (known to the individuals) and the interest differences (indicated by signals). Yet another possible explanation stems from the fact that threat signals are themselves elicitors of attack as well as of escape in reactors. For example, a territorial intruder may be more likely to flee from a threatening conspecific than from one who is not threatening, but a territory owner is more likely to attack a threatening individual than one who is passive. Thus to use a signal that could be read as exaggerating the signaller's aggressive intent would be disadvantageous in augmenting the (admittedly small) probability of an attack by the reactor (Hinde, 1981).

A related issue concerns the tightness of the linkage between signal and internal state. A particular signal may be associated with a specific internal state, changing its form gradually as that state changes, or the signal may remain constant whilst the internal state changes over a considerable range (Morris, 1957). The question thus arises, what determines whether an individual would do better to be more or less vague about his internal state? Would it not pay to exaggerate your attack readiness in order to increase the probability that the rival will flee? Again the fact that threat postures elicit attack as well as fleeing may be crucial. Exaggeration of the probability of subsequent attack or minimization of the probability of escape might augment the probability or viciousness of an attack by a rival, whilst the opposite tendencies might invite attack from a rival who would otherwise be deterred (see also Smith, 1977). Thus evolution towards an *optimal degree of ambiguity* seems inevitable. A graded series of threat postures, each implying a range of internal states, can be seen as a compromise between, on the one hand, a close linkage between the internal state and the form of the signal, and on the other hand, gross ambiguity.

Finally, on a speculative note, recognition of the continuum from expression to negotiation could be relevant to the as yet unsolved problem of the factors determining the ontogeny of signal movements. It is often implied that developmental changes depend on reward that is consequent upon the use of the signal, or on modelling of a signal used by others. It would seem possible that the crucial issue is successful negotiation, involving, for example, getting the rival to reveal his or her intentions—whether or not it leads to winning or losing the dispute. A similar principle is also likely to apply to signals used in nonagonistic contexts. Whether revelation of intentions acquires effectiveness as a secondary reinforcer is of course a further issue.

Conclusions

We see then, that understanding of both animal and human communication may be facilitated by acknowledging a continuum between *expression* and *negotiation*. Although discussion here has been limited mainly to signals exchanged in agonistic contexts, the principle is probably of wide application: for example, the analysis even of infant communication has been facilitated by an emphasis on its intentional as well as on its expressive aspects (Stern, 1977). However it must be recognised that signals vary along the whole range of this continuum, from those that are entirely or primarily expressive to those that involve almost pure negotiation. The continuum is similar to that between the expressive and instrumental use of signals, and can sometimes be related to that between information about Resource Holding Potential and intention. Recognition of the role of negotiation may lead to a deeper understanding of the causal bases of threat postures and of behaviour in conflict situations. It may also throw light on the ontogeny of signal movements.

Finally, one theme, implicit in much of what has been said, needs to be emphasized. Further progress in research on nonverbal communication must depend on full understanding of the cognitive as well as the emotional and motivational processes involved. Threat postures depend in part on an assessment of the probable response of the other and, in man at least, often on an assessment of the reactor's probable assessment of the signal; and the response of the reactor depends on his or her assessment of the actor's probable subsequent behaviour, which is only partially conveyed by the signal. The behaviour of babies playing peek-a-boo can be understood only on the basis of attributing to them some expectation of their partner's next move, and we must not be too chary of using cognitive variables if we are to make progress in analysing nonverbal signalling in other species, at least in higher vertebrates.

Summary

Since Darwin's classic book, much research on signal movements has treated them as if they were "expressive" of internal motivational states. Ethologists have used the sequelae of a signal as evidence for the nature of the internal state associated with it. It is argued here that the classic view has tended to underemphasize the cognitive contribution to signal movements and that their sequelae may depend in part on the behaviour of the respondent. Signals may involve negotiation as well as expression.

Acknowledgments

This work was supported by the Royal Society and the Medical Research Council. I am grateful to Clive Hambler, Jaap Kruijt, and Nick Thompson for their comments on earlier versions of the manuscript.

References

Baerends, G. P. An evaluation of the conflict hypothesis as an explanatory principle for the evolution of displays. In G. P. Baerends, C. Beer, & A. Manning (Eds.), *Function and evolution in behaviour.* Oxford: Clarendon Press, 1975.

Blest, A. D. The concept of ritualization. In W. H. Thorpe & O. L. Zangwill (Eds.), *Current problems in animal behaviour.* Cambridge: Cambridge University Press, 1961.

Bossema, I., & Burgler, R. R. Communication during monocular and binocular looking in European jays (*Garrulus g. glandarius*). *Behaviour,* 1980, *74,* 274-283.

Caryl, P. G. Communication by agonistic displays: What can games theory contribute to ethology? *Behaviour,* 1979, *68,* 136-169.

Caryl, P. G. Escalated fighting and the war of nerves: Games theory and animal combat. In P. P. G. Bateson & P. H. Klopfer (Eds.), *Perspectives in ethology,* (Vol. 4). New York: Plenum, 1981.

Caryl, P. G. Animal signals: A reply to Hinde. *Animal Behaviour,* 1982, *30,* 240-244.

Clutton-Brock, T. H., & Albon, S. D. The roaring of red deer and the evolution of honest advertisement. *Behaviour,* 1979, *69,* 145-170.

Darwin, C. *The expression of the emotions in man and animals.* London: Murray, 1872.

Davies, N. B., & Halliday, T. M. Deep croaks and fighting assessment in toads *Bufo bufo. Nature,* 1978, *274,* 683-685.

Dawkins, R. *The selfish gene.* Oxford University Press, 1976.

Dawkins, R., & Krebs, J. R. Animal signals: Information or manipulation. In J. R. Krebs & N. B. Davies (Eds.), *Behavioral Ecology: An Evolutionary Approach.* Oxford: Blackwell, 1978.

Ekman, P. Biological and cultural contributions to body and facial movements. In J. Blacking (Ed.), *The anthropology of the body, ASA Monograph 15.* London: Academic Press, 1977.

Ekman, P. Mistakes when deceiving. *Annals of the New York Academy of Sciences,* 1981, *364,* 269-278.

Ekman, P., & Friesen, W. V. The repertoire of nonverbal behaviour: Categories, origins, usage and coding. *Semiotica,* 1969, *1,* 49-98.

Ekman, P., & Friesen, W. V. *Unmasking the face.* New Jersey: Prentice-Hall, 1975.

Hamilton, W. D. The genetical theory of social behaviour. *Journal of Theoretical Biology,* 1964, *7,* 1-52.

Hinde, R. A. *Social behavior and its development in subhuman primates* (Condon Lectures.) Eugene: Oregon Press, 1972.

Hinde, R. A. The concept of function. In G. P. Baerends, C. Beer & A. Manning (Eds.), *Function and evolution in behaviour,* pp. 4-5. Oxford: Clarendon Press, 1975.

Hinde, R. A. Animal signals: Ethological and games-theory approaches are not incompatible. *Animal Behaviour,* 1981, *29,* 535-542.

Hinde, R. A. Was the expression of the emotions a misleading phrase? *Animal Behaviour,* in press.

Lack, D. *The natural regulation of animal numbers.* Oxford: Clarendon, 1954.

Marler, P. Animal communication signals. *Science,* 1967, *157,* 769-774.

Menzel, E. W. Communication about the environment in a group of young chimpanzees. *Folia Primatologica,* 1971, *15,* 220-232.

Maynard Smith, J. Evolution and the theory of games. *American Scientist,* 1976, *64,* 41-5.

Maynard Smith, J. Game theory and the evolution of behaviour. *Proceedings of the Royal Society of London, B.* 1979, *205,* 475-488.

Morris, D. "Typical intensity" and its relation to the problem of ritualisation. *Behaviour,* 1957, *11,* 1-12.

Moynihan, M. Some aspects of reproductive behavior in the black-headed gull (*Larus ridibundus ridibundus* L.) and related species. *Behaviour Supplement*, 1955, *4*, 1–201.

Parker, G. A. Assessment strategy and the evolution of animal conflicts. *Journal of Theoretical Biology*, 1974, *47*, 223–243.

Schachter, S., & Singer, J. E. Cognitive, social and physiological determinants of emotional state. *Psychological Review*, 1962, *69*, 379–399.

Simpson, M. J. A. The displays of the Siamese fighting fish, *Betta splendens. Animal Behaviour Monogrographs*, 1968, *1*, 1.

Smith, W. J. *The Behavior of Communicating: An ethological approach.* Harvard: Harvard University Press, 1977.

Stern, D. *The first relationship: Infant and mother.* London: Fontana Open Books, 1977.

Stokes, A. W. The comparative ethology of great, blue, marsh and coal tits at a winter feeding station. *Behaviour*, 1962, *19*, 208–218.

Tinbergen, N. Comparative studies of the behaviour of gulls (*Laridae*): A progress report. *Behaviour*, 1959, *15*, 1–70.

van Rhijn, J. G. Communication by agonistic displays: A discussion. *Behaviour*, 1980, *74*, Parts 3–4, 284–293.

van Rhijn, J. G., & Vodegel, R. Being honest about one's intentions: An evolutionary stable strategy for animal conflicts. *Journal of Theoretical Biology*, 1980, *85*,(4), 623–641.

Williams, G. C. *Adaptation and natural selection.* NJ: Princeton University Press, 1966.

Zivin, G. Preschool children's facial gestures predict conflict outcomes. *Social Science Information*, 1977, *16*(6), 715–730.

Zivin, G. Watching the sands shift: Conceptualizing development of nonverbal mastery with the assistance of instabilities and discontinuities. In R. S. Feldman (Ed.), *The Development of Nonverbal Communication in Children.* New York: Springer, 1982.

Chapter 6

Experiential Influences on the Development of Expressive Behaviors in Rhesus Monkeys*

William A. Mason

Relationship to Other Chapters and to the Field

Relevant Issues in the Field

Mason's chapter elegantly illustrates two approaches noted in this volume's framing chapter as of contemporary importance. One is the newer understanding of animal behavior and cognition that recognizes the subtlety of animals' social cognitions and behaviors plus the combinations of inherited and experiential forces that influence them. The second is an especially rich form of the most frequently held idea of the cumulative interaction of biological and environmental forces over the course of development. In applying the latter to expressive behavior, he explicitly notes the initial and the continuing potentiations and limitations of inherited patterns and sensitivities, finds evidence for effects of general experience on specifiable mechanisms of emotional expression, checks the plausibility of the effects against their adaptive value, and sees—in monkeys—the developmental trend to learn to emit expressive behaviors in accord with the acquired knowledge of social status and context.

In his conclusion, Mason organizes the studies he has reviewed as evidence for effects of general experience on rhesus expressive-behavior development

*Preparation of this chapter was aided by grants from the United States Public Health Service HD 06367 and RR 00169. I am grateful for the comments of M. W. Andrews, A. Butler, T. Heckmann, S. P. Mendoza, C. R. Menzel & C. P. Yeager.

through the three components of Ekman's neurocultural model *of emotion. He finds the greatest impact on the* appraisal mechanism: *here, the entire course of differentiation and integration in perception and cognition affects this mechanism such that the animal can increasingly understand his or her situation and thus increasingly respond with fitting emotion to it. On the* central-affect program, *there appears a notable split effect: it acquires increased differentiation, integration, and coordination of the motor and cognitive systems that produce expressive behaviors, but there is no effect of experience on the programs' production of the form of facial expressive behaviors, although there may be effect on vocal-expressive behaviors. He also finds effects on the* mechanism for managing emotions: *management assimilates social experience such that expressive behaviors are emitted in accord with status and context, rather than by putative state alone.*

Relationship to Other Chapters

Mason's view of the link between emotional state and specific expressive behaviors finds a parallel in Lewis and Michalson's (Chapter 7): as they do, Mason notes the evidence for the lack of definite correspondence in early life of specific state and specific behavior; and in great similarity to their view of the second stage of development, Mason sees most of rhesus development working to make more frequent the appraisal that brings together emotion and emotional expression. Again, similar to their third stage—which resembles the lengthy and final second stage for Malatesta (Chapter 8) and Cole (Chapter 11)—Mason further finds the trend in the rhesus to disconnect emotional conditions from expression according to rudimentary rules concerning status and context.

Mason's sensitivity to the necessity that an observer attend to context and multiple cues, and not simply read one signal in order to judge what emotion an individual may have, is central to concerns of Smith (Chapter 3) and Hinde (Chapter 5). Smith has been one of the first animal-communication theorists to codify the integral part that context plays in interpreting messages by conspecifics. In his chapter, Hinde further specifies this insight into the interplay of context and optional expressive behaviors as the process of negotiation of mutual stances, which he contrasts with simple expression. As do Gouzoules, Gouzoules, and Marler (Chapter 4) and Smith, Mason explicitly struggles with sound criteria for empirical evidence of a signal's referent. An interesting contrast appears between Mason and Smith on the question of the prevalence of change in the form of prewired signals: Mason finds form changes rare as the result of general experience in rhesus ontogeny, occurring in vocal signals and not in facial ones. Smith suggests, when emphasizing phylogeny, that form change is one of the two primary means of evolving new signals. This may lead to an apparent contradiction with Mason's conclusions. The apparent discrep-

ancy between these two positions seems to be more due to their general frames of reference—phylogeny versus ontogeny, and all channels of all species versus two channels of one species—than to any true disagreement.

*In attending to the impact of general experience on all three components of the neurocultural model of emotion, Mason treats in one chapter the concerns that are the separate foci of several others. It is interesting that this concordance holds even though the experiential variables that Mason examines are much less fine grained than those of the other contributors to this volume. In emphasizing the appraisal mechanism as accounting for one's emotional condition, and in avoiding the univariate concept of state as synonymous with emotional condition, Mason resembles Lewis and Michalson (Chapter 7), and even more closely Feinman (Chapter 12). Mason's notice of rhesuses' expression management depicts the capacities necessary for Hinde's (Chapter 5) negotiation by animals. And Mason's considerations of the central-affect program link with suggestions by the Gouzouleses and Marler (Chapter 4), Smith (Chapter 3), Thelen (See Chapter 9), and Fogel (Chapter 10): Mason concludes that the form of facial signals is not influenced by experience and thus does not serve to create new signals with new referents but that this may not be true for vocal signals. The question of the existence of signals with external reference is central to the chapter by Gouzoules, Gouzoules, and Marler. They present evidence that there are indeed vocal signals with external reference, but they leave open the question of whether these arose as experiential modifications of innate signal forms. The question Mason raises as to how much form-modification could occur and still allow recognizability is the primary question that Smith's chapter addresses. By noting that the central-affect program is influenced by experience in how it integrates (preformed) signals with other neurological and cognitive systems, Mason suggests the role assigned by Fogel to the coordinative structures of motor-action theory. And by asserting that it is the initiation and use of signals, rather than their form, that experience affects, Mason parallels on a broader level Thelen's minute analysis of how the exact timing and the strength of preformed movement are the variables over which an infant can gain voluntary control with experience.—*ED.

Introduction

From the standpoint of a modern behaviorist, the organism can be viewed as an enterprise that is basically concerned with extracting information from its surroundings, with comparing this in some fashion with its own needs, values, and expectancies, and with acting, or at least preparing itself to act, based on the outcome of this epistemic and evaluative process. I take it that this characterization will be acceptable to almost everyone. Although some might object to my choice of terms and wish to substitute others that have less mentalistic connotations, the basic model is commonplace. It is the familiar cybernetic view of the organism as an information-processing system.

Here I am mainly concerned with using this framework to examine the development of expressive behaviors in nonhuman primates, chiefly rhesus monkeys. I focus on a few relatively stereotyped facial expressions and vocalizations. My central thesis is that these expressive behaviors are the product or output of systems whose development is influenced, but never fully determined, by experience. In other words, I believe we are dealing with organized information-processing units or schemata in the Piagetian sense. These units constitute the basic framework within which information is assilimated, and they undergo change as they accommodate to the specific nature of that information. The contributions of experience are more diverse, however, than this simple formulation implies. My aim is to illustrate this diversity, and to show that useful conclusions about the role of experience in the ontogeny of expressive behavior must take general as well as specific contributions into account.

At the risk of doing a serious injustice to the rich expressive repertoire of the rhesus monkey, I deal mainly with three types of facial expressions and three classes of vocalizations. The facial expressions are the *grimace* (lips drawn back revealing the teeth), *lipsmacking* (rhythmic opening and closing of the lips), and *facial threat* (a variable pattern that includes among its components, staring, an open mouth with lower jaw slightly protruding, drawing back the ears, and jerking movements of the head). These patterns, which are generally believed to be associated with fear, friendliness, and hostility, respectively, are described in greater detail in several publications (e.g., Andrew, 1965; Chevalier-Skolnikoff, 1973; Hinde & Rowell, 1962; Redican, 1975; van Hooff, 1976). The vocalizations I consider are the *clear call* (''coo'' or ''whoo''), the *screech*, and the *bark*. Clear calls and screeches in the young monkey appear to be associated with anxiety or fear, and in some studies we have combined them into a single measure (*distress vocalizations*); a bark most often appears to be associated with hostility and is a frequent accompaniment of the threat display.

Stimulus Attributes, Age, and Experience

The first issue I address is the interaction between stimulus attributes, age, and experience in the development of expressive movements in relatively naive monkeys. These three variables are treated together because, as becomes evident, the age at which the animals begin to show expressive movements, the frequency with which they respond, and the effectiveness of stimuli in eliciting responses depend on experience.

Consider first the relationship between age and stimulus conditions. This was investigated in one of our first experiments on the development of expressive behaviors. We used 47 laboratory-born rhesus monkeys, arranged in five age groups (1, 3, 7, 16, and 25 months of age) and four sets of stimuli, each based on a crude representation of an animal. The monkeys had all been housed individually in wire cages from the first days of life in a standard nursery environment. Each stimulus set was scaled to provide three levels of complexity (Figure 6.1), and

Figure 6.1. The four sets of stimulus objects. The complex stimuli included, from top to bottom: 1. *Beetle*. Orange plastic 4½ inches high, and 6 inches in diameter, with moving wire feelers, a flashing light in its red plastic nose, and moving wheels. When in operation, a distinct noise was produced by the moving parts. 2. *Dog*. 5 inches high at the head and 6 inches long; covered with simulated black fur. In operation emitted a continuous high-pitched "bark." 3. *Grasshopper*. Green plastic, 6½ inches high at the head and 11 inches long, with large eyes, red and yellow wheels, and a red hat. 4. *Snake*. Constructed of multisectioned bamboo, mottled yellow and brown; 1 inch high, 18 inches long. Each object was fixed to a 12¼ inch by 6¼ inch gray base. (Bernstein & Mason, 1962).

the stimuli were presented individually on a moving belt that carried the object from the rear of a 5.5 foot chamber toward the monkey. As a control condition, we also presented the moving belt devoid of objects (Bernstein & Mason, 1962).

The stimuli were clearly effective, and the closer the resemblance to the animal form, the more effective was the stimulus. Results are presented for the combined age-groups for the grimace, for lipsmacking, for two components of the threat response (ears back, bark), and for distress vocalizations in Table 1. It is evident that all responses tended to become more frequent as the stimuli increased in complexity and in approximation of the animal form.

The effects of age were also clear, but the developmental trends for grimace, lipsmack, and threat (ears back, bark) were different from that for distress vocalizations. Results for the first three measures (combined) are presented in Figure 6.2. It is evident that these responses showed a general tendency to increase in frequency and to differentiate stimulus conditions more sharply with advancing age ($p < .001$). In contrast, distress vocalizations were most frequent in the two youngest groups, although their relationship to stimulus complexity was somewhat sharper in the three older groups (Figure 6.3).

To provide a further assessment of the specificity of the stimulus configurations in eliciting expressive behaviors, a comparison was made of the responses of the four older groups to food frustration (Bernstein & Mason, 1970). The results for grimace, lipsmacking, and the two components of the threat response are presented in Figure 6.4 (combined measures). It is evident that although this measure tended to increase somewhat during frustration, the magnitude of the effect was much less than that obtained with the stimulus objects (the fear stimuli). It is also

TABLE 1

Responses to Animal-like Objects at Three Levels of Complexity
and to the Moving Conveyer Belt Devoid of Objects (Combined Age Groups)[a]

Response	Stimulus conditions				
	Complex	Intermediate	Simple	Empty	p
Bark	114	19	6	0	.02
Ears back	115	89	64	47	.05
Grimace	36	2	2	0	NS
Lipsmacking	82	10	3	0	.01
Distress vocalizations	330	206	181	151	—

[a] Adapted from Bernstein & Mason, 1962.

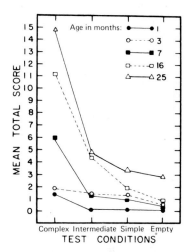

Figure 6.2. Mean total scores for combined responses of bark, ears back, fear grimace, and lipsmacking in relation to age and to stimulus conditions. (Bernstein & Mason, 1962).

clear that the difference in response to specific objects and to frustration increased with age. Distress vocalizations, shown in Figure 6.5, were most frequent in the youngest group but did not differentiate among the three older groups. In these three groups, distress vocalizations were more frequent to the stimulus objects than to frustration, and in all four groups they were higher to frustration than to the food or to empty conditions.

The relevance of age and of stimulus attributes to the elicitation of facial expressions was confirmed in a subsequent longitudinal study (Kenney, Mason, & Hill, 1979). In addition, this experiment established that lipsmacking and grimace (the only expressive behaviors measured) did not follow the same developmental course and were differentially related to eliciting stimuli. Moreover, we found that the tendency to display either response was influenced by experience.

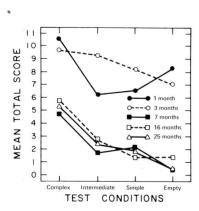

Figure 6.3. Mean total scores for the combined measures of clear calls (coo) and screech. (Bernstein & Mason, 1962).

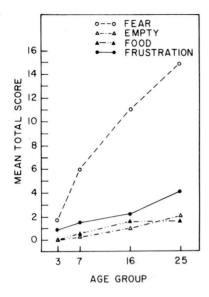

Figure 6.4. Mean total scores for bark, ears back, grimace, and lipsmacking. (Bernstein & Mason, 1970).

The subjects were 26 rhesus monkeys maternally separated as neonates and housed in individual cages in the same room. The cages were identical, except for the following variations, which defined the rearing conditions:

1. *Enclosed*—the walls and ceilings were covered with opaque material
2. *Visual*—the front of each cage was constructed of clear plastic, al-

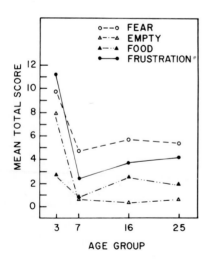

Figure 6.5. Mean total scores for distress vocalizations. (Bernstein & Mason, 1970).

lowing the monkeys to see human caretakers and other monkeys also housed in cages with plastic fronts or in wire cages
3. *Neighbor*—the cages were constructed in pairs such that two adjoining cages were separated by a transparent plastic wall, allowing each monkey to see only its age-mate and the interior of the adjacent cage.

All cages were illuminated continuously. The number of subjects per rearing group ranged from 6 to 10.

The monkeys were tested in their living cages. Testing started during the first week of life and continued into the fourth month of life. Two stimulus conditions were presented:

1. *Human face*—the observer with his or her face at the level of the cage attempted to maintain eye contact with the monkey
2. *Monkey face*—a mirror was held motionless at the front of the cage.

Stimulus conditions were presented for 15 seconds, 3–5 days a week, for a total of 80 presentations per subject for each condition.

Consider first the developmental course of lipsmacking and grimaces. This is shown for the combined rearing groups and stimulus conditions in Figure 6.6. It is evident that both responses showed a similar rapid increase during the first month of life and then diverged sharply. The frequency of grimaces continued to rise, whereas lipsmacking declined steadily followed a peak at around 35 days of age.

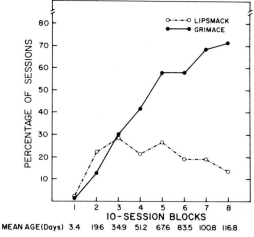

Figure 6.6. Percentage of lipsmacking and grimaces by 10-session blocks. (Mean age calculated for the first session of each block.) (Kenney, Mason, & Hill, 1979).

In addition to showing contrasting developmental courses, lipsmacking and grimaces were also differentially related to stimulus conditions. This is evident from Figure 6.7, which presents the frequency of the two responses in relation to the mirror and to the human face (combined rearing groups). It is apparent that the human face elicited many more grimaces than lipsmacks, whereas the mirror elicited slightly more lipsmacks than grimaces. Of total grimaces, 77% were elicited by the face and 23% by the mirror; of total lipsmacks, 76% were elicited by the mirror and 24% by the human face. Stimulus conditions also interacted significantly with age: the mean age of occurrence of first response (i.e., lipsmack or grimace) was earlier to the mirror than to the human face (33.5 days versus 41.0 days, $p < .01$). Eleven of the monkeys never lipsmacked to the face, whereas only one failed to do so to the mirror. For the monkeys that lipsmacked to both face and mirror, the mean age of first response was 29 days to the mirror, as compared to 51 days to the face ($p < .01$). Contrariwise, the mean age of first grimace was lower to the human face than to the mirror. For monkeys that grimaced to both stimuli, mean age of first grimace was 55 days to the mirror as compared to 45 days to the face ($p < .02$).

The effects of experience are clear. In general, the visual group was the first to respond, showed the highest level of responsiveness, and differentiated stimulus conditions most sharply; the neighbor group was intermediate on these comparisons, and the enclosed group consistently occupied last place.

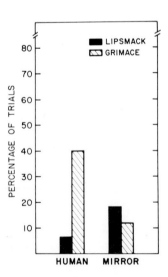

Figure 6.7. Percentage of trials in which lipsmacking and grimaces were elicited by human face and mirror image. (Kenney, Mason, & Hill, 1979).

With respect to age of first response (regardless of eliciting stimulus or type of response), mean values are 27, 28, and 47 days for visual, neighbor, and enclosed groups, respectively. The level of responsiveness, as measured by the percentage of trials on which at least one of the two types of responses occurred, also differentiated groups. The obtained values were 45%, 31%, and 23% for visual, neighbor, and enclosed groups, respectively.

Figure 6.8 presents the findings by response class, stimulus condition, and rearing group. Note that the neighbor group, which had had continuous visual contact with one other young monkey, showed the highest level of lipsmacking in the first half of testing and that this was most evident in their reactions to the mirror.

The results of these two experiments suggest the following conclusions: first, the tendency to display species-typical facial expressions follows an age gradient. In the first experiment, which was a cross-sectional study, the tendency to grimace, lipsmack, or threaten a complex, novel stimulus configuration increased with age over the first 2 years of life. In the second, a longitudinal study, the mean age at which the first response occurred was about 35 days, although the lower limit

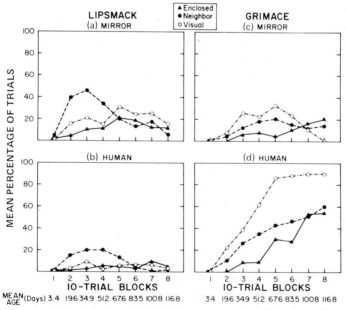

Figure 6.8. Effects of age, rearing conditions, and stimulus on lipsmacking and grimaces. (Mean age calculated for first session of each block.) (Kenney, Mason, & Hill, 1979).

was 12 days. It is noteworthy that the subjects in both studies were housed individually in a single, well-regulated environment from birth and had no opportunity for physical interaction with other monkeys. It seems likely from these findings and from the results of other investigators (Hinde, Rowell, & Spencer-Booth, 1964; Mendelson, 1982; Sackett, 1966) that the age of onset of these expressions and the likelihood that they will be displayed are dependent on fundamental changes, possibly relating to the growth and differentiation of central nervous system structures. These changes do not appear to be produced by individual experience, although they may be accelerated or retarded by it. I concur with Redican's (1975) view that it is futile to try to pinpoint a precise age of onset for these responses.

Second, the findings suggest that the developmental course of expressive behaviors varies with the particular behavior. Thus, the tendency to screech and give clear calls was strongest in the two youngest groups in the cross-sectional study, even though these responses occurred in all groups and were systematically related to stimulus conditions. In the longitudinal study, lipsmacking was the first facial expression shown by 65% of the monkeys. The frequency of this response peaked at about 35 days and had declined to a low of 13% by the last block of test sessions. In contrast, grimace was somewhat later to appear (mean age of first response was 43 days) but continued to rise until the end of testing, in spite of the fact that the same eliciting stimuli were used throughout the experiment. The possibility should also be noted that the developmental course of expressive behaviors are most likely affected by test schedules, settings, and specific procedures, although these variables have not been examined.

Third, the results I have presented show that expressive movements are systematically related to stimulus configurations. In the first study, expressive behaviors were much more frequently elicited by specific stimulus objects than by frustration, and the more complex the stimulus, the greater the likelihood that a response would occur. The most effective stimuli were crude representations of animals which were unlike anything the monkeys had previously encountered. The longitudinal study demonstrated that the age at which the first response was given, the form of the first response, and developmental changes in response frequency were strongly influenced by the stimulus configuration, apart from any specific differential contributions of experience. Mean age of first response was lower to the mirror than to the face in all rearing groups, and for a substantial majority of monkeys (80%), the first response to the mirror was a lipsmack. Mean age of first response to the human face was not only about a week later than that to the mirror, but the form of the modal response also differed. The initial re-action to the human face for 76% of the monkeys was grimace. The fre-quency of grimace to the human face increased in all groups with advancing age; the frequency of lipsmacking, however, declined with advancing age, regardless of the eliciting stimulus.

What can be said about the effective stimulus configuration for evok-ing expressive behaviors? The two most radical positions are impossible to defend. At one extreme is the view that the association between stim-ulus configurations and responses is based entirely on individual ex-perience. This was the position advocated by Schiller: "The innate constituents of complex patterns are not perceptual organizations but motor patterns" (Schiller, 1952, p. 187). Another attempt to account for stimulus effectiveness that places a heavy emphasis on prior experience is Hebb's *incongruity hypothesis* (Hebb, 1946). This hypothesis suggests that one of the essential conditions for a fear reaction in primates is a discrepancy between a perceived object and a set of familiar objects. Thus, the sight of a disembodied head of a chimpanzee is expected to evoke fear in normally socialized chimpanzees but not in those that have had no prior experience with members of their own species. I cannot see how Schiller's view or Hebb's can explain the differential responses to stimulus complexity obtained in the experiment by Bernstein and Ma-son (1962) or can account for the contrasting responses to the mirror and the human face by monkeys that had had minimal prior experience with either monkeys or people or can explain the differential responses to color slides shown by monkeys raised in total isolation (Sackett, 1966).

At the opposite extreme of explanatory possibilities is the idea that highly specific visual configurations function as innate releasers of ex-pressive behaviors. In its strict form this hypothesis asserts that an in-variant relationship exists between a specific configuration and the particular form of expressive response. So far as I can recall, no one has advanced such a claim for the nonhuman primates. To be sure, Sackett did suggest that "the visual stimulation involved in threat behavior ap-pears to function as an 'innate releasing stimulus' for fearful behavior" (Sackett, 1966, p. 1473). It is clear, however, that Sackett was not refer-ring to a specific response pattern. His measure of fearful behavior was based on a composite of several different responses (rocking, huddling, self-clasping, fear, withdrawal); some of these are seen only in monkeys deprived of early social stimulation and bear a different relationship to eliciting conditions than do discrete expressive behaviors such as lip-smacking, facial threats, and grimaces (Bernstein & Mason, 1962, 1970; Mason & Berkson, 1975; Mason & Green, 1962). Moreover, pictures of threatening monkeys did not merely elicit fear; they were also more effective than those of any other class in evoking play and exploration (although they were closely rivalled in this respect by pictures of infant monkeys). Thus, Sackett's results clearly demonstrate that certain visual configurations have "prepotent general activating properties"; the specifity of response usually implied by the concept of innate releasing stimulus, however, was not established.

Two kinds of additional findings cast doubt on a strict specificity hypothesis. First, a wide array of objects has been shown to elicit expressive behaviors (Bernstein & Mason, 1962; Green, 1965; Mason, Green, & Posepanko, 1960). The physical diversity of these objects renders unlikely the possibility that they possessed a common and specific set of visual attributes. Second, the same stimulus configuration has been found to evoke different expressive behaviors. For example, a doll's head evoked lipsmacking, grimaces, and threats from adult rhesus monkeys (Mason et al., 1960). Similar results were obtained with the animal representations used in our cross-sectional developmental study (Bernstein & Mason, 1962). In the longitudinal study, individuals tended to differ consistently in the modes of response, as well as the level of responsiveness to the same stimulus configurations. This is indicated by high-positive correlations between the percentage of responses to the mirror and to the human face for lipsmacking ($r = .81$, $p < .01$) and for the grimace ($r = .65$, $p < .01$), by a positive within-subject correlation between the ages at which the two responses first appeared ($r = .54$, $p < .01$), and by a positive (but nonsignificant) correlation between total scores for the two responses.

It thus appears that neither of the extreme hypotheses regarding the effective stimulus configuration is tenable. We are left on the uncertain middle ground: there appear to be inherent differences in the potency of visual configurations as evokers of expressive behavior in primates; the same configurations are capable of evoking different expressions, such as lipsmacking, grimace, or the threat face; the effective stimuli are physically heterogeneous, and the relevant dimensions are apparently broad.

Although these dimensions are yet to be delineated systematically, the following are likely to be found among the principal effective variables of a visual configuration for "naive" primates: size, complexity (including shape and internal features), and direction, rate, and regularity of movement (Bernstein & Mason, 1962; Green, 1965; Haslerud, 1938; Mason, Davenport, & Menzel, 1968; McCulloch & Haslerud, 1939; Menzel, 1962, 1964; Mineka, Keir, & Price, 1980; Schiff, Caviness, & Gibson, 1962; Valentine, 1930; Wolin, Ordy, & Dillman, 1963; Yerkes &

Yerkes, 1936). As to the relative effectiveness of these variables, it is likely that movement deserves first place, although it is clearly not an essential feature; how the remaining variables might be weighted is problematic.

In my view, two of the more interesting questions for future research are whether a particular configuration of variables will prove to be uniquely effective, and what factors dispose the animal toward a specific form of expressive response. With respect to the first question, my guess is that the larger the number of elements in the stimulus, the greater the magnitude of the individual elements, and the closer the approximation of the elements to a coherent gestalt, the greater the likelihood that an expressive behavior will be evoked. Several experiments suggest that eye patterns may be a particularly potent element in this gestalt (e.g., Coss, 1978; Keating & Keating, 1982; Mendelson, Haith, & Goldman-Rakic, 1982). As to the relationship between a configuration and the specific form of the response, it is already clear that this will not be constant, even in naive animals. It is safe to assert that a satisfactory account will have to reckon with factors that go beyond the stimulus configuration, such as the context in which the encounter occurs, the state of the individual (e.g., level of arousal), and its prior experience in general and with the eliciting stimulus in particular.

A fourth conclusion suggested by these results is that experience has a definite influence on the genesis of expressive responses to novel stimulus configurations. In the longitudinal study the primary variable that defined the three rearing groups was the nature of their visual exposure to stimuli similar to those presented in the test conditions. Within this rather restricted range of rearing conditions, the principal effects of experience were on the age of onset, the overall level of responsiveness, and the degree of differentiation of stimulus conditions. The visual group, which had the most varied visual contacts with people and other monkeys, responded at an earlier age than the other two groups, showed a higher level of responsiveness, and differentiated most sharply between the mirror and the human face; the neighbor group, which had received intensive visual exposure to one other young monkey, fell between the visual and enclosed groups on most measures, with the interesting exception of an initially high level of lipsmacking to the mirror; the enclosed group, which had minimal exposure to people or monkeys, was oldest at the age of first response, was least responsive throughout testing, and showed the poorest differentiation of stimulus conditions. I view these results as analogous to Humphrey's finding that discrimination among photographs increases in rhesus monkeys as the result of mere exposure, and as supporting perceptual-differentiation theory (Gibson, 1969; Gibson & Gibson, 1955; Humphrey, 1974).

Form, Social Functions, and Experience

This section considers the effects of experience on the form of expressive behaviors and on their functions in the regulation of social interactions. Functional aspects are examined with reference to the agent, that is to say, the use of expressive behaviors as a means of influencing others, and with reference to the recipient, which is to say, the social significance or meaning of such behaviors. Although there is some suggestion that both the structural and the functional aspects of expressive behavior are influenced by experience, it will become clear that the evidence is, for the most part, inconclusive.

This is nowhere more apparent than in regard to the form of expressive behaviors. Lipsmack and grimace appear in clearly recognizable form in isolation-reared monkeys within the first few weeks of life; screech and coo vocalizations are essentially present at birth. Facial threat is later to appear; its development appears to be more gradual. And it is, in any event, a more complex and variable pattern than the other two facial expressions; its recognition, therefore, is more problematic (Redican, 1975). In general, however, facial expressions are sufficiently stereotyped and distinctive that they can be recognized by experienced observers, even when the subjects are young or have been raised under highly atypical conditions. In this respect, they appear to be resistant to experiential influences. It is impossible to be more precise.

The problem is that unless the deviations in form are rather gross, observers' judgments are not likely to be useful. More refined methods are available for detecting and describing subtle variations in the structural features of expressive behaviors, but, so far as I know, they have seldom or never been applied to the assessment of experiential influences in nonhuman primates. The techniques that have been developed for the analysis of human facial expressions (Ekman & Oster, 1979) have not been applied to nonhuman primates; spectrographic analysis is used routinely in research on animal vocalizations, but I know of only one instance[1] in which this method has been used to detect possible experiential influences (Green, 1975). In the absence of systematic data, such as these methods could supply, the principal basis for assessing the ef-

[1]At the time of this writing, the report by Newman and Symmes (1974) was overlooked.

fects of experience on the form of expressive behaviors are observers' impressions and some indirect experimental evidence.

One pattern that appears to be grossly distorted in captive rhesus monkeys is the threat display. Many observers have noted the tendency among socially deprived monkeys to direct a portion of this display— usually, the components of lunging, biting, grasping, fur-pulling— toward their own bodies (e.g., Cross & Harlow, 1965; Mason & Sponholz, 1963). It is not altogether clear, however, that this deviation is entirely the result of early developmental influences, inasmuch as a similar pattern may occasionally be seen in individually housed wild-born monkeys, although the intensity of the reaction may be less than that shown by socially deprived animals. Moreover, it has not been shown that the facial expression per se that accompanies a self-directed threat is different from that shown in an externally directed threat, either by normal or socially deprived monkeys. Possibly, as Redican suggests, the variations in the form of facial threat resulting from early developmental influences are subtle. He describes the case of a mature male isolate he observed who displayed a conventional facial threat pattern, except that he kept his mouth wide open for exceptionally long intervals (Redican, 1975).

Berkson and Becker in a study of expressive movements in monkeys blind from early infancy did not comment on the facial expression of threat in these animals, beyond noting that it was seldom seen, although the monkeys "did threaten by shaking the environment and lunging at other animals" (1975, p. 523). They judged the form of grimace and lipsmacking, however, as grossly normal.

Although some experimental findings indicate that facial expressive behavior is atypical in socially deprived juvenile macaques, it is not clear whether this refers to the form of the expressive movement or to other aspects of responsiveness. Miller, Caul, and Mirsky, (1967) gave rhesus monkeys an opportunity to avoid shock by reacting to the televised facial expression of a stimulus-animal who was forewarned that shock was impending. This was the only information available to the responder that shock was about to be delivered. When the stimulus-monkey and the responder were both wild-born, an avoidance response was performed on 77% of the trials. In other words, the respondent was able with considerable success to read the facial expression of its partner. When the stimulus-monkey was an individual who had spent its first year of life as a social isolate, however, this value fell to 62%; furthermore, the rate of responding between trials increased, suggesting that the wild-born responder may have been confused by the behavior of the isolation-raised stimulus monkey.

The authors suggest that for the isolates "expressive reaction . . . to avoidance stimuli may be impaired" (p. 237). No analysis was provided of the actual expressions shown by either normal or isolation-raised monkeys in response to the signal for impending shock, however, so the nature of the impairment is unknown.

Inasmuch as isolation-raised monkeys are able to show clearly recognizable and mutually discriminable forms of lipsmacking, grimace, and facial threat, the most reasonable interpretive possibilities are either that such responses were not elicited in this situation or that they occurred so erratically or (as the authors suggest) that they were displayed so frequently throughout the testing session as to impair their utility to the responders as discriminative stimuli.

The evidence concerning the effects of experience on the functional aspects of expressive behaviors is also mostly circumstantial, although it is more persuasive than information on the form of these behaviors. On the basis of my original comparisons between wild-born monkeys and monkeys with restricted social experience, I suggested that the specific stimuli eliciting stereotyped gestures, vocalizations, and postures, and the effectiveness of these behaviors in controlling and coordinating social activity were heavily dependent on the experience of the actor, as well as that of the perceiver (Mason, 1960, 1961, 1965). As an example of the kind of evidence that led to this conclusion, in one experiment I determined the frequency with which a threat response by a dominant monkey was followed within 5 seconds by withdrawal of the subordinate monkey. This sequence occurred 135 times in 11 of 15 pairs of monkeys raised in the wild and 6 times in only 2 of the 15 pairs of monkeys with restricted social experience (Mason, 1961).

Supporting data were obtained in subsequent research. Miller *et al.* (1967) in their investigation of the communication of affect used isolation-raised monkeys as responders, as well as stimulus-monkeys. Their results indicate that the isolates in the responder role were vastly inferior to wild-born monkeys in reading the facial expressions of the stimulus-monkeys, regardless of whether the latter were wild-born or other isolates. For example, the percentage of avoidance responses when isolation-reared responders were paired with wild-born stimulus-monkeys was 7, as compared to 77 for wild-born responders with the same partners. Although the specific patterns evoked in the stimulus-monkey by the avoidance conditioning situation are not known, it is clear from these results that experience has a large effect on a monkey's ability to use the information conveyed by the facial expression of another animal.

Expressive behaviors may also be used selectively, seemingly as devices for manipulating social events. It is likely that the full development of this skill is dependent on early social experience. This was suggested by a comparison of social organization in two groups of captive-born monkeys by Anderson and Mason (1974, 1978). One group of six monkeys, (experienced) had been raised with their mothers and had extended contact with age-mates; the other group of six monkeys (deprived) were raised in individual cages. In neither social group had the animals had physical contact with each other before the groups were formed.

Both groups showed the conventional facial expressions and at comparable frequencies. So far as we could judge, there were no obvious intergroup differences in the form of these responses. A major difference was found in the way these expressions were used, however. For example, in a situation in which a single water bottle was available to six thirsty monkeys, a monkey subordinate to the monkey at the water bottle in the experienced group might approach the area near the bottle and direct facial threats toward the drinker, alternating this with facing and making grimaces toward a monkey whose status was higher than that of the monkey at the bottle; the drinker's usual response to such a sequence was to leave. Another pattern observed in the experienced monkeys was for the waiting animal to threaten a third party that was subordinate to the drinker, while directing grimaces toward the latter, which, in most instances, led to the drinker's leaving the bottle to chase after the third party. A third pattern consisted of two monkeys, both subordinate to the drinker, alternating glances toward each other with threats toward the drinker, with the usual outcome that the latter stopped drinking, faced both monkeys, then left. Thus, in the experienced group a subordinate monkey often was able to displace a dominant animal from the bottle by enlisting the support of an animal of higher status than the drinker or by inciting the drinker to leave the bottle to chase after a third monkey or by forming an alliance with another subordinate monkey also waiting for a turn at the bottle. Expressive behaviors played a conspicuous role in these maneuvers. Similar maneuvers were not shown by the monkeys in the socially deprived group; in spite of the fact that the same expressive behaviors were available, they were not used in the same manner.

Apparently, the critical difference between groups was that the experienced monkeys knew not only their own status vis-à-vis the other members of the group (as did the deprived monkeys) but also the status of the other group members in relation to each other (which the deprived monkeys seemingly did not). Thus, by combining relatively stereotyped expressive behaviors with their knowledge of the status relations between two other individuals, experienced monkeys were able to manipulate social events so as to gain an advantage in competition or in agonistic encounters beyond that which their own status could directly provide. Furthermore, the expressive behaviors shown in these maneuvers, while in accord with the status relations between the other parties, were often at variance with the affective tone that might be expected based on the manipulator's social status. For example, if the animal at the water bottle was dominant to a third party, the manipulator threatened the third monkey, even though he was subordinate to that monkey and most probably would never threaten it in a simple dyadic encounter; similarly, if the third party was dominant to the drinker, the drinker might be the target of the manipulator's threats, even though the manipulator had lower status than the drinker.

Although it is clear from these results that the experiences responsible for the differences between the two social groups must have occurred before the groups were formed, the relevant features of that experience are not known. Anderson and I suggested that the opportunity to interact simultaneously with at least two companions might be an important factor (Anderson & Mason, 1974). Recently, however, Capitanio has obtained evidence that experience with more than one companion, or even with conspecifics, may not be necessary for the development of the more complex forms of social interaction observed in the experienced group. Capitanio compared social groups consisting of monkeys that had been raised in outdoor cages either with a single canine-mother substitute or with an inanimate surrogate (Mason, 1978). In social groups, the monkeys raised with dogs were much more likely to interact in trios than were the monkeys raised with inanimate surrogates; the patterns of interaction within the trios were also more complex in monkeys raised with dogs and occasionally gave rise to social strategies similar to those displayed by the more socially experienced monkeys studied by Anderson and Mason (Capitanio, 1982). Thus, although the ability to use expressive behaviors as a means of altering social events appears to be dependent on experience, these results suggest that the development of this skill in at least rudimentary form does not require that the experience occur within the context of a multianimal group, or for that matter, even with another primate.

In summary, the aim of this section is to consider the effects of experience on the form of expressive behaviors and on their functions in the regulation of social events. As to form, a major problem is the paucity of systematic data and the need to depend on observers' judgments. It appears that the development of the three facial expressions considered here is relatively resistant to environmental influences. This is most clearly the case with respect to grimace and to lipsmacking; most observers would probably agree with Berkson and Becker's conclusion that these displays are grossly normal, even in monkeys with minimal social experience (Berkson & Becker, 1975). The effects of experience on the development of the threat face is more problematic, owing chiefly to the fact that the facial expression is itself variable and it is only one component in a complex and changing pattern involving postural adjustments, whole body movements, and vocalizations. So far as I know, no one has demonstrated that the structure of vocalizations in macaques is influenced by experience,[2] although Green (1975) has suggested social learning as one possible mechanism that might account for locale-specific structural differences in the calls of Japanese macaques. A systematic analysis of sound spectrographs will obviously be required. If one accepts Rowell's (1962) contention, however, that the agonistic sounds of rhesus monkeys form a continuous series, are not independent of the postures and gestures which they accompany, and cannot be studied in recordings alone, spectrographic analysis will be only the first step in a more elaborate process.

As to the functional development of expressive behaviors, the evidence that experience is influential is more persuasive, although it is mostly circumstantial. It is clear that monkeys raised in social isolation differ from wild-born monkeys in some aspect of their facial responses to impending shock; it is also clear that they are substantially inferior to wild-born monkeys in the ability to make use of the information conveyed in this situation by the facial expression of others; more limited data suggest that monkeys lacking normal socialization experience do not respond reliably to the facial expressions displayed by another in agonistic encounters. Finally, there is a clear suggestion that monkeys raised without companions are deficient in the ability to use expressive behaviors selectively and instrumentally as part of the means for manipulating social events.

Responsiveness, Expressive Behaviors, and Experience

To this point I have tried to maintain a focus on the input and output aspects of expressive movements. Experience has been treated as though it acted rather specifically and directly on one or the other of these two

---

[2]Newman and Symmes (1974) report structural abnormalities in the clear calls of rhesus monkeys raised in isolation.

external components or on the association between them. Thus, we considered how experience influences the age of onset and early development of expressive behaviors in response to specific stimuli, the stimulus configurations that are effective in evoking such behaviors, the form of expressive behaviors, and their functions in conveying information and regulating social events.

So far, I have not dealt with such problems as the individual's affective states and cognitive sets—emotionality, central motive states, levels of arousal, coping strategies, and the like—and the relation of such factors to experience and to expressive behaviors. This issue constitutes the principal concern of this section. The question is whether variations in experience contribute to generalized and abiding changes in the way an individual characteristically responds to novel events or stressful situations, including the likelihood that it will show expressive behaviors. The answer is unequivocally affirmative.

Although this is obviously not the place for a detailed examination of the effects of experience on the cognitive, motivational, and emotional aspects of development, it appears that the responsiveness of rhesus monkeys experiencing early social deprivation may differ from that of their normally socialized counterparts in at least two respects that are relevant to the topic of expressive movements: first, the deprived animal develops a variety of self-directed responses—notably, body-rocking, self-clasping, and nonnutritive sucking—that are most prominent under conditions of high-emotional arousal and that may have the function of reducing arousal (Berkson, 1967; Mason, 1971). Although these behaviors clearly do not preclude the development of expressive movements, once they have become established in an individual's repertoire they can serve as readily available alternative responses in emotion-provoking situations, thereby affecting the likelihood that specific expressive behaviors will occur. Second, social experience appears to have pervasive effects on the individual's basic stance toward the world, as reflected in its characteristic modes of interacting with the environment and of responding to stress (Mason, 1971; Sackett, 1970). For example, in our early comparisons of the behavior of wild- and laboratory-born monkeys we observed the animals while they were alone in a novel room. As compared to the laboratory-born monkeys, those born in the wild more frequently engaged in gross motor activities (jumping, backward somersaults), had higher vocalization and locomotion scores, defecated or urinated in more sessions, and more frequently touched the objects that were placed in the room (Mason & Green, 1962). More recently, we have found precisely the same pattern of differences in similar test situations between monkeys raised with canine mother-substitutes, as compared to those raised with inanimate surrogates. In addition, we obtained physiological measures and found that the dog-raised monkeys had higher heart rates in novel situations and higher levels of plasma cortisol. In tests of problem-solving behavior, the dog-raised monkeys also made more contacts with the problems, and consequently were more successful, than those raised with inanimate surrogates. When given an opportunity to view projected color-transparencies, they spent more time looking and appeared to be more responsive to the specific visual details, as compared to the monkeys raised with inanimate surrogates, in spite of the fact that the general level of visual stimulation in the rearing environment was high and equivalent for both groups (Mason, 1978). In other research, Green compared the responses of wild- and captive-born juvenile macaques to a variety of stimuli representing animate objects and found that fewer threats and grimaces were displayed by the captive-born monkeys (Green, 1965).

Many additional examples could be given that support the generalization that early experience has pervasive and persistent effects on the individual's emotional responsiveness, including the frequency with which it displays expressive behaviors. It is also clear, however, that measures of frequency do not show a simple and invariant relation to experience. In some research the frequency of expressive movements is lower in restricted monkeys, as in the aforementioned study by Green (1965); in other investigations the frequency is higher in the animals with more restricted experience, as in Capitanio's comparison of dyadic interactions of juvenile monkeys raised with dogs or with inanimate mother substitutes (Capitanio, 1982). The explanation for such discrepancies is not known. One factor that may be relevant is the extent to which the environment is a source of active or of passive stimulation. Under conditions in which stimulation is not forcibly imposed on the animal or can be readily avoided, the frequency of expressive displays may be lower among individuals with restricted experience than among control subjects; in situations in which stimulation is imposed on the individual, however, the frequency among animals whose experience has been restricted may be equal to or higher than that of the controls. Thus, the finding that laboratory-raised macaques show a lower level of grimaces, threats, and lipsmacking than do wild-born monkeys to live snakes and snakelike objects presented in transparent boxes or secured in place on a test tray (Joslin, Fletcher, & Emlen, 1964; Mineka et al., 1980) might reflect generalized differences in the tendency to display expressive behaviors in response to passive stimulation rather than the specific effects of prior experience with snakes. A similar explanation may account for the differences in responsiveness to novel objects and situations between rhesus monkeys raised in rural or in urban environments (Singh, 1966, 1969).

In any event, such findings suggest several conclusions that are relevant to the development of expressive behaviors. The first conclusion concerns the factors that influence the probability that an expressive behavior will occur. The data suggest that an individual's basic stance toward the world, its characteristic modes of perceiving and relating to environmental events, is dependent on broad features of its rearing history. The likelihood that a monkey will display expressive behaviors, therefore, depends on more than the specific attributes of the object or the individual's previous experience with it or with similar objects; a monkey's habitual reactions to novelty, ambiguity, challenge, and change are clearly influential. The second conclusion concerns the issue of what is being expressed. In previous sections, evidence was presented indicating that the relationship between the eliciting stimulus-configuration and the specific expressive movement it evokes is not invariant. The same configuration may elicit lipsmacks, grimaces, or threat faces, even from the same individual. In this section the findings we consider suggest that the coupling between expressive movements and the presumptive emotional state is similarly loose. An individual that readily and frequently grimaces or gives the threat face is not necessarily more fearful, aggressive, or emotionally aroused, as measured by physiological responses, than one that rarely displays these patterns. To illustrate: monkeys raised in social isolation showed more "fear-disturbance-emotional behavior" than did monkeys raised with peers during social interaction in a novel environment, but did not differ from them in the rise in cortisol induced by the situation (Sackett, Bowman, Meyer, Tripp, & Grady, 1973, p. 209). At the very least, such findings demonstrate that inferences regarding internal emotional states based entirely on behavioral measures can be unreliable and misleading. The third conclusion concerns the functional elaboration of expressive movements. To the extent that expressive movements serve a communicative function, persistent individual differences in the tendency to display such behaviors carry obvious implications for the regulation and control of social intercourse. The monkey that fails to show expressive behaviors, or shows them at a level that deviates substantially from the norm, may experience immediate difficulties in relating to other monkeys. In addition, inasmuch as behaviors that do not occur or occur erratically or infrequently are less available for modification by response-contingent social feedback, opportunities for the acquisition of normal functions will be to that extent curtailed.

Conclusions

The principal objective of this chapter is to examine the development of some expressive movements in rhesus monkeys and to characterize environmental influences on this process. Limited though they are, the findings plainly show that traditional dichotomies, such as cognitive versus emotional, innate versus acquired, and associative versus non-associative, have little to contribute to an account of the development of expressive behaviors in these primates. Although such categorical distinctions may serve as useful shorthand devices for referring to particular experimental conditions or testing procedures, they do not provide a satisfactory description of the changing organization of expressive behaviors as development proceeds. No one should be surprised by this conclusion. The idea that psychological development is epigenetic—which is to say the cumulative result of the continuing interaction between a living system and its environment—is now commonplace. The question is, do the data go beyond confirming the relevance of this general viewpoint and suggest a definite model of the epigenetic process at work?

I believe they do, and presenting such a model is the aim of this final section. I draw on Ekman's neurocultural model of emotions (Ekman, 1977; Oster & Ekman, 1978). Although Ekman's concern is with human behavior, the general framework he presents readily accommodates the developmental data on rhesus monkeys. The major components in his model are an *appraisal mechanism,* capable of analyzing and evaluating potential elicitors of emotional responses, a *central-affect program* that organizes the activity of the various systems comprising an emotional response, and a mechanism for *managing emotional responses* that serves as a repository of the display rules that govern when, where, or to whom an emotional response will be expressed.

The starting point of our inquiry in this chapter is the neonatal rhesus macaque. We know of course that it enters the world as a highly organized ongoing enterprise, impressively well equipped to extract what it requires to sustain itself from the environment it is likely to encounter. One of the most important features of this environment is its mother, the principal and unique source of nourishment, warmth, protection, and so on. It is equally obvious that our starting point imposes no constraints in principle on what we can discover about how the neonate's behavior is organized; it does, however, place strict limits on our understanding of how this organization came about. For example, we know that a host of factors, such as the quality of maternal nutrition, the level of maternal hormones, the presence of specific diseases and dysfunctions, and countless other events during gestation and the period immediately surrounding birth may have significant, sometimes irreversible effects on the organization of behavior in the neonate. Contrariwise, normal development presupposes the orderly interaction of myriad variables, the precise import of which we can only surmise. The essential idea, then, is that at the beginning of the present inquiry into the factors influencing the development of expressive movements, the individual is already an actively developing system whose organization has proceeded a considerable distance. Whatever the environment offers or imposes is in relation to the existential state of this system.

In the normal neonate we encounter an individual that is either already prepared to display most of the expressive behaviors we have considered in their species-typical form, or soon will be. The basic organization of the motor patterns themselves—part of the central-affect program of Ekman (Ekman, 1977; Oster & Ekman, 1978)—appears to require little if any specific environmental input or support in order to produce these responses. This is not to say that their form is totally fixed of course but that any effects of experience are probably slight. In any event, one might ask what purpose experiential modifications in the form of expressive movements might serve if they did occur and how such modifications might be brought about.

The most obvious general purpose that might be served is semantic or referential. That is to say, learned modifications could constitute the means for generating a large array of discriminable signals, each with a different meaning or referent, from a few basic movement patterns. The mechanisms by which such modifications could be brought about are easiest to discern with respect to vocalizations. In this case the actor has the benefit of immediate auditory feedback from its own sound productions plus the examples provided by other animals with which its sounds could be compared. In principle, this situation should lend itself readily to learned modifications in individual sound production. Some such process appears to be responsible for the acquisition of song patterns shown by many species of birds, and there is no a priori reason to assume that the same phenomenon could not occur in the nonhuman primates. In fact, however, there is little hard evidence in support of such a possibility. Although regional variants in sound structure have been described for the Japanese macaque, it remains to be shown that they are learned (Green, 1975). With respect to experiential influences on the form of facial expressions, the mechanism through which systematic variants could be brought about is not apparent. To be sure, a monkey probably experiences some distinctive proprioceptive sense of giving a threat face or making a grimace that might allow it to monitor its own performance, but on what basis could the motor pattern be altered to conform to some local norm? Even if the individual was able to change the form of its facial expressions readily, the social-learning process through which a particular variant was selected is likely to be so slow and inefficient as to all but preclude a significant and generalized effect of experience on the form of facial expressions. In any event, with the possible exception of the threat face, there is no indication that the form of facial expressions in the rhesus macaque is much affected by experience. This is consistent with the evidence from humans that the major facial expressions (happiness, surprise, fear, anger, disgust, sadness) show essentially the same form in widely different cultures, and in blind as well as sighted children (Ekman, 1977; Oster & Ekman, 1978). It appears then, the effects of individual experience on the form of expressive movements are negligible, providing another instance in support of the familiar generalization that motor patterns are rather tightly constrained in ontogeny and phylogeny and are resistant to environmental influences.

If one accepts this characterization of the motor component of expressive movements as accurate, then it follows that the patterns should be present at birth (as indeed they are with respect to vocalizations) or follow a definite developmental schedule (as they appear to do with facial expressions). Nevertheless, we have seen that experiential factors influence the age at which these responses first appear and the ease with which they can be elicited following their initial onset. In terms of Ekman's (Ekman, 1977; Oster & Ekman, 1978) neurocultural model, it appears that the critical experiential effects are operating on the appraisal mechanism. The hypothesized role of this mechanism is to analyze and evaluate potential elicitors of expressive movements. Based on the data we have considered three generalizations seem warranted:

1. The appraisal mechanism is coarsely tuned to stimuli and events independently of specific previous experience. The coo and screech sounds are the clearest example; they are elicited in the newborn monkey by a variety of conditions, among which loss of contact or support, cold, and possibly hunger are salient. The facial expressions of lipsmacking and grimace appear later than these vocalizations, usually not

before the infant is a few days old, and they are elicited by a broad range of stimuli, including the human face, photographs, crude representations of animals, or the monkey's own image in a mirror. It thus appears that the dimensions of a visual stimulus that are effective in eliciting these facial expressions are general ones, such as the direction, rate, and regularity of the movement of the stimulus, its size, its complexity, and possibly the configuration of its elements. Lipsmacking and grimace are not sharply differentiated initially with respect to eliciting stimuli. In spite of the general view that these responses are associated with different emotional states or convey different messages in the older monkey, both responses may be elicited in the neonate by the same stimulus. Some differentiation is present almost from the beginning, however, although even in the adult the same configuration may elicit either response, particularly if the stimulus is ambiguous and unfamiliar, such as a crude representation of an animal.

2. The appraisal mechanism becomes more responsive during the neonatal period and beyond this. We have seen that once lipsmacking and grimacing appear, they tend to become more readily elicited, even when the same stimulus configuration is encountered on successive days. Thus, in the early stages of development, there is no evidence of habituation, which is the common response of adults to repeated exposure to stimuli that lack important biological consequences. On the contrary, as noted, the opposite trend is observed. Furthermore, we have seen that the tendency to give these responses on first encounters with animal representations increases progressively, at least throughout the first 2 years of life. The threat face is relatively late to appear in its complete form, but it is present by early adolescence (e.g., 2 years) and at around this time appears to show a noticeable increase in probability of occurrence. Thus, in the course of development the apparent general trend is for the appraisal process to become increasingly likely to result in an expressive movement.

3. The process of fine-tuning of the appraisal mechanism begins in early infancy. We have seen that experience affects the precise age of onset, the level of responsiveness, and the degree to which stimuli are responded to differentially. Infants with the most varied visual experience tend to respond earlier, more frequently, and more discriminatingly. We have also seen that frequency of responding and degree of differentiation of stimuli of graded complexity increases with age for at least the first 2 years of life. Humphrey (1974) has shown that young rhesus monkeys allowed to view colored slides of domestic animals also become more discriminating with increasing experience. It seems likely

that the effective process in all these findings is perceptual differentiation resulting from mere exposure to visual stimuli (Gibson, 1969).

Perceptual differentiation is only one possible source of fine-tuning of
the appraisal mechanism. The neonatal macaque is capable of classical
and instrumental conditioning, and it is reasonable to suppose that early
in the socialization process expressive movements are becoming selectively associated with specific stimuli. So far as I know this has not been
investigated. An interesting possibility is that certain configurations will
be much more effective as conditioned stimuli than others are. Associative learning will therefore be *constrained*—either facilitated or retarded—by the nature of the configuration.

Ontogenetic changes in expressive behaviors are not occurring in isolation, of course, but as part of a broad suite of related developments.
Most relevant among these are changes in perception, in exploratory
behavior, in motor skills, and in the tendency to make more refined
spatial adjustments. For example, in Bernstein and Mason's (1962) cross-
sectional study we found that the three older groups of monkeys made
more use of the available floor space to create distance between themselves and the approaching stimuli than did the younger animals, even
though the latter had the motor capabilities to make such adjustments.
Collectively these changes describe a general trend in the organization
of behavior toward increasing differentiation and selectivity with respect
to environmental events, and greater integration and coordination with
respect to the responses evoked by these events. The individual becomes more fully engaged with its environment, appears to become
more discriminating, more aware of novelty and change, and has more
ways available to it for dealing with its world. Under normal conditions
these changes are promoted by experience, and this leads in turn to
more extended and varied experience, a process which has been characterized as *deviation amplifying* (Maruyama, 1963).

These general changes are presumably reflected in each of the components of Ekman's (Ekman, 1977; Oster & Ekman, 1978) model. As we
have seen, that facet of the central-affect program governing the form
of expressive movements appears not to be much affected by experience. On the other hand, its presumptive role in the integration and
coordination of different response systems (e.g., endocrine, autonomic),
in the elaboration of coping behaviors (fleeing, fighting), and in the in-
corporation of memories, expectations, and the like is expected to be
heavily influenced by experience. We have, in fact, considered evidence
that the individual rhesus monkey's basic stance toward the environ-

ment, as reflected in its physiological and behavioral responses to emotion-provoking situations, is profoundly influenced by its early experiences. One consequence of particular interest in the present context is that experience may result in abiding individual differences in expressivity. These general developmental trends are presumably also reflected in greater refinement and differentiation of the functions of the appraisal mechanism, which analyzes and evaluates potential elicitors of emotional responses.

These two components of Ekman's (Ekman, 1977; Oster & Ekman, 1978) model seem to provide suitable hypothetical accommodations for most of the changes in expressive movements of rhesus monkeys resulting from experience. Is there any need then to invoke his third component, the mechanism for managing or interfering with emotional responses? It would seem so, for as we have seen, there are indications that one of the consequences of experience is that the rhesus monkey becomes not only more adept at using expressive movements to manage others but does so in a manner that suggests the behaviors are used in ways that are more socially expedient than expressive. The specific pattern and sequence of expressive movements that an experienced monkey displays, the conditions under which they were displayed, and the apparent social stimuli that elicit or receive such displays seem to be determined in the socially experienced monkey by *rules* that relate more to the power structure and dynamics of social groups than to the individual's presumptive affective state. Although this achievement is probably a far cry from the highly conventionalized use by human beings of species-typical gestures—the polite smile, the disapproving frown, the sympathetic, sad face—which may be almost completely detached from the underlying affective state, the similarity is close enough to suggest that the management function hypothesized by Ekman is present in rudimentary form in the macaque monkey.

In brief, we may conclude that the early development of expressive movements proceeds in accord with the Piagetian concepts of assimilation and accommodation within established structures, or with Lashley's suggestion that "the nervous system seems to consist of schemata or basic patterns within which new stimuli are spontaneously fitted" (Lashley, 1949, p. 35). It is as though the infant macaque is equipped at birth with a broad set of perceptual categories that are loosely associated with, for example, the tendencies to lipsmack or to grimace. As a function of growth and of continued visual exposure, expressive responses become more frequent, and their relationships to stimulus configurations become better differentiated and more precise, but the basic process occurs within these primordial structures.

While this is going forward, there is, in the ordinary course of events, ample opportunity for the rhesus monkey growing up in a normal social context to develop general expectancies about the kind of world it lives in—to form its basic stance toward the environment—and to acquire specific information about the probable causes and consequences of the expressive movements that it receives from others and (somewhat later, one would guess) that it displays toward them. In addition, while still in adolescence the socialized individual demonstrates that it has acquired the ability to select from its repertoire of relatively stereotyped expressive movements a specific pattern or sequence of responses that is related less to its emotional state than to its knowledge of the power structure and dynamics of a social group.

Perhaps the most important general message that can be drawn from these findings is that experience has little influence on the motor patterns that characterize expressive behaviors. At the motor level the organization of these patterns is virtually impervious to wide variations in the environment. Experience has its major influence on the functions that the patterns serve. As the result of functional elaborations, refinements, and transformations of the schemata present in early infancy, experience creates new sources of social order, new possibilities for the regulation and control of social life.

Summary

1. This chapter examines the development of some expressive behaviors in rhesus monkeys and attempts to characterize the influences of experience on this process.

2. The stereotyped, species-typical form of most expressive behaviors shown by rhesus monkeys is seen early in the neonatal period, suggesting that the organization of these patterns at the motoric level is relatively impervious to environmental influences. Similarly, the age at which different expressive behaviors appear, the ease with which they can be elicited, and the stimulus conditions that elicit them appear to follow the same definite and predictable schedule in all individuals, despite broad variations in rearing conditions. This suggests that the early development of these behaviors is mainly dependent on fundamental changes in structures within the central nervous system and requires no specific input from the environment.

3. In spite of strong evidence that experience does not produce the overall trend in early development of expressive behaviors, it is known

to affect the precise age at which these patterns appear, the likelihood that they will occur, and the extent to which they are elicited differentially by distinct stimulus configurations.

4. These findings are considered in terms of Ekman's (Ekman, 1977; Oster & Ekman, 1978) neurocultural model of emotions. This model postulates a central affect program that organizes the activity of the various systems comprising an emotional response and an appraisal mechanism capable of analyzing and evaluating potential elicitors of emotional responses. Both of these components of Ekman's model appear to be present in the normal neonatal rhesus monkey at birth, or shortly thereafter.

5. In the beginning the appraisal mechanism is coarsely tuned to the environmental events. With respect to visual stimuli, the effective dimensions are probably broad, such as the direction, rate and regularity of the movement of the stimulus, its size, its complexity, and the configuration of its elements. The potency of these dimensions is not dependent on individual experience and probably persists throughout life.

6. The appraisal mechanism becomes more selective and discriminating as development proceeds. The process of fine-tuning starts in early infancy and is facilitated by experience. Perceptual differentiation, resulting from mere exposure to varied stimulation, as well as the more specific and directional effects of associative learning probably are important contributors to this process.

7. Expressive behaviors do not develop in isolation but as part of a broad suite of changes in the organization of behavior. Collectively, these changes describe a general trend in which the individual becomes more fully engaged with the environment, more discriminating, more responsive to novelty and change, and more versatile in dealing with its world.

8. The rate at which these general developmental changes proceed and their specific form and content are heavily influenced by the individual's experience and by the opportunities afforded by its environment. For example, the monkey growing up as the sole occupant of a small cage is necessarily exposed to different experiences and to different developmental opportunities than is the animal that has grown up within an established social group.

9. The effects of such broad differences in personal history on the form of expressive behaviors is slight, however, whereas their influence on the level of responsiveness and on the social functions that expressive behaviors perform is considerable. Because the socialized monkey has had opportunities to acquire information about the probable causes and consequences of the expressive behaviors that are directed toward it by others and to learn about the social reactions to its own displays,

one might expect that it will be a more skillful and effective communicator. Indeed, this seems to be the case. A more surprising finding is that experienced monkeys have apparently reached another level of function in which they use expressive behaviors as devices for manipulating social events. When this stage is reached the behaviors are expressive in name only, for the particular pattern an animal displays does not provide reliable information about its affective state (e.g., fear, anger) or its probable responses (e.g., submit, attack). Instead, the specific patterns and sequences that are shown and the social stimuli that seemingly elicit or receive them are selected according to rules that derive from the perceived power structure and anticipated dynamics of the social group. This achievement suggests that the third component in Ekman's (Ekman, 1977; Oster & Ekman, 1978) neurocultural model of human emotions, a mechanism for managing emotional responses, is also present in nonhuman primates in rudimentary form.

10. It thus appears that the principal contribution of experience to the development of expressive behaviors is not to the organization of these patterns at the motor level but to the refinement, elaboration, and transformation of the social functions they perform.

References

Anderson, C. O., & Mason, W. A. Early experience and complexity of social organization in groups of young rhesus monkeys (*Macaca mulatta*). *Journal of Comparative and Physiological Psychology*, 1974, *87*, 681–690.

Anderson, C. O., & Mason, W. A. Competitive social strategies in groups of deprived and experienced rhesus monkeys. *Developmental Psychobiology*, 1978, *11*, 289–299.

Andrew, R. J. The origins of facial expressions. *Scientific American*, 1965, *213*, 88–94.

Berkson, G. Abnormal stereotyped motor acts. In J. Zubin & H. F. Hunt (Eds.), *Comparative psychopathology—Animal and human.* New York: Grune & Stratton, 1967.

Berkson, G., & Becker, J. D. Facial expressions and social responsiveness of blind monkeys. *Journal of Abnormal Psychology*, 1975, *84*, 519–523.

Bernstein, S., & Mason, W. A. Effects of age and stimulus conditions on the emotional responses of rhesus monkeys: Responses to complex stimuli. *Journal of Genetic Psychology*, 1962, *101*, 279–298.

Bernstein, S., & Mason, W. A. Effects of age and stimulus conditions on the emotional responses of rhesus monkeys: Differential responses to frustration and to fear stimuli. *Developmental Psychobiology*, 1970, *3*, 5–12.

Capitanio, J. P. *Early experience, behavior and organization in rhesus monkey (Macaca mulatta) social groups.* Unpublished doctoral dissertation, University of California, Davis, 1982.

Chevalier-Skolnikoff, S. Facial expression of emotion in nonhuman primates. In P. Ekman (Ed.), *Darwin and facial expression.* New York: Academic Press, 1973.

Coss, R. G. Perceptual determinants of gaze aversion by lesser mouse lemur (*Microcebus murinus*): Role of two facing eyes. *Behaviour*, 1978, *64*, 249.

Cross, H. A., & Harlow, H. F. Prolonged and progressive effects of partial isolation on the behavior of macaque monkeys. *Journal of Experimental Research on Personality*, 1965, *1*, 39–49.

Ekman, P. Biological and cultural contributions to body and facial movement. In J. Blacking (Ed.), *The anthropology of the body*. London: Academic Press, 1977.

Ekman, P., & Oster, H. Facial expressions of emotion. *Annual Review of Psychology*, 1979, *30*, 527–554.

Gibson, E. J. *Principles of perceptual learning and development*. New York: Appleton-Century-Crofts, 1969.

Gibson, J. J., & Gibson, E. J. Perceptual learning: Differentiation or enrichment? *Psychological Review*, 1955, *62*, 32–41.

Green, P. C. Influence of early experience and age on expression of affect in monkeys. *Journal of Genetic Psychology*, 1965, *106*, 157–171.

Green, S. Dialects in Japanese monkeys: Vocal learning and cultural transmission of locale-specific vocal behavior. *Zeitshrift für Tierpsychology*, 1975, *38*, 304–314.

Haslerud, G. M. The effect of movement of stimulus objects upon avoidance reactions in chimpanzees. *Journal of Comparative Psychology*, 1938, *25*, 507–528.

Hebb, D. O. On the nature of fear. *Psychological Review*, 1946, *53*, 259–276.

Hinde, R. A., & Rowell, T. E. Communications by postures and facial expressions in the rhesus monkey (*Macaca mulatta*). *Proceedings of the Zoological Society of London*, 1962, *138*, 1–21.

Hinde, R. A., Rowell, T. E., & Spencer-Booth, Y. Behaviour of socially living rhesus monkeys in their first six months. *Proceedings of the Zoological Society of London*, 1964, *143*, 609–649.

Humphrey, N. K. Species and individuals in the perceptual world of monkeys. *Perception*, 1974, *3*, 105–114.

Joslin, J., Fletcher, H., & Emlen, J. A comparison of the responses to snakes of lab- and wild-reared rhesus monkeys. *Animal Behaviour*, 1964, *12*, 348–352.

Keating, C. F., & Keating, E. G. Visual scan patterns of rhesus monkeys viewing faces. *Perception*, 1982, *11*, 211–219.

Kenney, M. D., Mason, W. A., & Hill, S. D. Effects of age, objects, and visual experience on affective responses of rhesus monkeys to strangers. *Developmental Psychology*, 1979, *15*, 176–184.

Lashley, K. S. Persistent problems in the evolution of mind. *Quarterly Review of Biology*, 1949, *24*, 28–42.

McCulloch, T. L., & Haselrud, G. M. Affective responses of an infant chimpanzee reared in isolation from its kind. *Journal of Comparative Psychology*, 1939, *28*, 437–445.

Maruyama, M. The second cybernetics: Deviation-amplifying mutual causal processes. *American Scientist*, 1963, *51*, 164–179.

Mason, W. A. The effects of social restriction on the behavior of rhesus monkeys: I. Free social behavior. *Journal of Comparative and Physiological Psychology*, 1960, *53*, 582–589.

Mason, W. A. The effects of social restriction on the behavior of rhesus monkeys: III. Dominance tests. *Journal of Comparative and Physiological Psychology*, 1961, *54*, 694–699.

Mason, W. A. The social development of monkeys and apes. In I. DeVore (Ed.), *Primate behavior: Field studies of monkeys and apes*. New York: Holt, 1965.

Mason, W. A. Motivational factors in psychosocial development. In W. J. Arnold & M. M. Page (Eds.), *Nebraska Symposium on Motivation* (pp. 35–67). Lincoln: University of Nebraska Press, 1971.

Mason, W. A. Social experience and primate cognitive development. In G. M. Burghardt

& M. Bekoff (Eds.), *The development of behavior: comparative and evolutionary aspects* (pp. 233–251). New York: Garland Press, 1978.

Mason, W. A., & Berkson, G. Effects of maternal mobility on the development of rocking and other behaviors in rhesus monkeys: A study with artificial mothers. *Developmental Psychobiology*, 1975, *8*, 197–211.

Mason, W. A., Davenport, R. K., & Menzel, E. W. Early experience and the social development of rhesus monkeys and chimpanzees. In G. Newton & S. Levine (Eds.), *Early experience and behavior* (pp. 1–41). New York: Thomas, 1968.

Mason, W. A., & Green, P. C. The effects of social restriction on the behavior of rhesus monkeys: IV. Responses to a novel environment and to an alien species. *Journal of Comparative and Physiological Psychology*, 1962, *55*, 353–368.

Mason, W. A., Green, P. C., & Posepanko, C. Sex differences in affective-social responses of rhesus monkeys. *Behaviour*, 1960, *16*, 74–83.

Mason, W. A., & Sponholz, R. R. Behavior of rhesus monkeys raised in isolation. *Journal of Psychiatric Research*, 1963, *1*, 299–306.

Mendelson, M. J. Clinical examination of visual and social responses in infant rhesus monkeys. *Developmental Psychology*, 1982, *18*, 658–664.

Mendelson, M. J., Haith, M. M., & Goldman-Rakic, P. S. Face scanning and responsiveness to social cues in infant rhesus monkeys. *Developmental Psychology*, 1982, *18*, 222–228.

Menzel, E. W., Jr. The effects of stimulus size and proximity upon avoidance of complex objects in rhesus monkeys. *Journal of Comparative and Physiological Psychology*, 1962, *55*, 1044–1046.

Menzel, E. W., Jr. Responsiveness to object-movement in young chimpanzees. *Behaviour*, 1964, *25*, 147–160.

Miller, R. E., Caul, W. F., & Mirsky, I. A. The communication of affects between feral and socially-isolated monkeys. *Journal of Personality and Social Psychology*, 1967, *7*, 231–239.

Mineka, S., Keir, R., & Price, V. Fear of snakes in wild- and laboratory-reared rhesus monkeys (*Macaca mulatta*). *Animal Learning and Behavior*, 1980, *8*, 653–663.

Newman, J. D. & Symmes, D. Vocal pathology in socially deprived monkeys. *Developmental Psychobiology*, 1974, *7*, 351–358.

Oster, H., & Ekman, P. Facial behavior in child development. In W. A. Collins (Ed.), *Minnesota Symposium on Child Psychology* (Vol. 11, pp. 231–276). Hillsdale: Erlbaum, 1978.

Redican, W. K. Facial expressions in nonhuman primates. In L. A. Rosenblum (Ed.), *Primate behavior* (Vol. 4, pp. 103–194). New York: Academic Press, 1975.

Rowell, T. E. Agonistic noises of the rhesus monkey (*Macaca mulatta*). *Symposium of the Zoological Society of London*, 1962, *8*, 81–96.

Sackett, G. P. Monkeys reared in isolation with pictures as visual input: Evidence for an innate releasing mechanism. *Science*, 1966, *154*, 1468–1470.

Sackett, G. P. Innate mechanisms, rearing conditions, and a theory of early experience effects in primates. In M. R. Jones (Ed.), *Miami Symposium on the Prediction of Behavior*. Coral Gables, University of Miami Press, 1970.

Sackett, G. P., Bowman, R. E., Meyer, J. S., Tripp, R. L., & Grady, S. S. Adrenocortical and behavioral reactions by differentially raised rhesus monkeys. *Physiological Psychology*, 1973, *1*, 209–212.

Schiff, W., Caviness, J. A., & Gibson, J. J. Persistent fear responses in rhesus monkeys to the optical stimulus of "looming". *Science*, 1962, *136*, 982–983.

Schiller, P. H. Innate constituents of complex responses in primates. *Psychological Review*, 1952, *59*, 177–191.

Singh, S. D. The effects of human environment upon the reactions to novel situations in the rhesus. *Behaviour*, 1966, *26*, 243–250.

Singh, S. D. Urban monkeys. *Scientific American*, 1969, *221*, 108–115.

Valentine, C. W. The innate bases of fear. *Journal of Genetic Psychology*, 1930, *37*, 394–420.

van Hooff, J. A. R. A. M. The comparison of facial expression in man and higher primates. In M. von Cranach (Ed.), *Methods of inference from animal to human behaviour* (pp. 165–196). Chicago: Aldine, 1976.

Wolin, L. R., Ordy, J. M., & Dillman, A. Monkeys' fear of snakes: A study of its basis and generality. *Journal of Genetic Psychology*, 1963, *103*, 207–226.

Yerkes, R. M., & Yerkes, A. W. Nature and conditions of avoidance, (fear) response in chimpanzee. *Journal of Comparative Psychology*, 1936, *21*, 53–66.

Chapter 7

Faces as Signs and Symbols

Michael Lewis and Linda Michalson

Relationship to Other Chapters and to the Field

Issues Relevant to the Field

This chapter illustrates the interrelationship of all the issues of the field that were reviewed in the framing chapter: it initially emphasizes the learned versus innate dichotomy both for states and expressive behaviors and characterizes the field as thus polarized between learning and nativist theorists; it puts forth the model of biology–environment interaction described in the framing chapter as one that sees environment taking the active role in using and shaping biological givens; and it employs the semiotic concepts of signs and symbols to characterize the nature of expression as it changes with development.

Lewis and Michalson's idea of the three stages of expression development is one of the field's most empirically challenging conceptions. In the first stage of expression—and of emotion—development there is no innate coordination of states and the behaviors that express them. It is socialization into rules of what to feel and how to show it that greatly, if not totally, brings about the coordination, in the second stage, of state and veridical expression of state. In a final stage, state and expression become greatly disconnected through voluntary control of expressive behaviors, as taught by socialization.

Although most theorists of infant emotional development would allow that in early infancy there appears little capacity to experience all the basic emotions or to perform the fully differentiated and coordinated facial expressions that express them, most developmental theorists who use the state concept hold, in

153

contrast to Lewis and Michalson, that a latent innate program is soon largely responsible for the infant or the toddler's concurrence of basic emotional states and their prewired facial expressions. Thus, Lewis and Michalson see two stages whereas others see one, and they give a much greater role to environmental factors in bringing about the coordination of state and expression seen in the toddler and preschool years. They are in full agreement with most other theorists about a final stage as the transition via complex social learning from the stage of concurrent state and expression to their voluntary disconnection. They coincide with other developmentalists, notably Haviland, Izard, and Malatesta (see Chapter 1) in characterizing the final stage of disconnection as one in which expressive behaviors function more symbolically than as the signs they had previously been. They agree also with most theorists of emotional development that a theory of emotional development must accompany one of expressive behavior.

Relationship to Other Chapters

As suggested in the preceding, this chapter contrasts with views of more differentiated, enduring, and active biological influences in the early years of human emotion and expressive development, views that are represented by the exclusively human development chapters in the last section of this volume. The contrast is most clearly made with Malatesta (Chapter 8) who articulates a theory of emotion and expressive development that assigns detailed biological roles and stages in the first year of life (including preadaptive emotional responses) and that sees increasing socialization as facilitated by inherited scheduled tendencies. Lewis and Michalson's emphasis on the coordinating function of social experience suggests a stance similar to Feinman's (Chapter 12) and to Mason's (Chapter 6). These latter hold the social psychological position that cognitive appraisal of one's circumstances, more than evocation of state, is the factor that leads to emotion experience and expressive behavior. As stated previously, however, all contributors, regardless of their positions on the role of state and its correlation with expressive behaviors, agree that the last stage of emotion and expression development is the socialization of expressive behaviors as social signals.

The observational data presented by Lewis and Michalson on the early ways that parental reinforcements and attentions teach rules for feeling and expressive behavior parallel in intent that of Malatesta's (Chapter 8) reviewed and original data on infants. They likewise set the stage for Cole's (Chapter 11) review of data on how such rules are conveyed to children, for her original data documenting the use of rules for expressive behavior in preschoolers, and for Feinman's (Chapter 12) review of how infants learn appropriate emotional reactions to new stimuli through social referencing.

Fogel's (Chapter 10) conception of independent start-up schedules for elements of emotion and expression development is much more reliant upon biological maturation for the eventual coalescence of emotional subsystems. However, it is congenial to Lewis and Michalson's view of the variably timed, multiple coordinations needed by partially potentiated and partially learned elements of state and expression.

For Consistent Terminology

Sign is used in this chapter in a manner that has acquired use in the psychology of communication, although it is a modification of Pierce's classic semiotic coinage that is explicated in the framing chapter. The modification is along the lines of Kroeber's distinction (see Chapter 1) between signs for emotional communication and symbols for communication of cognitions: sign, in opposition to symbol, labels all indicators that are not symbol-like, that is, nonarbitrary in their relationship to their referents and noncognitive in their conveyed information. This use of sign encompasses both index, *as an indicator naturally connected to its referent, and* icon, *as an indicator that resembles its referent. Slightly more poetic, but shared with some few other expressive-behavior theorists who want to describe the same trend, is Lewis and Michalson's use of* symbol. *They use it to describe an expressive behavior whose performance has become, through socialization, disconnectable from the state that is its naturally connected referent. Thus, symbol here is not arbitrarily connected with the meaning of its referent: it bears an iconic (or indexical) relationship to the state that it is supposed to represent. Nevertheless, when an expressive behavior is unreliably connected to the presence of the state it represents, symbol is used as a label to underline the cultural determination and the physical arbitrariness of the cooccurrence of expressive behavior and state.—*ED.

Introduction

The distinction between signs and symbols can be used to understand and to study facial expressions. *Signs*[1] refer to those events that have a one-to-one relationship with the object, person, or action that they are supposed to represent. That is, the representation of an object actually resembles that object. Thus a picture of an apple is a sign of that apple. The representation of an apple has a one-to-one correspondence to an

[1]The complexities of this use of *sign* are discussed in the brief introduction immediately preceding.

actual apple. Whereas the sign *apple* may not represent any one particular apple, it does represent apple rather than any other object. The degree to which the sign–object does not represent any particular apple is the degree to which a sign can be said to serve as a representation.

The case for a *symbol* is somewhat different. Here the representation in no way resembles the object, person, or action. In general, some arbitrary marking is used to represent the object. In the case of writing, the use of the written word *apple* in no way resembles an apple. It is an arbitrary social convention to use a particular marking to represent a real object.

This difference between sign and symbol is a good analogy for the study of facial expressions and their development. It may be the case that human facial expressions develop first as signs and then, as the result of socialization pressures within any given group, become symbols. In this chapter we argue that at some point in development, facial expressions have a strong one-to-one correspondence with internal emotional states but that one important aspect in the socialization of any individual in any culture is the separation of expressions from internal states so that facial expressions need not act as signs. Socialization processes both convert and create a symbolic system wherein facial expressions become somewhat arbitrary vis-à-vis internal states. This process of converting facial expressions from signs to symbols begins early in children's lives and continues throughout the life of the individual.

It is important to note that our use of the term symbol is particular. Technically, a signal is a symbol when it bears an arbitrary relationship to the object it represents. Mature expressions may continue to bear an iconic relationship to the states that the face maker intends to represent. However, they are no longer icons of the state that the observer is likely to infer as the referent of the expression. (See Smith, Chapter 3, this volume, on the problem of discovering the referents of expressions.)

Examples of Faces as Signs versus Symbols

Example 1

Lucy is 18 months old. While her mother is working on a law brief at home, Lucy is playing quietly in the back yard. Through the window the mother witnesses the following scene: Lucy runs to get a toy at the far end of the yard. She falls on her knees and starts to cry. Immediately she looks up but sees that no one is paying any attention. She stops crying and walks to the back door of the house. As she approaches the door, she starts to cry again.

Here we have an example of facial expressions and vocal behaviors that are not totally determined by the precipitating event or the internal state. Whereas Lucy's first cry is probably related to her pain, her subsequent cry has more to do with her attempt to communicate a specific message to her mother. This conclusion is supported by the fact that Lucy first looked around to see if anybody was watching. Lucy's ability to produce her facial expressions and vocal behavior at will suggests that these behaviors are under her control and not necessarily related to an underlying state of pain.

Example 2

Matthew, a four-month-old, is playing in his playpen. While examining a toy, he starts to laugh and babble. His mother calls to him from the other room, responding quickly to his vocalization. Ten minutes later he starts to fret and shakes the bars of his playpen. This time his mother does not respond immediately. In fact, she closes the door to the kitchen in order to shut out his sound.

This example illustrates the direct reinforcement (in this case the extinction) of particular emotional expressions that are deemed socially inappropriate. The reinforcement of specific emotional expressions begins early in children's lives and can be seen to modify behaviors that reflect particular emotions. In this case, Matthew's fretting and other displays of anger at being kept in the playpen are not tolerated by his mother, who will extinguish them through lack of response or even through negative reinforcement. The extinction of behaviors can occur either through direct reinforcement by parents, siblings, teachers, and peers or more indirectly through children's modeling of the behavior of other people in particular situations. Thus, for example, in families in which laughing is unusual, young children may learn to eliminate the vocal components of enjoyment through modeling their parents' behavior. In this example, Matthew will eventually express his anger through behaviors other than fretting and shaking.

Example 3

Casey has gone to his grandfather's house for the weekend. At 2 years old, Casey is a verbally precocious child who is highly sociable and enjoys being with other people. His grandfather is an actor who encourages Casey's dramatic flair. One game they like to play together is "make a face." In this game, the grandfather asks Casey to make different kinds of faces. First, he may ask Casey to make a sad face, for example. Casey indeed makes something resembling a sad face, narrowing his eyes and frowning. Next, the grandfather may ask Casey to make a happy face. For an instant, Casey's face resumes its neutral position and the frown disappears. His eyes then open wide and a grin fills his face. Casey's grandfather follows these faces with requests for others including, possibly, a sleepy face and an angry face. Before he becomes bored with this game, in each instance Casey produces a face that approximates that of the adult version of the appropriate face.

This example highlights the fact that, around 2 years of age, children are capable of producing some facial expressions when requested to do so. It also indicates that the verbal labels of particular emotions are already associated with particular facial configurations. Had we observed the game further between Casey and his grandfather, we would have seen the grandfather ask Casey what kind of face a little boy would make if he got a big, chocolate ice cream cone. We would have seen that Casey was capable of producing a happy face as a consequence of either his learned association between past ice cream cones and his feelings when receiving them or his general knowledge about what people usually feel in certain situations. Thus, either as a function of past associations, the common knowledge of emotions associated with particular situations, or of empathy, Casey is able to produce facial expressions appropriate to imagined situations. Specific events and facial expressions are mediated by cognitive processes that may be as simple as associations or as complex as empathy.

Summary

These three examples raise an issue that we wish to address: namely, the developmental relationship between facial expressions and emotional states. These examples underscore the fact that there is not necessarily an isomorphic relationship among emotional elicitors, states, and expressions. In fact, we would argue that emotional expressions are a function of both a complex neuromusculature involving facial, bodily, and vocal responses as well as the socialization rules governing these behaviors in any particular society. Viewing emotional development from the perspective of biology–environment interaction, we suggest that these unlearned and biologically programmed neuromuscular patterns constitute universal attributes (when facial expressions can be viewed as signs), whereas the social rules represent the environmental contribution to emotional development and the force that converts facial expressions from signs to symbols. To understand facial expressions, both the development of neuromuscular configurations (the biological factor) as well as the socialization history of emotion (the environmental factor) need to be considered.

A Structural Analysis of Emotion

In the previous section we mentioned three different features of emotion and implied that they are structurally separate. Rather than defining emotion, we choose to represent emotion in terms of a structural analysis. We approach the study of emotion from this point of view to test the proposition that the components comprising emotion are independent. After defining the components of emotion, we contrast two views of emotion, one of which, in fact, makes little distinction among the components.

Emotions consist of five major components that together constitute *emotion*. These five components are labeled elicitors, receptors, states, expressions, and experiences (Lewis & Michalson, 1983; Lewis & Rosenblum, 1978). Although others have also stated that a complete description of emotion must take into account the experience (conscious, subjective feeling), the neurophysiological state, and the expression of emotion (e.g., Izard, 1977), little attention has been given to an analysis of each component, to its role in the total structure or process that we call emotion, or to its developmental course.

In our model, *emotional elicitors* refer to situations or stimulus events that trigger an organism's emotional receptors. These stimuli may be either internal or external, and the capacity of these elicitors to evoke responses may be either innate or learned. *Emotional receptors* are relatively specific loci or pathways in the central nervous system (CNS) that mediate changes in the physiological and/or cognitive state of the organism. The process through which these receptors attain their emotional function and the types of events that trigger their activity may be genetically encoded or may be acquired through experience. *Emotional states* are the particular constellations of changes in somatic and/or neuronal activity that accompany the activation of emotional receptors. *Changes in* is the critical aspect of this definition. Emotional states are largely specific, transient, and patterned alterations in ongoing levels of physiological activity. *Emotional expressions* are the potentially observable surface features of changes in face, body, voice, and activity level that accompany emotional states. The constituent elements and their patterning as well as the regularity with which they are associated with particular emotional states may be either learned or innate. Finally, *emotional experiences* are an individual's conscious or unconscious perception, interpretation, and evaluation of his or her own emotional state or expression. This cognitive process is influenced by a range of prior social experiences in which the nature of the eliciting stimuli and the appropriateness of particular expressions have been partially articulated and defined for the individual by others.

These components are depicted in Figure 7.1 as they participate in the ongoing emotional process. This emotional process is set in motion by either internal or external elicitors. These elicitors activate receptors that produce emotional states. Emotional states in turn generate emotional expressions. Emotional states and expressions become emotional experiences through self-mediation and other cognitive processes and through socialization experiences. This description attributes a unidirectional quality to the emotional process that is not intended. Although most models of emotion portray the emotional process as unidirectional, strong cycling effects probably occur in the process. The multidirectional quality between emotional components is indicated in the diagram through the use of double arrows. Multidirectionality can be found in

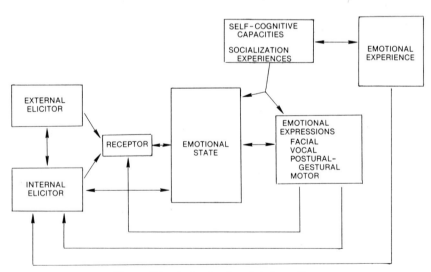

Figure 7.1. A structural model of emotion.

the specific relationships between pairs of these components. This model can be used to illustrate (1) the unfolding of a particular emotion at a fixed point in time, (2) the cycling of emotions (either as a continuation of one emotion or a sequence of different emotions) in the life of an organism, and (3) the ontogenesis of emotional processes. Elsewhere, we present numerous examples of the feedback system among the components of the model (Lewis & Michalson, 1983).

The model in Figure 1 is useful for describing two very different approaches to emotional development, one more biological and the other more environmental. Although our specific concern in this chapter is with the connection between emotional states and expressions, it helps to understand this connection by contrasting the two views in terms of the various connections in the emotional process. The subsequent discussion touches upon some developmental issues concerning all five components of emotion.

A strong biological approach to emotional development is based on the assumption that emotional behavior has an evolutionary history and specific biological programs. In the case of facial expressions, the evolutionary trend seems to involve an increasingly differentiated neuromusculature, which results in different emotional expressions. According to this view, the development of emotion occurs as a consequence of strong biological forces that rely on maturational changes rather than on cultural factors. Biological interpretations of emotion posit (1) specific elicitor–receptor connections, such as innate-releasing mechanisms, (2) specificity of CNS receptors, and (3) unlearned connections between receptors and states, between states and expressions, and among states, expressions, and experiences.

The biological interpretation of emotion is represented in the work of Izard (1971, 1977; Izard and Dougherty, 1982), who asserts,

> Emotion expressions are innate and emerge ontogenetically as they become adaptive in the life of the infant and particularly in infant-caregiver communication. (Izard & Dougherty, 1982, p. 98).

Moreover,

> The data from these investigations [studies showing that certain emotions have similar facial expressions across widely different cultures] provide a sound basis for inferring that the fundamental emotions are subserved by innate neural programs that are part of the substrate of qualitatively distinct states of consciousness. (Izard & Dougherty, 1982, p. 98).

A strong connection between particular emotional expressions and experiences, as well as between expressions and states is also postulated:

> It is reasonable to infer that the link between facial expression, neurochemical processes and emotions, and certain actions or action tendencies *is* the inner emotion experience and its motivational properties. (Izard & Dougherty, 1982, p. 101, emphasis added).

Izard's view of an isomorphic relationship among states, expressions, and experiences, with little attention given to the role of socialization factors, represents a strong biological view of emotional development. To the extent that socialization factors enter the process at all, socialization is seen as a force that can alter innate facial configurations or emotional expressions once they have developed (Ekman, Friesen, & Ellsworth, 1972; Izard, 1978).

The assumptions of biological models concerning the development of elicitor–receptor connections, the specificity of receptors, and the connection between receptors and states and between states and expressions derive from the same data base (i.e., the universality of facial expressions). States are defined by expressions; thus, a one-to-one correspondence between them is assumed. This assumption in turn implies a specificity of emotional states based on a demonstration of differences in emotional expressions. The idea of specific states requires the assumption of specificity of receptors insofar as specific elicitors produce specific expressions. Evidence of the universality of emotional expressions is used to argue that these expressions are not culturally controlled but are determined by biological mechanisms. The data for such claims are limited to the demonstration that particular emotions have specific expressions (Ekman *et al.*, 1972; Izard, 1977).

We do not mean to undermine the importance of data on facial expressions. Such data certainly seem to support the view that particular configurations of facial muscles are the result of biological and maturational processes. The slowly accumulating evidence of the emergence of different facial expressions as a function of age (Izard, 1978), if verified, would implicate a systematic unfolding of emotions in emotional development.

The crux of the issue is the degree to which this maturational process is connected to other developmental processes, either maturational and/or cultural (including both learning and socialization processes). Thus, certain facial patterns may be subject to a slow and sequential maturational unfolding. What is the relationship between this maturational process on the one hand and the development of states and elicitors on the other? Fear faces, for example, may be elicited by fear stimuli only after the maturation of particular facial muscles. This process may take approximately 6 to 8 months and occur independently of other processes. Could one say, in the absence of a fear face, that a child younger than 6 months of age had a fear state? If a one-to-one correspondence is postulated between expressions and internal states, one would have to conclude that a fear state cannot exist in the absence of a fear face. However, under this same assumption one would be forced to recognize the existence of certain emotional states that probably do not occur until well after their facial expressions appear. For example, the observation of a puzzled face in the presence of a discrepant stimulus in 3- to 4-week-old infants is difficult to attribute to the cognitive process of problem solving as Oster (1978) does. Thus, emotional expressions may appear according to a biological timetable, independent of any internal state, yet dependent on certain elicitors.

The maturation of the facial musculature and facial expressions can be viewed as cooccurring with, although independent of, the growth of other processes and structures that are primarily cognitive. In some sense, then, biological models of emotion, at least as they explain facial expressions, may involve two separate processes: the development of the facial musculature and the simultaneous development of some other processes.

Implied in this discussion of the limitations of biological models is the assumption that states and expressions, states and experiences, and expressions and experiences do not necessarily share a one-to-one correspondence, at least in adult members of a particular society. This notion is the basic premise of socialization models of emotion. Indeed, the literature on the socialization of *feeling rules* (social rules that govern the expressions of personal feelings) suggests that children as young as 3 years are capable of disassociating their expressions from their internal emotional states (Lewis & Michalson, 1983; Saarni, 1979, 1980, 1982). Indeed, as adults we know that our own emotional expressions do not always correspond to the way we feel. Clinical psychologists tell us that the conscious awareness of people and their particular emotional states are often discordant. In fact, part of the therapeutic process may involve teaching patients to identify correctly and to monitor their internal states.

The socialization rules that affect emotional expressions, states, and experiences are quite complex (Lewis & Michalson, 1983). After considering the development of the connection between states and expressions, we discuss two of these feeling rules: how to express emotions and when to express emotions. Two empirical studies that illustrate the acquisition of these feeling rules are described.

The Development
of the State–Expression Relationship

In the preceding analysis a relationship between expressions and states was posited. Two questions must be asked: (1) When is there a relationship? (2) What is the nature of the socialization process that affects this relationship? In the following developmental model to be delineated, facial-musculature maturation is related to emotional states in a curvilinear fashion. Figure 7.2 illustrates this relationship for two different emotions. For both emotions the facial expression is unrelated to the state in Period 1, there is a correspondence or synchrony between the expression and the state in Period 2, and the expression is once again only loosely related to the state in Period 3.

The first period of development, indicated by the numeral 1, is viewed as biologically asynchronous. Here, internal states are undifferentiated for the most part and are unrelated to differentiated facial configurations. Examples of the early asynchrony are found in research on early infant smiling (e.g., Emde & Koenig, 1969; Wolff, 1963). An infant's

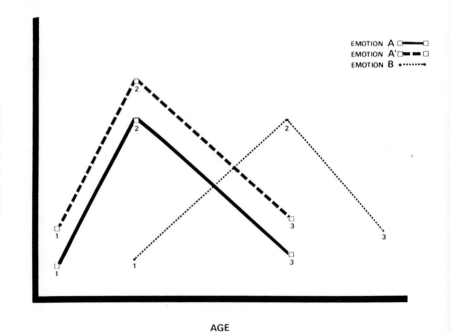

Figure 7.2. The developmental relationship between emotional states and expressions.

earliest smiles are considered *endogenous* because they do not occur in response to external elicitors and do not seem to be related to positive states. Endogenous smiles often are observed when the infant is asleep and appear to be correlated with spontaneous CNS activity and REM sleep. Endogenous smiles decrease rapidly over the first 3 months of life. One would be reluctant to think of these facial expressions as related to anything more than a general excitation of the nervous system.

A similar explanation may apply to observations of specific faces observed in very young infants (Izard, Huebner, Risser, McGinnes, & Dougherty, 1980; Oster & Ekman, 1978). In this period the neuromusculature and the patterning of facial muscles are probably related to a start-up or rehearsal mechanism in which facial expressions share little synchrony with underlying emotional states. This speculation receives support from the fact that many of the specific faces observed early in life do not match the nonspecific bipolar internal states assumed to exist in young infants. (For a detailed analysis of such initial asynchrony, see Fogel, Chapter 10, this volume). In other words, infants may show differentiated facial expressions in the absence of differentiated internal states. Alternatively, asynchrony may exist if the facial musculature of very young infants is not sufficiently developed to correspond with the highly differentiated emotional states that some theorists assume exist in early infancy. Whether the early emotional states of the infant emerge from an undifferentiated state (Bridges, 1932; Emde, Gaensbauer, & Harmon, 1976; Sroufe, 1979) or emerge as differentiated from the start (Izard, 1978) is an unsettled issue. In either case, asynchrony could exist if the facial musculature of the infant is either more differentiated (in the first case) or less differentiated (in the second case) than the internal state.

The second period of development, indicated by the numeral 2, is marked by a greater synchrony between facial expressions and emotional states. In this phase, different patterns of facial expressions correspond to differentiated emotional states. This relationship may exist because (1) biological factors link states and expressions, and socialization factors are not yet sufficiently powerful to disengage the two; and (2) children's cognitive structures have not matured enough to enable them to control their emotional expressions apart from underlying states. That is, even if social reinforcement and socialization rules are operative, the cognitive structures necessary for emotional deception may not yet exist, and the social knowledge about what constitutes appropriate emotional behavior may not yet be acquired. During this second period, then, one is likely to find the greatest synchrony between facial expressions and internal emotional states.

We have so far implied that a biological force creates the synchronous relationship between emotional expressions and states in the second period of emotional development. Equally likely is the possibility that the child's socialization experiences create the synchrony between emotional expressions and states (Lewis & Michalson, 1983). Support for this proposition comes from two sources. First, one must show that facial expressions are subject to socialization effects. In fact, various investigators have shown that caregivers socialize particular infant expressions (e.g., Brooks-Gunn & Lewis, 1982; Malatesta & Haviland, 1982). Our own data indicate that mothers of 1-year-olds respond differentially to their infant's distress, depending on what they believe the child is feeling (Lewis & Michalson, 1982). These socialization practices result in the selective display by the infant of particular facial expressions; they also result in the acquisition by the child of particular beliefs about emotional displays (Michalson & Lewis, 1983). Second, one must show that facial expressions and beliefs are related to internal states and that facial expressions and beliefs can at times produce certain states (for supporting data, see Laird, 1974). On the basis of these pieces of evidence— the socialization of facial expressions and the connection between faces and internal states—one can logically argue that socialization practices, by acting on expressions, beliefs, and internal states, may produce a synchrony between expressions and states. Thus, for example, when mothers reinforce certain facial expressions of their children, they are also likely to be influencing the actual connection between these expressions and the discriminable internal states that develop from an original, undifferentiated form.

In the third period of emotional development, facial expressions and internal emotional states are once again independent. Unlike Period 1, however, when the lack of correspondence is due either to undifferentiated internal states or to an inability to express discrete states through a finely articulated facial musculature, the asynchrony of Period 3 is due to the acquisition and maturation of cognitive structures and to the cumulating effects of socialization. Although children may have a particular emotional state and the corresponding expression, they may have learned to mask the state by disassociating from it the appropriate facial expression (Saarni, 1980, 1982). The result is that the emotional expression–emotional state relationship is a function of the interaction between biological and environmental factors.

The three periods are schematized in Figure 2 in terms of children's age and the degree of synchrony between facial expressions and internal emotional states. The courses of two different emotions (A and B) are depicted in this figure, from which several points can be made. First, as already noted, asynchrony may exist at different times for two different reasons: (1) the biological immaturity of the organism (in Period 1) or (2) the impact of socialization and cognitive forces (in Period 3). Although all emotions follow a three-stage process, different emotions may develop according to different time schedules. Because each emotion has its own timetable (determined in part by both biological and socialization factors), it is not possible to state the specific ages for the emergence and developmental sequence of emotion. Synchrony may exist for one emotion at the same time another is in a period of asynchrony, as noted by the different time courses for A and B.

Emotions that emerge from an undifferentiated state will probably reach a period of synchrony earlier than emotions that appear later. Thus, a fear face that reflects a fear state should appear earlier than a guilt face that reflects guilt. In fact, the fear face that corresponds to the internal state of fear (Period 2) might occur at the same time as the guilt face that does not correspond to an internal state (Period 1). If this is the case, the assumption cannot be made that by demonstrating a correspondence between a facial expression and internal state for one emotion, we have learned anything about the correspondence for any other emotion. Each emotion has a unique temporal sequence in terms of the first appearance of the facial expression and its correspondence with an internal state. There is no reason to believe that all emotions should follow the same timetable even though they follow the same developmental course.

Implicit in our discussion has been the notion that the time frame between any two developmental periods is equal and independent of the specific emotion. This may not be the case, however. The third point illustrated in Figure 2 is that emotions differ not only in their time of emergence but also in the rate at which they pass through the three periods. Thus, for Emotion A the amount of time between Periods 1 and 2 is shown to be shorter than for Emotion B, whereas the time between Periods 2 and 3 is longer for Emotion A than for Emotion B.

Furthermore, the asynchrony of the third period may vary, with some emotions (e.g., Emotion B in Figure 2) retaining more synchrony than others (e.g., Emotion A). The degree of asynchrony in the third period may be a function of (1) the nature of the particular emotion, (2) the degree to which its expression has been the target of socialization, (3) the particular situation that elicits the emotion, and (4) the degree to which the expression is under the child's cognitive control. Thus, some emotions (e.g., anger) are probably more quickly and more intensely socialized than other emotions (e.g., happiness). Furthermore, although an emotion may have been the focus of intense socialization, it may be more or less appropriate to express that emotion in certain circumstances. For example, it may be acceptable for a boy to express fear when a large dog lunges but not when going to the doctor ("big boys don't cry"). If the child has not yet fully acquired the necessary cognitive capacity for controlling the expression apart from the underlying state, then the state–expression relationship in Period 3 may be less asynchronous.

Finally, two levels of Emotion A (A and A') are portrayed in Figure 2. Each shows the course of the same emotion for different intensities of eliciting stimuli. The course of Emotion A' reflects the fact that greater synchrony is possible as a function of the intensity of the eliciting stimulus (and thus the intensity of the underlying state). It may be more difficult to disassociate emotional expressions from emotional states that are very intense. Thus, intense stimuli are more apt to produce greater synchrony between facial expressions and internal emotional states than are less intense stimuli (Lewis, Brooks, & Haviland, 1978). In fact, one way to judge the power of an emotional elicitor may be to establish the degree of synchrony between the subsequent expression and the state.

In studying facial configurations and their relationship to internal emotional states, it is crucial to keep this hypothesized developmental sequence in mind. With this analysis, researchers can study faces and their relationships to internal states while recognizing that faces and states may not be related to one another for very different reasons.

Socialization Rules: Converting Signs into Symbols

Given our belief that the relationship between states and expressions is mediated by socialization rules as well as by a biologically programmed neuromusculature, the explication of these environmental factors is of some interest. Such a task is formidable and involves a discussion not only of the socialization of emotional expressions but also of the other components of emotion and their interconnections. The strong form of socialization models posits a learned connection between elicitors and states, between states and expressions, and among states, expressions, and experiences (Lewis & Michalson, 1983). We have relatively little empirical data on how individuals acquire the capacity for altering their expressions vis-à-vis their internal states. We do not mean to imply that total control over emotional expressions is ever achieved but rather that emotional expressions can be viewed as the product of internal states (i.e., as signs) and as the product of socialization (i.e., as symbols). Even though such a discussion is well beyond the scope of this chapter, we address at least some aspects of the socialization of emotional expressions in order to examine the relationship between states and expressions as it is mediated by socialization rules.

We subscribe to Geertz's (1973) view that "not only ideas but emotions too are cultural artifacts" (p. 81). Elsewhere, we have specified five particular feeling rules that are subject to socialization forces (Lewis & Michalson, 1982, 1983). The two rules that we shall consider here are *how* to express emotions and *when* to express emotions. It is clear that adults sometimes express humor by laughing at an employer's joke, even though they do not feel amused. Just as often they suppress expressions of internal states that they judge to be inappropriate to the situation. For example, boys learn to suppress expressions of fear in order to demonstrate their bravery.

Ekman and Friesen (1969) list four categories of modification of facial expressions which Saarni (1979) has adapted to describe the rules young children use to disguise their internal states. *Personal or idiosyncratic display rules* are familial and individual rules that result from a child's personal history. *Deception* is a second category that as its label implies, involves intentionally falsifying an internal state through deceptive behavior. *Cultural display rules* pertain to the way cultures differ in the rules governing emotional expressions. For example, the resting neutral face of the Occidental contrasts with the smiling neutral face of the Oriental. Finally, *dramatic rules* for pretense are theatrical rules that involve "putting on" a particular expression.

Children as young as 6 years (Saarni, 1980) and even preschoolers (Cole, Chapter 11, this volume) are capable of deception. Both researchers have found that there tends to be a sex difference in this ability. Studies of the *acquisition* of display rules, however, are unusual. (See Cole, Chapter 11, this volume, for a review of what is known about children's knowledge and use of display rules.) Recently, we conducted two studies on the ways in which emotional expressions may be socialized. Each is subsequently described.

How to Express Emotions:
A Study of Mother–Infant Interaction

Observations of mother–child interaction patterns suggest the existence of cultural as well as individual differences that may underlie the acquisition of early socialization rules governing emotional expressions. For instance, whether a culture condones crying will affect the rules learned by the child that apply to emotional displays. Caudill and Wein-stein's (1969) study of the interactions between Japanese and American infants and their mothers reveals strong cultural differences in levels of emotional expressions as a function of different socialization rules. What the literature lacks, however, are developmental studies of mother–child interactions that focus on facial expressions.

Recently, we conducted a study in which we looked at three sets of behavior in mother–child interactions in the first 2 years of life: mother or infant vocalization, mother or infant smiling, and infant crying (Brooks-Gunn & Lewis, 1982). Interesting developmental patterns were found in the mothers' socialization rules pertaining to emotional expres-sions (see Table 1). During the first half year of the infant's life, mothers were significantly more responsive to infant crying than in the second half of the first year or in the second year of the infant's life. This de-crease in responsivity occurred despite the fact that maternal respon-sivity to other behaviors increased over this same period. For example, maternal responses to infant smiling increased between the time the in-fant was 6 and 12 months of age and then showed little developmental change: mothers were as responsive to their child's smile when the child was 1 year old as when the child was 2 years old. These data suggest that different socialization rules govern positive and negative emotional behavior. In the patterns we found mothers increased their responsive-ness to positive emotions but became unresponsive to negative emo-tions as children grew older. (See Malatesta, Chapter 8, and Cole,

TABLE 1

Proportion of Maternal Response to Infant Behavior

Infant behavior	Maternal response to infant (age in months)		
	2–7[a]	8–16[b]	17–27[c]
Infant vocalization			
Nonhandicapped	.13	.35	.50
Handicapped	.34	.25	.30
Infant smile			
Nonhandicapped	.07	.23	.27
Handicapped	.11	.17	.10
Infant cry			
Nonhandicapped	.21	.08	.06
Handicapped	.31	.13	.09

[a] Nonhandicapped $n = 193$, handicapped $n = 16$.
[b] Nonhandicapped $n = 167$, handicapped $n = 27$.
[c] Nonhandicapped $n = 156$, handicapped $n = 39$.

Chapter 11, this volume, for findings on the socialization of negative and positive affects in young children.)

The data for a small sample of handicapped children were similar to those for the nonhandicapped sample, confirming the reduction in responsivity to infant crying over the first 2 years of the infant's life. Mothers of handicapped children were somewhat more responsive to infant crying than were mothers of nonhandicapped children, however. This observation suggests that, even though it may have become less appropriate to respond to infant crying in the later stages of infancy, it is still more appropriate if the child is handicapped. In responding to infant smiling, the behaviors of mothers of handicapped children showed less of a developmental pattern and mothers responded less to infant smiling. Responses to infant vocalization also failed to show a developmental pattern in the handicapped sample. Mothers of handicapped infants seemed to be less responsive to infant vocalizations than were mothers of nonhandicapped infants.

These data are important to the study of emotional expression for several reasons. First, they suggest that maternal responsivity to crying signals of distress decreases as children get older. The rule seems to be "it is inappropriate for older children to express distress through crying; other 'more appropriate' means should be used." Feiring and Lewis (1979) showed that expressions of an infant's distress, caused by separation of the infant from its mother by a barrier, change from crying to asking for help over the second year of the child's life. This developmental change corresponds to a decrease in maternal responsivity to infant crying and to an increase in maternal responsivity to infant vocalization that are observed during this same age period.

Second, the data showed that mothers were less responsive to the crying of male infants than to the crying of female infants with the developmental function being steeper for males. This finding reveals a socialization rule dictating (at least in our culture) that "boys should not cry."

Third, the data showed differences in maternal socialization rules as a function of the status of the child. In this particular study, the status of the child was defined in terms of nonhandicapping versus handicapping characteristics. In both conditions crying was less reinforced as the appropriate expression of distress but less so for handicapped children. Other differences in maternal responsivity suggest that the socialization rules may be modified according to the developmental level of the child. Thus, maternal reinforcement patterns to children's early emotional expressions appear to underlie some of the known socialization rules that govern children's later emotional behavior.

Issues pertaining to parent–child emotional exchanges and the differential reinforcement patterns of specific emotional expressions need to
be explored further. The study just described exemplifies processes by
which particular emotional expressions, distress and smiling, may be
disassociated from internal states. Reinforcement practices constitute one
influence on children's emotional expressions and provide a process
through which society can separate emotional expressions from internal
emotional states, thereby converting expressions as signs into symbols.

When to Express Emotions: A Study of Children's Knowledge of Faces as Symbols

A second way in which emotional states and expressions can be separated is through a person's *knowledge* of the social and cultural rules
that govern emotional expressions. We shall consider this knowledge in
terms of the feeling rule: when to express emotions. This means of disassociating states and expressions differs from the reinforcement process by suggesting that children may acquire knowledge about emotional
expressions apart from their actual experiences concerning which emotions occur in particular situations. The situational knowledge about
emotional expressions precludes a logical necessity that emotional expressions are always elicited by a stimulus situation.

The knowledge that adults have about socially appropriate emotional
expressions in the context of particular situations can be demonstrated
in everyday examples such as we have already given (e.g., laughing at
jokes). A more direct test is to ask people directly about what emotions
or emotional expressions will occur in particular situations. Children's
knowledge about how other people will feel in certain situations is an
area of research that has received some attention because it overlaps
with two other important areas: the development of social knowledge
and empathy. Whether knowledge of others' feelings is derived through
empathy or other learning processes is a problem beyond the scope of
this chapter. Of specific interest to the present discussion are studies
showing that at relatively young ages children know about how others
feel in certain situations.

The source of children's situational knowledge about expressions may
be their understanding of facial or other expressive behaviors observed
in the situation rather than an explicit understanding of the emotions
associated with a situation per se. Thus, for example, children's knowledge about situations may be derived through their observation of an-

other person's behavior in a particular context (Feinman & Lewis, 1983; Lewis & Feiring, 1981). This observation of emotional expression may in turn provide information about the situation. Alternatively, children may understand the situational requirements *apart* from the participants' emotional expressions.

If we are primarily interested in what children know about when to express emotions and not whether children can recognize the expressions of others and associate them with situations, the studies most relevant to this knowledge are those that do not include emotional behaviors as cues to the emotion associated with the situation. In most research on this topic children are told a brief story and shown a picture of the situation (e.g., Borke, 1973; Feshbach & Roe, 1968). For example, the story might be about a birthday party or a broken toy. The subject is asked, "How does the child in the story feel?" Or, "How would you feel?" The extent to which the picture does not contain clues about emotional behavior is the extent to which the subjects' answer reflects knowledge of situations apart from knowledge of emotional expressions. The results of such studies suggest that by 4 years of age, and sometimes as young as 3, children can give what would be considered by adults to be the correct response to the situation (Borke, 1971, 1973; Mood, Johnson, & Shantz, 1974). In a review of this literature, Shantz (1975) suggests that simple situations eliciting happy responses are reliably understood by children as young as 4 years of age. Between 4 and 7 years children show an increasing ability to recognize situations eliciting fear, sadness, and anger.

Similar results are reported by Camras (personal communication), who interviewed kindergarten children about their knowledge of appropriate emotions in situations and the varying intensities of these emotions. Camras told the children a number of different stories, including the following: "My friend came home from school one day and his mother told him that the family dog had just had puppies. My friend didn't even know his dog was going to have puppies." The children were asked about the presence or absence of several emotions and about the intensity of the emotion ("a lot" or "a little"). The results indicated that the kindergarteners were able to judge both the presence and the intensity of the emotions that other children might have in various situations. They also recognized that more than one emotion may be elicited by a situation. In the example about the dog, the children reported the feelings associated with this situation included equal amounts of happiness and surprise and some disgust.

The process of identifying feelings appropriate to particular situations appears to be enhanced by a similarity between the subject and the child in the story. When the person in the situation is more like the subject (i.e., similar in age or gender), the subjects' ability in accurately reporting the emotion is facilitated (Shantz, 1975). Such findings suggest that empathy may be an important aspect of this process.

It is interesting to note that when both situational and facial cues are provided in the story, younger children tend to rely more on the information provided by the situational cue. Studies containing ambiguity because of a discrepancy between the situational and facial cues have shown that children differentially use situational and facial cues in judging the emotion of the person in the story. In one study preschool children were found to base their judgments more in accord with situational cues, whereas elementary school children used expressions more often (Burns & Cavey, 1957). Too few data exist on this topic to confirm a developmental trend, especially because there is evidence that adults, like the younger children, frequently use situational cues (Tagiuri, 1969) and that situational cues have a more powerful effect on adults' emotional response than do their own facial expressions (Laird, 1974). Nevertheless, regardless of the source, it appears that children as young as 4 years have already acquired some situational knowledge about when emotions occur.

In most studies of children's knowledge of emotions, investigators ask children to use verbal labels or line drawings rather than human facial expressions to identify the appropriate emotion. Rarely are children asked to identify how a human face would look in particular situations.

We tested a group of eight middle-class 2-year-olds about their understanding of other peoples' facial expressions. We showed the children Polaroid snapshots of a 10-year-old girl (Felicia) posing six different facial expressions. For each photograph we asked the subjects, "What kind of face is Felicia making? The array of faces included happy, sad, surprised, angry, fearful, and disgusted. After testing the 2-year-olds' ability to *produce* verbal labels for the faces (i.e., to label the faces), we tested their ability to *recognize* different facial expressions by asking them to point to the face that matched the emotional label provided by the experimenter. The correct face was embedded in a set of four different faces that were displayed in a photograph album. Each subject received two different orders of the recognition test. To receive a correct score for each face, the subject had to point to the correct face on both orders. The production and recognition tasks assessed the subjects' understanding of the verbal labels of emotion.

The next task we presented to the subjects tested their situational knowledge of emotional expressions. In this task we told the subjects stories in which the main character (Felicia) is involved in situations that are likely to elicit the emotions of happiness, sadness, anger, fear, surprise, and disgust. For example, in the "fear story" Felicia gets lost in a grocery store and cannot find her mother. For each story the subjects were shown (1) a simple drawing that illustrated the situation but in which the faces of the characters in the story were left blank and (2) four pictures of Felicia making different faces. The experimenter asked the subjects to point to the face Felicia made in the story. We also gave this test to 10 adults to compare the children's judgments of the situationally "appropriate" emotion with the adults' judgments.

The results showed that by 2 years, many children understand the verbal labels corresponding to the facial expressions of six basic emotions and that the ability to recognize the label–face relationship precedes the ability to produce the labels (see Figure 7.3). Although only 12%

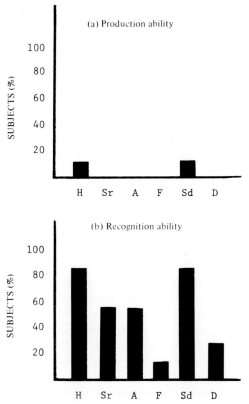

Figure 7.3. The ability of 2-year-olds to match verbal labels of emotions with facial expressions: happiness (H), surprise (Sr), anger (A), fear (F), sadness (S), and disgust (D).

of the 2-year-olds were able (and willing) to produce the labels "happy" and "sad," 86% could recognize the happy and sad faces. Likewise, 57% of the subjects recognized surprised and angry faces, although none could or would label these faces. Interestingly, only 14% could recognize the fearful face although 29% recognized the disgusted face.

In the situational knowledge test, between 25 and 71% of the 2-year-olds could select the appropriate face in the context of the happy, sad, and surprised situations. Their understanding of these situations paralleled the adults' understanding. The 2-year-olds did not understand the association between the disgusted face and the situation of eating a disliked food, an association that was agreed upon by 90% of the adults. The situations thought to elicit a fearful or an angry face also showed that at least some children by the time they are 2 years old have the same understanding as adults. More than 50% of the adult subjects did not associate the fear and anger situations with fearful and angry faces, respectively, which suggests that our choice of situations may not have been appropriate. For the fear situation, the adults were as likely to pick a sad face as they were to pick an angry face. The 2-year-olds showed this same tendency as well.

These data are also useful in understanding the socialization process that connects an expression to a particular situation (or elicitor). Although we thought the context "knocking over a tower of blocks" should elicit anger, the results suggest that individual subjects' socialization experiences can create elicitors that are idiosyncratic. For example, one 2-year-old subject selected a *happy* face as the expression that goes with the situation, "Sister knocks over Felicia's tower of blocks." Adults generally interpret this situation as either eliciting anger or sadness. From an adult's point of view, then, the 2-year-old who selected the happy face was wrong. However, the mother of this subject explained that at home they play knock-over-the-tower-of-blocks as a fun game. Thus, this subject's response is actually correct from the point of view of the personal context of the situation.

These data lend some support to the proposition that children acquire knowledge quite early about the contexts for socially appropriate emotional expressions. It is not known whether children in different cultures with different feeling rules have this same knowledge. To test the proposition, one would need to find two *different* cultural rules governing the expression of emotion within the same situation. For example, in the United States, when someone reaches a goal, "Be proud" is the rule. This emotion can be expressed through smiling and general excitement as well as verbally. In another culture, such as that of the Zuñi Indians, however, "Feel embarrassed" is the rule taught as the appropriate response to personal achievement (Benedict, 1934). The successful child here may be taught to lower the eyes, hang the head, and maintain a neutral mouth.

The socialization rules about how and when to express emotions, illustrated by the studies just described, are two topics in the study of the socialization of emotional expressions. The richest area on socialization effects is found in the literature on nonverbal communication (Harper, Wiens, & Matarazzo, 1978; Key, 1977; Knapp, 1978; Siegman & Feldstein, 1978; Weitz, 1974, 1979) and in Goffman's (1971) analysis of behavior in public places. One particular area of this literature in which the effects of socialization are most profound is the disassociation of vocal expressions from emotional states. If vocalizations are one component of emotional expression, then the reduction or elimination of vocal manifestations from emotional states or the alteration of vocal expressions to mask a particular internal state are important topics of investigation (Scherer, 1979, 1982; Streeter, Krauss, Geller, Olson, & Apple, 1977; Williams & Stevens, 1972).

The demonstration of socialization influences on expressive behaviors returns us to our original proposition, namely that facial expressions can be both signs and symbols. They are signs when there is a one-to-one correspondence between the expression and the internal state and they are what may be called symbols when the expression is unrelated to the underlying state.

Summary

In this chapter we argue that facial expressions must be viewed in terms of their functions both as signs and as symbols. Socialization rules are the forces that convert expressions from signs to symbols. A developmental sequence for the connection between facial expressions and internal emotional states is articulated based on the assumption that expressions and states are not necessarily or always connected to each other. Three periods in early development are described. In the first, which typically occurs between birth and 3 months of age, facial expressions are not synchronized with internal states. This lack of synchrony is posited on observations that although a variety of facial expressions can be observed early in infancy, the infant's internal emotional states are thought to be largely undifferentiated. In addition, very young infants lack the necessary cognitive prerequisites necessary to produce these faces in the absence of underlying internal states. The second period of emotional development is characterized by an integration of facial expressions and internal states. This integration, or the synchrony, is the result of biological programs, the development of particular cognitive structures, and important socialization factors that connect facial expressions to internal states. This period can be characterized for the most part by the statement, "What is expressed is what is felt." Yet during this same period, typically between 3 and 18 months of age, socialization forces are acting in such a way to disassociate facial expression from internal states. The third period of emotional development, then, is marked by an asynchrony between facial expressions and internal states as children practice the social rules that govern the expression of emotion in particular contexts. This period in emotional development, from 18 months onward, corresponds with the emergence of the child's sense of self and a notion of agency as well as an ability to engage in reciprocal relationships. Through these mediating structures—empathic behavior and a cognitive ability to judge what is appropriate—the child is able to disassociate facial expressions from internal feeling states. Although in the third period children are capable of separating many facial expressions from internal states, one cannot assume that they always do so. That is, facial expressions and states may be synchronous as well as asynchronous in the third period, depending on the circumstances and the child's understanding of the rules that govern the expression of emotion.

References

Benedict, R. Anthropology and the abnormal. *Journal of Genetic Psychology*, 1934, *10*, 59–82.

Borke, H. Interpersonal perception of young children: Egocentrism or empathy? *Developmental Psychology*, 1971, *5*, 263–269.

Borke, H. The development of empathy in Chinese and American children between three and six years of age: A cross-cultural study. *Developmental Psychology*, 1973, *9*, 102–108.

Bridges, K. M. B. Emotional development in early infancy. *Child Development*, 1932, *3*, 324–334.

Brooks-Gunn, J., & Lewis, M. Affective exchanges between normal and handicapped infants and their mothers. In T. Field & A. Fogel (Eds.), *Emotion and interaction: Normal and high-risk infants*. Hillsdale, NJ: Erlbaum, 1982.

Burns, N., & Cavey, L. Age differences in empathic ability among children. *Canadian Journal of Psychology*, 1957, *11*, 227–230.

Caudill, W., & Weinstein, H. Maternal care and infant behavior in Japan and America. *Psychiatry*, 1969, *32*, 12–43.

Ekman, P., & Friesen, W. The repertoire of nonverbal behavior: Categories, origins, usage, and coding. *Semiotica*, 1969, *1*, 49–98.

Ekman, P., Friesen, W., & Ellsworth, P. *Emotion in the human face.* New York: Pergamon, 1972.

Emde, R. N., Gaensbauer, T., & Harmon, R. Emotional expression in infancy: A biobehavioral study. *Psychological Issues,* 1976, *10*(1, Whole No. 37).

Emde, R. N., & Koenig, K. L. Neonatal smiling and rapid eye-movement states. *Journal of the American Academy of Child Psychiatry,* 1969, *8,* 57–67.

Feinman, S., & Lewis, M. Social referencing at ten months: A second-order effect on infants' responses to strangers. *Child Development,* 1983, *54,* 878–887.

Feiring, C., & Lewis, M. Sex and age differences in young children's reactions to frustration: A further look at the Goldberg and Lewis subjects. *Child Development,* 1979, *50,* 848–853.

Feshbach, N. D., & Roe, K. Empathy in six- and seven-year-olds. *Child Development,* 1968, *39,* 133–145.

Geertz, C. *The interpretation of cultures.* New York: Basic, 1973.

Goffman, E. *Relations in public: Microstudies of the public order.* New York: Basic, 1971.

Harper, R. G., Weins, A. N., & Matarazzo, J. D. *Nonverbal communication: The state of the art.* New York: Wiley, 1978.

Izard, C. E. *The face of emotion.* New York: Appleton-Century-Crofts, 1971.

Izard, C. E. *Human emotions.* New York: Plenum, 1977.

Izard, C. E. On the development of emotions and emotion-cognitive relationships in infancy. In M. Lewis & L. A. Rosenblum (Eds.), *The development of affect.* New York: Plenum, 1978.

Izard, C. E., & Dougherty, L. M. Two complementary systems for measuring facial expressions in infants and children. In C. E. Izard (Ed.), *Measuring emotions in infants and children.* New York: Cambridge University Press, 1982.

Izard, C. E., Huebner, R. R., Risser, D., McGinnes, G. C., & Dougherty, L. M. The young infant's ability to produce discrete emotion expressions. *Developmental Psychology,* 1980, *16,* 132–140.

Key, M. R. *Nonverbal communication: A research guide and bibliography.* Metuchen, NJ: Scarecrow, 1977.

Knapp, M. L. *Nonverbal communication in human interaction* (2nd ed.). New York: Holt, 1978.

Laird, J. I. Self-attribution of emotion: The effects of expressive behavior on the quality of emotional experience. *Journal of Personality and Social Psychology,* 1974, *29,* 475–486.

Lewis, M., Brooks, J., & Haviland, J. Hearts and faces: A study in the measurement of emotion. In M. Lewis & L. Rosenblum (Eds.), *The development of affect.* New York: Plenum, 1978.

Lewis, M. & Feiring, C. Direct and indirect interaction in social relationships. In L. Lipsett (Ed.), *Advances in infancy research* (Vol. 1). New York: Ablex, 1981.

Lewis, M., & Michalson, L. The socialization of emotions. In T. Field & A. Fogel (Eds.), *Emotion and early interaction.* Hillsdale, NJ: Erlbaum, 1982.

Lewis, M., & Michalson, L. *Children's emotions and moods: Developmental theory and measurement.* New York: Plenum, 1983.

Lewis, M., & Rosenblum, L. A. Introduction: Issues in affect development. In M. Lewis & L. A. Rosenblum (Eds.), *The development of affect.* New York: Plenum, 1978.

Malatesta, C. Z., & Haviland, J. M. Learning display rules: The socialization of emotional expression in infancy. *Child Development,* 1982, *53,* 991–1003.

Michalson, L., & Lewis, M. What do children know about emotional expressions and when do they know it? In M. Lewis & C. Saarni (Eds.), *The socialization of affect.* New York: Plenum, in press.

Mood, D., Johnson, J., & Schantz, C. U. *Affective and cognitive components of empathy in young children.* Paper presented at the Southeast Regional Meeting of the Society for Research in Child Development, Chapel Hill, NC, 1974.

Oster, H. Facial expression and affect development. In M. Lewis & L. A. Rosenblum (Eds.), *The development of affect.* New York: Plenum, 1978.

Oster, H., & Ekman, P. Facial behavior in child development. In A. Collins (Ed.), *Minnesota symposia on child psychology* (Vol. 11). Hillsdale, NJ: Erlbaum, 1978.

Saarni, C. Children's understanding of display rules for expressive behavior. *Developmental Psychology*, 1979, *15*, 424–429.

Saarni, C. *Observing children's use of display rules: Age and sex differences.* Paper presented at the Annual Meeting of the American Psychological Association, Montreal, September 1980.

Saarni, C. Social and affective functions of nonverbal behavior: Developmental concerns. In R. Feldman (Ed.), *Development of nonverbal behavior.* New York: Springer-Verlag, 1982.

Scherer, K. R. Nonlinguistic vocal indicators of emotion and psychopathology. In C. E. Izard (Ed.), *Emotions in personality and psychopathology.* New York: Plenum, 1979.

Scherer, K. R. The assessment of vocal expressions in infants and children. In C. E. Izard (Ed.), *Measuring emotions in infants and children.* New York: Cambridge University Press, 1982.

Shantz, C. U. The development of social cognition. In E. M. Hetherington (Ed.), *Review of child development research.* Chicago, IL: University of Chicago Press, 1975.

Siegman, A. W., & Feldstein, S. (Eds.), *Nonverbal behavior and communication.* Hillsdale, NJ: Erlbaum, 1978.

Sroufe, L. A. Socioemotional development. In J. D. Osofsky (Ed.), *Handbook of infant development.* New York: Wiley, 1979.

Streeter, L. A., Krauss, R. M., Geller, V., Olson, C., & Apple, W. Pitch changes during attempted deception. *Journal of Personality and Social Psychology*, 1977, *35*, 345–350.

Tagiuri, R. Person perception. In G. Lindzey & E. Aronson (Eds.), *The handbook of social psychology* (Vol. 3). Reading, MA: Addison-Wesley, 1969.

Weitz, S. *Nonverbal communication: Readings with commentary.* New York: Oxford University Press, 1974.

Weitz, S. *Nonverbal communication: Readings with commentary* (2nd ed.). New York: Oxford University Press, 1979.

Williams, C. E., & Stevens, K. N. Emotions and speech: Some acoustical correlates. *Journal of the Acoustical Society of America*, 1972, *52*, 1238–1250.

Wolff, P. H. Observations on the early development of smiling. In B. M. Foss (Ed.), *Determinants of infant behavior* (Vol. 2). New York: Wiley, 1963.

PART II

Processes of Expressive Development in Humans

Chapter 8

Developmental Course of Emotion Expression in the Human Infant*

Carol Zander Malatesta

Relationship to Other Chapters and to the Field

Relevant Issues in the Field

Malatesta's summary of emotional and expressive development in the infant's first year furnishes an unusual degree of detail for the most frequent general model of biology–environment interaction in expressive development: the model of environmental forces increasingly acting upon biological givens. Malatesta's view stands out from others' by invoking the strongest and most active biological component and by articulating many precise points at which biological and environmental forces come together. She draws her information on biological factors from reviewing work on neuroanatomy, embryology, hormonal influence, and ethological thinking. Her ideas on learning factors in early socialization come from her own naturalistic observations of mother–infant interaction. She synthesizes the trends in the first year of expressive development into three stages during which socialization factors become continuously and specifiably more influential.

*The writing of this chapter was supported in part by an NIMH National Research Service Award 1 F32 MH08773-01 and a grant from the Foundation for Child Development.

THE DEVELOPMENT OF EXPRESSIVE BEHAVIOR: BIOLOGY-ENVIRONMENT INTERACTIONS   183

Relationship to Other Chapters

Contrast with the chapter by Lewis and Michalson (Chapter 7) occurs on many parallel points. Both see their theories of expressive development as built upon their theories of emotional development. Whereas Lewis and Michalson acknowledge a definite role for inherited biological predisposition to response tendencies, Malatesta is more precise about the multiplicity of biological schedules and mediators, more insistent on the presence of differentiated emotional states in early infancy, and she sees their effects as considerably longer term in shaping the course of development. Lewis and Michalson attribute the guiding organization of emotional–expressive development primarily to the confluence of learning experiences, while Malatesta attributes it to a biological schedule that opens to facilitate the cascade of new learning processes and experiences. Lewis and Michalson assert that there is no inherited correspondence either between emotional state and expressive behavior or between emotional experience and expressive behavior; for them the task of development is to bring them all together and then to learn to separate them under voluntary control, in accord with cultural rules. Malatesta assumes that emotional experience comes out of an emotional state and that both innately coincide with some expressive behaviors; for her the task of development is more simply to learn to separate them under voluntary control, also in accord with cultural rules.

Malatesta's strong position, assuming the presence of rather differentiated emotional states and their innate pairing with categorical behaviors in the young infant, also contrasts with other contributors who question the traditional concept of state in expression. These are Mason (see Chapter 6) and Feinman (see Chapter 12), who emphasize the role of differentiated cognition which may or may not determine states on the way to generating expressive behaviors, and Smith (Chapter 3), who analyzes the internal condition that is correlated with animal signalling as more physiological–motivational than emotional. It is interesting to note a different contrast with Dolgin and Azmitia (Chapter 13). Although their position is approximately as richly biological as is Malatesta's, Malatesta is more ready to accept others' evidence of neonatal ability to perceive categorically emotional facial expressions.

In this chapter, Malatesta makes explicit application to expressive-behavior development of Thelen's (Chapter 9) earlier characterization of infant motor stereotypies. She sees in Thelen's ideas a type of early behavior that has the complexity and gradual malleability that fits the expressive behavior of the young infant. Thelen details this process of gradual control in her chapter's interpretation of stereotypies as expressive behaviors, and Fogel (Chapter 10), in concord with Malatesta, further builds on Thelen's stereotypes as revealing the integrative structure underlying coordinated emotional expressions.

For Consistent Terminology

As do many writers in the field, Malatesta uses emotion *and* affect *interchangeably. That is how they appear throughout this volume, although* affect *includes inner states beyond emotions.*—ED.

Introduction

Donald Hebb once summarized the plight of the nature–nurture controversy within developmental psychology by equating it with the task of trying to determine how much of a playing field is due to its length and how much to its width. More recently Wachs and Gruen (1982) have dismissed the controversy as "irrelevant, immaterial, and wasteful of scientific time." It is obvious, they go on to say "that both heredity and environment play a part in the developmental process . . . and the critical question is not so much which is more relevant but rather *how biology and environment interact to influence development*" (p. 11). While we are essentially in agreement with their disposition, we would modify the critical question to include attention to how these factors interact at *varying points* in the developmental course. We can assume that the relative weights of these developmental factors vary as a consequence of the maturity of the organism as well as changes in the environment, because the environment includes other living beings (like caregivers) who are themselves modifiable.

In this chapter we discuss the nature of biological factors and social forces that determine the course of development in a selected domain of behavior, that of emotion expression. Discussion is restricted to the period of infancy because that is where our most recent and substantive advances in understanding the nature of organism–environment interactions have been made. To be sure, infancy is a particularly exciting time of development both for parents and for students of behavior because it encompasses a period of rapid and dramatic behavioral change and a chance to examine the interpenetration of the dual developmental forces of biology and socialization.

This chapter is organized around the assumption that there are a variety of biological and social inputs that determine emotion expression, each making its own unique contribution. However, we also assume that emotional development involve stagelike changes in both the formal and the functional aspects of behavior and that it is the distinctive *pattern* of interplay among maturational and environmental factors at different points in time that serves to distinguish one developmental period from another.

For the aforementioned reasons we first examine the various contributions of biological and social forces individually and then consider their mutual interaction. Before we begin, however, it is necessary to address certain theoretical issues—issues that are invariably invoked whenever the nature of emotional development in infants is considered.

Theoretical Considerations

It is helpful to start with a general discussion of the nature of the affect system before proceeding to a discussion of the unique issues that inhere in any consideration of infant emotion.

The Nature of the Affect System

The *affect system* shows features of both innateness and modifiability. The *innate* features are directed by genetic programs; the *malleable* aspects derive from programmed allowances for learning, or developmental modifiability, at least for some parameters of emotion expression. *Genetically determined* aspects of development include provisions for (1) innate elicitors of affective reactions (e.g., distress crying associated with hunger sensations; smiling associated with tactile and social stimulation; disgust expressions associated with noxious substances), (2) innately determined morphology of expressions before learned modifications have occurred (e.g., the "classic" anger or fear face), (3) a natural coherence (at least initially) between state and behavior (distress feelings associated with distress crying), and (4) predictable timetables for the initial emergence in behavior of discrete patterns of emotional behavior (for example, cross-cultural concurrences in the time of emergence and peak of infant smiling and separation anxiety, as reported by Super & Harkness, 1982). Elements of *developmental modifiability* include (1) capacity for acquiring *learned* elicitors of affect (e.g., fear reactions associated with furry objects such as white rats), and (2) modification of expressive behavior through instrumental learning and exercise of deliberate control (developing idiosyncratic facial mannerisms or learning to dissimulate).

In combination, early genetic programs and later developmental modifiability assure a tremendously adaptive behavioral system. Genetic predispositions impose limits on phenotypic diversity, thereby preserving the adaptive social significance of expressive behavior. Unbridled phenotypic variation in eliciting conditions, in pattern and timing of emotion expression, in morphology of expression, and in linkage between state and behavior would render the human social world functionally chaotic. (See Smith, Chapter 3, this volume, for an evolutionary-semiotic analysis to a similar conclusion for vertebrate state–signal relations in general.) If, for example, the link between particular states and particular expressive behaviors were random, the usefulness of emotion expressions as social signals indicating motivational states and response probabilities would be completely foregone. In such a world, a person who said they loved you might be just as likely to beat you as to embrace you.

On the other hand, developmental modifiability in the use and control of certain emotional expressions, for example, ensures a fit between individuals and their social niche. The pursuit and expression of happiness is taken for granted in certain cultures and even guaranteed by constitutional law in one but in others suppression of excited positive affect may be the norm, especially in cultures characterized by a high population density or extreme economic or emotional interdependence; under such conditions, calm rather than elated behavior is more adaptive, in that it helps deter occasions for escalation of feelings, loss of control, and resultant interpersonal strife (Lutz, 1982; Malatesta & Haviland, in press).

In sum, there are adaptive advantages to both prewiring and later contextual flexibility. Genetically-derived programs may direct behavior initially, ensuring a certain degree of universality in the expression of emotion among individuals reared in disparate environments, but cultural norms and social-learning experiences provide the occasion and developmental modifiability that means to modify the original programs while preserving their fundamentally adaptive nature.

The Nature of Infant Affect

Affect theorists generally make a distinction between the various components or aspects of emotion, the most general distinction being that between expressive behavior and feeling. It is our practice in this chapter to use the terms *affect* and *emotion* to refer to the general system. The terms *emotional* (or *affective*) *expression* refers to the motoric, behavioral responses and *state* or *feeling* refers to the internal, subjectively experienced component.

There are several issues related to infant emotion and to the distinction between feeling and expression that require some discussion before we proceed to a presentation of our model of infant expressive development. These issues concern (1) whether or not infants have feelings and when they might first experience them, (2) the hierarchical organization of units of motoric-expressive behavior and their integration with feeling components, and (3) the importance of the signal value of affect for the detection, the interpretation, and ultimately, the transformation of feeling. We consider each of these issues in turn.

Do Infants Have Feelings?

The feeling component of emotion, historically, has given the field of emotions research more trouble than might seem reasonable. From the collective assaults of the reductionism of late introspectionism, through the virtual obliteration of feeling from stimulus–response (S–R) psychology, and to its cerebralization in the hands of cognitive psychology, it is a small wonder that the feeling component of emotion has survived at all as a conceptual entity in psychological theory. The issue of feeling is especially problematic in infancy research because inferences about what appear to be feelings cannot be verbally confirmed by the infant, and the very *unformedness* of infants makes them appear to be not yet quite human and therefore incapable of emotion. It is somewhat of an irony that although adult self-reports of emotional feeling are often discounted because of the sophistication of the organism and the capacity to dissimulate, infant feelings are suspect because of the naïveté of the organism.

As a rule, people in Western societies, especially psychologists, expect infants to be affectless (Haviland, 1976). As Haviland notes, "pleasurable affects are thought to be 'gaseous' until linked to eye contact and the mother's smile" (p. 375). Many theorists concerned with emotions or emotion–cognitive development defer the emergence of feeling until several months into development (Sroufe, 1979) or even later, into the second half of the first year of life (Kagan, in press, Lewis & Brooks, 1978); Emde, Kligman, Reich, & Wade, 1978). Lewis and Michalson (1983, and Chapter 7, this volume) suggest a complex course to coordinate feelings or emotional experiences with states and expressive behaviors. The justification for deferring emotion until later in infancy has rested on citing the cognitive immaturity of the young infant and on assuming a dependence of affect upon cognition. Such assumptions have been challenged, with some psychologists willing to concede the likelihood that emotions may be capable of functioning independently of cognition and that infants do indeed experience some form of emotional feeling well within the opening months of life (Chevalier-Skolnikoff, 1973; Demos, 1982a, 1982b; Fogel, 1982, Izard, in press; Malatesta & Haviland, in press). Rarely, however, has this assumption been substantiated by more than intuition. It is probably the case that a solution to the problem lies outside the realm of confirmation by behavioral psychologists and must await developments in the field of neurophysiology. For example, if one were to adduce evidence of localized neural activation with a subjective report of an adult on his or her feeling and also were able to find a similar localized site of activation under appropriate eliciting conditions in the infant, the position would be empirically strengthened, although not entirely resolved. In the meantime, we must rely on inference and intuition, although Izard (in press) has advanced a persuasive argument based on analogy. Izard views early infant affect as a type of sensory information that the brain utilizes in its interaction with the environment, much like taste or other sensory experience. In the case of emotion, the relevant sensory experience consists of neural events associated with motor-expressive behavior, such as feedback from contraction of the facial muscles. What emotion sensation and gustatory sensation have in common is that they both provide the organism with cues that can guide approach and avoidance behavior—experiences that are basic to animal adaptation. Like gustatory experience, emotion may exist at the subjective-experiential level as feeling that can occur in consciousness without being symbolized or represented cognitively. Early emotion-expressive behavior (such as the endogenous smile) is probably processed in the brain stem, but, as with gustation, an intact limbic system is probably necessary for the generation of motivational feeling states. Although the limbic system is not completely myelinated in the human infant at birth (Konner, 1982), the limbic brain is capable of conducting impulses, nevertheless, and myelinization proceeds apace between the second and tenth postnatal months.

To return to the question of whether or not infants have feelings, we conclude this section by acknowledging that this is a highly controversial issue, an issue that is patently unresolvable at the present state of empirical knowledge. However, it is our preference to make the assumption that infants *do* have feeling states, rather than that they do not, and moreover, that there is a correspondence between feeling states and motor expressive behavior. First, infants display facial behaviors that bear a striking resemblance to facial patterns of emotion in adults (Izard, 1978; Malatesta & Haviland, 1982); in adults these differential facial patterns are associated with differential emotional states at least when the expressive behaviors are spontaneous and not dissimulated

(Izard, 1971, 1977). Secondly, infant facial and vocal behaviors *appear* to index emotional states because interpretations of state by caregivers based on these behaviors (Emde, 1980) are normally reinforced by subsequent infant behaviors. For example, behavioral interventions by caregivers, designed to correct inferred negative emotional disturbances, effectively terminate the negative expressive behavior. That is, certain infant facial and vocal behaviors are commonly interpreted by mothers as signs of their infants' subjective distress, and the mothers then make appropriate interventions. Such interventions are typically rewarded by the cessation of infant distress behavior, thereby increasing the likelihood of similar sequences in the future. To take an unlikely contrast, if distressed facial and vocal behaviors were instead interpreted as signs of pleasure or as completely meaningless activity, there would be eventual extinction of the distress behavior, not to mention the baby itself. Finally, Izard's analogy serves as a useful reminder that emotion has a sensory component. Such elemental experience is probably independent of cognitive appraisal. Although adult emotional experience is frequently imbued with all kinds of cognitive embroidery, cognitive activity is not *prerequisite* for emotional responding, as Zajonc (1980, in press) and others have substantiated. Physical parameters of stimuli, alone, are capable of arousing behavioral dispositions. There is no reason to believe that this is not the case with infants as well. However, this is *not* to claim that the quality of emotional experience in infants is the same as that experienced by adults. It is surely different, given the different levels of consciousness available to infants versus adults.

In contrast to the previously mentioned position, some psychologists argue that infants do not have feeling states and that they must acquire them developmentally. Others argue that the relationship between feeling states and facial behaviors is originally disjoint and that the developmental task of childhood is to acquire a coordination between state and behavior. These arguments are counterintuitive and more developmentally complicated than seem warranted.

First, to argue that children must *acquire* feelings begs the question of who will teach them. As Zajonc (1980) has pointed out, feelings are among the most difficult experiences for adults to describe. Our verbal descriptions surely do not match the complexity of experience each of us is capable of having. Where does such complexity come from and are we really dependent on others to teach us these subtleties? It seems more reasonable to assume that feelings are inherent to human nature and that the process of development is one of struggling to learn more articulate ways of describing our experiences.

The argument that state and behavior are originally independent, that they are disjoint and that development consists of learning to bring these two aspects together (Lewis & Michalson, 1983; Chapter 7, this volume) is at variance with research on children's comprehension of and observance of display rules (Demos, 1974; Saarni, 1979, 1982). The developmental task of childhood appears to be one of learning *dissimulation* and this appears to require a great deal of skill. *Coherence* between state and behavior is easy, according to the work of Demos (1974) and Saarni (1979), it is dissimulation that is difficult and attendant on the maturation of cognitive skills. A young child presented with a disappointing gift is not likely to smile and accept it gracefully but to react with expressed anger, disappointment, or distress. It is only later that these immediate feeling–behavior reactions are controlled and emotion is masked. It seems unnecessarily complicated and at variance with the developmental continuities that are found in other subsystems of personality to assume that state and behavior are disjoint during infancy, become coupled sometime thereafter, resist uncoupling until late childhood, and then become behaviorally variable once again.

The foregoing discussion of issues concerning infant feeling and the relationship between state and behavior serves as a notice of theoretical bias. Additional empirical evidence to support the preceding assumptions is presented in the next two sections.

The Motor Side: Early Infant Affect as Complex Reflexive Behavior

Developmentalists have long alluded to the reflexive quality of early infant affect. References to neonatal-gustofacial responses (Steiner, 1965), to startle and interest responses (Herzka, 1965), to REM-state smiles, frowns, and grimaces (Emde, Gaensbauer, & Harmon, 1976), indicate that the motor components of at least some of the fundamental human emotions (i.e., the *categorical* emotion expressions of distress, disgust, and so forth) exist from the earliest days of birth, and there is even evidence of their existence prenatally as evidenced by ultrasound pictures of infant facial expressions in utero (Field, personal communication, 1982). To some psychologists, these early behaviors appear to be analogous to the classic infant reflexes of rooting, stepping, and the startle response, and devoid of any real affective content (Malatesta & Haviland, in press). However, to our mind, these expressive behaviors have qualities that would distinguish them from other early infant reflexes, as discussed later.

It may be helpful to consider facial motor behaviors as a subclass of motor behaviors and to consider motor development from a larger developmental perspective. In a recent article on rhythmical stereotypies, Thelen (1981; Chapter 9, this volume) presents a general model of motor development during infancy that provides a useful way of thinking about the expressive aspect of affective behavior. Rhythmical stereotypies are a class of spontaneously emitted repetitive motor behaviors such as rocking, waving, bouncing, banging, rubbing, scratching, and swaying. Thelen proposes that infant *rhythmical stereotypies* are a preprogrammed source of timing mechanisms for gross motor behavior, which, in combination with simple motor reflexes of the classic type, make up the essential subroutines for the assembly of coordinated movements. They are, in essence, early building blocks for more complex and variable motor behavior to be seen later in development. These behaviors are distinguished from simple reflexes in two ways: (1) in the nature of their developmental profiles and (2) in terms of their eliciting circumstances.

1. **Developmental profiles:** Most simple infant reflexes appear during the neonatal stage and largely disappear by the end of the second month. In contrast, the various stereotypies have developmentally different timetables, depending on the complexity of the stereotypy and degree of neuromuscular maturation necessary for its expression. For example, stereotypies involving the legs begin gradually increasing at about 1 month and peak at 5–6 months, whereas those involving the arms gradually increase with age also but have a later age of onset and peak.

2. **Eliciting circumstances:** The simple reflexes of infancy are released by highly specific stimuli, whereas rhythmical stereotypies are typically reactive to a wide variety of relatively nonspecific stimuli and internal states. For example, the rooting reflex is elicited by gentle pressure applied to the infant's cheek or lip. On the other hand, rhythmical cycling or kicking of the legs can be elicited by a variety of arousing circumstances—approach of a caregiver, intensifying hunger, etc.

With the foregoing distinctions in mind, early infant affective expressions seem to conform more to the more complex rhymical stereotypies of infancy than to the simple reflexes of the opening weeks. In the first place, emergence of the "fundamental" emotions have different developmental timetables, with some in evidence within the first few days of life and others taking months to become manifest. Second, the various facial expressions of emotion are each capable of being elicited by a variety of eliciting circumstances. Smiles can be elicited by the right pattern of light–dark contrast, simple patterns of dots or angles, objects suddenly moving into the visual field, pleasurable tactile sensations, and so forth. Fear responses can be elicited by looming objects, the perception of the deep side of the visual cliff, strangers, and so on.

The motoric expression of emotion in young infants also bears a resemblance to rhythmical stereotypies on other counts, in its early rhythmical or cyclical manifestations, in its resemblance to transitional behavior and in terms of its capacity for instrumental conditioning. The rhythmical nature of early infant crying has been noted by Wolff (1966), Emde, Gaensbauer, and Harmon (1976) and Tronick, Als, and Adamson (1979); crying fluctuates rhythmically within crying bouts, and early unexplained fussiness has a diurnal rhythmicity. Oster (1978) has noted the cyclic nature of brow knitting and smiling in young infants.

The term *transition behavior* is used by Thelen (1981) to represent a stage in motor maturation that is more complex than spontaneous motility or simple spinal reflexes, yet is less variable and less flexible than that of fully voluntary behavior. While they are available, stereotypies are released by generalized arousal shifts triggered by relevant exogenous or endogenous stimuli. As structures mature and adaptive needs change developmentally, the relevance or potency of a particular stimulus for eliciting the motor behavior also changes. This would seem to apply to early affective behavior as well. The developmental course of smiling is from weakly articulated REM-state smiles (Emde *et al.*, 1976; Oster, 1978) through exogenously elicited but nonspecific smiles, to the social smile. Crying proceeds from distress crying to a wide variety of stimuli, through a long interval of unexplained fussiness, to more differentiated cries of hunger, pain, and anger (Malatesta, 1981; Wolff, 1966), and finally to instrumental crying.

Stereotypies are also viewed as primary operants for the development of more complex, coordinated motor acts. Like other forms of unlearned, spontaneous behavior, the rhythmical stereotypies may be brought under control of environmental contingencies to produce more developmentally mature behavior. For example, the rhythmical stereotypic kicking of infants exposed to contingent movement of an attractive mobile will develop instrumental kicking (Thelen & Fisher, 1983). Thelen suggests that the process of molding instrumental behavior from wired-in components may be the very prototype of motor skill learning. Early infant motoric components of emotional behavior once again appear to conform to the preceding model. Smiles given in response to patterns of dots and angles and to moving objects (Ahrens, 1954; Wolff, 1966) would seem to be more developmentally complex than the apparently spontaneous discharges seen during the REM state, and yet they are nonspecific and do not appear to be under voluntary control. It also appears that simple emotional expressions that are elicited by nonspecific stimuli may become operants conditioned to a variety of specific internal and external contingencies, as discussed in a later section.

In sum, the early expressions of affect have a reflexlike quality, but they appear to be more complex than simple infant reflexes. These behaviors may be seen as transition behaviors, organized patterns of response given to a wide array of stimuli. They stand midway between random, spontaneously generated responses and the more mature forms of instrumental behavior.

The fact that early infant affect is more reactive (reflexive) than voluntary is no grounds for ruling out an experiential component. Even the limbic brain of young infants is capable of conducting impulses and therefore capable of generating motivational feeling states, as discussed earlier.

The Signal Value of Affect

Infants make a variety of potentially informative facial expressions, and it is this overt aspect of infant affect that has important social consequences. Although psychologists, historically, have been reluctant to assign meaning to the expressions of young infants, it is clear that caregivers do not share this reticence and that they use facial expressions and other expressive behaviors to make inferences about infant state. As Emde and colleagues have documented (Emde, 1980; Emde et al., 1978), mothers and other individuals experienced with children readily apply almost the entire range of categorical emotional expressions to infants upwards of 2 months of age, including enjoyment, interest, distress, surprise, shame, disgust, anger, fear, passive–bored, and sleepy.

Buck (1981) has hypothesized that emotion has evolved as a process by which central nervous system (CNS) mechanisms dealing with homeostasis and adaptation signal or "read out" their condition, both internally to the subjective consciousness of the responder and externally to others via expressive behavior. Selection pressures would favor those infants who more accurately communicated their emotional and motivational states to their caregivers, who could then intervene to correct homeostatic imbalance. Other factors favoring read-out of emotion include the facilitation of bonding. Mothers of children with flattened affect, such as Down's syndrome babies and blind infants, often report difficulty in establishing a sense of rapport and bondedness (Emde, Katz, & Thorpe, 1978; Fraiberg, 1979).

The very fact of the baby's overt expressive behavior and the maternal tendency to draw attention to it by verbal or nonverbal commentary (Malatesta & Haviland, 1982) serves to bring emotion into the public domain, where it may be subject to further scrutiny, comment, and socialization.

The preceding discussion of the nature of affect and the nature of infant affect serves to illustrate the levels at which emotion may be considered to function. In the course of discussing these issues we began to touch upon some of the biological and social parameters that define the ontological course of emotion expression development. With this as a preface, let us now turn to a more detailed examination of the developmental inputs. We begin with biological factors because they have at least initial chronological primacy, and then discuss the social inputs and mechanisms of emotion socialization.

Developmental Inputs

Biological Factors: The Universal Features

Basic Neuromuscular Equipment and Programs

The basic neuromuscular equipment necessary for the reception of emotional stimuli and for the performance of emotional responses includes perceptual, motor, and central components. According to Carmichael's (1970) law of anticipatory function in prenatal neurogenesis, many structures that later become adaptive responses in organisms are functional at a period somewhat prior to the time they are actually called into use; this critical preadaptation prepares the animal to survive and to lead a life that is characteristic of its species. It is perhaps a testimony to the crucial adaptive importance of the affective system that infants enter the world rather well equipped to process and respond to affective stimuli, and to communicate their own emotional states.

Human infants demonstrate a precocial pattern of sensory development. All their sensory systems are capable of at least rudimentary function at birth and some systems, such as the vestibular, are rather well developed (Werner & Lipsitt, 1981). This means that the early elicitors of affect—sounds, tactile and vestibular sensations, pain, and visual events—can be detected and processed, at least at an elementary level. Neonates are also capable of signaling motorically what appear to be emotional states because the facial muscles and nerves innervating them are sufficiently developed and differentiated at birth and have reached their definitive points of insertion in the tissue of the skin by 18–29 weeks of gestation (Oster & Ekman, 1977). Oster (1978) has demonstrated that virtually all the component muscle-movement units of adult facial-emotional expressions can be identified in the facial movements of both premature and full-term infants and that the facial muscle actions of young infants are often well defined and highly discriminable, even when occurring in complex patterned configurations.

In addition to the preceding neuromuscular hardware, emotion expression apparently depends on central neural programs for the integration of elicitors and responses. Tomkins (1962, 1963) and Izard (1971, 1977) have proposed that there exist emotion-specific programs for the articulation of discrete emotional responses stored within subcortical regions of the brain. The very early emergence of the fundamental human emotions and their stereotypy across cultures would seem to support such a thesis (Ekman & Oster, 1979; Izard, 1977). Not only does the young infant possess the necessary neural equipment for emotion expression and experience (hindbrain structures for the detection of natural elicitors of emotion and for the execution of motoric patterns [see Isaacson, 1982] and limbic structures for the sensory motivational component), he or she actually does *show* the features we most associate with the emotions and shows them very early in life.

Discrete Expressions in Neonates and Older Infants

Reports of infant expressive capabilities rely on the use of objective coding systems that involve component analysis of facial expressions or that look for feature changes that are characteristic of the individual emotions. According to Izard (1978), the expressions of interest, joy, physical distress, and disgust can be seen during the neonatal period. Field and Walden (in press), observing the facial expressions of neonates undergoing the Brazelton examination procedures, also report the expressions of sadness and surprise. Malatesta and Haviland (1982) have coded anger responses in three-month-olds after separation from mothers who did not immediately pick them up upon reunion, and Stenberg (1982) has coded anger expressions in four-month-olds in response to mild limb restraint. Components of the fear expression have not been reliably coded until after 6 months of age (Izard, 1978).

The relatively late appearance of anger and of fear deserves further comment. It cannot be ascertained whether neural programs for fear and for anger are simply not mature during the opening weeks of life or whether the appropriate incentives have not been utilized under conditions of experimental elicitation. Earlier observers have reported anger and fear reactions in neonates (e.g., Watson, 1919; Stirnimann, 1940), though it is not always clear what aspects of behavior were used to infer these states. Moreover, eliciting conditions were sometimes more drastic than those commonly employed today (sudden loss of support, a push or shake); such studies are not likely to be replicated with the blessing of human subjects committees. Full-blown fear responses in the natural world are usually reserved for life-threatening circumstances that we are not likely to impose on anyone, much less young infants; eliciting conditions that might justifiably incite anger in extremely young infants would also be reluctantly imposed for experimental purposes. A study of abused infants, however, suggested evidence of fear responses much earlier than is usually reported (Gaensbauer, 1980). It is thus a moot point whether fear and anger responses require sophisticated forms of appraisal as some psychologists have suggested.

Elicitors of Discrete Emotions

Both Izard (1971, 1977) and Tomkins (1962, 1963) have suggested that there are a host of natural, unlearned elicitors of affect. Moreover, Tomkins (1962) has proposed a neural model that specifies a hypothesized relationship between gradients of stimulation and rates of neural firing, and emotional responses. In brief, this theory holds that it is the rate or density of neural firing in response to the timing, gradient, and quality of elicitors that serves to distinguish the various categorical emotions. A decrease in neural firing is said to elicit joy and laughter, whereas increase in neural firing produces interest, startle, or fear, depending on the rate at which stimulation or neural firing increases. Anger and distress are activated by continuing unrelieved levels of stimulation (with higher density of chronic stimulation needed for anger than for distress). Assumedly physical as well as psychological stimuli provoke neural firing, and different types of physical and psychological stimuli provoke different rates of firing. This theory, then, would predict that early infant affect would be almost exclusively elicited by physical stimuli and only later by psychological stimuli. Ontogenetically, this theory seems to fit the data. The spontaneous elicitors of affect in young infants are, in fact, various types of physical stimulation. Simple visual stimuli involving patterns of dots or angles can produce smiling, (Ahrens, 1954) as can an inanimate object suddenly moving into the visual field (Wolff, 1966); certain types of tactile stimulation, depending on intensity, can produce smiles or laughter (Sroufe & Wunsch, 1972; Guillory, Self, Biscoe, & Cole, 1982; Washburn, 1929). Auditory stimuli, depending on their onset, intensity, and pitch values, can elicit the startle response, smiling, and laughter (Guillory et al., 1982; Cicchetti & Hesse, 1983). Various visual events such as looming stimuli and the gradients associated with depth, as well as loud auditory events, can elicit fear (Campos & Stenberg, 1981; Cicchetti & Hesse, 1983). Sudden loud noises tend to produce startle responses. Distress crying is provoked by chronic unrelieved pain, hunger, and certain auditory events such as the crying of other infants (Sagi & Hoffman, 1976; Cicchetti & Hesse, 1983; Martin & Clark, 1982). Anger can be produced by sustained physical restraint (Wiesenfeld, Malatesta, & Deloach, 1981; Stenberg, 1982) and by low-level distress that persists over a prolonged period of time (Malatesta & Haviland, 1982).

Note that all of the aforementioned stimuli are strictly physical in nature. The type or quality of emotional response is conceivably related to the gradient features of the stimuli, such as level of intensity, rise time, and chronicity—exactly the parameters described by Tomkins (1962). The band of stimulation necessary to elicit a certain type of response may be narrowly defined. Not all tactile stimulation will produce smiling. There seems to be an upper and lower boundary. Low levels of stimulation may go undetected or may only elicit interest, whereas sufficiently strong tactile stimulation used to allay distress (as in the stroking or rocking of a colicky infant) may produce smiling; beyond a certain intensity level or a certain duration of stimulation, crying may be the result.

Later in development, physical stimuli remain potent elicitors of affective response, but now learned elicitors (previously neutral stimuli paired in time with innate elicitors) and psychological elicitors are also added in. Psychological elicitors involve psychological accomplishments such as the recognition of familiar persons (for the elicitation of smiling), the perception of strangeness (for the elicitation of fear), the perception of incongruity (for the elicitation of knit-browed perplexity or interest), and the resolution of incongruity (for the elicitation of joy), just to name some of the earliest psychological elicitors.

In summary, the very existence of early infant affect is dependent on mesencephalic and diencephalic brain structures, on sensory and motor components of the cranial nerves, and on sensitivity to the physical parameters of a wide band of stimuli. The specific nature of the response (smiling versus crying, for example) is presumed to be linked to both the gradient features of the stimuli and activation of discrete programs.

Hormone–Emotion Interactions

In this section we consider the impact of hormones on brain organization, on behavior, and on the emotional development of infants. We examine how hormones affect infant sensitivity to emotional stimuli as well as dictate patterns of behavioral response.

There are two broad classes of hormones within the neuroendocrine axis that have a rather profound effect on the organization of the brain and behavior with respect to emotions—those related to sexual development and those related to stress reactivity and management.

Hormones Affecting Sexual Differentiation and Development

Sex hormones have both organizational and activational effects on behavior (Beatty, 1979; Vernadakis & Timiras, 1982; Money, 1977). Organizational effects refer to early and enduring directive influences on brain development. Activational influences involve hormone interactions with the brain so as to modulate its immediate physiology. Organizational effects are seen primarily early in development, though changes in synaptic connections can occur throughout life. During gestation the presence of masculinizing hormones in the male fetus have a critical effect on the developing brain, transforming the basic pattern of female development into a specifically male program. As a result of this influx into the brain of steroid hormones from the gonads at developmentally critical points in gestation, and even shortly after birth in some species, actual structural changes take place in the male brain, not only in regions directly concerned with reproductive functions but in other areas as well. For example, grossly visible differences are known in the hypothalamus, the brain stem, and the spinal cord, and even the rate of maturation of the cerebral cortex is thought to differ between the genders (Beatty, 1979; Vernadakis & Timiras, 1982). More importantly for the present discussion, anatomical differences in the structure of the limbic system, a region of the brain known to be deeply involved in mediating emotional responses, have also been noted (Ehrhardt & Meyer-Bahlburg, 1981; Goldman, 1976; MacLean, 1973; Papez, 1937; Rubin, Reinisch, & Haskett, 1981). Papez, for example, in an early paper (1937), observed that in humans the precuneus region of the cingulate gyrus features a greater difference in size in the two genders than any other portion of the cortex and is more highly developed in the male; Papez suggested that the differences reflect a representation of the sex organs. Alternatively they may reflect structures subserving aggression; gender differences in aggression have been consistently documented and are among the most distinct behavioral differences in nonreproductive functions between the sexes (Maccoby & Jacklin, 1974, 1980). More subtle structural differences in the limbic brain at the level of the cell also have been reported (Goldman, 1976; Rubin et al., 1981).

The prenatal structural changes just cited set the stage for later activational differences between males and females that govern the pattern of gonodotrophin release from the pituitary gland, which determine whether there will be a steady or a cyclic pattern of secretion after puberty (Beach, 1976). Activational effects may exist prior to puberty as well. A number of investigators have determined differences in the concentration of testosterone in males and females during the newborn period (Forest, Sizonenko, Cathiard, & Bertrand, 1974; Maccoby, Doering, Jacklin, & Kraemer, 1979), with boys exposed to higher concentrations of circulating testosterone than girls. Testosterone production in males is said to peak postnatally towards the end of the first month of life (Beach, 1977). Interestingly, there are a number of gender-related differences in infant emotional behaviors, to be discussed later, and these may also be due to hormonal effects, although it is difficult to tell whether the observed differences in behavior reflect the impact of organizational or of activational influences. The very fact that gender-related differences in sensitivity to emotional stimuli and in emotional behavior show striking patterns of developmental continuity from infancy through childhood and into adulthood (Haviland & Malatesta, 1981) would seem to suggest that these differences owe their origin to organizational influences, although activational influences are not ruled out. The major gender differences in emotional behavior during infancy are subsequently described.

In surveying a wide array of empirical studies we find that there are early and clear differences in the socioemotional behaviors of male and of female infants. These are largely differences in state, in patterns of emotional expressivity, and in sensitivity to social and emotional stimuli.

Differences in State and Expressive Behavior

Boys appear to be more emotionally labile than girls, at least during the opening months of life. Young male infants show greater lability of state and a greater peak of excitement and rapidity to build up, as assessed by the Brazelton scale (Osofsky & O'Connell, 1977). They also show more facial grimacing (Phillips, King, & DuBois, 1978) and display a higher rate of facial emotional expression changes than do girls (Malatesta, 1980). Young males startle more readily than do females both during alert states and during sleep (Feldman, Brody, & Miller, 1980; Korner, 1969; Osofsky & Danzger, 1974; Osofsky & O'Connell, 1977), and they show more irritability and high-intensity crying (Crockenberg, 1982; Moss, 1967; Osofsky & O'Connell, 1977; Phillips et al., 1978). Once crying has begun, males are more difficult to sooth than females (Moss, 1967; Osofsky & O'Connell, 1977; Thoman, 1976).

Differences in Responsivity to Social Stimuli

Gender differences in responsiveness to social stimuli are found within the opening days of life. During neonatal assessment, female infants show greater orientation to faces and to the face combined with the voice (Osofsky & O'Connell, 1977). They also spend a greater percentage of eyes-open time in eye contact with an interacter, make more frequent eye contacts, and sustain eye contact for longer periods of time than do male infants (Hittleman & Dickes, 1979). By the time they are 3 to 6 months of age, girls show longer duration of visual fixation to photographs of faces and more smiling to realistic and distorted facial stimuli, although these differences are not pronounced (Kagan & Lewis, 1965; Lewis, 1969) perhaps owing to the artificial nature of the stimuli. Infant females in this age range, however, show a greater number of interest expressions when interacting with their mothers than do males. Differences in social responsiveness apparently persist into the second half year of life and beyond (Goldberg & Lewis, 1969; Gunnar & Donahue, 1980; Sorce & Emde, 1981; Sorce, Emde, & Klinnert, 1981; Stoller & Field, 1982; Tauber, 1979). Boys are shown to gaze avert more frequently from the opening days of life up through at least the second year of life (Hittleman & Dickes, 1979; Haviland & Lewis, 1976).

The two preceding sets of gender differences—those involving state and expressive behavior on the one hand and sensitivity to social and emotional stimuli on the other—are possibly connected. The greater lability of state and the greater irritability of male infants likely sets up conditions that operate against environmental sensitivity. Attention to commanding endogenous stimuli of necessity deflects attention from other events occurring externally. The interesting question residing in this difference in lability and in irritability is its origin. Studies of nonhuman primates also appear to demonstrate gender-linked differences in their pattern of early socioemotional behavior (Lewis & Sackett, 1980; Stevens & Mitchell, 1972), and Lewis and Sackett (1980) speculate that prenatal mechanisms, probably hormonal, underlie both male infant vulnerability and differential patterns of socioemotional response, an opinion with which we are in agreement.

Hormones Affecting Stress Management

Adrenocorticotropic hormone (ACTH) is released from the pituitary in response to environmental stressors; when it reaches the adrenal cortex through circulation, it stimulates the secretion of cortisol, a hormone useful in the body's management of stress. In newborn infants, the adrenocortical system is apparently active although somewhat immature

(Tennes & Mason, 1982). For example, infants respond to physically stressing circumstances such as circumcision with an adrenocortical response within hours after birth (Gunnar, Malone, & Fisch, 1984). Recently, it has been discovered that older infants vary in both circulating levels of cortisol under ordinary conditions and in the magnitude of response to stressful situations. Tennes (1982) rated the behavior and the cortisol levels of 1-year-olds reacting to maternal departure. She found a consistent linear relationship between the mean cortisol excretion level and the level of separation distress. Infants who were not at all behaviorally distressed by the mother's leave-taking had the lowest levels of cortisol and those who cried when she left and remained distressed during her absence excreted the highest levels of cortisol. Within the group of distressed children, two types were discerned—those showing withdrawal and those showing agitation. Distressed-agitated infants had significantly higher levels of cortisol than the distressed-withdrawn infants. These differences in behavioral response and in cortisol level in the experimental condition were found to be substantially related to individual differences in chronic levels of cortisol, that is, under ordinary, everyday conditions. Also found was a remarkable degree of intraindividual stability across a 2-year interval of time. Of course, without knowing what the individual patterns of adrenocorticol response were in the earliest days of life, it is impossible to determine whether cortisol and behavioral responses at 1 and 3 years of age were due to an innate physiological predisposition or whether specific patterns of hormone responsivity and attachment were forged early in life within the mother–infant relationship. Nevertheless, the foregoing data, as well as those pertaining to sex hormones and socioemotional development, indicate the very significant linkages between hormones and affective behavior early in life.

Other Innate Factors Involved in Early Emotional Communication

Contagion and Imitation

Young infants appear to have a precocious sensitivity to the emotional signals of others as manifested in the contagion of the affective behavior displayed by others and in their imitations of affective facial pattern. Neonatal contagion of crying has been repeatedly demonstrated. Simner (1971) was the first to demonstrate that newborns will cry to the tape-recorded cries of other infants at 70 hours after birth, and Sagi and Hoffman (1976) extended the finding to even younger infants. Recently, Martin & Clark (1982) determined a differential responsiveness to own-versus-other cries. These investigators found that the instigation of new-born crying is restricted to cries of other infants and that they do not cry to the sound of their own previously recorded cries. Moreover, crying infants who heard their own cry almost completely stopped crying. These latter findings suggest a keen discrimnation and a built-in regu-latory function in young infants. Contagion of other's affective behavior demonstrates a *tuned-in-edness* to others that probably facilitates inter-personal cohesion as in the case of infrahuman primates (see review by Malatesta & Izard, 1984); the ability to resist contagion of one's own ongoing or prior affect defines a self-regulatory mechanism that is also adaptive: the experience of uninterrupted negative affect is probably physiologically toxic and there must be of necessity some mechanism for turning off the response before total exhaustion sets in.

The question of early infant imitation appears to be more in dispute than is the case with contagion, to judge by the amount of controversy it has generated in the literature. At the heart of the controversy is the resistance of some psychologists to the use of the term *imitation* because it implies a voluntary component that would be beyond the cognitive skills of the young infant. It is therefore preferable to refer to *matching* responses. Our own review of the literature on the matching abilities of young infants (Malatesta & Izard, 1984) found that the empirical evi-dence runs more in favor of the capacity than against it. Infants as young as 1 to 2 months of age are capable of quite specific facial appearance changes including brow movements and lip and tongue movements (Burd & Milewski, 1981; Maratos, 1973). Because infants apparently ac-commodate their responses over time to match a model (Kaye & Marcus, 1978), the failure of some studies to demonstrate matching may have been a function of overly restrictive time sampling or overcontrolled ex-perimental paradigms unsuited to the detection of accommodations. Field, Woodson, Greenberg, and Cohen, (1982) have demonstrated that neonates can make facial expressions, in response to a model, that are recognizable as the categorical emotional expressions of sadness, hap-piness, and surprise. It is our hunch that this early ability to match whole-face appearances is a developmental precursor to the more ma-ture ability to match specific facial appearance changes (such as raised brows with no other movement in other regions of the face) and that the primary mechanism involved in the earliest matching is affect con-tagion, mediated by lower brain stem mechanisms. MacLean (1980) has suggested that hindbrain structures are critical for species-typical dis-play behavior and the related imitative factors in squirrel monkeys. Moreover, he notes that imitation is a primitive form of behavior and that full displays can be released by partial stimuli, which suggests a readiness to respond in species-typical fashion. Modulation of such displays only becomes possible with the maturation of limbic and neocortical structures.

Summary

Thus far we have looked at some of the basic biological factors involved in early emotion expression, including the basic neuromuscular equipment and central programs for affect displays, hormone–emotion interactions, and innate sensitivity to emotion elicitors. We can see that in the beginning the young infant is strongly influenced by immediate endogenous and exogenous events that serve to elicit complex motoric behaviors. These behaviors seem to be biologically determined in early form and elicitation. Nothing is as yet socialized nor brought under conscious control, and there are no early schemata based primarily on learning or experience. The emotional expressions at this level of development are viewed as *hard* signals, to use the pretransitional stage of Zivin's (1982) taxonomy, that is, biologically based and controlled. Eventually these signals come under a variety of other forces that serve to modify their form, function, and eliciting conditions. Even among nonhuman primates, emotional displays may be adapted for social purposes (see Hinde, Chapter 5, this volume).

We may view the previous factors as serving a preadapted readiness to enter the social world in a way that lends itself to accommodation within a variety of social niches and to an ultimate adjustment within a particular niche. Young infants are capable of performing a wide range of categorical emotional behaviors; they are also responsive to the expressive behaviors of others and show accommodation over time. The particular pattern of accommodation that they follow depends heavily on the social milieu into which they are born. In the following section we discuss some of the cultural determinants of emotion socialization and specify the learning mechanisms thought to be involved in transforming the originally hard-wired behavior patterns into the variable "soft" forms needed for social commerce within a particular culture.

Sociocultural Factors

Culture and Emotion

Despite the existence of certain universal facial configurations in the elicitation of fundamental emotions (Izard, 1971), there is tremendous cross-cultural variability in the rules governing when, where, and in what form these expressions will be given. That is, universal features are often overriden by culture-specific conventions. Children rapidly acquire knowledge of *cultural display rules* (Ekman & Friesen, 1975; Saarni, 1979, 1982), and they also acquire knowledge of *feeling rules* or those rules that govern a sense of how they should feel under various circumstances (Hochschild, 1979; Malatesta & Haviland, in press). These two sets of rules serve as a tacit system, culturally defined, and cross-culturally variable, governing which emotion can be expressed under what circumstances and governing how emotional events are to be experienced. However, as various investigators have noted, there has been little substantive work in delineating how it is that children acquire knowledge of the rules, nor for that matter, do we know what factors mediate the child's own modulated affect expression (Ekman & Oster, 1979; Lewis & Michalson, 1982). Developmentalists have begun speculating about the mechanisms involved in display rule acquisition, including classical and instrumental learning (Malatesta & Haviland, 1982; Malatesta & Izard, 1984; Zivin, 1982), as well as the involvement of cognitive–symbolic processes (Malatesta & Izard, 1984, Saarni, 1982; Zivin, 1982). See Cole, Chapter 4, this volume, for a review of processes contributing to display rule acquisition in early childhood.

In the following section we consider some of the data concerning the early course of emotion socialization. Because this chapter is focused on early infancy we will limit our discussion to the mechanisms hypothesized to exert an influence during the first year of life; we will also limit our treatment to facial (versus vocal and gestural) displays.

The Socialization of Emotional Facial Patterns in Infancy

Much of what we know about the socialization of infant emotional expressions comes from a detailed microanalytic coding of sequential patterns of facial displays of mothers and their 3- to 6-month-old infants (Malatesta & Haviland, 1982), which is subsequently described in some detail.

Reasoning that early face-to-face play provides mothers with some of the earliest opportunities to shape infant emotion expression and infants with some of the earliest experiences with the expressive modulation of affect, we undertook an investigation of the emotional expressions of mothers and infants during dyadic interaction. Mothers who agreed to participate in the study were simply asked to play with their infants while seated face-to-face. After 15 minutes of play, mothers left the room; when the infants cried, mothers returned for another minute of interaction. Videotape recordings of the middle 5 minutes and the last minute of reunion were coded using a fine-grained component facial affect coding system that allows for the identification of eight categorical emotions as well as other signals (Izard, 1979). Both mother and baby were coded. In considering the babies' data alone, we found that 3- to 6-month-olds show very expressive facial behaviors. They emit a wide range of categorical emotional expressive behaviors and signals including interest, enjoyment, surprise, sadness/distress, anger, knit brow, discomfort/pain, and brow flash. Their rate of facial change is high, with 3-month-olds changing their expressions once every 7 seconds, and 6-month-olds every 9 seconds. Maternal expressions, which tend to be restricted to the positive emotions of joy, surprise, and interest, and to a positive brow-flash signal (although some sad and angry expressions are displayed to older infants) are displayed at a similarly high frequency.

We next looked at the contingency between infant facial expression changes and maternal facial changes, using a sequential lag analysis (Sackett, 1979). This analysis demonstrated that maternal expression changes are nonrandom and related to the ongoing expressive behavior of the child. The lag between maternal expression changes and infant changes was found to be less than half a second; thus, mothers' responses fall within the most optimal range for instrumental conditioning. The predominant pattern is for mothers to match their infants expressions, especially in the case of younger infants. For example, the expression of interest in infants is met with an expression of maternal interest; the expression of infant brow-flash is met with maternal brow-flash or interest, and so on.

A further analysis by infant gender revealed another interesting pattern. Although males and females displayed the same types and rate of facial expression change (with the one exception that infant daughters displayed more interest expressions), mothers responded differentially to them. First, mothers showed a significant increase over infant age in contingent responding, especially smiling, to the smiles of their sons and showed the reverse pattern for daughters. (Lewis and Michalson, Chapter 7, this volume, comparably found that after 6 months mothers decrease response to boys' crying.) Second, mothers were more likely to imitate male expressions, whereas they were more likely to show a wider range of expressions, both imitative and dissimilar, to females.

The pattern of maternal response observed in this study affords some of the first evidence of early forms of emotion socialization:

1. Consistent with this culture's emphasis on overtness of emotional expression, at least with respect to the more sanguine, social emotions,

mothers model primarily positive affect and tend to use positive contingencies when responding to infant affect.

2. Congruent with this culture's notions about females as the more emotionally sensitive sex, mothers display a wider range of contingent emotional expressivity with daughters. If mothers continue this pattern as girls progress developmentally, then we have at least a partial explanation of why girls are better at decoding emotional expressions than boys at all ages (Hall, 1978).

3. Finally, mothers also encourage the initially more irritable and labile male (Haviland & Malatesta, 1981) to become more *stoic* by being sure to reinforce positive affect, when it occurs, with contingent smiles and by avoiding the kind of facial play that tends to overstimulate.

In summary, we find that mothers engage in practices that undoubtedly influence the course of expressive behavior in infants. They engage in *modeling* appropriate interpersonal affect and they do so with repetitive instances. We estimate that infants (at least 3- to 6-month-olds) are exposed to over 300 exemplars of emotion signals per day and over 32,000 during the third to sixth month (Malatesta & Haviland, in press), a period of time identified as the peak period in face-to-face play. Mothers also engage in *contingent responding* and this responding is selective, being governed by the age and gender of the child, as well as, one assumes, idiosyncratic personality factors. Selectivity in responding can be considered as constituting reinforcement and extinction training in patterns of emotional expression. The combination of selective modeling and selective responding to infant affect expressions probably constitute two very powerful parental socialization practices. These kinds of behavior are frequent, repetitive, and contingent, and the lag between infant and maternal expression changes is in the most optimal range for instrumental learning. When we add to this the biological preadaptation of infants to match expressions to which they are exposed, we have all the prerequisites that are necessary to ensure an early and rapid assimilation of culture-specific forms of expression management.

To recapitulate thus far, infants come equipped with certain preadaptations including the abilities to perceive and to respond to the emotional signals of others (see Dolgin and Azmitia, Chapter 13, this volume) and to generate recognizable emotional signals of their own. They are also born into a particular cultural milieu and are exposed to a variety of very powerful social influences. We have already discussed the component biological attributes and social influences in some detail. We turn now to a description of how these biological and social influences interact with one another at successive stages of development during the first year of life and how the relative balance of influence on behavior shifts over time. For heuristic purposes we have divided the first year into three developmental epochs.

Developmental Course of the Interplay between Biological and Social Factors in Expressive Behavior

The First 3 Months

The primary developmental task of early infancy is to moderate fluctuations in physiological state (Als, 1982; Brazelton, 1982; Cicchetti & Hesse, 1983; Fogel, 1982; Lamb, 1981; Stoller & Field, 1982). The young infant is a biologically labile organism, showing considerable fluctuation in states of consciousness as well as affective expression (Emde et al., 1976; Field, 1981; Field et al., 1982; Konner, 1982; Malatesta & Haviland, in press; Oster, 1978; Stoller & Field, 1982). Only gradually does the infant develop regularities in patterns of sleep, of arousal, and of feeding. In addition to the establishment of circadian rhythms, the young infant must begin to develop tolerance for increasing levels of stimulation and to develop the means of reasserting equilibrium should the level of stimulation, on occasion, exceed its level of tolerance.

The expression of affect during this early developmental stage is closely connected with state changes, according to the model presented previously in this chapter. Not only do affective expressions occur in the process of the infant's attempts to regulate physiological arousal (Field & Walden, in press), they also signal certain central motive states and changes in states (Demos, 1982a, 1982b; Malatesta & Haviland, in press). The earliest affect expressions appear as reflexlike responses to disruptions in physiological equilibrium—hunger, pain, hormonal fluctuations, and so forth. However, there rapidly develops an awareness of and a responsivity to certain patterns of environmental stimulation such as visual and auditory events and tactile stimulation. These distal stimuli are capable of eliciting a range of affective responses, as discussed earlier.

To summarize, the young infant is physiologically and expressively labile. Affective expression is largely under the influence of immediate endogenous and exogenous physical stimulation. The responses themselves are reflexlike and have an all-or-none, whole-body character (Malatesta, 1981), yet are more complex, resembling motor stereotypies. During this stage of development, caregivers play a crucial mediatory role in enabling the child to achieve regulation of state, although there are apparently certain preadapted self-regulatory mechanisms as well (Malatesta & Haviland, in press; Martin & Clark, 1982).

Transition

Between the second and third month of life there are significant maturational changes taking place in the nervous system of the infant that will produce qualitatively different patterns of response. These changes are manifest at the physiological as well as behavioral level. For example, there is a shift in the pattern of neural activity during sleep, with a change from the early postnatal pattern of beginning sleep states with active-REM sleep to the more mature pattern of beginning with quiet-NREM sleep. We also see the emergence of Grade II (mature form) sleep spindles (Emde et al., 1976). Qualitative changes in neuromotor patterns are also found in respiratory activity (Wilder & Baken, 1978). All of the foregoing reflect growth in neuromotor control. Because emotional expression is a neuromotor event as well, we might expect to find parallel developments, as we in fact do. Salient changes in emotional expressive behavior are manifest during the second and third months, including decreasing incidence of nonhunger fussiness (Emde et al., 1976) and endogenous smiling (Charlesworth & Kreutzer, 1973), and the emergence of social smiling and laughter (Charlesworth & Kreutzer, 1973; Dennis & Dennis, 1937; Washburn, 1929; Wolff, 1965) as well as cooing (Lenneberg, Rebelsky, & Nichols, 1965). The infant also begins to favor stimuli that are contingently responsive to its own behavior (Watson, 1972; Watson & Ramey, 1977) about this time.

From the preceding discussion it is clear that by the third or fourth month of life the infant will have achieved a greater regulation of physiological state and the ability to tolerate stimulation; he or she will have become decidedly more positive in his or her affective expression and will have become more responsive to social agents.

The Second 3 Months

The immediacy and stereotypy of affective response during the opening months of life clearly reflects the biological grounding of early expressive behavior. At this point emotional expressions can be regarded as fairly primitive and unformed. The hard-wired, preadapted emotional behavior pattern are as yet unsocialized. However, these very same expressions are the initial substrate upon which social forces will act. The fact that the young infant can produce a number of categorical facial expressions spontaneously (Izard, 1978), has the musculature to make all of the component movements of the fundamental emotional expressions and their variants at birth (Oster, 1978), and can discriminate facial expressions of others and imitate whole and partial configurations of emotional expressions in response to a model's demonstrations (Burd & Milewski, 1981; Field *et al.*, 1982; Maratos, 1973) means that the learning of socialized patterns of emotional expression may begin within short order once the infant has achieved a certain degree of stabilization in basic organic processes and rhythms. The second 3 months of life appear to afford copious learning opportunities for the assimilation of socialized forms of expression and of mutual social interchange, at least in most Western cultures in which face-to-face interaction between parents and infants is characteristic and intense (Field, Sostek, Vietze, & Leiderman, 1981).

Face-to-face interactions provide the infant with some of the earliest opportunities to learn culture-specific forms of emotional expression. Although these kinds of interactions certainly occur during the opening months of life, the period from 3 to 6 months is a peak time in face-to-face play (Ling & Ling, 1974; Field, 1979). With more stabilized physiological organization and more advanced perceptual skills, the infant is prepared to focus fairly sustained attention to interesting sights. Infants at about this age display a fascination for the animated facial games in which mothers and other adults engage while interacting with them. The human face appears to have a magnetic attraction for the infant (Mahrer, Levinson, & Fine, 1976). Various investigators have noted that mothers present exaggerated, slow-paced facial expressions to infants (Brazelton, Koslowski, & Main, 1974; Kaye, 1979; Stern, 1974; Tronick *et al.*, 1979). Such facial play captures and sustains infant attention. The slow pacing is apparently well suited to the slower visual information processing of young infants (Lasky & Spiro, 1980). Our own research (Malatesta & Haviland, 1982) has demonstrated that the infant's exposure to such expressions is repetitive and frequent during the peak 3- to 6-month period. The cumulative impact is presumed to be substantial. Because infant emotional expressions are linked to central motive states and occur under highly motivating circumstances, we assume that maternal instruction in emotional display occurs in an optimal learning context.

Infants, of course, have certain skills that enable them to assert some directionality in social interchange, even at this early age. They can cry or exercise gaze aversion to break contact with an intrusive or an overstimulating partner. Their appealing smiles and expressions of interest encourage adults to engage in entertaining behavior. Nevertheless, it is the adult who exerts the balance of power, through the magnetic appeal of his or her animated facial play, by initiating and terminating play sessions, and through the quality of stimulation that is offered.

By the 7th month of life there is a general lessening of the infant's interest in face-to-face play (Field, 1979) as infants become ambulatory and find other interesting aspects of their environments to explore. However, it is quite probable that significant social learning concerning facial expressivity has already taken place, as judged by the infant's ability to discriminate various positive and negative emotional expressions (Oster, 1981) and by evidence of family resemblance in the use of facial expressions (Malatesta & Haviland, 1982). During this peak in face-to-face play, the infant has been exposed to myriad opportunities to observe a restricted class of full-blown, boldly schematized facial expressions—ones selected unconsciously by the mother to represent exaggerated versions of her culture's conventional forms of interpersonal interaction, not to mention her own idiosyncratic version of these conventions. We assume the learning experience is not trivial.

The Second Half of the First Year

During the second semester of the first year of life the infant makes significant strides in its management of emotion expression. The older youngster demonstrates greater affect modulation and selectivity in attention, and also appears to exercise some intentionality in his or her expressions (Demos, 1982a, 1982b; Harding & Golinkoff, 1979; Malatesta & Haviland, in press). For example, infants appear capable of exaggerating their own affective behaviors for instrumental purposes, such as in the deliberate intensification of crying to bring mother (Wolff, 1965), although such an ability probably attends the emergence of the causal-developmental level (Harding & Golinkoff, 1979), that is, sometime after the 10th month. The latter half of the first year of life also heralds the emergence of discretionary (versus magnetic) social interchange. Kaye and Fogel (1980), for example, have shown that whereas the facial expressions of 1- to 3-month-olds are mainly under control of maternal elicitation, by 7 months of age babies are beginning to show their own self-initiated greetings. The older infants in the Kaye and Fogel study also selectively reduced the time they looked at their mothers, decreasing the time spent gazing at her resting face but maintaining attention during the time of maximal activity. The findings indicate that mothers continue to provide important information concerning social interchange and emotional regulation, and infants in the second half of the first year and beyond continue to avail themselves of the opportunity to learn. For example, they continue to reference the mother's facial behavior under situations of uncertainty (Campos & Stenberg, 1981) and use the information provided as a regulator of behavior. Such continued observance of the emotional behaviors of others provides further opportunities to learn about the display characteristics of people whose expressions transmit the larger culture's stance toward the overt display of affect, as well as provide further opportunities for the social world to influence the child's development of affect modulation. This kind of social comparison apparently continues throughout life (Shaver & Klinnert, 1982). The discretionary aspect of facial regard marks significant progress in the infant's ability to be in charge of and to modulate its own affective behavior. The infant can now "decide" whether or not to cry or hold back tears, whether to throw a temper tantrum or smile beguilingly and ask for what he or she wants, and so forth. Thus, in the course of the first year of life infant emotional expressive behavior proceeds from spontaneously emitted complex reflexive behaviors (akin to the motor stereotypies) through a period of susceptibility to instrumental conditioning, to the eventual capacity to use these behaviors voluntarily and instrumentally. In effect, operants have become operators.

Summary

The developing affect system is characterized by genetic programs for certain aspects of emotional behavior along with features of developmental modifiability. Behavior of the infant during the opening months of life is governed almost exclusively by preadapted propensities. The young infant's affect expressions are elicited by physical properties of endogenous and exogenous stimuli. These elicitors provoke stereotypies that are assumedly linked to central motive and feeling states. The various expressions appear in the child's repertoire as the underlying neuromuscular programs and sensory–perceptual support systems become mature. Plasticity enters the picture in the form of an innate readiness to add *learned* elicitors of affect and in the capacity to modulate expressions through exposure to social models.

In terms of the relative balance of influence between biological and social factors developmentally, we have seen that biological factors clearly predominate in the opening weeks and months of life. The young infant is strongly influenced by immediate endogenous and exogenous events that serve to elicit complex motoric behaviors. These behaviors resemble the species' specific displays described by ethologists. Expressions are relatively uncontaminated by social experience. However, the heavy biogenetic influence includes an innate preparedness to respond to social contingencies, especially during the next stage of development.

The 3- to 6-month period is a stage during which the infant is particularly susceptible to the socioemotional instruction of others. Parents exert selective pressures on the infant's affect communication by modeling a culturally defined and restricted class of emotional expressions. They also respond selectively to the child's own spontaneously emitted expressions. A preadapted magnetic attraction to human faces, susceptibility to contagion of affect, and a propensity to match or to imitate others' expressions all contribute to the child's assimilation of cultural display rules and eventual accommodation of expressive behavior.

By 7 months of age the child has begun to exercise more discretionary engagement in social interchange and has begun actively to modulate his or her expressive behavior, a practice that gains in strength over time. Expressive behavior from then on is increasingly used instrumentally for a variety of social-communicative purposes. The linkage between state and behavior has become more variable. It is at this point that we can speak of a decided social and individualistic component to emotion expression. However, it is important to recognize that humans are emotional creatures throughout their lives and that various physical and psychological stimuli generate intense emotional experiences, some of which will be reflected in spontaneously emitted expressions and others of which will be inhibited or transformed in some fashion. In that sense, the individual's expressive behavior continues to be affected by multiple influences throughout his or her life.

References

Ahrens, R. Beitrag zur Entwicklung des Physiognomie und Mimikerkennens. *Zeitschrift für experimentelle und angewandte Psychologie*, 1954, 2, 412–454.

Als, H. The unfolding of behavioral organization in the face of a biological violation. In E. Z. Tronick (Ed.), *Social interchange in infancy: Affect, cognition, and communication.* Baltimore: University Park Press, 1982.

Beach, F. A. Hormonal control of sex-related behavior. In F. A. Beach (Eds.), *Human sexuality in four perspectives.* Baltimore: The Johns Hopkins University Press, 1976.

Beatty, W. W. Gonadal hormones and sex differences in nonreproductive behaviors in rodents: Organizational and activational influences. *Hormones and Behavior*, 1979, 12, 112–163.

Brazelton, T. B., Koslowski, B., & Main, M. The origins of reciprocity: The early mother–

infant interaction. In M. Lewis & L. A. Rosenblum (Eds.), *The effect of the infant on its caretaker.* New York: Wiley, 1974.

Brazelton, T. B. Joint regulation of neonate-parent behavior. In E. Z. Tronick (Ed.), *Social interchange in infancy: Affect, cognition, and communication.* Baltimore: University Park Press, 1982.

Buck, R. The evolution and development of emotion expression and communication. In S. S. Brehm, S. M. Kassin, & F. X. Gibbons (Eds.), *Developmental social psychology.* New York: Oxford University Press, 1981.

Burd, A. P., & Milewski, A. E. *Matching of facial gestures by young infants: Imitation or releasers?* A paper persented at the Bienniel Meeting of the Society for Research in Child Development, Boston, MA, April, 1981.

Campos, J. J., & Stenberg, C. R. Perception, appraisal and emotion: The onset of social referencing. In M. E. Lamb & L. R. Sherrod (Eds.), *Infant social cognition.* Hillsdale, NJ: Erlbaum, 1981.

Carmichael, L. The onset and early development of behavior. In P. H. Mussen (Ed.), *Carmichael's manual of child psychology.* New York: Wiley, 1970.

Charlesworth, W. R., & Kreutzer, M. A. Facial expressions of infants and children. In P. Ekman (Ed.), *Darwin and facial expression.* New York: Academic Press, 1973.

Chevalier-Skolnikoff, S. Facial expression of emotion in nonhuman primates. In P. Ekman (Ed.), *Darwin and facial expression.* New York: Academic Press, 1973.

Cicchetti, D., & Hesse, P. Affect and intellect: Piaget's contributions to the study of infant emotional development. In R. Plutchik & H. Kellerman (Eds.), *Emotion: Research and theory* (Vol. II). New York: Academic Press, 1983.

Crockenberg, S. B. Antecedents of mother-infant interaction and infant irritability in the first three months of life. *Infant Behavior and Development,* 1982, 5, 105–1191.

Demos, V. *Childrens' understanding and use of affect terms.* Unpublished doctoral dissertation. Graduate School of Education, Harvard University, 1974.

Demos, V. The role of affect in early childhood: An exploratory study. In E. Z. Tronick (Ed.), *Social interchange in infancy: Affect, cognition, and communication.* Baltimore: University Park Press, 1982a.

Demos, V. Facial expressions of infants and toddlers: A descriptive analysis. In T. Field & A. Fogel (Eds.), *Emotion and early interaction.* Hillsdale, NJ: Erlbaum Associates, 1982b.

Dennis, W., & Dennis, M. G. Behavioral development in the first year as shown by forty biographies. *Psychological Record,* 1937, 1, 349–361.

Ehrhardt, A. A., & Meyer-Bahlburg, H. F. L. Effects of prenatal sex hormones on gender-related behavior. *Science,* 1981, 211, 1312–1317.

Ekman, P., & Friesen, W. V. *Unmasking the face.* Englewood Cliffs, NJ: Prentice-Hall, 1975.

Ekman, P., & Oster, H. Facial expressions of emotion. In M. R. Rosenzweig & L. W. Porter (Eds.), *Annual review of psychology.* Palo Alto, CA: Annual Reviews, 1979.

Emde, R. N. Levels of meaning for infant emotions: A biosocial review. In W. A. Collins (Ed.), Development of cognition, affect, and social relations. *The Minnesota Symposia on Child Psychology* (Vol. 13). Hillsdale, NJ: Erlbaum, 1980.

Emde, R. N., Gaensbauer, T. J., & Harmon, R. J. Emotional expression in infancy: A biobehavioral study. *Psychological Issues,* 1976, 10, 1–193.

Emde, R. N., Katz, E. L., & Thorpe, J. Emotional expression in infancy: II. Early deviations in Down's Syndrome. In M. Lewis & L. Rosenblum (Eds.), *The development of affect.* New York: Plenum, 1978.

Emde, R. N., Kligman, D. H., Reich, J. H., & Wade, T. Emotional expression in infancy: I. Initial studies of social signaling and an emergent model. In M. Lewis & L. Rosenblum (Eds.), *Development of affect.* New York: Plenum, 1978.

Feldman, J. F., Brody, N., & Miller, S. A. Sex differences in non-elicited neonatal behaviors. *Merrill-Palmer Quarterly*, 1980, *26*, 63–73.

Field, T. M. Visual and cardiac responses to animate and inanimate faces by young term and preterm infants. *Child Development*, 1979, *50*, 188–194.

Field, T. Affective displays of high-risk infants during early interactions. In T. Field & A. Fogel (Eds.), *Emotion and early interaction*. Hillsdale, NJ: Erlbaum, 1981.

Field, T. M., Sostek, A. M., Vietze, P., & Leiderman, P. H. (Eds.), *Culture and early interactions*. Hillsdale, NJ: Erlbaum, 1981.

Field, T. M., & Walden, T. A. Perception and production of facial expressions in infancy and early childhood. In H. Reese & L. Lipsitt (Eds.), *Advances in child development and behavior* (Vol. 16). New York: Academic Press, in press.

Field, T. M., Woodson, R., Greenberg, R., & Cohen, D. Discrimination and imitation of facial expressions by neonates. *Science*, 1982, *218*, 179–181.

Fogel, A. Affect dynamics in early infancy: Affective tolerance. In T. Field & A. Fogel (Eds.), *Emotion and early interaction*. Hillsdale, NJ: Erlbaum, 1982.

Forest, M. G., & Cathiard, A. M., Bourgeoise, J., & Genoud, J. *Androgenes plasmatiques chez le nourrisson normal et premature, relation avec la maturation de l'axe hypothalamo-hypophysogonadique* (Vol. 32). Paris: Inserm, 1974.

Forest, M. G., Sizonenko, P. C., Cathiard, A. M., & Bertrand, J. Hypophysogonadal function in humans during the first year of life. *Journal of Clinical Investigation*, 1974, *53*, 819–828.

Fraiberg, S. Blind infants and their mothers: An examination of the sign system. In M. Bullowa (Ed.), *Before speech*. Cambridge: Cambridge University Press, 1979.

Gaensbauer, T. Anaclitic depression in a 3½-month-old child. *American Journal of Psychiatry*, 1980, *137*, 841–842.

Goldberg, S., & Lewis, M. Play behavior in the year old infant: Early sex differences. *Child Development*, 1969, *40*, 21–31.

Goldman, P. S. Maturation of the mammalian nervous system and the ontogeny of behavior. *Advances in the Study of Behavior*, 1976, *7*, 1–83.

Guillory, A. W., Self, P. A., Biscoe, B. M., & Cole, C. A. *The first four months: Development of affect, cognition, and synchrony*. Paper presented at the Annual Meeting of the American Psychological Association, Washington, DC, August, 1982.

Gunnar, M. R., & Donahue, M. Sex differences in social responsiveness between six months and twelve months. *Child Development*, 1980, *51*, 262–265.

Gunnar, M. R., Malone, S. & Fisch, R. O. Deep sleep and levels of plasma cortisol during recovery from routine, circumcision in human newborns. Paper presented at the International Conference on Infant Studies, April, 1984, New York, NY.

Hall, J. A. Gender effects in decoding nonverbal cues. *Psychological Bulletin*, 1978, *85*, 845–857.

Harding, C. G., & Golinkoff, R. M. The origins of intentional vocalizations in prelinguistic infants. *Child Development*, 1979, *40*, 33–40.

Haviland, J. Looking smart: The relation between affect and intelligence in infancy. In M. Lewis (Ed.), *Origins of Intelligence: Infancy and early childhood*. New York: Plenum, 1976.

Haviland, J. M., & Lewis, M. *Infants' greeting patterns to strangers* (Research Bulletin 72-2). Educational Testing Service, Princeton, NJ, 1976.

Haviland, J. J., & Malatesta, C. Z. A description of the development of sex differences in non-verbal signals. In C. Mayo & N. Henley (Eds.), *Gender and non-verbal behavior*. New York: Springer-Verlag, 1981.

Herzka, H. S. *Das Gesicht des Sauglings: Ausdruck und Reifung*. Basel/Stuttgart: Schwabe, 1965.

Hittleman, J. H., & Dickes, R. Sex differences in neonatal eye contact time. *Merrill-Palmer Quarterly*, 1979, *25*, 171–184.

Hochschild, A. R. Emotion work, feeling rules, and social structure. *American Journal of Sociology*, 1979, *85*, 551–575.

Isaacson, R. L. *The limbic system*. New York: Plenum, 1982.

Izard, C. *The face of emotion*. New York: Appleton-Century Crofts, 1971.

Izard, C. E. *Human emotions*. New York: Plenum, 1977.

Izard, C. E. Emotions as motivations: An evolutionary-developmental perspective. In H. E. Howe, Jr. (Ed.), *Nebraska Symposium on Motivation* (Vol. 26). Lincoln: University of Nebraska Press, 1978.

Izard, C. E. The maximally discriminative facial movement coding system (Max). Newark, DE: University of Delaware, 1979.

Izard, C. E. Emotion-cognition relationships and human development. In C. E. Izard, J. Kagan, & R. Zajonc (Eds.), *Emotions, cognition, and behavior*. New York: Cambridge University Press, in press.

Kagan, J. Overview: Perspectives on human infancy. In J. D. Osofsky (Ed.), *Handbook of infant development*. New York: Wiley, 1979.

Kagan, J. The idea of emotion in human development. In C. E. Izard, J. Kagan, & R. Zajonc (Eds.), *Emotions, cognition and behavior*. New York: Cambridge University Press, in press.

Kagan, J., & Lewis, M. Studies of attention in the human infant. *Merrill-Palmer Quarterly*, 1965, *2*, 95–122.

Kaye, K. Thickening thin data: The maternal role in developing communication and language. In M. Bullowa (Ed.), *Before speech*. Cambridge: Cambridge University Press, 1979.

Kaye, K., & Fogel, A. The temporal structure of face-to-face communication between mothers and infants. *Developmental Psychology*, 1980, *16*, 454–464.

Kaye, K., & Marcus, J. Imitation over a series of trials without feedback: Age six months. *Infant Behavior and Development*, 1978, *1*, 141–155.

Konner, M. Biological aspects of the mother–infant bond. In R. N. Emde & R. J. Harmon (Eds.), *The development of attachment and affiliative systems*. New York: Plenum, 1982.

Korner, A. F. Neonatal startles, smiles, erections and reflex sucks as related to state, sex and individuality. *Child Development*, 1969, *40*, 1039–1053.

Lamb, M. E. The development of social expectations in the first year of life. In M. E. Lamb & L. R. Sherrod (Eds.), *Infant social cognition*. Hillsdale, NJ: Erlbaum, 1981.

Lasky, R. E., & Spiro, D. The processing of tachistoscopically presented visual stimuli by five-month-old infants. *Child Development*, 1980, *51*, 1292–1294.

Lenneberg, E., Rebelsky, F., & Nichols, I. The vocalization of infants born to deaf and hearing parents. *Human Development*, 1965, *8*, 23–37.

Lewis, J. K., & Sackett, G. P. Toward an ontogenetic monkey model of behavioral development. In J. S. Lockard (Ed.), *The evolution of human social behavior*. New York: Elsevier, 1980.

Lewis, M. Infants' responses to facial stimuli during the first year of life. *Developmental Psychology*, 1969, *1*, 75–86.

Lewis, M., & Brooks, J. Self-knowledge and emotional development. In M. Lewis & L. A. Rosenblum (Eds.), *The development of affect*. New York: Plenum, 1978.

Lewis, M., & Michalson, L. The socialization of emotions. In T. Field & A. Fogel (Eds.), *Emotion and early interaction*. Hillsdale, NJ: Erlbaum, 1982.

Lewis, M., & Michalson, L. *Children's emotions and needs: Developmental theory and measurement*. New York: Plenum, 1983.

Ling, D., & Ling, A. H. Communication development in the first three years of life. *Journal of Speech and Hearing Research*, 1974, *17*, 146–159.

Lutz, C. The domain of emotion words on Ifaluk. *American Ethnologist*, 1982, *9*, 113–116.

Maccoby, E. E., & Jacklin, C. M. *The psychology of sex differences*. CA: Stanford University Press, 1974.

Maccoby, E. E., & Jacklin, C. N. Sex differences in aggression: A rejoinder and reprise. *Child Development*, 1980, *51*, 964–980.

Maccoby, E. E., Doering, C. H., Jacklin, C. N., & Kraemer, H. Concentrations of sex hormones in umbilical-cord blood: Their relation to sex and birth order of infants. *Child Development*, 1979, *50*, 632–642.

MacLean, P. D. A triune concept of the brain. In T. J. Boag & D. Campbell (Eds.), *Hincks Memorial lectures*. Toronto: University of Toronto Press, 1973.

MacLean, P. D. Sensory and perceptive factors in emotional functions of the triune brain. In A. O. Rorty (Ed.), *Explaining emotions*. Berkeley: University of California Press, 1980.

Mahrer, A. R., Levenson, J. R., & Fine, S. Infant psychotherapy: Theory, research, and practice. *Psychotherapy: Theory, Research, and Practice*, 1976, *11*, 131–140.

Malatesta, C. Z. *Determinants of infant affect socialization: Age, sex of infant and maternal emotional traits*. A doctoral dissertation, Rutgers University, 1980.

Malatesta, C. Z. Infant emotion and the vocal affect lexicon. *Motivation and Emotion*, 1981, *5*, 1–23.

Malatesta, C. Z., & Haviland, J. M. Learning display rules: The socialization of emotion expression in infancy. *Child Development*, 1982, *53*, 991–1003.

Malatesta, C. Z., & Haviland, J. M. Signals, symbols and socialization: The modification of emotional expression in human development. In M. Lewis & C. Saarni (Eds.), *The socialization of affect*. New York: Plenum, in press.

Malatesta, C. Z., & Izard, C. E. The ontogenesis of human social signals: From biological imperative to symbol utilization. In N. Fox & R. J. Davidson (Eds.), *Affective development: A psychobiological perspective*. Hillsdale, NJ: Erlbaum, 1984.

Maratos, O. *The origin and development of imitation in the first six months of life*. Unpublished doctoral dissertation, University of Geneva, 1973.

Martin, G. G., & Clark, R. D. Distress crying in neonates: Species and peer specificity. *Developmental Psychology*, 1982, *18*, 3–9.

Money, J. Human hermaphroditism. In F. Beach (Ed.), *Human sexuality in four perspectives*. Baltimore: Johns Hopkins University Press, 1977.

Moss, H. A. Sex, age, and state as determinants of mother–infant interaction. *Merrill-Palmer Quarterly*, 1967, *13*, 19–36.

Osofsky, J. D., & O'Connell, E. J. Patterning of newborn behavior in an urban population. *Child Development*, 1977, *48*, 532–536.

Osofsky, J. D., & Danzger, B. Relationships between neonatal characteristics and mother–infant interaction. *Developmental Psychology*, 1974, *10*, 124–130.

Oster, H. Facial expression and affect development. In M. Lewis & L. Rosenblum (Eds.), *The development of affect*. New York: Plenum, 1978.

Oster, H. "Recognition" of emotional expression in infancy? In M. E. Lamb & L. R. Sherrod (Eds.), *Infant social cognition*. Hillsdale, NJ: Erlbaum, 1981.

Oster, H., & Ekman, P. Facial behavior in child development. In A. Collins (Ed.), *Minnesota Symposia on Child Psychology. Vol. 11*. Hillsdale, NJ: Erlbaum, 1977.

Papez, J. W. A proposed mechanism of emotion. *Archives of Neurology and Psychiatry*, 1937, *38*, 725–744.

Phillips, S., King, S., & DuBois, L. Spontaneous activities of female versus male newborns. *Child Development*, 1978, *49*, 590–597.

Rubin, R. T., Reinisch, J. M., & Haskett, R. F. Postnatal gonadal steroid effects on human behavior. *Science,* 1981, *211,* 1318–1324.

Saarni, C. Children's understanding of display rules for expressive behavior. *Developmental Psychology,* 1979, *15,* 424–429.

Saarni, C. Social and affective functions of nonverbal behavior: Developmental concerns. In R. Feldman (Ed.), *Development of nonverbal behavior.* New York: Springer-Verlag, 1982.

Sackett, G. P. The lag sequential analysis of contingency and cyclicity in behavioral interaction research. In J. D. Osofsky (Ed.), *Handbook of infant development.* New York: Wiley, 1979.

Sagi, A., & Hoffman, M. L. Empathic distress in the newborn. *Developmental Psychology,* 1976, *12,* 175–176.

Shaver, P., & Klinnert, M. Schachter's theories of affiliation and emotion: Implications of developmental research. In L. Wheeler (Ed.), *Review of personality and social psychology* (Vol. III). Beverly Hills: Sage, 1982.

Simner, M. Newborn's response to the cry of another infant. *Developmental Psychology,* 1971, *51,* 136–150.

Sorce, J. F., & Emde, R. N. Mother's presence is not enough: Effect of emotional availability on infant exploration. *Developmental Psychology,* 1981, *17,* 737–745.

Sorce, J. F., Emde, R. N., & Klinnert, M. *Maternal emotional signalling: It's effect on the visual cliff behavior of one-year-olds.* A paper presented at the Bienniel Meeting of the Society for Research in Child Development, Boston, MA, April, 1981.

Sroufe, L. A. Socioemotional development. In J. D. Osofsky (Ed.), *Handbook of infant development.* New York: Wiley, 1979.

Sroufe, L. A., & Wunsch, J. P. The development of laughter in the first year of life. *Child Development,* 1972, *43,* 1326–1344.

Stenberg, C. R. *The development of anger facial expressions in infancy.* Unpublished doctoral dissertation, University of Denver, 1982.

Stern, D. The goal and structure of mother–infant play. *Journal of the American Academy of Child Psychiatry,* 1974, *13,* 402–421.

Stevens, C. W., & Mitchell, G. Birth order effects, sex differences and sex preferences in the peer-directed behaviors of rhesus infants. *International Journal of Psychobiology,* 1972, *2,* 117–128.

Stirnimann, F. *Psychologie des neugeborenen Kindes.* München, Germany: Kindler Verlag, 1940.

Stoller, S. A., & Field, T. Alteration of mother and infant behavior and heart rate during a still-face perturbation of face-to-face interaction. In T. Field & A. Fogel (Eds.), *Emotion and early interaction.* Hillsdale, NJ: Erlbaum, 1982.

Super, C. M., & Harkness, S. The development of affect in infancy and early childhood. In D. A. Wagner & H. W. Stevenson (Eds.), *Cultural perspectives on child development.* San Francisco: Freeman, 1982.

Talbert, L. M., Draybill, E. N., & Potter, H. D. Adrenal cortical response to circumcision in the neonate. *Obstetrics and Gynecology,* 1975, *48,* 208–210.

Tauber, M. A. Sex differences in parent–child interaction styles during a free-play session. *Child Development,* 1979, *50,* 981–988.

Tennes, K. The role of hormones in mother–infant transactions. In R. N. Emde & R. J. Harmon (Eds.), *The development of attachment and affiliative systems.* New York: Plenum, 1982.

Tennes, K. H., & Mason, J. W. Developmental psychoendocrinology: An Approach to the study of emotions. In C. E. Izard (Ed.), *Measuring emotions in infants and children.* Cambridge: Cambridge University Press, 1982.

Thelen, E. Rhythmical behavior in infancy: An ethological perspective. *Developmental Psychology*, 1981, *17*, 237–257.

Thelen, E., & Fisher, D. M. From spontaneous to instrumental behavior: Kinematic analysis of movement changes during very early learning. *Child Development*, 1983, *54*, 129–140.

Thoman, E. B. *Development of synchrony in mother–infant interaction in feeding and other situations*. Proceedings of the 58th Annual Meeting of the Federation of American Societies for Experimental Biology, 1976.

Tomkins, S. *Affect, imagery, consciousness: Vol. I: The positive affects*. New York: Springer, 1962.

Tomkins, S. *Affect, imagery, consciousness. Vol. II: The negative affects*. New York: Springer, 1963.

Tronick, E., Als, H., & Adamson, L. Structure of early face-to-face communicative interaction. In M. Bullowa (Ed.), *Before speech*. Cambridge: Cambridge University Press, 1979.

Vernadakis, A. & Timiras, P. S. *Hormones in development and aging*. N.Y: Spectrum, 1982.

Wachs, T. D., & Gruen, G. E. *Early experience and human development*. New York: Plenum, 1982.

Washburn, R. W. A study of the smiling and laughing of infants in the first year of life. *Genetic Psychology Monographs*, 1929, *6*, 398–537.

Watson, J. B. *Psychology from the standpoint of a behaviorist*. Philadelphia: Lippincott, 1919.

Watson, J. S. Siling, cooing and "the game." *Merrill-Palmer Quarterly*, 1972, *4*, 323–339.

Watson, J. S., & Ramey, C. Reactions to response contingent stimulation in early infancy. *Merrill-Palmer Quarterly*, 1972, *13*, 219–228.

Werner, J. S., & Lipsitt, L. P. The infancy of human sensory systems. In E. S. Gollin (Ed.), *Developmental plasticity*. New York: Academic Press, 1981.

Wiesenfeld, A. R., Malatesta, C. Z., & DeLoach, L. L. Differential parental response to familiar and unfamiliar infant distress signals. *Infant Behavior and Development*, 1981, *4*, 305–320.

Wilder, C. N., & Baken, R. J. Some developmental aspects of the infant cry. *Journal of Genetic Psychology*, 1978, *132*, 225–230.

Wolff, P. H. The natural history of crying and other vocalizations in early infancy. In B. M. Foss (Ed.), *Determinants of infant behavior* (Vol. 4). London: Methuen, 1965.

Wolff, P. H. The causes, controls, and organization of behavior in the neonate. *Psychological Issues*, 1966, *5*, 1–99.

Zajonc, R. B. Feeling and thinking: Preferences need no inferences. *American Psychologist*, 1980, *35*, 151–175.

Zajonc, R. Affect and cognition: The hard interface. In C. E. Izard, J. Kagan, & R. Zajonc (Eds.), *Emotion, cognition and behavior*. New York: Cambridge University Press, in press.

Zivin, G. Watching the sands shift: Conceptualizing development of nonverbal mastery. In R. S. Feldman (Ed.), *The development of nonverbal communication in children*. New York: Springer-Verlag, 1982.

Chapter 9

Expression as Action: A Motor Perspective of the Transition from Spontaneous to Instrumental Behaviors

Esther Thelen

Relationship to Other Chapters and to the Field

Relevant Issues in the Field

Thelen explicates a particular process by which the earliest forms of expressive behavior may be transformed from inherited involuntary fragments to experientially coordinated voluntary communicative actions. In so doing, she makes explicit one aspect of the general model of biology–environment interaction in development that unites the chapters in this volume: the gradual voluntarization and coordination with other behaviors of early, rigid, inherited behavior patterns. Her research has demonstrated how infants' kicking patterns gradually become voluntarized by the infant acquiring control of the few variables in the motor structure of the pattern that are not locked together by inherited motoric architecture. These are the motor units' initiation, intensity, and interunit pauses. She interprets how the structure of this kicking pattern parallels the motor side of all expressive behaviors, and thus how it may be used to understand the process of the gradual voluntarization of expressive behavior. Along with Fogel (Chapter 10, this volume), as noted below, Thelen is the first to

THE DEVELOPMENT OF EXPRESSIVE BEHAVIOR: BIOLOGY–ENVIRONMENT INTERACTIONS

221

bring these sharpened views of the organization of behavior from motor action theory to the field of expressive-behavior development.

Relationship to Other Chapters

*Thelen's introduction into developmental psychology of the concept of co-*ordinative structures, *a general category for the* rhythmic stereotypies *that she has discovered in infant kicking, has found resonance in the thinking of Malatesta (Chapter 8) and Fogel (Chapter 10) as a particularly apt description of the very early form in which the packages of expressive behaviors appear. Although Malatesta's chapter does not focus on this characterization, she does offer it as the starting structure of expressive behavior. Fogel, by contrast, suggests coordinative structures as the central concept for understanding the co-ordination of many motoric and cognitive features into the general neurocognitive structure that underlies emotional expression. Through the route of examining broad patterns that characterize development, Mason (Chapter 6) also empha-sizes the increased central coordination of expressive-behavior patterns that oc-curs with general experience.*

A similar search for the constancy of form within necessary flexibilities relates Thelen's chapter with Smith's (see Chapter 3). Smith's chapter, taking a phy-logenetic as well as ontogenetic perspective, aims to analyze the evolutionary constraints within which a signal can vary in form and still be reliably recog-nized. Thelen, with an ontogenetic perspective, addresses the same issue at the end of her chapter by noting that the process of voluntarization that she describes leaves intact, during its transformation of structure, the form of the motor be-havior so that it remains usable in expressive communication.

For Consistent Terminology

Thelen uses spontaneous behavior *in a way that precisely fits her motor action orientation. It is different from, but compatible with, more general, com-mon characterizations of expressive behavior as spontaneous. The common meaning refers to behavior that is elicited by stimuli with little or no voluntary control of the behavior's presence or form. The behavior has no goal. This is the meaning used in this volume's framing chapter that cites the troublesome di-chotomy of spontaneous versus instrumental. Thelen, by contrast, specifies spontaneous behavior as an independent behavioral means that is not (yet) hi-erarchically coordinated with a centralized program for achieving a* goal. *The-len's special meaning implies that spontaneous behaviors are naturally adaptable toward instrumental goals.—*ED.

Introduction

My purpose in writing this chapter is to show how an action-based perspective can help answer one of the most central of all developmental questions: how the spontaneous movements of the infant can be transformed into skilled voluntary actions (Trevarthan, 1982). The theme of this volume is the development of a particular class of actions, expressive behaviors, from a biological core of simple percursors to complex, intentional, and subtle forms of intraspecific communication. I argue that we can begin to understand this transformation by considering expressive behaviors as a special kind of action and by considering their development as a special case of the more general problem of the development of motor control. In the sense that expressive behavior, like all movement, is ultimately muscle contraction, we can seek to discover some general principles by which the patterns of the infant are converted into intentional actions, with the belief that principles may well apply to all classes of motor output.

Despite the enormous influence of Piaget's action-based cognitive theories, we know almost nothing about the development of movement. Motor development is a much neglected area of study in contemporary developmental psychology. For example, a recent *Handbook of Infant Development* (Osofsky, 1979) contained no chapters on motor behavior, nor was motor development or action even mentioned in the index. This trend is in direct contrast to the earliest traditions of child study. Pioneers like Arnold Gesell, Mary Shirley, and especially Myrtle McGraw, established a fine American tradition of careful, descriptive work on infant motor progress, using techniques like home observation and frame-by-frame cinemagraphic analysis, which are being rediscovered by mainstream developmental psychologists.

Although each of these workers was interested in theory and process, McGraw as a neurophysiologist, Gesell as a thoroughgoing Darwinian, and all relied heavily on the comparative method, they were also all concerned with developmental norms. Thus as developmental psychologists became more interested in learning, perception, cognition, affect, and social interaction, the normative data of these early scientists seemed old-fashioned and static. But even more telling, the early motor researchers were primarily maturationists when environmentalism was in the ascent. The study of motor processes thus became associated with maturationism, the establishment of age norms, and little else, and has so remained the orphan of developmental research. With the renewed acceptance of the role of biology in the developmental equation, it is time to refocus our attention to the motor aspects of behavior.

A further reason for an action-based perspective is that since the 1930s and 1940s, there have been significant, and some say even revolutionary advances in our understanding of the control of movement in general. Yet with a few outstanding exceptions, these breakthroughs have not been applied to human infant motor development.

However, in applying an action-based analysis of expressive development, I want to emphasize that an action-based analysis does not trivialize the rich motivational and communicative aspects of expressive behavior into "nothing but" muscle contraction. Contemporary theories of action (e.g., Reed, 1982; Turvey, 1977) integrate many levels of the sensorimotor axis into an ecologically relevant single system. Rather, I base my ethological approach on the premise that fine dissection of movement, and especially its patterning in time and space, can reveal certain relationships and mechanisms that are unavailable from more macroanalyses of responses and their frequencies. (See Mounoud, 1981, for an elegant example of inferences about cognitive mechanisms derived from an analysis of action.)

In this chapter, I present experimental evidence for one *rule* by which the neuromuscular system gains voluntary control of early movement. But in order to view this rule in the larger matrix of the structure of motor control, I introduce a general model of infant motor development. The model is based on current notions of motor organization and my own work on stereotyped and transitional infant movements. The purpose of the model is to provide a framework for understanding all classes of motor output in infancy in their transition from the biological core to intentional action.

The Hierarchical Structure of Movement

Imagine yourself playing an infield position in a softball game when the batter hits a ground ball right to you. You perceive the hit, and after making the decision to attempt to catch the ball and throw the batter out at first base, your brain must command your muscles to bend your torso at precisely the right instant, position your arms for the catch, straighten up, and execute a strong, well-aimed throw of the ball. Your command must include stabilizing your posture and adjusting your locomotion for irregularities in the terrain at the same time your movements must anticipate changes in the path of the ball—and all in a very few seconds.

The enduring problem in understanding the motor control of such highly skilled activities is how the brain could possibly have enough storage space to encode all the possible plans for movement necessary to anticipate the variabilities of the ball and the terrain and then, how the brain could contain enough execution capacity to translate those plans to the nearly infinite number of combinations of joints and muscle groups (Bernstein, 1967). The central nervous system would be sorely overtaxed to store and retrieve the instructions for every possible movement in an individual's action repertoire (Clark, 1982).

Coordinative Structures

The most widely accepted solution to the problem of the nearly infinite *degrees-of-freedom* of the neuromuscular system envisions that the control of movement is hierarchically distributed (Bernstein, 1967). In this view, coordinated movement is built from a limited number of *subsets*, each of which deals with only a discrete part of the final motor sequence (Greene, 1982). The highest levels of the central nervous system do not direct individual muscles but issue *command* functions to initiate, coordinate, and tune interactions between the more peripheral centers of control. These command signals carry the goal or the intent of the movement, but they themselves specify only a few degrees of freedom. Command signals recruit lower pathways largely by *tuning* or potentiating their parameters, that is, by altering the relative ease by which they may be recruited.

In contrast, the specific kinematic details of the movement emerge from organization at much lower levels of the control hierarchy. These *subsets* of movements were dubbed *coordinative structures* by Easton (1972), and I will adopt that terminology. Coordinative structures have come to be defined as, "a unit of motor control which governs a group of muscles as it operates over one or more body joints" (Clark, 1982, p. 165). Thus, a coordinative structure is constrained to act as a single unit or a functional synergy, thereby reducing the individual elements to be recruited by the command signals. This distributed control system can be compared to building a house from modular, prefabricated units, which requires far fewer executive decisions than assembling the building from individual bricks, nails, and boards. This notion that the coordinative structure *constrains* the degrees of freedom afforded by the neuromuscular architecture is the central theme of contemporary thinking in motor control.

The most compelling and well-studied examples of hierarchical control come from the literature on vertebrate locomotion. A large body of evidence from a variety of nonhuman mammals (see reviews by Delcomyn, 1980; Grillner, 1975; Herman, Grillner, Stein, & Stuart, 1976; Shik & Orlovsky, 1976) has established that the spinal cord can generate patterned stepping movements even when it has been surgically isolated both from the brain and from sources of sensory feedback from the moving limb. In the dog, for example, stimulation of such isolated spinal control centers can produce locomotor movements that are not only coordinated within a single limb but show normal alternations between limbs (Shik & Orlovsky, 1976). The role of higher level command signals appears to be recruitment of the appropriate action, setting commands of speed and direction, and fine-tuning the resulting gait. Although normal movement does, of course, use information from the motor cortex and from ongoing sensory information, these experiments demonstrate that movement may have spatiotemporal organization within much lower levels of control. Within Easton's terminology, the dog's entire limb may be envisioned as a coordinative structure, as the muscles are controlled as a functional group.

We are, of course, not able to subject the coordinative structures underlying more complex, skilled human movement to such experimental dissection but must infer their nature from observation. One especially compelling demonstration of the *ensemble* character of motor recruitment is the nonindependence of the two arms in performing a bimanual skilled activity. For example, when Kelso, Putnam, and Goodman (1983) placed obstacles in the path of one limb, creating tasks of differing difficulty for each arm, they found that the space and time behavior of *both* limbs was affected. These multijoint movements, therefore, are organized to function as a single unit.

The coordinative structure concept is also well illustrated by the organization of facial-expression movements. In their Facial Action Coding System (FACS), Ekman and Friesen (1976, 1978) identify about 50 anatomically based, discrete *action units,* that constitute the minimally distinguishable actions of the facial muscles. Although a few human facial expressions use only one of these action units, most expressions use a combination. However, the number of combinations of action units actually seen in the human repertoire is far less than the possible combinations of muscle groups, suggesting that the control system is recruiting an assemblage of cooccurring movements.

In short, although the identification of coordinative structures, the nature of their recruitment and control, and the manner in which they may be modified into skilled action does not have a long history, the logical necessity and theoretical elegance of postulating some sort of biological substrate to movement is well accepted.

Developmental Implications of Hierarchical Control

The hierarchical structure of motor control has profound implications for understanding the development of action, and for the ontogeny of expressive behavior in particular. First, it is one of the cardinal rules of development (Trevarthan, 1982) that the spontaneous behavior of the infant contains the bits and pieces of adult voluntary action. Carmichael (1970) called this "the law of anticipatory function" (p. 448). Because natural selection has insured that behaviors necessary for the normal life of the individual are functional when they are needed, sequences of behavior may be observed *before* they are normally used in an adaptive manner. These selective demands to have certain behaviors functional at specific times can accelerate the maturation of very specific neuromuscular systems, for example, the rapid myelination of the tract of the eighth facial nerve, which innervates sucking (Anokhin, 1964). An additional important consequence of the law of anticipatory function is that the components of a final system may not mature synchronously or in a path of smoothly accelerating function. Rather, percursors to mature functioning may appear in modular form and undergo transitions and transformations as they become integrated with other subsystems of the final behavior.

The very prolonged duration of motor development in human infants gives us a window on those bits and pieces organized in anticipation of function. The theme of this chapter is that the spontaneous and often transitory behavior fragments of the young infant are indeed developmental manifestations of such fundamental coordinative structures. I propose that they encode certain constrained muscle combinations and as a consequence of their organization, a fundamental timing property. Some developmental coordinative strucures appear to be organized at birth, others become available through normal neuromuscular maturation, and still other distinctive muscle combinations of highly skilled movements must be constructed through practice. Thus, although certain elements of the patterns of erect locomotion can be detected at birth as the newborn stepping reflex, these must be combined with the later-developing synergisms of postural control for walking to occur (Thelen, 1983). Tap dancing, on the other hand, requires individual experience to establish the unique, higher-order pattern of intrajoint and interjoint control, although even such movements likely recruit more simple sub-units.

The second very important implication of hierarchical structure is that the higher-level command functions of a movement—that is, the motivation or goal—can be viewed separately from the organization of the constituent subroutines. I hope I show that during development these levels may not mature synchronously. In other words, the subroutines may appear seemingly unrelated to the normally appropriate motivation or goal direction, and conversely, we may detect in the infant certain desires and goals but the inability to recruit the corresponding movement pattern. In the first case, we call the movements *spontaneous*, because they appear to serve no immediate function. In the latter case, we simply call the infant incompetent to compete a goal, as in "he *wants* to grab the toy, but he cannot."

Some key questions, then, in understanding the development of action are considered, (1) What are the coordinative structures and how do they arise? (2) How are simple coordinative structures assembled into more complex, coordinated movement? (3) What is the nature of the linkages between the higher-level command function and these lower-level units of control, and how do these linkages change with development? To those of us who have been looking at the construction of movement in infancy, it seems clear that a developmental approach is full of promise for answering some of these questions.

What Are the Developmental Coordinative Structures and How Do They Arise?

Coordinative Structures in Young Infants

Studies of newborn infants have revealed a remarkable biological core of well-orchestrated muscle combinations. Best known are the well-studied *primitive reflexes* of early infancy such as the Moro reflex, the palmar and plantar grasp reflex, the Babinski reflex, or rooting reflex. These defined-muscle synergisms are elicited by discrete stimuli such as dropping the head or touching the soles, palms, or cheeks, and they seem to disappear with normal maturation. The functions of the reflexes at birth, the nature of their suppression during development, and their role in later movement control is really unknown but remains an area of active debate (e.g., Oppenheim, 1981; Prechtl, 1981). More salient to our discussion of expressive-behavior development, however, are several described coordinations in newborns that are not strictly reflexive in character and differ from the so-called primitive reflexes in their obvious continuity with later behavior.

Traditionally, limb movement in newborns has been viewed as disorganized, random thrashing (Peiper, 1963; White, Castle, & Held, 1964). Detailed microanalysis of movements in both upper and lower limbs has shown, however, that there is considerable organization, both within the muscles of the limbs and between the limbs. Forward-extension movements of the arm of infants who are alert and in a semireclining position show a synergistic opening of the fingers as the arm is extended (Trevarthan, 1974; von Hofsten, 1982). Hands are rarely fisted in these spontaneous forward extensions of the arm. In contrast, a passive extension obtained by pulling the arm at the wrist will elicit flexion in arm and hand.

Spontaneous movements of the leg similarly show synergistic activity over several joints. Leg kicks in newborn (Thelen & Fisher, 1982, 1983b) and 1-month-old infants (Thelen, Bradshaw, and Ward, 1981) consist of simultaneous, rapid flexions at hip, knee, and ankle. In addition, newborns exhibit a striking degree of coordination between legs; about two-thirds of the kicks in one leg are followed by a kick in the opposite leg (Thelen, Ridley-Johnson, & Fisher, 1983). Thus, not only are there consistent movement synergies within the limb but between limbs as well.

A second property of these early arm and leg movements in addition to the coactivation of several muscle groups, is an intrinsically generated timing function. The duration of both a single forward arm movement and a flexion movement of the leg in a kick is around 300 msec (von Hofsten, 1979; Thelen, Bradshaw, & Ward, 1981; Thelen & Fisher, 1982, 1983b). Forward-arm extensions and leg kicks, then, appear to be muscle collectives acting over several joints, with nonrandom temporal organization.

Coordinative Structures in Expressive Action

What about the coordinative structures underlying expressive behaviors? Can they be detected in the newborn? From her analysis of infant facial expression using the Ekman and Friesen FACS, Oster (1978) reported that with a single exception "all of the discrete elementary action units specified in FACS can be identified in the facial movements of both premature and full-term infants" (p. 255). Moreover, these facial movements were often well defined and highly discriminable, even when occurring in complex configurations.

Manual-expressive behaviors also appear in recognizable, differen-

tiated form within the first few weeks of life and long before they become associated with intentional action (Fogel, 1981; Papousek & Papousek, 1977; Trevarthan, 1977). These manual expressions do not occur
randomly, but each is associated with a unique pattern of internal states
and external stimuli (Fogel & Hannan, in preparation). Like infant limb
movements, early coordinated gestures of the hand are not diffuse but
highly structured patterns of muscle use.

How Are Simple Coordinative Structures Assembled into More Complex Movements?

We know very little about the detailed developmental progression
from the simple movement precursors of early infancy to skilled, intentional action. Several studies have described relatively short-term
changes in movement patterns and frequency in the development of
reaching (von Hofsten, 1984), of leg movements, (Thelen & Fisher,
1983b) and of manual (Fogel, 1981) and facial gestures (Oster, 1978), but
we are a long way from understanding the construction of movement
from simple building blocks, or the nature of the transitions, dips,
regressions, and asynchronies that characterize such development.

One study, however, has traced in a particularly elegant fashion the
structure of oral behavior, especially the organization of the so-called
oral reflexes and the emergence of functional chewing. Sheppard and
Mysak (1984) followed two infants from 1 to 35 weeks of age by eliciting
six oral reflexes (rooting, lip, lateral tongue, mouth opening, biting, and
Babkin) by appropriate stimuli and by eliciting chewing by placing a bit
of banana in the infants' mouths. Reflexes could be elicited in the infants
throughout the period tested, although with age the reflex responses
became more subtle: they showed fewer reverberating or repetitive
cycles, involved fewer structures, and had shorter response times and
smaller movement excursions.

Sheppard and Mysak described all the reflex and chewing responses
by a repertoire of 26-movement subsets, much like Ekman and Friesen
subdivided facial movement into action units. Most intriguingly, all the
reflexes shared a similar repertoire of 19–22 movements. What differentiated one oral reflex from another in form was the *response frequencies*
of these movement subsets. For example, the Babkin and biting reflexes
showed a nearly identical repertoire of 22 components. However, the
Babkin reflex had a high frequency of depressed-mandible lip-separate
and eyes-closed units, whereas the *biting reflex* showed high frequencies

of elevated-mandible and lip-approximate components. Thus, the overall movement pattern was a combination of many subcomponents in random and low frequencies and a few movements that defined each reflex. These reflexes appeared to diminish with age by losing complexity and by the movement amplitudes declining at the same time that the stimulus-response association weakened.

Chewing, on the other hand, was acquired by the gradual consolidation of the already available movement components, which were observed long before the onset of functional chewing. Most significantly, chewing was constructed at a time when the infantile oral reflexes were still active, suggesting that these more immature responses did not have to be inhibited before the later movement appeared. Although none of the infants were actually chewing food during this age range, when food was placed in their mouths, the reflex subcomponents were increasingly well reorganized into functional responses.

A study of neonatal facial expressions in response to gustatory stimuli shows movement organization in affect that closely parallels that described for oral-reflexive behavior. Ganchrow, Steiner, and Daher (1983) identified 25 response components in the faces of newborn infants fed varying concentrations of sweet, bitter, and neutral solutions. When the responses of 23 infants were tallied using this catalogue, they found that it was the *frequency distribution* of the facial features that defined the recognizable affective expression associated with the taste stimuli. For example, the responses to urea and quinine contained a high frequency of head turning, lower lip in, and wide-open mouth, whereas those to sucrose showed especially slightly open mouth, licking, sucking, and smiling. However, there was considerable overlap in many response components. The intensity of differential response frequencies was associated with the varying concentrations of the solutions.

The significance of both these studies is the identification of coordinative structures that could be combined with varying frequencies to produce recognizable movement outcomes in response to different stimuli and at different ages. Many of the early oral reflexes like rooting, lateral tongue movements, and mouth opening appear to serve adaptive purposes in nursing, and the gustofacial reflexes were shown by Ganchrow et al. (1983) to communicate affect. As infants mature to the ingestion of solid foods, the same movement components become integrated into the new functional pattern of chewing, and the nursing reflexes wane, replaced by more goal-corrected feeding. Similarly, infants eventually recruit facial expressions of pleasure and disgust for intentional communication.

It is precisely this transformation of the movement subsets, or coordinative structures, into goal-corrected action that I discuss in the remainder of this chapter. To do this, I first propose a model of motor development derived from my research into a particular class of developmental coordinative structures, *rhythmical stereotypies*. Although such rhythmical stereotypies are large movements of the limbs and torso, there are many correspondences between their developmental characteristics and those of the movements associated with affect. Thus, by examining one principle that governs the transformation of these muscle synergisms into voluntary behavior, we may be able to generalize to other such transformations whether the motive of the action is expression or other functional ends.

Rhythmical Stereotypies as Developmental Coordinative Structures

Research into a class of intriguing transient infant behaviors, rhythmical stereotypies, has provided important clues to the construction of early movement. These rapid, repetitious movements of the limbs and torso—rocking, kicking, waving, bouncing, banging, rubbing, scratching, and swaying, are extraordinarily common in the first year of life. Although developmental theorists have discussed these distinctive movements for many years, their origin and function have remained obscure (see Thelen, 1979, for review).

My studies of these movements both in natural settings and in the laboratory, and in longitudinal and cross-sectional designs, revealed certain striking characteristics that are described next.

The Nature of the Movements and Their Development

1. Movements could be catalogued into about 50 distinguishable motor patterns involving the arms, legs, head, or whole torso in various postures (Thelen, 1979).

2. Frame-by-frame analysis of one stereotypy, supine kicking, and electromyographic recording of the underlying muscle activations revealed a consistent synergistic cocontraction of muscle groups spanning two or more joints and a strong temporal patterning (Thelen & Fisher, 1982, 1983b; Thelen, Bradshaw, and Ward, 1981).

3. Each of these movement patterns had a characteristic developmental profile, that is, an age of onset, of peak frequency, and of de-

cline. The onset and peak frequency of a movement appeared to coincide with emerging motor control in that particular limb or posture. For example, rocking in the hands-and-knees position appeared after the infant gained postural control but before the onset of coordinated crawling (Thelen, 1979).

In sum, rhythmical stereotypies had the characteristics of coordinative structures: that is, *units* of motor control that govern groups of muscles operating over one or more body joints, in this case to produce very simple, repetitive flexions, extensions, and rotations. The distinctive developmental profiles of these movements suggested that they were associated with emerging voluntary control over a particular function. In other words, these behaviors looked like an intermediate stage between little or no neuromuscular coordination and full voluntary control. Because motor development in humans is so prolonged, we can actually observe the constituent parts of the movement before they become incorporated into a smooth, voluntary performance.

Eliciting Stimuli

The most potent elicitors of bouts of rhythmical behaviors in the first 6 months were changes of generalized *behavioral arousal* (Thelen, 1981a). For example, in the laboratory, kicking in both the newborn period (Thelen & Fisher, 1983b) and in the following months (Thelen, Ridley-Johnson, & Fisher, 1983) was highly correlated with measures of behavioral arousal, or *state*. While in the newborn period, high arousal and kicking was associated with distress; as infants matured, they would kick with joyous excitement as well. Occasionally, rhythmical movements were seen when infants were drowsy or in states of low arousal.

In the first months, it was usually difficult to identify a particular external event associated with the arousal state. However, beyond the neonatal period a wide variety of contexts appeared to be related to stereotyped behavior. These included social interactions, feeding situations, movement stimulation, either passively or actively produced, and looking at or manipulating objects. And during the first year, the salience of different eliciting contexts for producing rhythmical stereotypes changed. Interactions with the caregiver were strong elicitors of stereotypy in 3- to 5-month-old infants, and object-related stereotypy became relatively more common in the last half of the first year (Thelen, 1981a).

Most significantly, however, the *form*, of the resulting movement stereotypy had no apparent relationship to the specific eliciting context. In other words, kicking in response to distress appeared in form to be no different from kicking in a bout of joy. Thus, it seemed as though arousal level or state, rather than a particular task or goal, was the mediating mechanism. It was as though behavioral activation *tuned-up* the system and potentiated a constellation of coordinated movements. Specific situations indeed had changing efficacy in getting the system tuned-up— social stimuli at 3 months or an interesting toy at 6 months. But unlike in a goal-corrected task, the kinematic details of the resulting movement were more a product of neuromuscular maturation than of the demands of the specific context. In sum, these developmental coordinative structures did appear to be organized on the lower levels of the control hierarchy, with their kinematic details independent of the apparent command functions.

Early Functions of Stereotyped Movements

With early stereotypies, movement outcomes were related to the environmental context but in a very general way, that is, through the ability of certain events to elicit changes in arousal. However, as infants matured, I observed a growing ability to use these simple patterned movements as instrumental responses (Thelen, 1981a, 1981b). For example, a 1-month-old infant might kick when distressed, a 3-month-old infant might kick during social play with the mother, a 4-month-old infant might kick against a squeaky toy to reactivate the noise, and a 6-month-old infant might kick apparently to signal the mother to continue the feeding. Our observational and experimental evidence showed that infants actually converted simple synergisms to functional actions, using developmentally available motor patterns to serve useful ends, including contingent control of people and objects, self-stimulation, communication, and exercise. The same kick or bounce or rock that was earlier a function of nonspecific activation became *attached*, so to speak, to a specific goal.

This conversion of these coordinative structures from state to *goal activation* was paralleled by an increasing modulation of the extreme arousal shifts that were so effective in eliciting stereotypy in younger infants. Older infants spent less time crying and in performing stereotypy. As complex, voluntary movements increased, so did the alert *optimal* state. However, even year-old infants often reverted to the rhythmical movements characteristic of an earlier age when arousal levels were extreme during great distress or joy (Thelen, 1981a).

Expressive Behaviors
as Developmental Coordinative Structures

Rhythmical stereotypies are conspicuous movements using large muscle groups. However, as Malatesta also points out in this volume (Chapter 8), there are many correspondences between patterning, developmental profiles, elicitation, and functional transformations of rhythmical stereotypies and those of emerging expressive behaviors. The following points illuminate the correspondence between coordinative structures and expressive behaviors.

First, like rhythmical stereotypies, the different emotionally expressive behaviors have a characteristic age of onset, peak frequency, and decline, apparently paced by neuromuscular maturation. For example, Fogel (1981) showed that between 5 and 14 weeks, a range of expressive movements showed different frequency profiles. Many, like *smile,* showed gradually increasing frequencies, whereas others, like *yawn* and *cry,* decreased in occurrence.

Second, early expressive movements may first appear in a *transitional* form, that is, a coordinated muscle synergism but not a fully articulated, mature behavior sequence. Individual facial and body gestures are often quite adultlike in form but without the complex temporal and spatial sequencing of expressions in older children or adults (Fogel, 1981; Oster, 1978).

A number of investigators have noted the intrinsic *rhythmical* patterning of early expressive behaviors, including crying (Emde, Gaensbauer, & Harmon, 1976; Wolff, 1969), brow-knitting and smiling (Oster, 1978), and attention levels in social interaction (Brazelton, Koslowski, & Main, 1974). The extreme importance of this intrinsic-timing component in the transition into voluntary activity is subsequently discussed in detail.

In addition, the progression from generalized-state changes to nonspecific arousal to more specific stimulus situations of eliciting contexts associated with rhythmical stereotypies is paralleled in the development of emotional behaviors. The earliest smiles occur in REM sleep (Emde *et al.*, 1976) and in the nonalert state following a feeding. The first visually-elicited smiles can be released by simply patterned stimuli and only later become more specifically associated with social stimuli. Some theorists have proposed that the smile is a generalized response to a particular pattern of pleasurable-tension buildup and then release, and in this sense, the smile is a motor response to arousal changes. Only late in the first year do smiles become used as operants (Sroufe, 1979). Similarly, Malatesta (Chapter 8, this volume) described the course of crying, from undifferentiated state-related behavior, to more specific cries of hunger, pain and anger, and only then as operants in a social context. Finally, Fogel and Hannan (in preparation) reported co-occurrences of particular manual gestures with specific states of arousal, for example, the gesture *point* occurring with moderate arousal levels and the gesture *curl* associated with higher levels.

The development of expressive behaviors also parallels that of rhythmicities in the opportunistic use of available coordinations for what appear to be highly functional ends. In both cases, we see appropriation of what is developmentally available to fill an adaptive niche. Whatever the releasing stimuli of early smiles, caregivers interpret them as communication of pleasure and as social gestures, and these smiles undoubtedly are powerful promoters of social bonding. When the processes of mutual gazing and smiling are disrupted, as with blind infants, mothers reported great difficulty communicating with and understanding their infants (Fraiberg, 1977). Early crying is undifferentiated but not nonfunctional. Like rhythmicities, early expressions of affect are both the bits and pieces of more complex behaviors, and in their essential functions during infancy, highly useful behaviors in their own right.

Finally, the model of motor development derived from rhythmical behaviors can be generalized to expressive actions in the conversion of apparently nonintentional movements into instrumental action, as is detailed in the next section.

How Do the Developmental Coordinative Structures Become Connected to Mechanisms of Voluntary Control?

The common and striking transitional rhythmical movements of infancy, then, may be good prototypes for studying the appropriation of the organized substrata into intentional action. My observations of the use of rhythmicities for instrumental ends in natural settings (Thelen, 1979, 1981a) prompted me to look for a paradigm whereby this conversion could be studied in more detail in an experimental manipulation. In fact, one rhythmical behavior, supine kicking, had been used in such a design to study early learning and memory (e.g., Lindsley, 1963; Rovee & Rovee, 1969; Rovee-Collier, Morrongiello, Aron, & Kupersmidt, 1978; Rovee-Collier, Sullivan, Enright, Lucas, & Fagen, 1980).

In this experimental procedure, infants are placed supine under a colorful overhead mobile, with a ribbon connecting their ankles to the mobile. As infants kick their legs, the mobile responds with movement and often, sound. Infants apparently so reinforced by the mobile's response to their kicking increase their kick rate over their spontaneous baseline rates in which they view a stationary mobile. Control infants who see noncontingent mobile movements do not increase their kick rate. This reinforcement schedule in which the intensity of the reinforcement is proportional to the effort of the response in both rate and vigor—kicking more and kicking harder produces more reinforcement—has been called *conjugate reinforcement* and is believed to be an especially potent schedule for early infant learning (Rovee-Collier & Gekoski, 1979).

Conjugate reinforcement of supine kicking appeared to be an especially appropriate paradigm for studying the imposition of voluntary control because we already knew something about both the kinematic organization and motivational control of *spontaneous leg kicks,* that is, those apparently not under voluntary control (Thelen, Bradshaw, & Ward, 1981). The most striking characteristic of spontaneous kicking was the temporal stability of the movement phases of the kick. The *flexion* phase, in which hip, knee, and ankle bend simultaneously and the leg is brought toward the torso, averaged around 300 msec in duration. The *extension* phase, in which the joint angles increase and the leg is extended up and away from the torso, was slightly longer than flexion, around 400 msec, but both movement phases were remarkably stable both in individual infants and in the sample as a whole. Figure 9.1 illustrates the temporal characteristics of the movement phases in four independent samples of infants at the ages of 2 weeks, one month, and three months. *Movement* phases remained stable regardless of the overall rate of kicking; there was no relationship between the individual rates of kicking and the durations of the movement phases. In contrast to the stability of the movement phases, the *pause* phases of kicking, the spaces between the flexions and extensions, were much more variable (Figure 1) and indeed reflected the speed or rate of kicking. Infants who kicked at a higher rate had shorter pauses between kicks.

Kick rate, in turn, was directly related to overall behavioral arousal. In infants aged from 2 weeks to 6 months, there was a strong correlation between the moment-to-moment changes in behavioral arousal and the rate of kicking (Thelen, Ridley-Johnson, & Fisher, 1983). Infants who were distressed or excited kicked more, but both the duration of the movement and the bilateral coordination of kicks were not affected by the infant's degree of behavioral excitement.

Consistent with the aforementioned hierarchical control models, it appeared as though spontaneous kicking resulted from tonic or nonspecific activation tuning-up a kick-generating mechanism. However, the

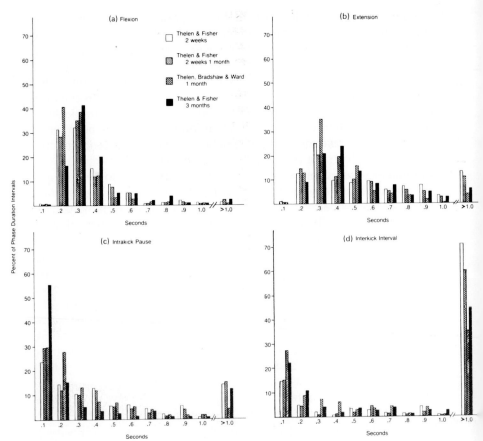

Figure 9.1. Frequency histograms of the durations of movement and pause intervals in spontaneous kicking of four samples of 2-week- to 3-month-old infants. Data are from Thelen and Fisher (1982, 1983a, 1983b); and Thelen *et al.* (1981). (a) *Flexion* is the movement of the leg toward the torso, with decreasing angles in hip, knee, and ankle. (b) *Extension* is the movement away from the torso, with increasing (straightening) angles in the joints. (c) *Intrakick pause* is the time of no movement between the cessation of the flexion phase and the onset of the succeeding extension. It is usually very short, so that flexion and extension are often nearly continuous. (d) The *interkick interval* or the pause between the end of the extension and the initiation of the next flexion shows a bimodal distribution. Some intervals are very short—kicks follow in quick succession—whereas others are many seconds in length.

control of the specific timing of the kick movements and the coordination between legs was unaffected by the generalized motivational component and was presumably organized, therefore, at independent and lower levels of a control hierarchy.

The intriguing question, then, was what would happen in the experimental procedure when a voluntary component was imposed on these nonspecific motor activities. How would the infant's higher-level, intentional-command signals control the nerves and muscles to activate the mobile? To answer this question, we replicated the conjugate reinforcement mobile design of Rovee-Collier and her associates (Rovee-Collier et al., 1978, 1980) but in addition to counting only the rate of kicking, we coded kinematic details of the temporal characteristics and amplitudes of the movements themselves. Thus, we were able to record the changes in the actual movement outcome as the infant converted an apparently spontaneous behavior into an instrumental one.

Six 3-month-old infants served as subjects, successively assigned to experimental and control groups. All infants were tested in their home cribs. We suspended a commercial mobile from a portable microphone stand so that the mobile hung about 20 cm from the infant's chest (See Figure 9.2). (The microphone stand isolated the mobile from movement transmitted by the crib). Infants' legs were bared and marked to facili-

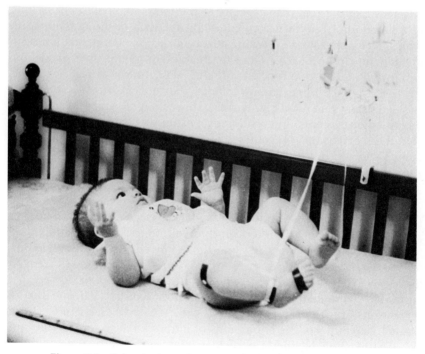

Figure 9.2. Infant in the mobile conjugate-reinforcement experiment.

tate movement analysis, and the entire test session was videotaped to give a lateral view of the infants' right legs.

All infants were given a 4-minute baseline condition in which they viewed a stationary mobile to establish operant levels of kicking. Immediately following baseline, the experimental group was reinforced for their kicking by attaching a ribbon from the right ankle to the mobile. The acquisition phase was 12 minutes. In order to provide the control group with a realistically moving mobile, an observer counted, in 30-second intervals, the jiggles of the mobile produced by the experimental infant. Control group infants had the ribbon attached to the crib bar and viewed the mobile moved by the experimenter at a rate provided by the previous experimental infant's jiggle schedule. Both groups were then given a 3-minute extinction period in which they again viewed a stationary mobile.

Kinematic analysis of the videotapes involved scanning each infant's entire 19-minute session frame-by-frame for the temporal and topographic characteristics of the kicks, according to methods reported elsewhere (Thelen, Bradshaw, & Ward, 1981; Thelen & Fisher, 1982, 1983a). A total of 400,000 frames were scanned and 1782 kicks analyzed.

Tables 1 and 2 report the results of the temporal analysis of kicking as a function of reinforcement condition for each of the individual infants. (To emphasize the learning effect, the acquisition period has been divided into two halves.) Despite changes in overall rate of kicking within each infant as a function of reinforcement and of individual differences in overall rate among infants, the movement phases, flexion and extension, remained highly stable for each infant and relatively consistent among infants. In each infant, flexion was shorter and less variable than extension. In contrast (Table 2), the nonmovement-pause phases showed much greater intra- and interindividual variability.

As in spontaneous kicking, infants appeared to adjust the overall rate of kicking by adjustments in the pauses between movements, rather than controlling the movement duration itself. There was a strong linear relationship between the duration of the kick cycle (the reciprocal of rate) and the duration of the interkick interval for each infant. Individual regressions of kick phases of cycle time showed that the interkick interval was always significantly ($p < .01$) related to cycle time (R^2 ranged from .665 to .999). In contrast, only 3 of 24 regressions of flexion against cycle time were significant (R^2 ranging from .039 to .100). Of the 24 regressions of extension against cycle time, 8 were significant (R^2 from .084 to .265) and 9 of the regressions of intrakick pause were significant (R^2, .054 to .218). Neither a particular infant nor a particular condition predicted significant regressions. Thus, although the flexion, extension,

TABLE 1

Duration of Movement Phases as a Function of Reinforcement Condition

Infant	Kick rate[a]	Flexion[b]		Extension[b]	
		$\overline{X}$	SD	$\overline{X}$	SD
Experimental					
DC (male)					
Baseline	12.1	.311	(.170)	.411	(.198)
Acquisition 1	21.5	.306	(.159)	.447	(.301)
Acquisition 2	25.2	.283	(.149)	.413	(.247)
Extinction	18.7	.278	(.142)	.604	(.420)
KS (female)					
Baseline	11.6	.346	(.179)	.378	(.204)
Acquisition 1	18.8	.272	(.116)	.308	(.167)
Acquisition 2	17.0	.305	(.139)	.303	(.158)
Extinction	14.2	.333	(.157)	.302	(.187)
TR (female)					
Baseline	17.8	.274	(.078)	.404	(.199)
Acquisition 1	7.2	.362	(.197)	.492	(.231)
Acquisition 2	17.8	.269	(.100)	.359	(.217)
Extinction	23.9	.312	(.127)	.483	(.304)
Control					
JB (male)					
Baseline	14.0	.299	(.194)	.435	(.194)
Acquisition 1	6.0	.228	(.131)	.396	(.190)
Acquisition 2	6.3	.243	(.151)	.354	(.199)
Extinction	4.0	.346	(.252)	.369	(.180)
MM (female)					
Baseline	20.3	.355	(.199)	.462	(.255)
Acquisition 1	13.9	.412	(.231)	.416	(.212)
Acquisition 2	17.4	.415	(.222)	.373	(.164)
Extinction	19.3	.408	(.198)	.448	(.225)
HB (female)					
Baseline	22.8	.394	(.191)	.584	(.384)
Acquisition 1	12.1	.459	(.256)	.734	(.370)
Acquisition 2	19.2	.415	(.205)	.585	(.342)
Extinction	26.1	.340	(.198)	.583	(.293)

[a] Measured as kicks/min.
[b] Measured in sec.

and intrakick pause were occasionally weakly related to kick rate, nearly all the variability could be accounted for by changes in the interval between kicks.

Thus, in both experimental and control groups, the absolute durations of the movement phases appeared to be stable features of the muscle collectives. Differences in rate of kicking, whether motivated by generalized arousal shifts, as in the control group, or by presumed operant

Duration of Pause Phases as a Function of Reinforcement Condition

Infant	Kick rate[a]	Intrakick pause[b]		Interkick interval[b]	
		$\overline{X}$	SD	$\overline{X}$	SD
Experimental					
DC (male)					
Baseline	12.1	.880	(2.891)	3.280	(4.310)
Acquisition 1	21.5	.097	(.307)	1.903	(2.982)
Acquisition 2	25.2	.084	(.383)	1.581	(3.226)
Extinction	18.7	.847	(2.330)	1.385	(2.229)
KS (female)					
Baseline	11.6	.484	(.459)	3.532	(6.612)
Acquisition 1	18.8	.648	(1.260)	1.880	(2.677)
Acquisition 2	17.0	.414	(.695)	2.284	(3.660)
Extinction	14.2	.476	(.698)	3.002	(5.561)
TR (female)					
Baseline	17.8	.136	(.239)	2.528	(4.382)
Acquisition 1	7.2	.102	(.205)	7.129	(18.509)
Acquisition 2	17.8	.110	(.230)	2.606	(3.704)
Extinction	23.9	.167	(.360)	1.432	(2.789)
Control					
JB (male)					
Baseline	14.0	.142	(.218)	3.115	(5.293)
Acquisition 1	6.1	.119	(.198)	9.391	(16.125)
Acquisition 2	6.3	.060	(.062)	8.275	(12.549)
Extinction	4.0	.072	(.042)	12.694	(16.421)
MM (female)					
Baseline	20.3	.427	(.789)	1.575	(2.554)
Acquisition 1	13.9	.374	(.539)	3.030	(4.744)
Acquisition 2	17.4	.194	(.308)	2.373	(4.000)
Extinction	19.2	.136	(.236)	1.997	(3.766)
HB (female)					
Baseline	22.8	.717	(1.046)	.739	(1.302)
Acquisition 1	12.1	1.007	(1.580)	2.512	(4.890)
Acquisition 2	19.2	.686	(1.059)	1.369	(2.536)
Extinction	26.1	.736	(1.020)	.545	(1.294)

[a] Measured as kicks/min.
[b] Measured in sec.

control, were accomplished nearly entirely by changes in the inter-movement intervals.

Rovee and Rovee (1969) noted anecdotally that when infants learned to control the mobile, they kicked with increased precision and vigor. We attempted to quantify these topographic differences in the quality of kicking as well as in the rate by measuring the amplitude of the kick as movement changes of the knee both parallel to the trunk in the supine infant and along a Y-axis, which represents the relative lift of the knee. We found that in all the experimental group infants, there was a strong increase in the horizontal trajectory of the knee in both flexion and extension over the conditioning session. Bigger kicks accompanied an increased kick rate. During extinction, however, two of the infants decreased their kick rate but continued to increase the kick amplitude. Lift of the leg also increased with the kick rate but not as dramatically as in the horizontal vector. However, control group infants whose kick rate varied not as a result of learning also showed a positive relationship between rate and amplitude, but again, two infants increased amplitude without a corresponding rate increase during one condition. Thus, it appears that there is a proportional relationship between the overall rate of kicking and the amplitude but that the two variables are not rigidly linked, that is, the amplitude of movement could be controlled independently of the rate.

Although kick rate and amplitude increased as a result of the reinforcement condition, reinforced kicks appeared more vigorous because the duration of the movement remained stable. The kicks are therefore of a greater velocity and the infants must exert correspondingly more muscle force.

A Motor Rule in the Transition from Spontaneous to Instrumental Action

The mobile study revealed that in these 3-month-old infants, certain characteristics of the organization of developmental coordinative structures remain stable when the motivation to move changed from generalized arousal to voluntary control. The duration of the movement itself, and perhaps its underlying muscle burst, were tightly constrained and apparently could not be altered by this learning task. In contrast, infants could readily adjust the "spaces" between movements in response to reinforcement contingencies. That is, they could control the initiation of a movement, but once the movement began, its temporal dimensions were fixed.

In addition, infants appeared able to adjust the strength of the muscle contraction to produce differences in amplitude or vigor, presumably by altering the number of motoneurons recruited or by adjusting the firing rate. Although infants in our studies generally increased both the rate and the amplitude when the action was reinforced, we also noted that the two parameters were not necessarily linked in that a few infants during extinction kicked less frequently but just as vigorously as when the mobile jiggled in response to their kick effort.

The results of imposing a voluntary component on a simple infant movement are consistent with contemporary notions of motor control. First, there is clear evidence of hierarchical levels of control. As infants kicked faster and harder to jiggle the mobile, the basic organization—the coordinative structure—of the kick was preserved. In short, the change of the motivation to move was not reflected in the recruitment of the muscle ensemble. The properties of the coordinative structure that were modifiable, that is, the rate of initiations and the force of the movement, allow flexibility to meet varying demands, while maintaining the integrity of the functional unit.

Indeed, it appears that early infant kicking conforms to a very general plan for motor control: that the duration and sequencing of muscle activations is relatively invariant and that the frequency and amplitude of movements are more modifiable. The best studied examples are in vertebrate locomotion, in which numerous studies (reviewed in Kelso & Tuller, 1984) show that the relative timing of the muscle groups involved is constant through a wide range of speeds and forces. Stability of timing relationships over metrical change has also been found to characterize postural adjustments, voluntary arm movements and speech (see Kelso & Tuller, 1984).

Constancy of relative muscle contraction times over a range of movement speeds and amplitudes is necessary to maintain the integrity of the coordinative structure. Freund and Budingen (1978) offer an explanation. They suggest that, at the neural level, the burst duration is constant but the firing rate is modulated. This type of control system is necessary to efficiently regulate several muscles working synergistically together. For a movement to occur, several muscles must contract in concert, but they each may work at a different effort level. If the amplitude of the resulting movement were dependent on the duration of the muscle discharge, these muscles working together would each have to start contracting at different times in each situation requiring adjustments of effort level. It is much simpler to achieve this coordination by regulating contraction amplitude instead of duration so that the peaks of contractions can be at the same time, or in the same fixed relationship, despite the effort by individual muscles. Infant leg kicks result from precise cocontraction of antagonist pairs (Thelen & Fisher, 1983b); as kick rate increases, this timing is preserved.

One motor rule, then, in the conversion of spontaneous into instrumental action might be: gain control of those variables in movement that can be modified without losing the essential construction of the movement. Because movement is structured as multimuscle coordinative structures, maintaining the timing and sequencing of the participating groups is essential. However, the numbers of initiations and/or the strength of the movement can be varied in scalar fashion. Similarly, numbers of coordinative structures can be sequenced and combined.

The examples of oral reflexes and chewing by Sheppard and Mysak (1984) obey well this motor rule. It is the frequency of the combining subsets that identifies a particular reflex. When the reflexes drop out, they diminish in amplitude or reverberations, but are still recognizable as coordinative structures. When chewing is constructed, it is essentially a task of filling the spaces with the appropriately timed and sequenced subsets.

The recognition of both facial and manual expressive behaviors in early infancy suggest that these may also follow such a motor rule. When the spontaneous smile of the infant is converted into a voluntary behavior, its form is preserved, but its initiation, and likely its strength or intensity, can be controlled by the infant. For an expressive gesture to function as communication, the movement must have some structural invariance that allows the receiver to correctly understand the message of the sender. On the other hand, gestures are not rigid but may vary in duration, intensity, and complexity, a flexibility that is essential for dealing with contextual variability. Motor theory has proposed one mechanism for providing flexibility within variability, and we show that this motor organization characterizes one infant behavior, kicking.

We have yet to ask whether the flexible-movement components of expressive behavior might similarly be assembled according to this more general motor rule of adjusting the spaces and the intensity of invariantly timed muscle collectives. Because of the similarities between transitional rhythmical stereotypies such as kicking and the early manifestations of expressive behavior, this model of conversion to voluntary control may be a promising direction for future research. For example, Ganchrow et al. (1983) have offered one possibility in their microanalysis of movement subcomponents of gustofacial expressions. Tracking the organization of these movements, especially their temporal and spatial characteristics, may yield valuable clues about the mechanisms of the transformation from state to voluntary control.

Summary

This chapter considers the question of how immature, innately given behaviors, such as some expressive ones, are transformed to flexible, voluntary use. It presents a model for the transformation of innately preprogrammed rigid actions into voluntary ones over whose initiation and temporal patterning the child gains control. Concepts from motor action theory on the hierarchical organization of action are discussed as a framework for the model. The argument is made that many infant expressive behaviors are structurally similar to ones previously studied from this perspective. Research is presented that shows how this control is achieved in infant kicking patterns, and it is argued that the same features of transformation from involuntary to voluntary control may apply to the infant's expressive behaviors.

Acknowledgments

I am indebted to Donna M. Fisher for her collaboration on the experiments reported here and to Alan Fogel and Scott Kelso for invaluable discussion of some of these issues. The research and preparation of this paper were supported by National Science Foundation grant BNS 804872 and by a NICHHD Research Career Development Award.

References

Anokhin, P. K. Systemogenesis as a general regulator of brain development. *Progress in Brain Research*, 1964, *9*, 54–86.

Bernstein, N. *Coordination and regulation of movements*. New York: Pergamon, 1967.

Brazelton, T. B., Koslowski, B., & Main, M. The origins of reciprocity: The early mother–infant interaction. In M. Lewis & L. A. Rosenblum (Eds.), *The origins of behavior: The effect of the infant on its caregiver*. New York: Wiley, 1974.

Carmichael, L. The onset and early development of behavior. In P. H. Mussen (Ed.), *Carmichael's Manual of Child Psychology* (3rd ed.). New York: Wiley, 1970.

Clark, J. E. The role of response mechanisms in motor skill development. In J. A. S. Kelso & J. E. Clark (Eds.), *The development of movement control and coordination*. New York: Wiley, 1982.

Delcomyn, F. Neural basis of rhythmic behavior in animals. *Science*, 1980, *210*, 492–498.

Easton, T. A. On the normal use of reflexes. *American Scientist*, 1972, *60*, 591–599.

Ekman, P., & Friesen, W. V. Measuring facial movement. *Environmental Psychology and Nonverbal Behavior*, 1976, *1*, 56–67.

Ekman, P., & Friesen, W. V. *Manual for the facial action coding system*. Palo Alto, CA: Consulting Psychologists Press, 1978.

Emde, R. N., Gaensbauer, T. J., & Harmon, R. J. Emotional expression in infancy. *Psychological Issues*, 1976, *10*(1), Monograph 37.

Fogel, A. The ontogeny of gestural communication: The first six months. In R. E. Stark (Ed.), *Language behavior in infancy and early childhood*. New York: Elsevier/North Holland, 1981.

Fogel, A., & Hannan, T. E. Manual expression in 9- to 15-week-old infants during face-to-face interaction with their mothers, in preparation.

Fraiberg, S. *Insights from the blind*. New York: Basic Books, 1977.

Freund, H. J., & Büdingen, H. J. The relationship between speed and amplitude of the fastest voluntary contractions of human arm muscles. *Experimental Brain Research*, 1978, *31*, 1–12.

Ganchrow, J. R., Steiner, J. E., & Daher, M. Neonatal facial expressions in response to different qualities and intensities of gustatory stimuli. *Infant Behavior and Development*, 1983, *6*, 189–200.

Greene, P. H. Why is it easy to control your arms? *Journal of Motor Behavior*, 1982, *14*, 260–286.

Grillner, S. Locomotion in vertebrates: Central mechanisms and reflex interaction. *Physiological Reviews*, 1975, *55*, 247–304.

Herman, R. M., Grillner, S., Stein, P. S. G., & Stuart, D. G. (Eds.), *Neural control of locomotion*. New York: Plenum, 1976.

Kelso, J. A. S., Putnam, C. A., & Goodman, D. On the space-time structure of human interlimb co-ordination. *Quarterly Journal of Experimental Psychology*, 1983, *35*, 347–375.

Kelso, J. A. S., & Tuller, B. A dynamical basis for action systems. In M. S. Gazzaniga (Ed.), *Handbook of cognitive neuroscience*. New York: Plenum, 1984.

Lindsley, O. R. Experimental analysis of social reinforcement: Terms and methods. *American Journal of Orthopsychiatry*, 1963, *33*, 624–663.

Mounoud, P. Cognitive development: Construction of new structures or construction of internal organizations. In I. E. Sigel, D. M. Brodzinsky, & R. M. Golinkoff (Eds.), *New directions in Piagetian theory and practice*. Hillsdale, NJ: Erlbaum, 1981.

Oppenheim, R. W. Ontogenetic adaptations and retrogressive processes in the development of the nervous system and behaviour: A neuroembryological perspective. In K. J. Connolly & H. F. R. Prechtl (Eds.), *Maturation and development: Biological and psychological perspectives*. London: Spastics and Heinemann, 1981.

Osofsky, J. D. *Handbook of infant development*. New York: Wiley, 1979.

Oster, H. Facial expression and affect development. In M. Lewis & L. A. Rosenblum (Eds.), *The development of affect*. New York: Plenum, 1978.

Papousek, H., & Papousek, M. Mothering and the cognitive head-start: Psychobiological considerations. In H. R. Schaffer (Ed.), *Studies in mother–infant interaction*. New York: Academic Press, 1977.

Peiper, A. *Cerebral function in infancy and childhood*. New York: Consultants Bureau, 1963.

Prechtl, H. F. R. The study of neural development as a perspective of clinical problems. In K. J. Connolly & H. F. R. Prechtl (Eds.), *Maturation and development: Biological and psychological perspectives*. London: Spastics International and Heinemann, 1981.

Reed, E. S. An outline of a theory of action systems. *Journal of Motor Behavior*, 1982, *14*, 98–134.

Rovee, C. K., & Rovee, D. T. Conjugate reinforcement of infant exploratory behavior. *Journal of Experimental Child Psychology*, 1969, *8*, 33–39.

Rovee-Collier, C. K., & Gekoski, M. J. The economics of infancy: A review of conjugate reinforcement. *Advances in Child Development and Behavior*, 1979, *13*, 195–225.

Rovee-Collier, C. K., Morrongiello, B. A., Aron, M., & Kupersmidt, J. Topographical response differentiation and reversal in 3-month old infants. *Infant Behavior and Development*, 1978, *1*, 323–333.

Rovee-Collier, C. K., Sullivan, M. W., Enright, M., Lucas, D., & Fagen, J. W. Reactivation of infant memory. *Science*, 1980, *208*, 1159–1161.

Sheppard, J. J., & Mysak, E. D. Ontogeny of infantile oral reflexes and emerging chewing. *Child Development*, 1984, *55*, 831–843.

Shik, M. L., & Orlovsky, G. N. Neurophysiology of locomotor automatism. *Physiological Reviews*, 1976, *56*, 465–501.

Sroufe, A. L. Socioemotional development. In J. D. Osofsky (Ed.), *Handbook of Infant Development*, New York: Wiley, 1979.

Thelen, E. Rhythmical stereotypies in normal human infants. *Animal Behaviour,* 1979, *27,* 699–715.

Thelen, E. Kicking, rocking, and waving: Contextual analysis of rhythmical stereotypies in normal human infants. *Animal Behaviour,* 1981a, *29,* 3–11.

Thelen, E. Rhythmical behavior in infancy: An ethological perspective. *Developmental Psychology,* 1981b, *17,* 237–257.

Thelen, E. Learning to walk is still an "old" problem: A reply to Zelazo. *Journal of Motor Behavior,* 1983, *15,* 139–161.

Thelen, E., Bradshaw, G., & Ward, J. A. Spontaneous kicking in month-old infants: Manifestations of a human central locomotor program. *Behavioral and Neural Biology,* 1981, *32,* 45–53.

Thelen, E., & Fisher, D. M. Newborn stepping: An explanation for a "disappearing reflex." *Developmental Psychology,* 1982, *18,* 760–775.

Thelen, E., & Fisher, D. M. From spontaneous to instrumental behavior: Kinematic analysis of movement changes during very early learning. *Child Development,* 1983a, *54,* 129–140.

Thelen, E., & Fisher, D. M. The organization of spontaneous leg movements in newborn infants. *Journal of Motor Behavior,* 1983b, *15,* 353–377.

Thelen, E., Ridley-Johnson, R., & Fisher, D. M. Shifting patterns of bilateral coordination and lateral dominance in the leg movements of young infants. *Developmental Psychobiology,* 1983, *16,* 29–46.

Trevarthan, C. The psychobiology of speech development. In E. H. Lenneberg (Ed.), Language and brain: Developmental aspects. *Neurosciences Research Program Bulletin,* 1974, *12,* 570–585.

Trevarthan, C. Descriptive analyses of infant communication behaviour. In H. R. Schaffer (Ed.), *Studies in mother–infant interaction.* New York: Academic Press, 1977.

Trevarthan, C. Basic patterns of psychogenic change in infancy. In T. G. Bever (Ed.), *Regressions in mental development.* Hillsdale, NJ: Erlbaum, 1982.

Turvey, M. T. Preliminaries to a theory of action with a reference to vision. In R. Shaw & J. Bransford (Eds.), *Perceiving, acting, and knowing: Toward an ecological psychology.* Hillsdale, NJ: Erlbaum, 1977.

von Hofsten, C. Development of visually directed reaching: The approach phase. *Journal of Human Movement Studies,* 1979, *5,* 160–178.

von Hofsten, C. Eye-hand coordination in the newborn. *Developmental Psychology,* 1982, *18,* 450–461.

von Hofsten, C. Developmental changes in the organization of prereaching movements. *Developmental Psychology,* 1984, *20,* 378–388.

White, B. L., Castle, P., & Held, R. Observations on the development of visually-directed reaching. *Child Development,* 1964, *35,* 349–364.

Wolff, P. H. The natural history of crying and other vocalizations in early infancy. In B. Foss (Ed.), *Determinants of infant behavior, IV.* London: Methuen, 1969.

Chapter 10

Coordinative Structures in the Development of Expressive Behavior in Early Infancy

Alan Fogel

Relationship to Other Chapters and to the Field

Issues Relevant to the Field

Fogel addresses the organizational substrate of the biological side of biology–environment interactions in action development. This general characterization includes the organization of the action of expressive behavior, across motor channels and cognitive features. By applying principles of evolutionary and functional economy, Fogel's view sees motor development as composed of cascades of reorganizations of the structure and function of subsystems. In this, he and Thelen (Chapter 9, this volume), as noted later bring a newly sharpened vision of the organization of expressive behavior development from motor action theory. This vision contrasts with the traditional one of gradual accretion of skill, scheme, or differentiation in one continuous direction. Fogel presents his own observational data on multiple-expressive subsystems to support the aptness of his characterization for expressive development and to demonstrate an observational strategy that is consistent with it.

In Fogel's characterization, the environment interacts with this fundamentally biological reorganization by providing the experiences that contribute to the restructuring of subsystems and that create the environmental press for necessary functions and their timing. He further puts forth a current position in evolutionary theorizing that suggests a broad-gauge relationship between inherited features and natural selection: contrary to the unfortunate tendency to

THE DEVELOPMENT OF EXPRESSIVE BEHAVIOR:
BIOLOGY–ENVIRONMENT INTERACTIONS   249

posit adaptive value for any inherited feature, for this position, extant inherited features need not be adaptive in the sense of having been selected by natural selection but need only be nonmaladaptive and ready when a truly selected system is needed to function. Thus, features may be inherited as genetic riders on other selected features and/or as contributions to the eventual organization and function of a selected system. Such a view urges theorists who posit adaptive value of inherited features to supply additional evidence of the feature's evolutionarily adaptive value beyond the mere fact of inheritance. Almost all theorists in the field of expressive development assume adaptive value of some inherited feature, making this caution a general issue for the field.

Relationship to Other Chapters

Fogel employs Thelen's (Chapter 9) identification of motor stereotypies as one starting place for his thinking on the organization of motoric development. The coordinative structures, which Thelen introduced into mainstream developmental psychology from motor theory, are the focus of Fogel's conception. Fogel emphasizes the cascading coordination of motor and cognitive subsystems, whereas Thelen emphasizes the transformation of immature motor systems into new voluntary organizations. Independently supporting the relevance of coordinative structures to expressive development, Malatesta (Chapter 8) also cites Thelen's characterization of motor stereotypies, a particular type of coordinative structure, as apt descriptions of the expressive behavior of the young infant. Fogel's conception of the organizing role of coordinative structures in organizing multiple-motor and cognitive systems suggests itself as a vehicle for a main primary effect of general experience cited by Mason (Chapter 6): the increased coordination of systems through Ekman's (See Chapter 1) central-affect program.

Fogel's implication of the inheritance of many behaviors that have not directly been naturally selected is consistent with Darwin's view of the inheritance of expressive behaviors, as explicated by Montgomery (Chapter 2). As Montgomery shows, it was important for Darwin to argue that expressive behaviors may be inherited, but were neither specialized, nor special creations, for the function of emotional communication.

For Consistent Terminology

As many other theorists and contributors to this volume, Fogel uses emotion and affect interchangeably, although affect includes internal states besides emotions. —ED.

Introduction

The development of expressive behavior in the first year of human life has attracted the attention of a number of scholars since the early 1900s. Although this period of time has seen the expansion and refinement of observational techniques, accounts of affective development are typically descriptive in nature. Theories that propose models of the developmental process are more often metaphors for the form in which the ontogenetic process has revealed itself to the investigator. Bridges's (1933) description of emotion expressions as differentiating gradually out of a small set of more global response states is a good example of this metaphorical approach.

Piaget's (1962) answer to the "How?" of development, was *equilibration*. Although it is likely that such a process is associated with development, too much is left unspecified. In particular, the invariant processes of equilibration—assimilation and accommodation—cannot explain why skills and affects emerge in their observed ontogenetic order. Why, to take one example, does social smiling not develop until 2 months of age? One can imagine evolutionary scenarios in which it would be adaptive for such things to have happened. Early smiling might serve a more immediate bonding function, for example. Fear of strangers is also relatively "late" to develop. If fear were to appear earlier, it could lead to a precocious, independent signaling response and lead to earlier control mechanisms that would serve to protect the infant against predators, if we are to follow Bowlby's (1969) reasoning to its logical conclusions.

On the other hand, there are many examples of affective behaviors that appear "too early" in development to serve any useful function. Investigators have seen components of all the mature emotional expressions in infants only months old (Oster, 1978), as well as manual expressions present in early life, such as pointing, that do not operate in the functional context of language development until the second year (Fogel, 1981; Fogel & Hannan, in press; Trevarthen, 1977, 1979). It seems that the solution to the apparent puzzle of expressions that appear "too early" and have no immediate functional significance for the infant and of expressions that appear "too late" and therefore leave the infant with the inability to complete intentions (such as wanting an object without being able to reach for it), or with the inability to express internal states that might yield potentially valuable information to caregivers, are common across many other realms of behavioral development (see Thelen, Chapter 9, this volume).

These apparent irregularities could be, and usually are, ignored as untidy sidelights in an otherwise orderly process. The concept of *decalage* seems to have been developed by Piaget and his followers to serve just such a theoretical function. Dacalage leaves intact the stage-sequence notion, and the invariant uniformity of assimilation and accommodation, by suggesting that certain skills develop at different times but in accord with the general structural principles of the particular stage of development. An alternative view offered by Fischer and Corrigan (1981) is that the basic unit of cognitive development is not the structural aspect of the stage but the morphological and neurological constraints of individual skills. Thus, individual motor skills and conceptual skills will have their own unique periods of ascendency and decline.

Rhythmical stereotypies involving different body parts, exemplify such unique patterns over time: the frequency of occurrence of each movement pattern (for example, kicking, banging, waving, and rocking) has a characteristic time of onset, rate of increase, and rate of decrease during the first year (Thelen, 1979). Facial expressions and manual expressions of affect also adhere to idiosyncratic patterns in the first year. Spontaneous finger-point expressions are relatively frequent in the first half year and decline in the second half of the first year, whereas finger-spread and grasp expressions are less frequent early and then increase (Fogel, 1981; Platzman, 1983). Frequency of occurrence of individual facial expressions show differences in their rise and fall times during the first year (Fogel, 1981).

So long as discussion of development adheres to a language of continuity, and to the assumption of a gradual accretion, we continue to repress these developmental observations as disturbing to our theoretical consciousness. If there is a defense mechanism operating to blind theory to the evidence, I suggest that it has to do with the fear of an anarchic chaos in which bits of action patterns and motor skills go rumbling through the ontogenetic terrain in a rather unlinked and random fashion. If this is indeed the case, we must accept its reality. However, because there are invariant developmental sequences, we know that components of action develop in some orderly fashion. It is now the time to take the existing order as a starting point and to no longer impose a model that lacks the ability to account for the intricacies of ontogenetic sequencing.

This chapter offers an example of how research in this area might proceed and some initial attempts to formulate a theoretical model to account for the findings. Breaking down expressive behavior into its component acts requires that we not ignore the motor aspects of expression. It is argued, therefore, that the most appropriate way to study ontogenetic sequences is to preserve the sequential and temporal aspects of expressive behavior during observation episodes. As in studies of kinematics, emphasis is placed on the morphology and temporal display properties of affective expressions. It is proposed that once we have a large corpus of such observations of the same infants at different ages, we will be in a better position to formulate some general developmental principles.

Sequential Patterns of Affect Expression:
Coordinative Structures

In the study of motor movement and motor development it has been shown that only a relatively few of the possible sequential patterns of component movements actually occur in nature. For example, given all the possible combinations of facial muscle movement, the relatively small number of facial affect expressions is of note. Discrete affect expressions are an example of what students of motor movement call *coordinative structures:* a group of muscles that have been constrained to act as a functional synergy (Thelen, Chapter 9, this volume). Unlike concepts of motor movement that posit only neuromotor constraints for behavior, the concept of functional synergy suggests that some movement patterns are constrained by the physical properties of the muscles—their strength, location vis-à-vis a movable joint, and mutual proximity—and by the nature of the task. Darwin (1872) had a similar view of facial expressions, which he saw as arising spontaneously (synergistically) from changes in blood pressure, muscle tension, jaw and eye movement that were associated with specific states of arousal.

The notion of synergy is intriguing and needs more specification than the goals of this chapter allow. For our purposes we need only note that real motor movements are discrete, coordinated units of mutually cooperating muscle groups. We can then propose that ontogeny is a process of breaking down and reconstituting new coordinative structures as the functional demands on the infant change over time. In order to demonstrate this we need to do the following:

First, the existence of discrete expressive behaviors must be documented. Although this has been done for the so-called basic affects, little is known about higher-order sequences of expressions that might constitute coordinative structures. An example of such a coordinated higher-order sequence is the newborn's state of arousal. As defined by Wolff (1966), each *arousal state* is a set of mutually complementary behaviors that cohere together in reliably repeating sequences of action. Second, we must demonstrate that the component movements of such sequences can become reorganized into new sequences, equally reliable, as the infant gets older. To continue with the example of states, consider the expression of smiling. It first appears only in drowsy states but by 2 months only in awake states (Sroufe, 1979). Furthermore, the pattern of behavior in waking and sleeping states is quite different at 2 months than it was at birth. Other examples of ontogenetic changes in behavioral sequences can also be found.

For example, some students of verbal and vocal development argue that later states of vocal production are merely reorganizations of the phonemic units that are present in early life. Stark (1978) suggested that the cooing of the 3-month-old is the creation of pleasurable vocalization out of the phonetic components found in the *vegetative* noises that all infants have at birth—crying, sneezing, coughing, burping, and so forth. Oller (1981) has suggested that the deliberate babbling of the 5-month-old infant is a form of vocal secondary circular reaction using the phonetic elements of vegetative and cooing sounds.

Trevarthen (1977, 1979) has argued that infants in the first few months of life show movements of the mouth that are not associated with sound production, nor are they clearly related to affect expressions. These movements take the form of mouth shape and tongue positionings that resemble those of later speech, such as the slightly protruded lip shape necessary to pronounce *wh-*, or the tongue-to-teeth (gum) proximity required to pronounce *th-*. It may be that these early motor patterns later become integrated with other speech-motor mechanisms that are maturing in the oropharyngeal anatomy and with perceptual changes in the neuronal auditory pathways (Kent, 1981; Netsell, 1981). Mature speech, therefore, could be conceptualized as a coordinative structure that uses some of the same elements found at birth, combined with other elements that have become operational at different times during development.

Do such developmental patterns exist for facial expressions? The work of Ekman and Oster (1979) has shown that the relatively few discrete facial expressions that we see are composed of a large number of component muscle groups that are organized into coordinative structures, and there is some evidence that the particular muscle groups used to produce an expression (a smile for example) change with development, with the ultimate effect of making the expressions more clearly discernible to the observer.

Demos (1982) and Riccuiti and Poresky (1972) have shown that initially discrete facial expressions of infants under 6 months become temporally reorganized in somewhat older infants to produce expressions of *mixed* affects. Components of anger from the brow region will be mixed with components of enjoyment from the mouth region to produce what Demos calls the "I've gotcha" expression. Another frequently occurring mixed expression observed by Demos is a smile combined with a nonaffective facial movement, such as a jaw drop, which occurs in situations of anticipated pleasure, such as when the mother approaches to nuzzle the child's neck. A distress expression with a lower-lip bite is another example of affective and nonaffective facial movements that combine to produce a new expression, in this case used to control the child's feelings of distress. Demos found that as the children in her sample got older, there was a higher percentage of mixed expressions, ranging from 50 to 75% of the child's repertoire.

Further Evidence for Expressive Behavior Sequencing in the First Year of Life

Data presented here come from a case study of two infants, a girl and a boy, videotaped at weekly intervals from the age of 2 weeks until 10 months, while engaged in face-to-face interaction on their mothers' laps. Interactions lasted between 5 and 10 minutes and took place in a laboratory playroom. Details of the procedures, coding, and other aspects of these data are available from Fogel (1981, 1982a, 1982b), Hannan (1982) and Platzman (1983).

In order to provide a large enough sample of occurrences at each observation point, successive sessions were pooled in groups of three sessions each. Because one infant (J) had more sessions than the other (H), J's data resulted in 13 groupings and H's, in 11 groupings, covering the same age span. The frequencies, by age-grouping for each expression category shown in Table 1, are given in Table 2. It should be clear from these tables that there is not a strict linear change in the frequency of each category from one age to the next. The session-to-session variation is even greater, so that pooling over three sessions has smoothed out the between-grouping variation somewhat. Some overall linear trends exist in these data, as shown from the correlation matrixes given in Table 3, but there are differences between the two infants in the pattern of significant correlations.

For example, both infants show a significant decrease in expressions

TABLE 1

Definitions of Categories of Facial Expression

Category	Definition
Smile	Positive affective expression, primarily smiling, but also includes an occasional occurrence of laughter.
Cry	Intense distress expressed by frown-face plus the vocalization of a cry.
Frown	Moderate distress in which lip corners are turned down; the eyebrows may be knit, and it may be accompanied by brief discomfort vocalizations.
Hand-mouth	Any contact of the infant's hand, fingers, or arm and the infant's mouth
Mouthing	Any nonexpressive movement of the mouth, such as tonguing, chewing, sucking, puckering, blowing bubbles, and so forth.
Rest	Relaxed facial expression, no mouth movement.

TABLE 2

Frequences of Occurrence of Individual Facial Expression
Categories, by Age Group

Grouping	Mean age (weeks)	Smile	Cry	Frown	Hand-mouth	Mouthing	Rest
Infant J							
1	3	1	3	8	0	20	27
2	5	6	9	22	0	24	28
3	9	4	11	10	4	30	36
4	12	13	4	7	15	45	32
5	15	20	22	26	6	46	29
6	20	12	3	7	24	42	37
7	24	19	4	4	14	41	62
8	30	31	18	2	10	28	43
9	34	23	7	0	15	21	43
10	36	33	3	4	20	28	63
11	42	25	8	6	46	29	66
12	44	27	18	5	7	33	66
13	46	40	16	6	9	21	71
Infant H							
1	3	0	11	6	0	14	6
2	7	13	13	13	2	25	28
3	10	10	0	0	9	45	47
4	13	22	0	4	22	53	40
5	17	34	1	5	26	65	67
6	25	18	5	2	31	42	61
7	30	22	1	0	26	23	55
8	33	20	0	0	37	37	78
9	37	7	0	5	30	18	43
10	40	14	0	1	33	23	40
11	42	33	13	1	28	14	39

TABLE 3

Intercorrelations of Facial Expression Categories and Age

	Smile	Cry	Frown	Hand–mouth	Mouthing	Rest
Infant J						
Age	.90***	.28	−.55*	.51*	−.20	.89***
Smile	—	.40	−.39	.33	−.13	.78***
Cry	—	—	.35	−.30	.04	.09
Frown	—	—	—	−.37	.27	−.53*
Hand–mouth	—	—	—	—	.16	.47*
Mouthing	—	—	—	—	—	.17
Infant H						
Age	.36	−.24	−.55*	.85***	−.33	.42
Smile	—	−.05	−.26	.51*	.44	.58*
Cry	—	—	.53*	−.54*	−.51*	−.60*
Frown	—	—	—	−.61*	−.08	−.50
Hand–mouth	—	—	—	—	.14	.74**
Mouthing	—	—	—	—	—	.57*

$*p < .05.$ $**p < .01.$ $***p < .001.$

of mild distress (*frown*) and a significant increase in hand-mouth activity with age. Although infant J significantly increases both *smile* and *rest* expressions with age, these do not significantly change for infant H. Another interesting difference is in the extent to which the *hand–mouth* activity is used by both infants. With infant H, *hand–mouth* is significantly and positively correlated with *rest* and with *smile* and is negatively correlated with *cry* and *frown*. This suggests that the *hand–mouth* expression is linked with both positive and neutral expressions of affect, and it may even serve to suppress expressions of negative affect. Similar trends were present for infant J, but only one correlation reached significance, between *hand–mouth* and *rest*. The behavior of *mouthing* was correlated significantly and negatively with *cry* and positively with *rest* for Infant H: similar to the pattern for *hand–mouth*. There were, however, no comparable trends for *mouthing* to be related to other categories in Infant J.

In order to clarify the sequential relationship between these expressive categories, a multiple-event lag analysis (Sackett et al., 1978) was done on the categories in Table 1. Data is reported here for the first lag, that is, whether contingent expressive behaviors were more likely to immediately precede or to immediately follow the target behavior. Event lags were calculated using each behavior category as the target. Two types of sequence can be identified from these data. (1) A simple *before–after* sequence in which one category is likely to either precede or to follow another and (2) an *alternating* sequence, in which two categories are likely to repeat, in alternating fashion, two or more times in succession.

Rather than present the rather long list of probabilities that were derived from this analysis, the highlights of the significant findings are presented. These are summarized in Table 4. In general, there was a good deal of consistency of event sequences, both within and between subjects. Within the same subject, significant sequences were highly likely to appear across two or more adjacent age-groups. This suggests

TABLE 4

Event Sequences for Target Behaviors

Target behavior	Infant J			Infant H		
	Age	Grouping	Sequence	Age	Grouping	Sequence
Smile	3	1	Frown (R)[c]	3	1	—
	5	2	Mouthing (A)[a]	7	2	Mouthing (A) Rest (B)
	9	3	—	10	3	Mouthing (A)
	12	4	Other[d] (R)	13	4	—
	15	5	Other (R)	17	5	Mouthing (A) Other (R)
	20	6	—			
	24	7	Rest(A)	25	6	—
	30	8	Rest(B)[b]	30	8	Rest(A) Other (R)
	34	9	Rest(A)	33	8	Rest(R)
	36	10	Rest(A)	37	9	Rest(R)
				40	10	Mouthing(R)
	42	11	—	42	11	Rest(R)
	44	12	—			
	46	13	Rest(A,B)			
Cry	3	1	Frown(R)	3	1	—
	5	2	Frown(A)	7	2	Hand–mouth(B)
	9	3	Other(R) Frown(B)	10	3	—
	12	4	Mouthing(B)	13	4	—
	15	5	Frown(R)	17	5	Mouthing(A)
	20	6	Other(R)			
	24	7	—	25	6	—
	30	8	—	30	7	—
	34	9	—	33	8	—
	36	10	—	37	9	—
				40	10	—
	42	11	—	42	11	Hand–mouth(A) Frown(R)
	44	12	Hand–mouth(A)			
	46	13	—			

TABLE 4 (*Continued*)

Target behavior	Infant J			Infant H		
	Age	Grouping	Sequence	Age	Grouping	Sequence
Frown	3	1	Cry(R) Smile(R)	3	1	Rest(B) Mouthing(A)
	5	2	Cry(B)	7	2	—
	9	3	Cry(A)	10	3	—
	12	4	—	13	4	Mouthing(A)
	15	5	Cry(R)	17	5	Rest(A)
	20	6	—			
	24	7	Rest(R)	25	6	Rest(R)
	30	8	—	30	7	—
	34	9	—	33	8	—
	36	10	Rest(A)	37	9	Hand–mouth(R)
				40	10	Hand–mouth(A)
	42	11	Rest(A)	42	11	Cry(R)
	44	12	Rest(A)			
	46	13	Rest(R)			
Hand–mouth	3	1	—	3	1	—
	5	2	Cry(A)	7	2	—
	9	3	—	10	3	—
	12	4	Rest(B)	13	4	—
	15	5	Rest(B)	17	5	—
	20	6	Other(R)			
	24	7	Mouthing(B) Other(R)	25	6	Rest(B)
	30	8	Rest(A)	30	7	Mouthing(A)
	34	9	Frown(R) Rest(A)	33	8	Cry(R)
	36	10	Rest(A) Frown(B)	37	9	—
				40	10	Rest(A) Frown(B)
	42	11	Rest(A)	42	11	Rest(A) Other(R) Cry(B)
	44	12	Cry(B)			
	46	13	—			

[a] A = Listed behavior comes *after* target behavior
[b] B = Listed behavior comes *before* target behavior
[c] R = Listed behavior is observed in *repeating* alternation with target behavior
[d] Other = One of several behaviors may occur in alternation with repeating target behavior.

that the sequences are not chance occurrences: they are persistent patterns of action that occur in a reliable fashion.

Sequences seem to change systematically with age in a way that is similar across infants. For example, repeated smiling begins at 12 weeks and continues until 15 weeks for infant J; it begins at 17 weeks and continues until the end of the observations at 42 weeks for infant H. (see Table 4). The results on the ontogeny of smiling clusters in these two subjects, and in a larger cross-sectional sample of subjects, has been reported elsewhere (Fogel, 1982b).

In infant J, although repeated smiling did not occur past 15 weeks, smiling either was preceded or followed by rest, analogous to the alternation of smile with rest and also with mouthing for infant H. Typically, the category "other" was either rest or mouthing. Therefore, smile is embedded in sequences in which the mouth is relatively nonexpressive, both before and after the smile. The fact that smile is not likely to occur in sequence with cry, frown or hand–mouth suggests that there may be a higher-order coordinative structure regulating the display of positively toned facial expressions.

Table 4 suggests that sequentially organized units may exist for other expressive behaviors and affective states. Cry, in the early weeks of life, is sequenced with the less intense frown (in Subject J, up to 15 weeks). Although *cry* is sometimes sequenced with *mouthing* for both subjects, it is never sequenced with *rest*, providing a striking comparison to *smile*. For at least half of the sessions, *cry* is not systematically sequenced with any other category of expression. These sessions occur primarily in the second half of the first year for both subjects, suggesting that *cry* is a sequentially isolated behavior later in the first year: it is no more likely to precede or to follow any particular behavior.

The patterning for *frown* is different than for cry. Because of the sequencing of *frown* with *rest* and *mouthing*, and the often repeating nature of the *frown–rest* pattern, it resembles *smile* patterns. However, *frown* is sometimes linked with *cry*, and sometimes with *hand–mouth*, neither of which is seen in *smile* sequences. Because *smile* and *frown* are both considered to be mildly arousing affects (Sroufe, 1979), it may be that the affective response system has enough resiliance to effectively return the infant to a *rest* or neutral state after both of these states. *Cry*, on the other hand, may reflect the presence of an overwhelmingly intense affect (see Fogel, 1982a). This experience may disrupt the affective system such that it cannot return systematically to a base state (the state after *cry* is unpredictable) of *rest* or *mouthing*. In this view, the *cry* disrupts the sequencing rules, or coordinative affective structures, that might otherwise maintain an optimally stable pattern of behavior.

One final behavior category of interest is *hand–mouth*. This behavior is often seen sequentially with *rest* and *mouthing*, but more often it precedes or follows *frown*. In all but one instance, *hand–mouth* follows these negative expressions, giving the impression that it may be used as a means of suppressing distress, once the distress starts. The instances in which *hand–mouth* is sequentially related to *rest* may be because the behavior has served successfully to eliminate the negative state. Indeed, this may account for the negative correlations of the frequency of *cry* and *frown*, with the frequency of *hand–mouth*.

By focusing on individual behaviors, their sequential interrelationships and their changes over age, the data suggest that stepwise progress and discontinuity become more salient to the observer than continuities and linear development progress. We find that the changes in coordinative structures are due to the reorganization of existing muscle movements into new coordinative structures over time. For example, cooing is a reorganization of vegetative sounds, and mature walking is a combination of earlier kicking movements combined with elements of postural control (Thelen, Chapter 9, this volume). Positive affective expression in the second half-year is a combination of earlier forms of discrete *smiles* with arousal controls that allow the infant to sustain positive engagement over a repeated series of smiles and laughs, and negative affective expression in the second half year moves away from the repeating cycles of *cry* and *frown* seen in the first half year and incorporates arousal regulatory components, such as *hand–mouth* and *mouthing*.

Theoretical Considerations

When the development of expressive behavior is considered from the perspective of reorganizations of components into coordinative structures, we may be in a better position to answer some of the questions posed at the outset. Why do some behaviors appear "too early" in development, whereas others seem to arrive "too late"? These labels, although enclosed in quotation marks, reflect the bias of continuity that pervades developmental thinking. Structures are late or early primarily by virtue of some presumed *function* or structure, one that is thought to be operating for the infant in the mind of the developmentalist. Aside from the bias of continuity by developmentalists, there is also an assumption of "adaptedness"; all behaviors must serve a purpose for the infant.

There is no a priori reason to believe that immature forms have adaptive value for the organism. Consider the behavioral development of the human fetus. The fetus develops a good many of the neonatal reflexes, not to mention reflexes having to do with respiration and heart function, during the second trimester of fetal life (Hooker, 1952; Trevarthen, 1973). Although neonatalists have been willing to speculate about the adaptive value of the newborn's reflexes (the Moro reflex, as a vestige of the primate clinging response, for example), few have seen fit to consider the adaptive value of the fetus's palmer reflex, or head turning responses to orofacial stimulation. On the contrary, it is presumed by most that these fetal behavior patterns are *preparatory* for the extrauterine environment of the newborn.

While it is no doubt true that the neonate comes to rely on many of the fetal reflexes for survival, there are many fetal coordinative structures that do not have any clear function for the neonate and thus appear to be "too early". There is some reason to believe that birth is not a major transition from the perspective of infant development. The timing of birth vis-à-vis gestation may have to do with ecological parameters of the live delivery of an organism with an extremely large head (about one-fourth of the body length at birth) and brain from a female whose pelvis size is limited by osteological constraints of bone weight, strength, and dimension.

There is good reason to believe that coordinative structure changes from the moment of conception, by a rather complex process that has been described as *heterochronic* (Anokhin, 1964). Based on studies of neuroembryology, Anokhin found that component elements of mature functional systems had their maturational onsets at different ages, and each component matured at a different rate. Heterochronic maturation may be an appropriate metaphor for some of the developmental processes that we have been describing in the realm of affective expression. Component expressions, which we have labelled coordinative structures, appear early in life and become reorganized with age.

Anokhin (1964) suggests that the explanation for heterochronicity is organismic economy. By this he meant that an organism that is so complex and that will be called upon to perform complex adaptive tasks cannot be prewired in such detail and for so many different skills. It is more economical to endow the species with a limited set of muscles—and coordinative structures of those muscles—and to provide a mechanism for creating new coordinative structures to handle age-appropriate adaptive tasks.

From the perspective of general organismic adaptation there seems to be a continuous development toward greater mastery over the environment and toward greater self-control of emotion. From the perspective of individual coordinative structures, development seems discontinuous. The heterochronic view does not presume that all coordinative structures are functionally adaptive. Indeed, some may be *transitional*, and some may be *preparatory*.

Some structures appear as part of one functional system, then another, and may sometimes drop out of the repertoire for a time, only to reappear later. The picture that emerges is of an opportunistic organism; one that is able to use the raw materials available to create transitional coordinative structures that serve as interim staging grounds for the further development of new or more functional coordinative structures. The young infant may, for example, use a palmer grasp in a situation in which, if available, a pincer grasp would serve much better. Because the fine motor control is not available, the opportunistic infant makes the best of what is available. While positive affect may be expressed more precisely with a smile or a laugh, younger infants often display rhythmical stereotypies, appealing thus to a more motorically available expression of the same inner state (Thelen, 1979).

In these examples, there is no need to impose consciousness or intention on the infant, but rather, an evolutionary endowment of individual opportunism. The implications of this view for our understanding of human development are profound. Rather than assume that palmer grasping *must* precede pincer grasping in an invariant sequence, it makes more sense to say that this happens only because the younger infant has opportunistically used the most available muscle movement to achieve a goal. There is no evidence that practice of the palmer grasp leads to the pincer, nor is there any evidence that the pincer movement differentiates out of the palmer movement. Instances of noninstrumental finger-to-thumb closure have been reported in infants as young as 2 months (Fogel, 1981).

Observed sequences in the development of affective expressions may be similarly opportunistic. When the pointlike gesture appears, in the first few months of life, it is tied to states of moderate arousal and interest in the environment. Its expression is nothing more than an epiphenomenon of the affect of interest (Fogel & Hannan, in press; Platzman, 1983). There is no reason to believe that pointing differentiates out of grasping at around 1 year, or that communicative pointing, in which the manual gesture is coupled with an extended arm, a look, and a vocalization to the mother, is built up by conditioning from earlier forms of the gesture. These reflect the more usual developmental theories of the ontogeny of pointing used by Leung and Rheingold (1981) and by Murphy (1978). Although much work is yet to be done on manual expression, the presence of discrete manual coordinative structures early in the first year and the changing organization of those coordinative structures with age (Platzman, 1983) suggest that each discrete manual behavior has a discontinuous path of development.

What is the adaptive value of early pointing? There may not be any for the infant at that age. Mothers tend not to notice the gesture, and infants do not use it intentionally. It may have its adaptive value only because the expression must, in a sense, cue up with the other components of later communicative pointing—arm extension, intentional vocalization, gaze control, joint reference, diexis—so that it is available to the infant when it is needed.

The Role of Evolution in the Development of Expressive Behavior

One of the questions that was raised earlier in this chapter was why behavior tends to emerge in development at specific ages and not at others. Why does social smiling, for example, appear at 2 months and not before? Why does the infant develop coordinated leg movements and the intention to get across a room considerably before the development of postural control mechanisms?

It seems that the answers to these questions must come from considerations of the evolutionary process as it has operated on the ontogenetic sequence, rather than from more proximal explanations of individual behavior. Even though we might refer to the use of a palmer grasp as an opportunistic behavior, the precedence of palmer grasping before pincer grasping is universally seen in infants. Could it be that human infants have evolved a set of coordinative structures without any ground plan for their ontogeny and development?

We cannot answer this question completely. However, we can make the assumption that evolution has selected for the most economical way of specifying the adaptive needs of the organism at any given age. We can also assume that there are limits on the number of functional behavior patterns that an organism with finite size and finite energy budgets can handle at any one time. From these assumptions we could postulate that a flexible and fluid ability to create functional synergies of behavior—as needed by functional demands, and as limited by motor assets and availabilities—may be more economically sound than the provision of a complex network of schemata, or a ground plan for the precise functional use of a particular coordinative structure. Strict schematization of behavior would not be very adaptive in the long run and would preclude the opportunistic use of available means to achieve needed ends. We have given a number of such examples, but others abound, such as the ability of handicapped individuals to meet their needs by using alternative motor and neural pathways that can be made available to serve adaptive purposes.

One could argue that the environment of evolutionary adaptedness imposed constraints on the young of the species and that these selection pressures led to the formation of the particular ontogeny we have today. The 2-month "delay" in the appearance of social smiling may have served to restrain parent–infant bonding in an ecology that supported a high rate of infant mortality and physical deformity. The logic of this kind of reasoning seems to be that if we cannot find an adaptive function for a behavior, or lack of one, in the individual's ontogeny, then we can certainly find a reason why such a pattern of behavior or developmental sequence might have been adaptive at more pristine ages in the history of man. If we carry this logic to its extreme, we fall into the trap of searching for the ultimate cause, moving it back or forward in time ad infinitum.

Consider the gesture of finger pointing. Why is it adaptive? In the first year we say that pointlike movements are preparatory for intentionally communicative pointing appearing the second year. But index finger extension is used in a wide variety of adaptive contexts later in life, such as ear scratching or sexual stimulation. Which is more important? Which is more mature? Which is more adaptive? What matters is that the index finger extension is a motor structure that is available and that can be used by an individual in order to meet the requirements of the contextual and functional goals at the moment. Not all people use index extensions to indicate, or to scratch their ears, but it works for those who do.

If we look at the morphology of the hand in other primate species, each species has a physically discrete set of digits, and species differ in the extent to which the digits are provided with neuromuscular articulation (Connally & Elliott, 1972). Humans seem to have inherited a unique form of articulatory control over their digits, not the ability to point per se. Furthermore, while only certain manual coordinations are possible, it is not as if evolution has selected only those with communicative signal value. It makes more economical sense to think that the use of manual expressions for communication, or whatever, is an opportunistic use of an available motor pattern by a clever organism. This notion is similar to that held by Darwin (1872) on facial expressions. Darwin did not think that expressions evolved primarily for communicative purposes but that they came to be used that way by members of the species (see Montgomery, Chapter 2, this volume).

It may be that some expressions have evolved to enhance mutual communication, but we need not think that all forms of expressive behavior are there because they are functionally adaptive. Developmentalists should place the concepts of opportunism and economy on a par with assimilation and accommodation, as they strive for a more realistic interpretation of the data taken from developing infants and children in the area of expressive development, and perhaps in other areas of development as well.

Summary

This chapter addresses the data on affective expression as it appears in infants during the first few years of life. The chapter argues that investigators need to preserve information on the temporal sequencing of individual affective expressions, both within the same observation session, and across ages. Such an approach yields a view of the developmental process that is inconsistent with prior notions of differentiation and of continuity of function. Instead, development appears as a discontinuous reorganization, into coordinative structures, of a finite number of motor movements. These coordinative structures change in composition and in function with age, as the same motor movements become used and reused for different purposes by the infant. From this perspective, development does not appear to be a gradual accretion of skill or schema but an opportunistic use of available motor elements to serve immediate adaptive functions. It is argued that this kind of ontogenetic process is consistent with evolutionary principles of economy within the finite size and the energy constraints imposed on biological organisms.

References

Anokhin, P. Systemogenesis as a general regulator of brain development. *Progress in Brain Research*, 1964, 9,54–86.
Bowlby, J. *Attachment and loss* (Vol. 1). London: Hogarth, 1969.
Bridges, K. M. B. A study of social development in early infancy. *Child Development*, 1933, 40, 36–49.
Connally, K., & Elliott, J. The evolution and ontogeny of hand function. In N. Blurton-Jones (Ed.), *Ethological studies of child behavior*. Cambridge University Press, 1972.
Darwin, C. *The expression of the emotions in man and animals*. New York: Appleton, 1872.
Demos, V. Facial expressions of infants and toddlers: A descriptive analysis. In T. Field & A. Fogel (Eds.), *Emotion and early interaction*. Hillsdale, NJ: Erlbaum, 1982.
Ekman, P., & Oster, H. Facial expressions of emotion. In M. R. Rosenzweig & L. W. Porter (Eds.), *Annual review of Psychology* (Vol. 30). Palo Alto, CA: Annual Reviews, 1979.
Fischer, K., & Corrigan, R. A skill approach to language development. In R. Stark (Ed.), *Language behavior in infancy and early childhood*. New York: Elsevier, 1981.

Fogel, A. The ontogeny of gestural communication: The first six months. In R. Stark (Ed.), *Language behavior in infancy and early childhood*. New York: Elsevier, 1981.

Fogel, A. Affect dynamics in early infancy: Affective tolerance. In T. Field & A. Fogel (Eds.), *Emotion and early interaction*. Hillsdale, NJ: Erlbaum, 1982a.

Fogel, A. Social play, positive affect and coping skills in the first six months of life. *Topics in Early Childhood Special Education*, 1982b, *2*, 53–65.

Fogel, A., & Hannan, T. E. Manual expressions of 3-month-old human infants. (In press)

Hannan, T. Young infant's hand and finger movements: An analysis of category reliability. In T. Field & A. Fogel (Eds.), *Emotion and early interaction*. Hillsdale, NJ: Erlbaum, 1982.

Hooker, D. *The prenatal origin of behavior*. Lawrence: University of Kansas Press, 1952.

Kent, R. D. Articulatory–acoustic perspectives on speech development. In R. Stark (Ed.), *Language development in infancy and early childhood*. New York: Elsevier, 1981.

Leung, E., & Rheingold, H. The development of pointing as a social gesture. *Developmental Psychology*, 1981, *17*, 215–236.

Murphy, C. M. Pointing in the context of a shared activity. *Child Development*, 1978, *49*(2), 371–380.

Netsell, R. The acquisition of speech motor control. In R. Stark (Ed.), *Language behavior in infancy and early childhood*. New York: Elsevier, 1981.

Oller, D. K. Infant vocalizations: Exploration and reflexivity. In R. Stark (Ed.), *Language behavior in infancy and early childhood*. New York: Elsevier, 1981.

Oster, H. Facial expression and affect development. In M. Lewis & L. Rosenblum (Eds.), *The development of affect*. New York: Plenum Press, 1978.

Piaget, J. *Play, dreams and imitation in childhood*. New York: Norton, 1962.

Platzman, K. *The ontogeny of pointing in the first ten months of life*. Unpublished doctoral dissertation, University of Chicago, 1983.

Riccuiti, M. N., & Poresky, R. H. Emotional behavior and development in the first year of life: An analysis of arousal, approach–withdrawal and affective responses. In A. Pick (Ed.), *Minnesota Symposium on Child Psychology* (Vol. 6). University of Minnesota Press, 1972.

Sackett, G. P., Holm, R., Crowley, C., & Henkins, A. A FORTRAN program for lag sequential analysis of contingency and cyclicity in behavioral interaction data. *Behavior Research Methods & Instrumentation*, 1978, *11*(3), 366–378.

Sroufe, L. A. Socioemotional development. In J. Osofsky (Ed.), *Handbook of infant development*. New York: Wiley, 1979.

Stark, R. E. Features of infant vocalization: The emergence of cooing. *Journal of Child Language*, 1978, *3*, 379–390.

Thelen, E. Rhythmical stereotypies in normal human infants. *Animal Behavior*, 1979, *27*, 699–715.

Trevarthen, C. Behavioral Embryology. In E. C. Carterette & M. P. Friedman (Eds.), *Handbook of perception (Vol. III): Biology of perceptual systems*. New York: Academic Press, 1973.

Trevarthen, C. Descriptive analysis of infant communicative behavior. H. R. Schaffer (Ed.), *Studies in mother–infant interaction*. London: Academic Press, 1977.

Trevarthen, C. Communication and cooperation in primary inter-subjectivity. In M. Bullowa (Ed.), *Before speech*. New York: Cambridge University Press, 1979.

Wolff, P. The causes, controls, and organization of behavior in the neonate. *Psychological Issues*, 1966, *5* (Monograph No. 17).

Chapter 11

Display Rules and the Socialization of Affective Displays

Pamela M. Cole

Relationship to Other Chapters and to the Field

Relevant Issues in the Field

This chapter exemplifies the most prevalent view of biology–environment interactions in expressive development: it characterizes environmental forces as actively seizing upon innate tendencies and bringing them under the control of social learning. Cole sees the child as developing from innately given pairings of state and expressive behavior through socialization processes and self-regulation facilitating processes that allow the individual control over performing expressive behaviors in accord with cultural and personal rules. Crucial in this socialization is children's learning of affective display rules—that is, the rules of when and how intensely to show which emotions. Cole reviews the work that is relevant to such learning, and from this, she characterizes what is currently known of the child's steps, from infancy through middle childhood, in display rule acquisition.

This chapter adds a particular richness to the data it presents. Cole's own data are the first to demonstrate experimentally the display rule knowledge and its use in young preschoolers. It is one of the few chapters—and few published reviews of expressive-behavior development—that includes consideration of voice tone and bodily movement as expressive behaviors.

The Development of Expressive Behavior: Biology-Environment Interactions

269

Relationship to Other Chapters

Processes that Cole mentions as preparing the way for display rule learning are reviewed in depth by other chapters in this volume. Feinman (see Chapter 12) reviews infant social referencing; Malatesta (Chapter 8) reviews many reinforcement behaviors and contingencies, including behavioral matching; Dolgin and Azmitia (Chapter 13) review infants' and young children's interpretations of expressive behaviors; and Lewis and Michalson (Chapter 7) present evidence that children as young as age 2 years have some display rule knowledge. Furthermore, Cole's characterization of the reinforcement contingencies that teach negative and positive emotions bear direct comparison and contrast with contingencies reported by Malatesta and by Lewis and Michalson in their chapters.

In agreement with Dolgin and Amzitia, Cole laments the current limitation of our knowledge due to the artificiality of experimental procedures and relative lack of naturalistic observation.

For Consistent Terminology

Display in display rule has acquired a widely used but different meaning from the display of ethology. In ethology it refers to a behavior, which as a product of evolution, has been specialized through natural selection for particularly effective communication-sending properties. In human psychology, however, display rule has no evolutionary implications. It simply means the rules—cultural, familial, or personal—that a person learns as appropriate to guide the behavioral demonstration of an emotional state. This general, nonevolutionary meaning holds even if the writer believes that an expressive behavior has, in fact, been specialized by evolution for its communicative properties.

Cole has chosen, as have some other chapter authors, to use the term affect rather than its close synonym, emotion. Affect encompasses internal states beyond the classic emotions and thus is more generally applicable. The terms appear interchangeably throughout this book.—ED.

Introduction

The well-adjusted child is expected to adapt to its milieu by learning and complying with a broad array of social conventions among which are cultural norms for the communication and control of affect. As such, the acquisition of the rules of the species, of culture, and of the family regarding affective display are an important aspect of socialization. The unexpressive infant and the tantruming 10-year-old child deviate from the expected norms of expressive behavior and present problems in their social relationships.

Acquiring the social norms of affective displays,[1] in the home or in the community, is not a simple matter. The conventions of affective display are not transmitted via formal instruction but are communicated in numerous, often subtle ways. It is probably less critical that members of the culture be able to cite the rules of affective display, than that they conduct themselves and regulate their behavior according to social standards. The socialization of affective display is an aspect of the child's developing self-regulation of behavior, or the organization of behavior in accordance with social norms.

In our culture, regulation of affective display entails a fair amount of suppression and minimization of spontaneous affective expression ("Wipe that smile off your face, young lady!" "Big boys don't cry." "Don't use that tone of voice with me!"). We seem to become so skilled at such affective suppression that the appropriate, open communication of deep-felt emotion is sometimes quite difficult, as psychotherapists often observe. On the other hand, in many settings one may need to master the ability to appear pleased when enraged or unaffected when disappointed. Affective display regulation is therefore a very critical aspect of social behavior and self-control. What do we know of the developmental course of self-regulated affective display and the acquisition of cultural and personal rules? The present chapter reviews conceptual and empirical contributions to the rudimentary literature on the development of affective display rules and regulation. To this end, we first summarize the conceptual contributions of Ekman and Friesen (1969) and Saarni (1981) and then summarize research on the socialization of the infant's affective displays. Then, we detail research on the development of self-regulation of affective display in children and of their knowledge regarding the rules and regulation of affective display. Finally, we offer a few initial conclusions on the course of self-regulation in affective displays.

Display is used in this chapter with its more popular, less ethological emphasis: a display or display behavior is assumed innately programmed but is not necessarily assumed to have been exaggerated or selected by evolution for its communicative function. This is the usage of almost all psychological but not of ethological writing (cf. Smith, Chapter 3, & Zivin, Chapter 1, this volume).

Display Rules

The concept of *display rules* was introduced to students of affective expressivity by Ekman and Friesen (1969). In their landmark studies of the relationship between emotional states and facial expression, Ekman and his colleagues asserted that universal, unlearned, biologically organized neuromuscular patterns prepare human beings with a basic set of emotionally communicative facial expressions. In addition to their documentation of pancultural recognition and production of these emotional expressions, Ekman and Friesen (1969, 1975) underscored the infrequency of such spontaneous displays and the degree to which culturally specified display rules interfere with spontaneous affective display.

Display rules are regarded as cultural norms that are learned and that underlie organized regulation of facial expressivity. Social conventions dictate whether a full, open, presumably unregulated display is expressed or whether one of four types of regulation are exercised (Ekman, 1977):

1. *Intensification* or *exaggeration,* such as feigning a very sad expression when your acquaintance is saddened over an event you care about only slightly
2. *Deintensification* or *minimization,* such as limiting oneself to a slight, fleeting smile when your professor trips over a chair while lecturing
3. *Neutralization,* such as maintaining a poker face when your competitor gets your goat
4. *Dissimulation* or *masking,* such as smiling at the tacky Christmas gift you received from your co-worker.

Saarni (1981) elaborated the discussion of display rules by adding the categories of *personal display rules, direct deception,* and *pretending* to the types of contexts in which affective displays are self-regulated. These display rules, which may or may not coincide with cultural display rules, may serve affect regulation and coping, impression management, and play or entertainment. Clearly, regulation of affective display pervades numerous aspects of psychological functioning.

Thus, the developing human must be capable of both the spontaneous expression of basic emotions (e.g., infant crying when in pain) and the regulated modification of affective display. Various developmental authors have discussed the emergence of the basic emotional displays (e.g., Malatesta, Chapter 8, this volume), the coordination of basic expressions and contextual elicitors (e.g., Lewis & Michalson, 1983; Sroufe, 1979), and the disengagement of expressive behavior from both felt experience and contextual elicitors (e.g., Saarni, 1978; Lewis & Michalson, Chapter 7, this volume; Zivin, 1982). Although not uncontroversial, the general consensus is that biologically prepared displays become organized and controlled with developing cognitive and social skills.

Ekman (1977) asserted that two separate sets of neuromuscular pathways serve spontaneous and voluntary facial displays and that individuals learn to interfere with the spontaneous triggering of facial display by exercising voluntary activity organized by cultural display rules. Differential patterns of cortical functioning have also been associated with spontaneous and voluntary affective displays—with left-hemispheric activity correlating with controlled, posed displays and right-hemispheric activity with spontaneous displays (Buck, 1982; Tucker, 1981). The nature of development is presumed to be ''a gradual transition from the automatic, uncontrolled expression of emotion in early infancy to the more modulated, subtle, and voluntary expression of emotion seen in older children and adults'' (Ekman & Oster, 1979, p. 537).

Dichotomizing displays into spontaneous and voluntary systems, while perhaps heuristic neurophysiologically, runs the risk of oversimplifying the complex nature of developing regulation of affective expression. For example, in a given moment, a facial display may entail elements of several spontaneous and counteractive, voluntary actions (Ekman & Friesen, 1969). Moreover, a specific display may be prewired but become more plastic with time. Zivin (1982) has offered five categories for conceptualizing the range of flexibility of expressivity and the degree to which particular displays are constrained by biological organization or are amenable to self-regulation.

The relationships between internal state, expressive behavior, cognitive appraisal, and situational context are subject to developmental influences, and the nature of the emergence of both the coordination and the independence of these elements is a topic of much research and controversy (e.g., Izard, 1978; Lewis & Michalson, 1983, Chapter 7, this volume; Sroufe, 1979).

In addition to intrapersonal aspects of the ontogeny of affect displays, developmentalists have discussed various socialization processes that transmit the rules a child comes to internalize and to use. *Contingent responding,* such as reinforcing appropriate displays and ignoring or punishing inappropriate displays, as well as the modeling of *affect displays* have been considered by social learning theorists (e.g., Maccoby, 1980). In addition, Campos and Stenberg (1981) have discussed *social*

referencing as a process in which the young child faced with its own emotional uncertainty in a situation refers to the mother, and by decoding
and responding emotionally to her affect display, resolves this uncertainty. This socialization process is hypothesized to communicate how
to feel and therefore, how to look, in particular contexts. A good example of this process is a mother's expressive communication of fear to
her crawling infant who then learns that the situation is dangerous and
comes to experience fear in that situation. Hence, the infant learns emotional expression-situational context relationships as well. Evidence supporting contingent maternal responsivity and social referencing of
mother has been reported in the infancy literature (e.g., Feinman, Chapter 12, this volume; Malatesta, Chapter 8, this volume).

Direct instruction—explicit do's and don'ts of affect display—is involved when a child is told that "big boys don't cry" or "keep a stiff
upper lip," but more subtle transmission may occur as well. Children
may infer certain display rules on the basis of observing their own or
others' interactions (Lewis & Michalson, 1983), or expectancies may be
developed on the basis of perceiving others' expectations of how you
feel or what you should reveal or hide (Saarni, 1983). The manner in
which the parent regulates affect in the child may also serve as a basis
for later emotional control; Sroufe (1983) has argued that the quality of
attachment provides such a basis for the child's later (preschool) affective control.

There have been more conceptual discussions of affective displays,
their socialization, and the development of self-regulation of affect. In
addition, a disorganized empirical base is emerging. Unsurprisingly it
provides many questions and few answers.

Infant Preparation for Affective
Display Self-Regulation

The emphasis of infant emotional-expression research has been tracking the emergence of basic emotional expressions, such as smiling,
laughing, fear, surprise, anger, sadness, interest, and disgust. Whatever
degree of biological preparedness is involved in infant affective display,
it is clear that socialization of display behaviors begins early in the life
of any expressive display. The burgeoning field of infant emotional-
expression research has been reviewed elsewhere (Charlesworth &
Kreutzer, 1973; Field & Walden, 1982a; Malatesta, Chapter 8, this vol-

ume), and the present discussion is restricted to those findings that bear on the regulation of affective display.

Perhaps the most studied affective display of infancy is the smile. In the first months, infant smiling is correlated with internal states of moderate arousal (Emde, Gaensbauer, & Harmon, 1976) or external stimulation (Sroufe & Waters, 1976). Quickly, smiling becomes a social phenomenon, with the emergence of the *social smile* generally placed at 2–3 months. This developmental milestone is considered to be critical to the development of attachment and of ego functioning (e.g., Sroufe, 1979). In regard to the socialization of affective display, the appearance of the social smile marks the infant's first entry into acculturation of expression—elicitor relationships: smiling at a human being. Over the first year, social smiling becomes increasingly selective. The infant may be said to be regulating display as a *function of the eliciting context*.

The *mother's responsivity* in the socialization of smiling is indicated in mother–infant interactional studies. Mothers become increasingly responsive to their infant's smiling between 3 and 6 months often imitating the child's smile (Malatesta & Haviland, 1982) while at the same time, infants smile contingently at their mothers' smiles (Field & Greenberg, 1981). Moreover, one study reported a decrease in maternal responsivity to crying accompanying the increased responsivity to smiling (Brooks-Gunn & Lewis, 1982). These interactions provide evidence of differential maternal consequences of affect displays and suggest socialization of positive and negative displays in the first year. Moreover, gender-specific norms may be communicated via these maternal responses: maternal decreases in responsivity to crying (Brooks-Gunn & Lewis, 1982) and increases in responsivity to smiling (Malatesta & Haviland, 1982) were greater for boys than girls. (Cf. contingencies reported by Malatesta (Chapter 8) and by Lewis & Michalson, Chapter 7, this volume.)

In addition to selective responding to infant displays, there is evidence that mothers supply infants with additional expression–elicitor combinations. The supposition is that mothers communicate how to feel (or at least how to look) in situations for which the infant is affectively uncertain, a phenomenon referred to as *social referencing* (Campos & Stenberg, 1981; Feinman, Chapter 12, this volume). Research indicates that around 8–9 months, a mother's affective display can lead the infant's affective display (Feinman & Lewis, 1983; Klinnert, Campos, Sorce, Emde, & Svedja, 1982), which may reflect the infant's emotional reaction to the mother's display and to the context to which it refers. We presume that these early socialized displays represent the infant's spontaneous displays and the learning of specific expression–elicitor relationships. That is, through its relationships the infant is associating specific affective states and displays with particular contexts (e.g., fear on the visual cliff) and is decreasing certain states and displays (e.g., crying, Lewis & Michalson, 1983). We presume there is synchrony between the affective state and the display behavior.

What, if any, control do infants have over their affective displays? A controversial issue is the age at which infants can voluntarily imitate facial displays. Some capacity for imitation of gross facial movement in very young infants has been indicated (Field, Woodson, Greenberg, & Cohen, 1982; Meltzoff & Moore, 1977). Although such *matching* behavior may not be entirely voluntary, it may indicate a precursor skill in an incipient segregation of spontaneous and voluntary display. *Voluntary imitation* seems more certain by 6 months of age. Reports of instrumental crying (Wolff, 1969) and delays in distressful displays (Sroufe, 1983) in the latter part of the first year suggest that some self-initiated control skills may develop during infancy.

In sum, the contribution of infant experience to the ontogeny of affective display regulation is unclear. Yet, it seems plausible to state that some of the cultural and/or familial rules constraining affective displays are transmitted and perceived by the young infant who is developing the ability to use others' facial displays to interpret situations and whose distress displays are decreasing and perhaps coming under some voluntary control. From the self-regulatory point of view, we would speculate that the infant is learning a great deal about when to display (or how to feel) specific expressions and about the consequences of certain displays. Most likely, the rudiments of expressive regulation are acquisitions of the first year and precursors to fully developed self-regulation.

Childhood Developmental Self-Regulated Affective Displays

In general, self-regulatory abilities are thought to emerge during the preschool years during which time children become increasingly agile and refined in their gross and fine motor activities and can voluntarily initiate, maintain, and cease activities. This period is marked by the increasing use of language (Zivin, 1979) and play to mediate behavior and by awareness of one's own actions and of others' actions. By kindergarten age children should have learned the social conventions of waiting, taking turns, attending, persisting, and considering others' needs and perspectives. Although limited in efficacy, self-regulation is thought to be descriptive of the self-initiated controlled behavior of the preschool years (Kopp, 1982). During the elementary school years, behavioral regulation appears to become more sophisticated and flexible. Children can plan long sequences of activity, reflect upon their inner experiences as well as their actions, and infer the thoughts, feelings, and intentions of others. These self-reflective, inferential, abstractive skills serve increasingly sophisticated self-regulatory skills. Although the importance of affective modulation is unquestioned, the development of self-regulation of affective experience and display is only now drawing systematic empirical attention.

Research on Voluntary Simulation

One avenue of research has been children's ability to simulate a particular emotion-related facial action or expression when instructed. Such an approach provides documentation of the ability to generate voluntarily an affective display in a situation of minimal emotional context. An early investigation of such simulative control required kindergarteners and fifth-graders first to identify and then to reproduce eight basic emotional expressions (Odom & Lemond, 1972). Both recognition and reproduction improved with age, and recognition was easier than reproduction for both ages. Accuracy was greater for positive than for negative expressions.

Later research has provided a similar pattern of age-related improvements in simulating affective expressions. Investigations of the ability deliberately to produce component facial movements and facial configurations of emotional expressions have indicated that the greatest improvements occur sometime between 6 and 9 years (Ekman, Roper, & Hager, 1980; Hamilton, 1973; Yarcowzer, Kilbride, & Hill, 1979). Consistently, negative expressions are simulated less accurately than positive expressions.

Investigating preschoolers' (3–5-year olds) ability to simulate facial expressions, Field and Walden (1982b) found that visual aids, such as photographic stimuli and mirrors enhanced preschoolers' reproductive accuracy more than did mere verbal prompting. Negative expressions were again more difficult than positive ones for preschoolers (Buck, 1977; Field & Walden, 1982b). Happy expressions are easy to simulate at all ages, and the ability deliberately to appear sad, mad, or fearful may be more sensitive to developmental change.

Youngsters' difficulties in simulating negative expressions may reflect difficulties in control of facial muscles or in deficiencies in knowledge about how negative expressions look or are made. However, even adults, presumably with more motoric control and knowledge of expressive displays and control, encounter more difficulty in simulating negative versus positive emotional expressions. Possibly, difficulty in simulating negative displays involves the simulator's countering an already learned tendency to minimize or to mask negative displays. In this regard, Yarcowzer et al. (1979) found that elementary school children's reproductions of negative displays were more accurate when children were alone than when the examiner was present. Alone, the children may have experienced less interference from previously acquired display rules about displaying negative emotion in the presence of relatively unfamiliar others.

In our work, preschoolers have easily generated happy faces with no more than a verbal prompt but appear reticent to generate negative (sad, mad) expressions. They initially move their faces in the appropriate configuration and then stop; some then state "but I'm not mad" or "I don't want to be sad." It is conceivable that preschoolers can simulate negative expressions but at the price of feeling the negative emotion. The ability to disconnect affective expression from the felt experience is clearly a developing phenomenon (Lewis & Michalson, 1983; Saarni, 1981; Sroufe, 1979), and it may be that generating a face without the associated feeling is more problematic for preschoolers. Possibly the preschooler's failure to realize that one's emotional expression can be discrepant from one's felt emotion interferes with their willingness to try to discover that looking sad is not the same as feeling sad. However, we have observed preschoolers try and then discontinue their attempts, which might suggest their discomfort. Even adults report increases in negative feeling when simulating its display (Laird, 1974).

Research on Voluntary Deception

These direct-instruction studies of simulated expressions generally provide little situational context for the child. Another approach involves *directions to deceive* in which the child's ability to dissimulate intentionally upon command is investigated (see DePaulo & Jordan, 1982, for a review). The typical experimental paradigm involves the child's drinking sweetened and unsweetened beverages with the explicit instructions to appear to dislike the former and to like the latter. Age differences emerge in these studies (Feldman, Devin-Sheehan, & Allen, 1978; Feldman, Jenkins, & Popoola, 1979). In one study, school-age girls seemed to improve in their control of their facial displays but their body movements became more ''leaky.'' Boys' deceptive facial expressions became increasingly obvious whereas their body movements became more deceptive (Feldman & White, 1980). Thus, the age improvement in a single expressive channel may not indicate more generalized expressive control in several channels. Utilizing a different deception paradigm, Shennum and Bugental (1982) found that while fifth-graders were more successful than first-graders in pretending in facial expression to like or to be neutral about something they didn't like, neither group could mask vocal tone. Gender differences in this deception study suggested that boys were better deceivers (facially) than girls; boys neutralized affective expressions in negative conditions, whereas girls engaged in exaggerated dissimulation, tending to intensify positive expressions, which was a less convincing deception. Additional studies involving instructions to deceive have consistently found that the ability to dissimulate via facial expression is better developed by age 10 or 11 years (Allen & Atkinson, 1978; Morency & Krauss, 1982). Gender differences often emerge but consistent patterns are difficult to distinguish, given variations in methodology.

In sum, developmental trends in the ability to simulate a facial display when instructed, or to dissimulate, have been found with successful facial modifications appearing between ages 7 and 9. It should be noted that younger children respond to the instructions by attempting to adjust their faces in the correct direction, but their attempts are inadequate to produce the desired simulation or deception. Therefore, although regulation of affective expressivity is not smoothly mastered, these younger children seem to comprehend the directions and to have some organizing strategy for modifying display. These paradigms are fairly contrived and unusual circumstances, and their findings may not generalize to children's spontaneous displays in more naturalistic sequences of events.

Research in Naturalistic and Quasi-Naturalistic Situations

Very little systematic research has been conducted on the developmental course of children's affective displays in naturalistic settings or in experimental situations in which display instructions are not provided. The few existing studies in this category support the presence of self-regulation of facial display in preschoolers but also developmental changes in the school-age years.

In naturally occurring interpersonal conflicts, facial displays have been identified that predict the eventual outcome of the conflict (Camras, 1977; Zivin, 1977a). The *plus* (win predicting) and *minus* (loss predicting) faces are not included in the "basic set" of emotional expressions, but their similarity in use to conflict displays of nonhuman primates has been taken to suggest that these may be basic, spontaneous displays (Zivin, 1982). Three findings are of particular interest in regard to the development of regulated affective display. First, Zivin (1977a) noted that the appearance of the plus face in 4 to 6½-year-olds occurred more frequently in an experimental conflict situation when the competitor could be seen; this observation could suggest the young child's voluntary control of the display. A shift in context has also been reported with the plus face extending to nonconflictual contexts for 7- to 10-year-olds, perhaps suggesting generalization and the development of the flexibility of this presumably hard-wired display (Zivin, 1977b). Finally, Hottenstein reported in a 1977 doctoral dissertation that cross-sectional samples of the plus face (3 years through adulthood) revealed a substantial decrease in the fully articulated winning expression with a concomitant increase in partial, or more subtle, versions of the expression.

Such systematic study of spontaneous, basic affective displays is rare (see Charlesworth & Kreutzer, 1973), presumably because children's increasing mobility and the developing control, subtlety, and complexity in their facial expressions creates methodological difficulties. Cheyne (1976) attempted a cross-sectional study of naturally occurring smiling in preschoolers' free play. Closed smiles occurred in similar proportions among 2-, 3-, and 4-year-olds in the context of solitary activity, whereas the upper, or social, smile (upper teeth exposed) increased with age. Notably, the increases in social smiling entailed selective displays in social interactions: increases in the older preschoolers' upper smiles were accounted for by increased smiling in interactions with same-gender peers. While social facilitation of smiling and laughing has been studied in preschoolers (e.g., Chapman & Wright, 1976), control of positive affective displays in naturalistic settings has not been examined.

A longitudinal study of distress between the ages of 18 and 24 months suggests that children as young as 2 years may delay negative displays and socially direct their affective communications. Van Lieshout (1975) created an experimental situation in which the children were frustrated in their play by their mothers. A decline in the frequency of angry, distressed displays was noted. Perhaps an increasing sense of agency decreased the degree of frustration the child felt. Increased approaches to the mother after frustration were also noted but gender differences emerged: there was an increase in positive approaches to the mother at age 2 years for boys and girls, but decrease in negative displays to the mother emerged only for the 2-year-old girls.

Speculative but intriguing questions arise from such findings. Were cultural display rules already directing two-year-olds' expressive signals to their mothers? Is the situation just much less frustrating for two-year-olds or are they signaling for help, in gender-specific ways, and delaying their frustrated anger at the toy? Initial delays and use of mother to regulate affect may contribute to self-regulated affective processes. The attachment relationship has been correlated with positive-affect expression and control and social competence in preschoolers (Sroufe, 1983). Sroufe has offered anecdotal reports in his separation studies of 12-month-olds who delay or minimize their distressed displays; some of the children are observed to "fight back their tears" and burst into full-blown distress upon mother's return. The transitions from infancy to toddlerhood to preschool years will eventually provide crucial information about the socialization and developing self-regulation of affective displays.

A more direct approach to the study of negative display regulation was designed by Saarni (1980). She developed an experimental situation in which first-, third-, and fifth-grade children were disappointed by receiving undesirable gifts for their participation. Their nonverbal reactions to the disappointing prize (a baby's toy) were recorded and coded as positive, negative, or transitional displays. The predicted age-related decreases in negative-affect displays when receiving the disappointment were found, as were gender-specific effects. The youngest boys were more likely to display negative expressions, whereas the youngest girls and most of the older children neutralized (i.e., appeared unaffected). The oldest girls managed to appear pleased, presumably dissimulating their disappointment.

This approach was extended downward in a study adapted for younger children (Cole, 1984a). Ekman's Facial Action Coding System (Ekman & Friesen, 1978) was used to code all facial activity in the expressions of preschoolers, first-graders, and third-graders. Gender-specific positive and neutral displays suggested that preschoolers were spontaneously controlling their affective displays (Cole, 1983). Cross-sectional analyses of all three age groups provided a pattern of developmental decreases in negative displays: preschool boys displayed virtually the only sad expressions (lip depressions), girls consistently smiled, and boys were more stoic (Cole, 1984a). Verbal self-reports, indicating sad and mad feelings and a unanimous willingness to trade the disappointing gift, strengthened the inference that the preschoolers were controlling their facial expressions.

To further investigate the likelihood that preschoolers were regulating affective displays via some social norms, we replicated the study with a sample of 3- and 4-year-old girls. The examiner remained with the child in some cases and not in others after the disappointment was administered (Cole, 1984b). Significantly more smiling occurred when the examiner remained versus when he or she left, even in the youngest 3-year-old. Young children, ages 7 years and under, may have more developed spontaneous regulatory control than is tapped in direct instruction studies.

Yet another report of regulated negative-affective displays comes from Blurton-Jones' (1972) observation of kindergarteners' play. He noted that children's distressed displays were more intense when an adult was present, a finding reminiscent of Maccoby's (1980) anecdote of the injured 4-year-old who didn't cry because, as he told his mother, ''I didn't know you were home!'' (p. 178).

If it is possible to draw a tentative conclusion from these various studies of socialized and regulated affective displays; it seems that younger children are aware of social aspects of their interchanges, have absorbed some gender-specific norms, and can delay and even control their expressive displays. Older children have more conscious control of facial expressions and are less dependent upon contextual sequences to deliberately simulate or dissimulate a display. Whether their expressive control can encompass multiple nonverbal channels (e.g., voice, face, body movement) seems questionable. It would thus seem that even young children have learned some display rules, both personal and cultural, which brings us to the next topic of display rule knowledge.

Display-Rule Knowledge

Children's knowledge of the emotional expressions associated with emotional labels and contexts is perhaps better documented than their regulated behavior (Field & Walden, 1982a; Shantz, 1975). Research has clearly indicated that preschool age children detect and utilize expressive behavior in interpreting events (Abramovitch, 1977; Abramovitch & Daly, 1979; Camras, 1980), although there are limitations to preschoolers' decoding or integration of displays in some situations, such as adjusting their behavior in response to a listener's puzzled expression (Peterson, Danner, & Flavell, 1972).

Preschoolers have some socially normed expectancies of how a child would feel and look in a given situation and what the consequences of certain emotional states are (Barden, Zelko, Duncan, & Masters, 1980; Cole, 1983; Felleman, Fischer, & Masters, 1982; Lewis & Michalson, 1983). With age, children seem to adjust their expectations of how one should feel. Discrepancies in these data do emerge, however. For example, both age-related increases and decreases have been found in the endorsement of sadness (Barden et al., 1980; Glasberg & Aboud, 1982). These apparent discrepancies may actually reflect age-related changes in managing emotion, for example, denial in younger children and minimization (intellectualization) in older children, and differences in the contexts children assume relevant.

The course of children's knowledge of expressive appropriateness is not clear. A persistent problem in social-cognition research is the question of what criteria we accept for evidence of knowledge. If we rely upon methods of verbal reports, we risk underestimating younger children's knowledge (Shantz, 1975). If we infer knowledge on the basis of the organization of behavior—as Michael Lewis (personal communication) argues, "If the rat doesn't run into the wall, I assume he knows the wall is there"—then we may be surprised at how even young infants detect, discriminate, and adjust behavior to others' expressive signals (see Dolgin & Azmitia, Chapter 13, this volume; LaBarbera, Izard, Vietze, & Parisi, 1976) and at what young children know of display rules and expressive control.

However, the data on knowledge of display rules is sparse. Saarni (1979) investigated 6-, 8-, and 10-year-olds' display rule knowledge by having them select the final frame in an emotional scenario about a child. The incidence of spontaneously stated display rules and the complexity of subsequent reasoning increased significantly between ages 8 and 10. Only the 10-year-olds consistently articulated their reasons in terms of social norms whereas younger children were concerned with avoiding interpersonal problems. In our cross-sectional study of children's display rule knowledge and regulated displays (Cole, 1984a), we gave children a similar task of assigning feeling labels and then faces to story characters who had fulfilled and had disappointed expectancies. Preschoolers rarely chose a facial configuration that was discrepant with the attributed feeling, whereas half the 6-year-olds and most of the 8-year-olds did so for one story in particular: receiving a disappointing birthday present from parents. The 6-year-olds using a label–face mismatch explained that the parents would get mad at the child if they knew his or her negative feeling, whereas 8-year-olds were concerned about hurting the parents' feelings.

We also asked our children how they felt when they received their disappointing gifts (usually a broken toy) and if the examiner knew their feelings, thinking that reasoning about a recent actual experience might tap knowledge more successfully than hypothetical stories. Only 1 of 20 preschoolers offered knowledge of facial self-regulation and masked affective communication ("She didn't know I was sad 'cause I kept my mouth a straight line!"). About 89% of the 6-year-olds felt they had hidden their feelings from the examiner by control of verbal and/or facial expression, and 85% of the 8-year-olds expressed trying to do so. However many assumed the examiner inferred their feelings despite regulated displays.

An interview study of 6-, 11-, and 15-year-old English children (Harris, Olthof, & Terwogt, 1981) entailed knowledge regarding the identification, control, and effects of expressive behavior. All three age groups cited appropriate strategies for hiding feelings, but there were age-related increases in the use of inner-state manipulation (changing how you feel) and masking strategies. In general, the age increases reflected the advanced abstractive thinking of the adolescent group.

Children's ability to detect deception appears to emerge in late childhood (see DePaulo & Jordan, 1982, for a review) with younger children apparently having difficulty coordinating the multiple features that lead to inferring deception. Younger children generally respond to a single expressive channel (Bugental, Kaswan, Love, & Fox, 1970; Volkmar & Siegel, 1982).

Age effects in studies of children's knowledge of display rules and regulation seem to vary with the methods employed. Future studies that systematically study task features as well as subject's age may cast a more integrative light on present findings. Nonetheless, it seems that the tacit knowledge of cultural display rules may be present in 3- and 4-year olds. With time, observations of their own and others' behavior may lead to the conscious awareness of general principles of display regulation.

Initial Conclusions

Infancy

The socialization of affective displays begins very early in infancy as indicated by mother–infant interaction research focused on expressive displays. Selective, contingent responsivity, imitation, and social referencing have emerged as early processes in the socialization of affect. Although some changes in infant affective displays may be governed by neurological maturation, infants appear quickly to enter the social stream and to organize their expressive behavior around cultural conventions, for example, smiling at mother. Such socially organized regulation is an antecedent to later self-regulated control and explicit knowledge of display rules. The anatomical components of facial actions seen in adults are present in the first year (Oster, 1978), but the developmental status of the neuromuscular pathways for spontaneous and voluntary action has not been studied. Some voluntary imitation appears in the first year but the precise onset of deliberate imitation is controversial.

Toddlerhood

The transition from infancy to preschool age has been described as a transition from sensorimotor modulation to intentional but limited control and finally to some awareness of the social conventions of behavior involving delay, awareness of self and others, and cognitive mediation (Kopp, 1982). As such, these transitional years deserve much more systematic investigation of affective display processes. The small collection of observations of children between 12 and 36 months suggest that affective display control, in the form of delayed displays and increased utilization of vocalization–verbalization and appeals to adults, is part of emergent affect regulation skills. (And see Lewis and Michalson, Chapter 7, this volume, for observations suggesting that 2-year-olds have some knowledge of face–label pairs and face–situation pairs.)

Preschool

While having very limited abilities to produce simulating and dissimulating expressions upon command, preschoolers appear to have some ability to intensify, minimize, and mask affective displays in their spontaneous behavior stream. These expressive modifications appear to be nonconscious adjustments implying tacit personal and/or cultural display rules. The preschooler's cognitive limitations in self-reflective, inferential, and abstractive social reasoning may render such tacit knowledge inaccessible.

Middle Childhood

This seems to be a period when regulation of affective display becomes more flexible and subtle. Simulative accuracy and deceptive skill emerge during the elementary school years as does the ability to consider and reason about the social circumstances of affective display regulation. While we expect that ages 7 to adolescence would be marked by increasingly sophisticated detection and knowledge of display rules and by less effortful regulation of affective display, this period is more representative of refinement than emergence of the rules and regulation of affective display.

Negative versus Positive Displays

The consistent finding of greater accuracy in the production of positive rather than negative displays is difficult to interpret. Given the initial evidence that preschoolers are capable of minimizing and/or masking negative displays, one may wonder why they seem unable to generate the negative displays voluntarily. Are they poor encoders with poor control of facial action units or can they not inhibit intervening display rules? Even adults are more successful at encoding (and decoding) happy faces. Perhaps the more interesting ability is that of producing an affective expression while maintaining a different affective state. We know almost nothing of children's development of ability to do this.

These conclusions are tentative because of their scanty empirical base. Low comparability between methods of assessment (e.g., Field & Walden, 1982b) indicate that posed, experimentally induced, and naturalistic contexts tap different aspects of expressive control and underscore the need for more systematic studies employing multiple methods of measurement. In addition to variance due to method and to degree of spontaneity in observed behavior, researchers have employed a variety of systematic (Ekman & Friesen, 1978; Izard, 1979) and idiosyncratic methods of coding affective expression.

Discussion

Display rules, or the ability to recognize and verbalize them, seem to be but one aspect of expressive regulation. To understand the transmission, internalization, detection, and utilization of affective display rules, we would do well to organize our thinking around the developmental constructs of modulation and self-regulation. Such larger organizing concepts would span the nonproductive disputes of the simple and narrow issues that have retarded the field. These disputes include theoretical controversies about whether discrete emotional states are biologically specified (e.g., Izard, 1977) or are socially specified (e.g., Hochschild, 1979), about when discrete facial expressions and emotional experiences first emerge, and about whether discrete emotions are neu-rologically prewired (e.g., Izard, 1977) or differentiated from general arousal states (Sroufe, 1979). It would seem that the average infant brings into the world a biological preparedness to quickly accommodate to the social milieu and that human biology prepares the child with both the initial signalling and the flexibility to evolve into a self-regulating, so-cially integrated member of the species. We may now ask for the details of the processes by which modulation and self-regulation come to turn biologically given propensities and limits into social constructions.

Summary

Although little is known about children's acquisition of cultural dis-play rules or, more generally, about the manner in which children ac-quire socially acceptable methods of regulating affect and affect display, the importance of these acquisitions is clear. There are some conceptual and empirical contributions to these topics but organized theoretical frameworks are lacking. The rudimentary research findings reviewed in the present chapter indicate that the ontogeny of socialized affect dis-play may well follow the general course of self-regulation with precur-sory skills developing in the first 2 years, self-initiated regulation emerging in the preschool years, and mastery of both expressive be-havior and explicit social knowledge of display rules and regulation un-folding during childhood. This developmental course has its roots in biologic propensities and in socialization processes that interface in the first year. The nature of the transition to a well-adjusted, emotionally regulated individual remains to be described and understood.

References

Abramovitch, R. Children's recognition of situational aspects of facial expression. *Child Development*, 1977, *48*, 459–463.
Abramovitch, R., & Daly, E. M. Inferring attributes of a situation from the facial expres-sions of peers. *Child Development*, 1979, *50*, 586–589.
Allen, V. L., & Atkinson, M. L. Encoding of nonverbal behavior by high-achieving and low-achieving children. *Journal of Educational Psychology*, 1978, *70*, 298–305.
Barden, R. C., Zelko, F. A., Duncan, S. W., & Masters, J. C. Children's consensual knowl-edge about the experiential determinants of emotion. *Journal of Personality and Social Psychology*, 1980, *38*, 968–976.
Blurton-Jones, N. (Ed.) *Ethological studies of child behavior.* Cambridge, England: Cambridge University Press, 1972.
Brooks-Gunn, J., & Lewis, M. Affective exchanges between normal and handicapped in-

fants and their mothers. In T. Field & A. Fogel (Eds.), *Emotion and early interaction.* Hillsdale, NJ: Erlbaum, 1982.

Buck, R. Nonverbal communication of affect in preschool children: Relationships with personality and skin conductance. *Journal of Personality and Social Psychology,* 1977, *35,* 225–236.

Buck, R. Spontaneous and symbolic nonverbal behavior and the ontogeny of communication. In R. S. Feldman (Ed.), *Development of nonverbal behavior in children.* New York: Springer-Verlag, 1982.

Bugental, D. E., Kaswan, J. W., Love, L. R., & Fox, M. N. Child versus adult perception of evaluative messages in verbal, vocal, and visual channels. *Developmental Psychology,* 1970, *2,* 367–375.

Campos, J. J., & Stenberg, C. Perception, appraisal and emotion: The onset of social referencing. In M. E. Lamb & L. R. Sherrod (Eds.), *Infant social cognition: Empirical and theoretical considerations.* Hillsdale, NJ: Erlbaum, 1981.

Camras, L. A. Facial expression used by children in a conflict situation. *Child Development,* 1977, *48,* 1431–1435.

Camras, L. A. Children's understanding of facial expressions used during conflict encounters. *Child Development,* 1980, *51,* 879–885.

Chapman, A. J., & Wright, D. S. Social enhancement of laughter: An experimental analysis of some companion variables. *Journal of Experimental Child Psychology,* 1976, *21,* 201–218.

Charlesworth, W. R., & Kreutzer, M. A. Facial expressions of infants and children. In P. Ekman (Ed.), *Darwin and facial expression.* New York: Academic Press, 1973.

Cheyne, J. A. Development of forms and functions of smiling in preschoolers. *Child Development,* 1976, *47,* 820–823.

Cole, P. M. *Preschoolers' emotional display rules: Grin and bear it?* Paper presented at the meetings of the Society for Research in Child Development, Detroit 1983.

Cole, P. M. *Age and sex differences in the rules and regulation of affective display.* Unpublished manuscript, 1984a.

Cole, P. M. *Self-regulation of affective display: Politeness in preschool girls.* Unpublished manuscript, 1984b).

DePaulo, B. M., & Jordan, A. Age changes in deceiving and detecting deceit. In R. S. Feldman (Ed.), *Development of nonverbal behavior in children.* New York: Springer-Verlag, 1982.

Ekman, P. Biological and cultural contributions to body and facial movement. In J. Blacking (Ed.), *The anthropology of the body.* London: Academic Press, 1977.

Ekman, P., & Friesen, W. V. Nonverbal leakage and clues to deception. *Psychiatry,* 1969, *32,* 83–105.

Ekman, P., & Friesen, W. *Unmasking the face.* Englewood Cliffs, NJ: Prentice-Hall, 1975.

Ekman, P., & Friesen, W. *Facial action coding system: A technique for the measurement of facial movement.* Palo Alto, CA: Consulting Psychologists Press, 1978.

Ekman, P., & Oster, H. Facial expressions of emotion. *Annual Review of Psychology,* 1979, *30,* 527–554.

Ekman, P., Roper, G., & Hager, J. C. Deliberate facial movement. *Child Development,* 1980, *51,* 886–891.

Emde, R. N., Gaensbauer, T., & Harmon, R. Emotional expression in infancy: A biobehavioral study. *Psychological Issues Monograph Series,* 1976, *10* (Monograph No. 37).

Feinman, S., & Lewis, M. Social referencing at 10 months: A second order effect on infants' responses to strangers. *Child Development,* 1983, *54,* 878–887.

Feldman, R. S., Devin-Sheehan, L., & Allen, V. L. Nonverbal cues as indicators of verbal dissembling. *American Educational Research Journal,* 1978, *15,* 217–231.

Feldman, R. S., Jenkins, L., & Popoola, O. Detection of deception in adults and children via facial expressions. *Child Development,* 1979, *50,* 350–355.

Feldman, R. S., & White, J. B. Detecting deception in children. *Journal of Communication,* 1980, *30,* 121–128.

Felleman, E. S., Fischer, M. J., & Masters, J. C. *Children's expectancies about the behavioral consequences of their emotional states.* Paper presented at the meetings of the American Psychological Association, August 1982.

Field, T., & Greenberg, R. *Facial expressions of 2- and 3-month-old infants during face-to-face interactions.* Unpublished manuscript, 1981.

Field, T., & Walden, T. Production and perception of facial expressions in infancy and early childhood. In H. Reese & L. Lipsitt (Eds.), *Advances in child development* (Vol. 16). New York: Academic Press, 1982a.

Field, T., & Walden, T. Production and discrimination of facial expressions by preschool children. *Child Development,* 1982b, *53,* 1299–1300.

Field, T. M., Woodson, R., Greenberg, R., & Cohen, D. Discrimination and imitation of facial expressions by neonates. *Science,* 1982, *218,* 1979–181.

Glasberg, R., & Aboud, F. Keeping one's distance from sadness: Children's self-reports of emotional experience. *Developmental Psychology,* 1982, *18,* 287–293.

Hamilton, M. L. Imitative behavior and expressive ability in facial expression. *Developmental Psychology,* 1973, *8,* 138.

Harris, P. L., Olthof, T., & Terwogt, M. M. Children's knowledge of emotion. *Journal of Child Psychology and Psychiatry and Allied Disciplines,* 1981, *22,* 247–261.

Hochschild, A. Emotion work, feeling rules, and social structure. *American Journal of Sociology,* 1979, *85,* 552–575.

Hottenstein, M. P. *An exploration of the relationship between age, social status, and facial gesturing.* Unpublished doctoral dissertation, University of Pennsylvania, 1977.

Izard, C. E. *Human emotions.* New York: Plenum, 1977.

Izard, C. E. The emergence of emotions and development of consciousness in infancy. In J. M. Davidson & R. J. Davidson (Eds.), *The psychobiology of consciousness.* New York: Plenum, 1978.

Izard, C. E. *The maximally discriminative facial movement coding system (MAX).* Newark, DE: Instructional Resources Center, 1979.

Klinnert, M. D., Campos, J. J., Sorce, J. F., Emde, R. N., & Svedja, M. Emotions as behavior regulators: Social referencing in infancy. In R. Plutchik & H. Kellerman (Eds.), *Emotions in early development.* New York: Academic Press, 1982.

Kopp, C. B. Antecedents of self-regulation: A developmental perspective. *Developmental Psychology,* 1982, *18,* 199–214.

LaBarbera, J. D., Izard, C. E., Vietze, P., & Parisi, S. A. Four- and six-month-old infants' visual responses to joy, anger, and neutral expressions. *Child Development,* 1976, *47,* 535–538.

Laird, J. Self-attribution of emotion: The effects of expressive behavior on the quality of emotional experience. *Journal of Personality and Social Psychology,* 1974, *29,* 475–486.

Lewis, M., & Michalson, L. *Children's emotions and moods.* New York: Plenum, 1983.

Maccoby, E. E. *Social development.* New York: Harcourt, 1980.

Malatesta, C., & Haviland, J. Learning display rules: The socialization of emotion expression in infancy. *Child Development,* 1982, *53,* 991–1003.

Meltzoff, A. N., & Moore, M. K. Imitation of facial expressions and manual gestures by human neonates. *Science,* 1977, *198,* 75–78.

Morency, N. L., & Krauss, R. M. Children's nonverbal encoding and decoding of affect. In R. S. Feldman (Ed.), *Development of nonverbal behavior in children.* New York: Springer-Verlag, 1982.

Odom, R., & Lemond, C. M. Developmental differences in the perception and production of facial expressions. *Child Development*, 1972, *43*, 359–369.

Oster, H. Facial expression and affect development. In M. Lewis & L. Rosenblum (Eds.), *The development of affect*. New York: Plenum, 1978.

Peterson, C. L., Danner, F. W., & Flavell, J. H. Developmental changes in children's response to three indications of communicative failure. *Child Development*, 1972, *43*, 1463–1468.

Saarni, C. Cognitive and communicative features of emotional experience, or do you show what you think you feel? In M. Lewis & L. A. Rosenblum (Eds.), *The development of affect*. New York: Plenum, 1978.

Saarni, C. Children's understanding of display rules for expressive behavior. *Developmental Psychology*, 1979, *15*, 424–429.

Saarni, C. *Observing children's use of display rules: Age and sex differences.* Paper presented at the meetings of the American Psychological Association, Montreal, September 1980.

Saarni, C. *Emotional experience and regulation of expressive behavior.* Paper presented at the meetings of the Society for Research in Child Development, Boston, April 1981.

Saarni, C. *Suggestion and expectancy in emotional socialization.* Paper presented at the Biennial Meeting of the Society for Research in Child Development, Detroit, April 1983.

Shantz, C. U. The development of social cognition. In E. M. Hetherington (Ed.), *Review of child development research* (Vol. 5). Chicago: University of Chicago Press, 1975.

Shennum, W. A., & Bugental, D. B. The development of control over affective expression. In R. S. Feldman (Ed.), *Development of nonverbal behavior in children*. New York: Springer-Verlag, 1982.

Sroufe, L. A. Socioemotional development. In J. D. Osofsky (Ed.), *Handbook of infant development*. New York: Wiley, 1979.

Sroufe, L. A. Infant-caregiver attachment and patterns of adaptation in preschool: The roots of maladaptation and competence. In M. Perlmutter (Ed.), *Minnesota Symposium in Child Psychology* (Vol. 16), Hillsdale, NJ: Erlbaum, 1983.

Sroufe, L. A., & Waters, E. The ontogenesis of smiling and laughter: A perspective on the organization of development in infancy. *Psychological Review*, 1976, *83*, 173–189.

Tucker, D. M. Lateral brain function, emotion, and conceptualization. *Psychological Bulletin*, 1981, *89*, 19–46.

Van Leishout, C. F. M. Young children's reactions to barriers placed by their mothers. *Child Development*, 1975, *46*, 879–886.

Volkmar, F. R., & Siegel, A. E. Responses to consistent and discrepant social communications. In R. S. Feldman (Ed.), *Development of nonverbal behavior in children*. New York: Springer-Verlag, 1982.

Wolff, P. H. The natural history of crying and other vocalisations in early infancy. In B. M. Foss (Ed.), *Determinants of infant behavior* (Vol. 4). London: Methuen, 1969.

Yarcowzer, M., Kilbride, J. E., & Hill, L. A. Imitation and inhibition of facial expression. *Developmental Psychology*, 1979, *15*, 453–454.

Zivin, G. Preschool children's facial gestures predict conflict outcomes. *Social Science Information*, 1977a, *16*, 715–730.

Zivin, G. On becoming subtle: Age and social rank changes in the use of a facial gesture. *Child Development*, 1977b, *48*, 1314–1321.

Zivin, G. (Ed.). *The development of self-regulation through private speech*. New York: Wiley, 1979.

Zivin, G. Watching the sands shift: Conceptualizing development of nonverbal mastery. In R. S. Feldman (Ed.), *Development of nonverbal behavior in children*. New York: Springer-Verlag, 1982.

Chapter 12

Emotional Expression, Social Referencing, and Preparedness for Learning in Infancy— Mother Knows Best, but Sometimes I Know Better

Saul Feinman

Relationship to Other Chapters and to the Field

Issues Relevant to the Field

Feinman employs a predominantly sociological and social psychological understanding of emotion and emotion expression. In the tradition of Schachter and other theorists who emphasize the social construction of meaning, *Feinman sees one's emotional condition to be the result of the interpretation of one's situation. Thus, the common concept of* emotional states, *as specific internal conditions with probable physiological components that are necessary for feeling specific emotions, holds a background and supersedable role in Feinman's analysis of emotion, except perhaps as the outcome of interpretation. Where others might refer to states determining emotions, Feinman refers to interpretations; he leaves unspecified whether the interpretations result in states.*

With this orientation, Feinman examines in detail the process of emotional social referencing *by infants, which he characterizes as a mechanism by which the infant uses another person's apparent interpretation of the current situation to determine his or her interpretation and thus how to feel in it. Feinman does not address the mechanisms that link the infant's interpretation to the infant's expressive behavior but seems to assume that in infancy the expressive behaviors follow from the condition of having the interpretation. He therefore sees social*

THE DEVELOPMENT OF EXPRESSIVE BEHAVIOR:
BIOLOGY–ENVIRONMENT INTERACTIONS

291

referencing as a process that contributes to expressive-behavior development as well as to emotional development.

Social referencing is the particular process that Feinman focuses upon by which biology and social influence interact. The biological givens for the interaction are not specific to emotional state nor to patterns of expressive behavior. Rather, they are the biologically programmed capacities for perception and social interpretation, for the inherited bias to attend to information from one's caregiver, and, as he newly suggests, for a particular bias in preparedness for learning *such that individuals search for social referencing information in conditions of uncertainty but resist social influence when certain or when in situations for which preprogrammed responses are most adaptive. The tendency to seek emotion-determining environmental information through social reference appears inherited in conjunction with its adaptive boundaries. Despite his emphasis on the need for and on the effect of acquired environmental information, Feinman implies a rather active biological component in the interaction.*

In keeping with the more subtle understandings of primate behavior, Feinman hints at the cognitive complexity of nonhuman primates' social interactions by citing studies in which social referencing appears among them. Social referencing is thereby presented not as a product of culture, but as an inherited adaptive strategy among social animals.

Relationship to Other Chapters

Social referencing is an important process for expressive development that is included in Cole's (see Chapter 11) and in Lewis and Michalson's (see Chapter 7) broad considerations of similarly important mechanisms. Although Lewis and Michalson are particularly interested in the disconnection of emotional condition from expressive behavior and Feinman is not, there is no incompatibility between their use of the concept—as a primary mechanism by which one learns how to feel about and/or act in a situation—and Feinman's.

In certain ways Feinman's approach is more global than that of his more psychological colleagues in this book. For example, his criteria for evidence of infants' interpretation of nonverbal emotional information accept grosser reactions to less minute stimuli than do those of Dolgin and Azmitia (Chapter 13). He cites studies that use general emotional impact as evidence for emotional interpretation of others' signals.

Mason (Chapter 6), however, shares both Feinman's attention to more general stimuli and his emphasis on the centrality of appraisal of circumstance. Unsurprisingly, Feinman cites studies of social referencing in nonhuman primates that fit the level of Mason's discussion. Mason also shares with Feinman, as perhaps do Lewis and Michalson (Chapter 7), the more classic social psychological view that emotion is first the result of interpretation of circumstance rather than of specific emotional state.—Ed.

Introduction

Several years ago, a young woman came to my office to ask a question. Although it is common for college students to ask questions of their professors, the significance of this incident is that the student was holding her 8-month-old infant in her arms. As mother and infant entered the office, the infant looked at me—a person whom she had never met before—and a puzzled look appeared on her face. Then, she squirmed around and looked at her mother's face. Upon seeing her mother smile, the infant turned back to look at me once again, but this time she displayed a big smile rather than a look of concern.

The question that logically arises is: what cognitive and social processes form the foundation of this sequence of behavior and emotional expression? Infant watchers—both the majority of humankind who have maintained their amateur status in this activity and the small minority who are paid professionals—have noted that when a stranger approaches, infants often look to and fro, alternatively attending to the stranger and to the mother. Such observations have elicited a wealth of explanations, including those derived from psychoanalytic, discrepancy, and attachment theories. This chapter considers a theoretical perspective that focuses upon the impact of others' expressive behavior on the formation of the individual's emotional response.

One interpretation of such behavior asserts that the infant looks to the mother in order to learn from her how to feel about the stranger. The infant's lack of cognitive clarity about the stranger stimulates interest in the mother's emotional interpretation of the stranger, which she provides to the infant when she smiles in response to the infant's look. It may be that the mother's smile in this situation is an emotional message about the stranger that helps the infant in determining whether this person is someone at whom to smile or to frown. Thus, the mother's emotional message about the stranger may serve to socialize the infant's affective reaction and expression to the stranger. This process, in which the infant uses another person as a base of information about persons or objects, has been called *social referencing* (Feinman, 1982; Klinnert, Campos, Sorce, Emde, & Svejda, 1983).

Social referencing has been formally defined as a "process characterized by the use of one's perception of other persons' interpretations of the situation to form one's own understanding of that situation" (Feinman, 1982, p. 445). The central purpose of the present chapter is to examine the role of social referencing in human infancy. It is suggested that social referencing is an important mechanism by which infants use the expressive behavior of others to form and to modulate their own emotional reactions and behavior. Five major sets of issues are considered.

First, what are the origins of the social referencing concept, how has it been applied to humans other than infants, and how did the concept come to be considered in the study of infants? Second, what are the major characteristics, dimensions, and social and cognitive prerequisites of social referencing, both for humans in general and for human infants in particular?

Third, what does the extant research literature on infant social referencing indicate about the inclination of infants to rely upon input from others in forming their own emotional and behavioral reactions to people, objects, and events? In other words, what evidence is there to suggest that the infant acts as if he or she believes that the mother—or another person—may know best about the appropriate emotional interpretation of the situation? Fourth, what are the limits of the process, that is, under what circumstances do infants (1) make mistakes in social referencing or (2) resist social referencing and act as if they believe that they know better than their mothers do as to how to interpret the situation? To what extent are such errors and resistance (1) indicative of preparedness in learning and (2) associated with adaptational benefits?

The first four sets of issues addressed in this chapter focus on the operation of social referencing exclusively in humans, and particularly in human infants. The fifth and final issue considered is whether there is evidence that this phenomenon occurs in other primate species. Discussion of this issue serves two major purposes. First, it provides a broader, cross-species perspective on infant social referencing. Furthermore, it considers whether the utility of the social referencing concept in understanding behavior and emotional expression extends beyond humans.

The Concept of Social Referencing:
Origins and Applications

The term *social referencing* derives (Feinman, 1982) from the concept of reference group, an idea that has had a long and venerable tradition in sociological and social psychological theory. A *reference group* is a "set of significant others with whom the individual may compare his attitudes, beliefs, and behaviors" (Webster, 1975, p. 115) and can apply, as Merton and Rossi (1968) have noted, to individuals and social categories as well as to groups per se. The investigation of the behavior of adults and verbal children has often focused on understanding the ways in which people influence each other, how behavior and thought are shaped by what others do and think, and the way in which people refer to each other for guidance in understanding not only the world around them but themselves as well. This theoretical and research tradition is a major conceptual source of the interest in infant social referencing.

Many theorists have noted that human reaction may not always be a direct response to the inherent characteristics of the situation but is often a function of the way that the individual defines the situation. The quintessential expression of the definition-of-the-situation view of human action is the assertion, often known as the *W. I. Thomas theorem*, that "if men define situations as real, they are real in their consequences" (Thomas, 1928, p. 584). Along this line, the classical sociological theorist, Max Weber (1964, pp. 87ff.) suggested that the individual's reaction to a situation is a function of the subjective meaning (*verstehen*) that he attributes to that situation.

Furthermore, the individual's definition of the situation is often influenced, as symbolic interactionist theorists have long noted, by other people (Mead, 1934), and especially by persons whom the individual particularly likes and respects, that is, *significant others* (Sullivan, 1947). As Lewis and Michalson (1983) and Hochschild (1979) have noted, such social influence upon the individual's definition of the situation is not limited to instrumental understanding, that is, what to do, but extends to emotional interpretation as well, that is, how to feel. Indeed, even perceptions of and feelings about oneself can be influenced by other people, as suggested by Cooley's theory of the *looking-glass self* (1902).

Similarly, phenomenologists (e.g., Berger & Luckmann, 1966) have proposed that the individual (1) does not respond directly to stimuli but, rather, constructs reality by converting sensation into meaning and (2) is influenced in this construction process by what other people think and do. In other words, human action is based upon images of the world that are created through the sociocognitive process that Berger and Luckmann (1966) have termed *social construction of reality*. The first element of this perspective—the construction component—is quite similar to Schachter's (1964) two-stage theory of emotion that proposes that emotional experience requires not only arousal but the interpretation of that arousal as well, for example, excitement can be defined as either pleasure or fear. It is important to note that social referencing is, in essence, a social-construction-of-reality mechanism in which the transformation of sensation into meaning is influenced by other persons' interpretations of such sensation.

Much research on adults and on older children has emanated from this social influence perspective, be it called social construction of reality, definition of the situation, reference group theory, or social referencing. For example, Schachter (1959) noted that one common motivation for affiliation is to learn about and to be influenced by others' interpretations of the situation. Similarly, Festinger's (1954) theory of social comparison hypothesized that a major pathway towards understanding is the comparison of one's own opinions with those of other people.

The strong influence of modeling both on adults (Latané & Rodin, 1969; Phillips, 1974) and on children (Baron, 1977; Freidrich & Stein, 1973) also reflects a process in which the individual appears to rely upon others for guidance and direction. Studies of social influence, such as Sherif's (1958) investigation of how other people's judgments modify the individual's judgment of the apparent movement of a point of light, indicate that individual cognition is affected by how others define the situation. These studies of affiliation, social comparison, modeling, and social influence are prominent examples of a zeitgeist that has pervaded much behavioral science research and theory about human behavior, orienting investigators to focus on the ways in which the individual is influenced by other persons' interpretations of the situation.

The Application of Social Referencing Theory
to Infancy

It is this social construction of reality perspective that underlies my interest in infant social referencing. From this vantage point, social referencing appears to be a mechanism by which infants learn about the world and about themselves. Through this process, other people may socialize the infant's appraisal of events and, as a consequence, his or her instrumental and emotional reactions to these events. A similar view of the socialization role of social referencing can be found in the work of Rogoff and her colleagues on the processes by which adult–infant interaction enables the infant to learn about the world (Rogoff, Gilbride, & Malkin, 1983). Along the same line, Lewis and Feiring's (1981) theory of social transitivity—a type of social referencing—emphasizes the impact of social learning upon infants' interpretations of other people.

Some researchers who have investigated infant social referencing were attracted to this process because of its explanatory value in understanding variations in emotional experience and expression during infancy (Campos, 1983; Campos & Stenberg, 1981; Klinnert, Campos, Sorce, Emde, & Svejda, 1983). Thus, Campos (1983) has suggested that social referencing is important primarily because it is one mechanism through which infant behavior is modulated by affective communication from others.

From this emotional-modulation-and-communication perspective, social referencing that influences instrumental responses, that is, what to do, is of little significance. Rather, the important issues are believed to reside in how social referencing modifies infants' emotional experiences and expression. But from a social construction of reality viewpoint, both instrumental (what to do) and emotional (how to feel) social referencing are important. An exposition of these two respective views of the importance and the parameters of infant social referencing can be found in the recent exchange between Campos (1983) and myself (1982, 1983). The convergence of these two divergent interests upon a common process of social referencing would seem to be an indication of the pervasiveness and significance of the process.

Basic Features of Social Referencing

As noted in an earlier paper (Feinman, 1982), there are two essential hallmarks of social referencing. First, action is at least partially based upon constructionist mental activity in which meaning is created from sensation through an evaluation and appraisal process. Second, such evaluation is influenced by the interpretations provided by other people. Furthermore, there are three entities involved in the social referencing process. First, the person who seeks out and/or is influenced by another individual's interpretation of the situation is the *referer*. The person whose opinion influences the referer is the *referee*. And, the situation, person, object, or event that is the focus of the information provided by the referee is the *referent*. When a mother conveys an affective message about an unfamiliar person to her infant, the infant is the referer, the mother is the referee, and the unfamiliar person is the referent.

Dimensions of Social Referencing:
A Typology of Social Influence

Social referencing episodes can be classified along several dimensions. First, interpretation can be explicitly requested by the referer, as when an infant sees an unfamiliar animal in the zoo and, with a look of puzzlement, turns to the caregiver as if asking "what is that?" Direct solicitation of evaluation can also be noted in adults, as when a husband asks his wife whether or not she likes a new work of fiction. But social referencing can also occur when interpretation is offered by the referee and used by the referer, even though the information was not solicited by the referer. For instance, the mother whose 9-month-old is afraid of the new family pet may intercede to try to alter the child's opinion of the animal despite the child's apparent lack of interest in the mother's interpretation. Similarly, a campaigning politician may attempt to modify a potential voter's interpretation of the opposition candidate even though this interpretative input has not been requested by the voter.

Within the category of requested social referencing, it is possible to detect variation in the way that information is solicited. Particularly in adults and verbal children, an explicit expression of the need for interpretative assistance may be displayed by the referer. For example, a third grader who cannot decide whether or not she likes a new teacher may ask another girl in the class for an interpretation of the teacher. On the other hand, the initiation of social referencing by the referer may be a more subtle matter, as when the individual looks toward a potential referee for cue information.

Social referencing can also be classified according to whether the interpretation is conveyed directly or indirectly by the referee. In the direct form of referencing, others inform the individual of their interpretations. The indirect pathway occurs when the individual infers others' interpretations from their behavioral responses to the situation. Direct social referencing may occur when an older sister points to a new toy, saying to her infant sibling "Look! Look at the pretty toy!" in a happy and enthusiastic tone of voice. Indirect social referencing may take place when a 12-month-old observes an infant peer's response to an unusual noise. In older individuals, direct referencing may transpire when a husband tells his wife how he feels about moving to a new city. In contrast, an example of indirect referencing may be noted when a wife observes her husband's reaction to a new food and infers his emotional interpretation of that food from the expression on his face.

At least conceptually, social referencing can be categorized into those episodes that provide affective information and those that provide instrumental information. In other words, the referee's communication may provide guidance about how to feel or about what to do with regard to the referent. A father may endeavor to convince his 11-month-old daughter that watching the nightly news is fun (affective referencing), or he may try to show her how to drink milk from a cup (instrumental referencing).

The distinction between feeling and doing is rarely clear-cut in actual situations. For example, socialization of an infant's emotional experience of a stranger—whether to fear or to like the stranger—implies strategies for how to behave with regard to the stranger—to avoid or to approach, respectively. Similarly, if a caregiver wishes to show a toddler how to build a tower of blocks, the affective tone of the demonstration is likely to influence the child's emotional reaction to the block building activity.

In practice, the affective and instrumental components of referencing are, more or less, confounded. Nonetheless, the distinction is useful as a conceptual and heuristic device that makes us aware that emotions as well as instrumental responses can be socialized through referencing. Furthermore, it is reasonable to speculate that, in some situations, affective referencing and learning temporally precede instrumental referencing and learning. Perhaps the formation of a basic emotional reaction to a new person or object is a prerequisite for learning about more specific instrumental behaviors concerning that person or object.

Social referencing messages from the referee can vary according to the mode by which they are communicated to the referer. The most basic distinction is that an interpretative message can be conveyed verbally or nonverbally. Within the nonverbal mode, various channels can be utilized, for example, facial expression, hedonic tone of voice, tactile cues. For instance, a father's interpretation of a novel toy can be conveyed to the infant when he either smiles at the toy or speaks happily about it. Given the relatively low level of semantic comprehension during the first year of life (Bates, Benigni, Bretherton, Camaioni, & Volterra, 1979), the verbal component of the referee's communication is likely to be of limited significance for referencing in infancy. The verbal content of the message should come to be more salient as semantic comprehension expands in toddlerhood and childhood.

Children and adults in literate societies may also refer to written material, and even toddlers can utilize electronic media to some degree. Sociocultural evolution and technological development have made available additional methods of social referencing in which it is possible to utilize a referee with whom one does not have direct face-to-face contact. From an ontogenetic perspective, one part of growing up in a technologically advanced society is that the range of potential referees expands as printed and electronic media become comprehensible to the developing child.

Social and Cognitive Skills Needed for Social Referencing

The social and cognitive prerequisites for social referencing are related to the basic characteristics of the process itself. First, referencing is unlikely to occur when a purely mechanistic link exists between sensation and action. Rather, social referencing requires that infants be at least part-time constructionists, that is, that they act to some degree as if they are constructing meaning out of sensation rather than responding solely to inherent qualities of the situation. It is within such appraisal and evaluation that others' interpretations can influence the infant.

The behavior of second-semester infants often suggests that they are engaging in what Lazarus (1968) has called *appraisal*, a process in which they appear to evaluate prospectively the probable consequences of contact with an object, person, or situation (Piaget, 1952). When a stranger approaches, the looking behavior of 6- to 12-month-old infants seems to facilitate appraisal of the stranger (Sroufe, Waters, & Matas, 1974). Similarly, the stronger inclination of infants older than 8 months to delay reaching for a novel object until they have taken the time to visually inspect the object (Schaffer, Greenwood, & Parry, 1972) may also reflect a greater inclination for appraisal.

A second condition to be satisfied for social referencing to become an active component of the infant's repertoire is that the infant must be interested in and receptive to *cues* that provide interpretative messages about the situation. Such cues can be observed by attending to others' behavior and emotional expressions. By 6 months, a common action upon encountering an ambiguous or novel event is looking towards a caregiver (Bretherton, 1978; Carr, Dabbs, & Carr, 1975; Feinman, 1980; Gunnar, 1980; Haviland & Lewis, 1975; Rheingold & Eckerman, 1973). Fein (1975) and Sorce and Emde (1981) have found that 15- and 18-month-olds appear to be distressed when they are with their mothers in a strange room and their mothers are distracted by other activities. Such distress could, of course, derive from the infant's desire to seek emotional comfort from the caregiver (the caregiver as a base of security) and/or it could derive from the infant's desire for interpretation of the unfamiliar situation from the caregiver (the caregiver as a base of information).

Whereas *infant looking* toward other people may be a major channel through which information about others' interpretations is obtained and could be an important initiator of social referencing episodes, it is important to note that not all such looking—or attending through other communication channels—is associated with referencing. Looking to others may signify a request for information, but it may also serve to express emotion, initiate interaction, sustain ongoing social interaction, or share information. One interesting question for future research on infant social referencing would be the investigation of how a potential referee determines whether information is being solicited. In other words, how does an adult, child, or infant peer discriminate between infant looking that requests information and looking that serves other functions?

In affective social referencing, it is important that infants be able to detect and utilize information about others' emotional responses. Even young infants attend preferentially to two major sources of emotional information—human faces and voices (Dolgin & Azmitia, Chapter 13, this volume; Eisenberg, Griffin, Coursin, & Hunter, 1964; Hainline, 1978; Schaffer, 1971; Wolff, 1963). By 5 months, visual inspection of faces focuses on features in the interior of the face, particularly the eyes and mouth, that reflect emotional expression (Caron, Caron, Caldwell, & Weiss, 1973; Salapatek, 1975). Furthermore, discrimination of and appropriate reaction to facial emotional cues occurs by 6 months (Klinnert, Campos, Sorce, Emde, & Svejda, 1983), if not sooner (Dolgin & Azmitia, Chapter 13, this volume).

By this age, infants appear to respond appropriately to vocally expressed emotion when it is juxtaposed with facial expression (Charlesworth & Kreutzer, 1973) and perhaps to vocal expression alone (Bühler & Hetzer, 1928). Unfortunately, there is a dearth of research on infants' ability to detect emotions in vocalization. Even less is known about infants' ability to derive emotional data from tactile and tension cues emitted by other people. There has been some interest, though, in the possibility that such sensations may generate artifactual effects in investigations of other phenomena during infancy (e.g., LaBarbera, Izard, Vietze, & Parisi, 1976).

The limited verbal comprehension skill of infants (Bates et al., 1979; Benedict, 1979) implies that early affective social referencing must rely primarily, if not exclusively, upon nonverbally expressed emotion such as facial expression and paralinguistic cues. Consequently, the apparent capacity of infants 6 months and older to derive affective information from others' facial expressions, and perhaps from their vocalization, would seem to be a significant milestone on the road to social referencing.

For social referencing to be of benefit to the infant, it is necessary that the infant be able to identify the referent of the referee's communication. As Smith (1981) has noted, nonverbal communication can provide information about many referents such as "what (the signaler) may be doing or (is) about to do, aspects of its internal state, and things or events other than itself" (p. 1273). Consider a case in which the mother tries, through smiling and speaking happily, to communicate to her infant that she likes the family's new cat which the infant fears. The social referencing message will yield the intended effect only if the infant accurately identifies the cat per se as the referent of the mother's smile. If the infant mistakenly considers the smile to be data about the mother's mood, or a maternal overture to interaction, then the infant's interpretation of the cat will not be modified.

In human adults, the verbal content of communication can inform the referer of the identity of the referent. For example, it is possible to express in words the fact that the referent of a fearful response is one particular individual within a group rather than the group as a whole. But infants' restricted verbal understanding implies that nonverbal gestures and cues are the primary source of information that infants can use to identify the referent.

One referent-identifying gesture that infants seem to understand is pointing. A mother may point to a new toy while joyfully saying to her 9-month-old son "Look at the pretty toy. Let's play with that wonderful toy!" Leung and Rheingold (1981) found that infants visually follow maternal pointing before the end of the first year. Similarly, Murphy and Messer (1977) reported that infant ability to follow maternal pointing improves significantly between 9 and 14 months.

Another gesture that may indicate the referent of the message is the direction of the referee's visual regard. For example, a 4-year-old may speak sadly to her infant sibling while looking at the broken pieces of what was once the soup bowl that she just knocked off the kitchen table. Scaife and Bruner (1975) reported that while only about one-third of 2- to 7-month-old infants visually follow the line of their mothers' visual regard, two-thirds of those between 8 and 10 months, and all of those between 11 and 14 months demonstrate this skill. Thus, infants possess some ability to identify referents—at least through visual means—by the end of the first year of life. By this point in development, infants appear to be ready, socially and cognitively, for social referencing.

The Investigation of Social Referencing

The optimal experimental design for the investigation of infant social referencing requires the deliberate variation of the affective or instrumental message that is provided to the infant by another person. For example, upon encountering a new toy, some infants in such a study would hear their mothers speak happily about the toy whereas others would hear their mothers speak fearfully about the toy. The central data analysis would consider whether happy-message and fearful-message infants differ in consequent reaction to the toy.

Because infant behavior patterns consistent with the social referencing hypothesis can also be generated through other mechanisms, it is critical that the investigator build into the design of the study some means of discriminating between social referencing and alternative explanations. Consider, for example, a study in which the mother provides an affective message about a new toy, but the infant mistakenly identifies the mother's mood instead of the toy as the referent of her communication. Thus, a happy communication about the toy is utilized by the infant as an indication that his mother is happy, but nothing is learned about the toy. Perhaps the infant's own mood consequently changes in accordance with his perception of the mother's mood, and the infant's altered mood subsequently influences behavior to the toy. The resulting pattern of behavior with regard to the toy would be consistent with the social referencing hypothesis despite the fact that it is the product of a mood modification process. This same outcome could also be produced by a simpler mood modification process in which the infant does not perceive the mother's communication as referential but, instead, experiences nonreferential mood contagion.

Studies of Infant Social Referencing

In 1981, findings from three experimental investigations of infant social referencing were reported: (1) Klinnert's (1981) toy study; (2) Sorce, Emde, Klinnert, and Campos's (1981) modified visual cliff study; and (3) Feinman and Lewis's (1981, 1982, 1983) stranger study. In Klinnert's (1981) toy study, 36 twelve-month-olds and 36 eighteen-month-olds along with their mothers encountered, in counterbalanced sequence, a stuffed toy dinosaur, a life-size bust of the "Incredible Hulk," and a remote control toy that resembled a large black spider. When the child looked towards the mother after noticing each toy, she posed a facial expression of either fear, neutrality, or joy. Each child was exposed to all three toys and all three facial expressions of emotion. Toy stimuli were randomly paired with emotional expressions. The subsequent toy-related behavior was consistent with the social referencing hypothesis, although the relationship between such behavior and the mother's facial affect was not strong. Movement toward the toy was greater after the mother displayed joy than after she displayed fear, whereas neutrality produced an intermediate effect. Similarly, latency to approach the toy was lower in the joy condition than in the fear condition, with an intermediate effect found for the neutral condition. None of these differences, however, were reported to be statistically significant.

Sorce *et al.* (1981) investigated the impact of social referencing upon 12-month-olds' behavior on a modified visual cliff with an apparent drop of 12 inches, that is, a *visual step,* so to speak. The mother stood at the deep side of the visual cliff (step) apparatus and the infant was placed on the shallow side. When the infant reached the dividing boundary between the shallow and deep sides and looked to the mother, 19 mothers smiled and 17 mothers displayed fear, in accordance with the experimenter's request. Although 74% of the infants in the smiling condition crossed over the apparent 12-inch drop to their mothers, none of the infants in the fear condition crossed. This pattern of results is compatible with the hypothesis that the infants engaged in social referencing by using their mother's facial expressions in interpreting the 12-inch visual step.

The preliminary results of Feinman and Lewis' stranger study were reported in 1981 (Feinman & Lewis, 1981); additional and more detailed analyses have been performed subsequently (Feinman & Lewis, 1982, 1983). Eighty-seven 10-month-olds and their mothers participated in the study. Infant and mother were approached by a female stranger. In the control condition, the mother did not speak during the stranger's approach. In the two direct referencing conditions, mothers spoke to their infants about the stranger in either a positive or a neutral tone of voice. The two indirect referencing conditions called for mothers to allow their infants to observe them greet the stranger in either a positive or a neutral tone of voice. Then, the stranger sat next to the infant for a 1-minute period during which she did not initiate interaction with either the infant or the mother.

When the mothers had spoken directly to their infants about the stranger, infants initiated a higher frequency of friendly behavior to the stranger during the 1-minute period (smiling to, moving near, and offering a toy to the stranger) in the positive affect condition than in the neutral affect condition—a pattern of behavior predicted by the social referencing hypothesis. This effect was especially striking for infants of easier temperament. But the opportunity to hear the affective tone of the mother's voice as she greeted the approaching stranger in the indirect referencing conditions did not influence infant behavior to the stranger.

It is important to note that data reported in the toy study and in the visual cliff study included only those infants who were observed to actively solicit information from the mother by looking to her after noticing the toy or the modified visual cliff, respectively. Thus, both of these investigations focused on requested social referencing. In contrast, mothers in the stranger study were asked to provide an affective message about the stranger without waiting for the infant to solicit such evaluation. Whether the message was solicited or unsolicited, the resulting infant behavior was consistent with the social referencing hypothesis. Furthermore, it is interesting to note that stronger evidence for social referencing was found in the two studies that focused on uncertain situations—a visual step or an adult stranger—than in the study that presented toys that may have initially produced fear rather than ambiguity.

Subsequent experimental investigations have provided further evidence of infant behavior that is in line with the social referencing hypothesis. In a study of 48 6- to 10-month-olds, Garland (1982) asked half of the mothers to show joy and the other half to show fear when a stranger came into the room. Nonlocomotor infants were not influenced by the mother's affective communication. But those infants who were locomotor and could integrate vision with locomotion did not approach or reach toward the stranger when in the fear condition.

Svejda and Campos (1982) requested that mothers vocally express either happiness, anger, or fear shortly after their infants noticed and began to approach a remote control toy. There were 72 infants in this investigation, equally divided between two ages—8½ and 11 months. Three different remote control toys were presented to each infant in a repeated-measures design. Lower latency to resume locomotion to the toy was found in the happiness condition than in the fear and anger conditions. Similarly, the speed of approach to the toy after hearing the mother's vocally expressed emotion was greater in the happiness condition than in the anger or fear conditions.

In Klinnert, Emde, and Butterfield's (1983) study, 46 12-month-olds observed a remote control robot toy. During this encounter, the mother was present but was instructed to appear puzzled if the infant looked to her. Instead, an affective message about the robot was provided by a stranger with whom the infant was familiarized just prior to the experimental session. The stranger either smiled or showed fear in response to the infant's glance as the robot appeared. Speed of infant locomotion to, and duration of play with, the robot were greater in the smile condition than in the fear condition.

Boccia and Campos's (1983) study of 19 8½-month-olds focused on the impact of mother's affect upon infant behavior to a stranger. As the stranger began to approach the infant, the mother said "Hello" either in a joyful or a worried manner and then posed a congruent facial expression throughout the stranger's approach and brief contact with her infant. Infants in the joy condition smiled more at the stranger than did infants in the worry condition. In addition, infant cardiac acceleration was greater in the worry condition than in the joy condition, and this physiological distinction was especially marked for those infants who, in a previous test, had been found to comprehend maternal pointing, a referential gesture.

Another study (Zarbatany & Lamb, 1983; Zarbatany, 1983, personal communication) investigated whether the responses of 52 13- to 15-month-olds to a remote control black felt spider was influenced by the emotional expression provided either by the mother or by an adult with whom the infant had become acquainted in a 10-minute interaction just prior to the social referencing episode. As the spider appeared and moved around the floor of the experimental room, the mother or other adult posed a facial expression either of happiness or fear. Considering the results for mother and for other adult together, it was found that infants were marginally more inclined to move towards the spider (combined measure of movement toward and of latency to move) in the happiness than in the fear condition.

In general, the patterns of infant behavior observed in these studies are consistent with the social referencing hypothesis. Reactions to the relevant object or person—toys, strangers—appear to have been correlated with others' emotional expressions. As was the case for the earlier studies, the weakest support for the social referencing hypothesis among these later investigations was found when a stimulus that may have been fearful rather than uncertain—a moving toy spider—was used.

Social Referencing or Mood Modification

The pattern of behavior noted above are consistent not only with the social referencing process but also with the process of mood modification that was described earlier. In social referencing per se, the infant accurately identifies the referent of the mother's communication as a stranger (e.g., Feinman & Lewis, 1981, 1983), a toy (Klinnert, Emde, & Butterfield, 1983), or a modified visual cliff (Sorce et al., 1981). But in mood modification, the infant commits an error either (1) by judging the referent of the mother's affective communication to be the mother's mood or (2) by failing to realize that the communication is indeed referential.

In either of these errors, the infant may subsequently respond sympathetically to the perceived maternal mood. The result is that infants whose mothers express positive affect are likely to experience a more favorable overall mood than are those infants whose mothers express neutral or negative affect. Such alterations in the infant's general mood may then be reflected in her or his behavior with regard to people, objects, and events in the environment. This effect would be detected in behavior to the intended referent of the mother's message, but it would also be noticed in behavior directed to other people, objects and events in the environment. In contrast, social referencing would influence infant behavior specifically with regard to the referent of the referee's message.

The comparison of the social referencing hypothesis with the mood modification explanation is relatively straightforward in the Feinman and Lewis (1981, 1982, 1983) stranger study because that investigation was designed specifically to consider this comparison. If social referencing truly has occurred, then infant behavior to the mother should not be influenced in the same manner as behavior to the stranger. In contrast, mood modification should produce parallel effects upon behavior to the mother and behavior to the stranger, that is, behavior to mother as well as to stranger should be friendlier in the positive condition than in the neutral condition.

To compare these two explanations, we analyzed the impact of affect of the mother's message upon infant behavior to the mother during the 1-minute period when stranger and mother sat near the infant. When the mother had spoken directly to her infant about the stranger—the condition under which mother's affect influenced the behavior to the stranger (as noted earlier)—the affect of the mother's message to her infant did not, on the average, produce a parallel effect upon behavior to the mother.

Although other studies of infant social referencing have not, as a rule, purposively aimed to discriminate among competing explanations, data relevant to such comparisons have been collected. Klinnert, Emde, and Butterfield (1983) reported that whereas a stranger's affective communication influenced 12-month-olds' reaction to a robot, behavior to their mothers, who were also in the room during the experimental episode, was not similarly influenced by the stranger's affect. But the results reported for 8½-month-olds by Boccia and Campos (1983) indicated an effect of the mother's affect upon infant smiling to the mother that paralleled that noted to the stranger. Infants smiled more to the mother as well as to the stranger in the joyful condition than in the worry condition.

The results reported for 10-month-olds by Feinman and Lewis (1981, 1983) and for 12-month-olds by Klinnert, Emde, & Butterfield (1983) appear to be more consistent with social referencing than with mood modification. The primary impact of emotional communication was found for affective and behavioral reaction to the referent of that communication—the stranger and the robot, respectively. In contrast, behavior to other elements of the environment—the mother—was not influenced in a similar fashion by the affective message. But the parallel effects of the mother's emotional expression upon infant smiling to the mother and the stranger noted by Boccia and Campos (1983) may indicate that these 8½-month-olds mistakenly used the mother's affect as information about the mother's mood, or that they perceived such messages as nonreferential.

Social Referencing or a Perceived Threat to the Mother's Emotional Availability

When mothers in the Feinman and Lewis (1981, 1982, 1983) stranger study let their infants observe them greeting the stranger, the affective tone of this communication did not influence infant behavior to the stranger. But affective tone did influence infant behavior to the mother. Infants were less friendly to the mother when she had spoken positively to the stranger than when she had spoken neutrally to the stranger. This pattern of behavior in the indirect referencing condition suggests that infants did not associate the affective message with its intended referent—the stranger.

One possible, but as yet untested, explanation of these results is that the infant identified the mother's emotional availability as the information conveyed by the maternal greeting to the stranger. Observation of friendly communication from mother to stranger could suggest to the 10-month-old that he or she will be ignored by the mother now that another adult has arrived. Consequently, the infant may become angry or annoyed with the mother—a reaction that is consistent with the occurrence of less friendly behavior to her in the positive than in the neutral condition. Perhaps the salience of the attachment relationship with the mother prepares the 10-month-old to be biased to utilize the mother's communication to the stranger as information about maternal availability rather than as information about the intended referent, the stranger.

Social Referencing Errors and Preparedness for Learning

The finding that affective communication that is transmitted as information about a particular referent can also influence the infant's behavioral and emotional reaction to other elements in the environment suggests that infants make mistakes in social referencing. One potential explanation of some of these errors relies upon the concept of *preparedness for learning*. In contrast to the general process theory of learning, it has been noted that animals—human as well as nonhuman—are especially prepared to learn some associations and behavioral sequences more easily than others (Seligman, 1970). Analogously, animals may be contraprepared and disinclined to learn still other associations and sequences.

Furthermore, Seligman (1970) has also suggested that patterns of preparedness and contrapreparedness form the biological boundaries of learning. Responses that are easy to learn may be especially important for adaptation, whereas those that the animal is particularly reluctant to learn may be detrimental and maladaptive. An often-cited example is Garcia and Koelling's (1966) finding that rats were more easily classically conditioned to avoid the taste of an ingested substance when it was associated with subsequent nausea—a naturally occurring association of considerable importance for the future avoidance of poisonous foods—than when it was associated with electric shock—a sequence that probably is found only in the laboratory.

Because infants usually depend greatly upon primary caregivers for survival, it is not unreasonable to expect that they will be especially motivated to acquire information about these persons. Indeed, the survival and fitness-enhancing benefits of caregiver–infant relationships have been discussed by attachment theorists (Ainsworth, Blehar, Waters, & Wall, 1978; see Lamb, Thompson, Gardner, Charnov, & Estes, 1984, for a somewhat different view). One possible general impediment to social referencing in infancy is that infants may be prepared and biased to extract information about attachment objects from the behavior of these individuals. Thus, the mother's communication to the stranger in the indirect referencing condition (Feinman & Lewis, 1981, 1982, 1983) may be interpreted by the infant as information about the mother because the infant is more interested in learning about the mother's emotional availability than about the stranger.

A bias to learn about primary caregivers may also underlie the pattern of infant smiling to mother and to stranger reported by Boccia and Campos (1983). But it is important to note that any such bias is unlikely to be overcome unless the infant understands referential gestures such as pointing or visual gaze. The finding that many of the 8½-month-olds in this study did not exhibit evidence of such ability suggests that these infants may have been guided—by an adaptational bias and a lack of cognitive sophistication—either to link the mother's affect with her mood or to simply respond contagiously to it. Indeed, the finding, noted previously, that the tendency for greater cardiac acceleration in the worry than in the joy condition was particularly dramatic for infants who understood pointing is consistent with this interpretation.

Social referencing would appear to be a complex juggling act in which the infant must (1) attend to the referee's message, (2) observe the referent of that message, and (3) connect the former with the latter specifically. Especially when the referee is a primary caregiver, preparedness to learn about the caregiver may interfere with the formation of the specific link between the message and the intended referent. The comprehension of referential gestures such as pointing and direction of visual attention would seem to be an essential development for the infant at least to be cognitively able to override any such special interest in the condition of the caregiver and of the caregiver–infant relationship.

Uncertainty, Preparedness to Learn, and Social Referencing

It was noted earlier that human adults are often influenced by the thought and behavior of others (e.g., Festinger, 1954; Schachter, 1959; Sherif, 1958). But there appears to be an especially strong bias to seek out other people's interpretations when the situation is ambiguous. For example, Festinger (1954) proposed that the individual's interest in social comparison is strongest when objective standards for evaluation are not available. It may be that humans are prepared for learning from others under conditions of uncertainty.

In contrast, humans and other animals seem to be resistant to learning from others when the situation is easy to interpret, and especially when the situation is either clearly dangerous or obviously safe. Such contrapreparedness against learning from others seems to be particularly prominent when biologically based responses with clear adaptive value are present in the animal's repertoire of behavior in that situation.

A nonhuman example of such contrapreparedness can be found in Breland and Breland's (1961) account of their attempt to train a raccoon to insert two coins into a container. When given two coins, the raccoon could not be conditioned to perform the task even though the situation was structured to reward this behavior. Instead, the coins were repeatedly rubbed together and dipped in and out of the container. As the Brelands (1961) noted, such behavior resembles the food-washing actions that this species often performs in the wild. Thus, when an animal has within its repertoire a response that clearly contributes to survival, contrapreparedness against learning other responses in that situation is likely to be found.

There is some evidence that infants' receptivity to others' interpretations is influenced by a similar set of biases. Uncertainty appears to be associated with preparedness for social referencing whereas clear danger or safety, especially when combined with the possession of adaptive and possibly prewired responses, seem to be associated with contrapreparedness against accepting others' interpretations of the situation. As noted earlier, variation among investigations in the strength of the observed social referencing effect appears to be correlated with the degree of uncertainty. Strangers are somewhat ambiguous because they can vary in friendliness. A 12-inch drop is also likely to have variable consequences. But a toy that resembles a large black spider may present more obvious cues of danger, resulting in less receptivity to social referencing information.

The visual cliff study (Sorce *et al.*, 1981) discussed earlier provides some interesting data that are relevant to uncertainty and to danger. Two other variations of this experiment indicated that there are conditions under which infants' emotional and behavioral reactions are not influenced by their mothers' affective interpretations of the situation (Campos, 1981, personal communication; Sorce *et al.*, 1981). First, when the full visual cliff, with its apparent drop of 3½ feet, was utilized, the mother's affect did not influence the infants' crossing behavior. Instead, the pattern of locomotion was similar to that usually noted in visual cliff studies (Walk, 1966), that is, infants strongly resisted going across the deep side of the cliff. Similarly, when the cliff apparatus was covered with a cloth so that depth cues were not visible, the mother's facial expression did not have an impact upon whether infants crossed over the surface.

Both the 3½-foot drop and the no-drop condition are relatively clear-cut situations. Falling 3½ feet will very likely hurt the average 12-month-old, whereas crossing a flat and solid surface will most probably do no harm. Under such ambiguous circumstances, infants act as if they are contraprepared to learn from their mothers, that is, they act as if they believe that they know better than their mothers do as to what is appropriate under the circumstances. Indeed, it would probably be quite maladaptive for locomoting infants to be convinced by their mothers that a fall of 3½ feet is anything but dangerous. Such infants appear to be averse to crossing a surface that displays depth cues. This strong response may be one source of the infant's resistance to the mother's attempts to socialize the infant's emotional and behavioral reaction to the cliff.

One social referencing study (Gunnar & Stone, 1983; Gunnar, 1983, personal communication) has purposively varied uncertainty and aversiveness. Forty-eight 12- to 13-month-olds were each exposed two times to a pleasant toy (a musical ferris wheel), an aversive toy (a chimp that clapped cymbals together), and an ambiguous toy (a nonmobile robot that "spoke" in a machinelike voice). In counterbalanced order, mothers provided a positive and a neutral message about each toy. No social referencing effects were observed for the first presentation of the toys. At the second presentation, infants moved closer to the ambiguous toy and farther from the mother in the positive condition than in the neutral condition. But mother's communication about the pleasant and the aversive toys did not influence infant behavior concerning these toys. Regardless of the mother's affect, infant behavior to the ferris wheel and to the chimp with cymbals seemed to reflect the qualities of the toys, that is, more favorable responses were displayed to the pleasant toy.

This patterning of response suggests that infants may be counterprepared against attempts to influence their affective interpretations of clearly safe or of aversive objects. Indeed, receptivity to social influence with regard to such clear-cut situations might not be especially adaptive. Learning to avoid situations that are pleasant and to approach those that are dangerous seems unlikely to be of benefit to the infant. On the other hand, receptivity to socialization about ambiguous situations would be helpful for the infant.

Does Social Referencing Occur in Nonhuman Primates?

The systematic investigation of social referencing in nonhuman primates has been pursued to only a very limited degree. Mason (Chapter 6, this volume) includes some studies in which social referencing or a similar process may influence expressive behavior in nonhuman primates. Indeed, there is tangential evidence that suggests that this phenomenon is not uniquely human. First of all, social learning activities such as modeling and imitation commonly occur in monkeys and apes (Hall, 1968). For example, the transmission of food-handling practices within monkey groups (*precultural behavior*: Kawai, 1965) and of food preferences (Itani, 1958) appears to proceed through social learning. Social referencing may be one component of such learning.

Similarly, there is considerable evidence that nonhuman primates attend to each other (Chance, 1967; Pitcairn, 1976). While looking and other attending behaviors do not guarantee that social referencing will occur, the former is clearly a necessary condition for the latter. Along this line, it is interesting to note that such behavior has been reported for other mammals, such as wolves (Mech, 1970, p. 73). Indeed, King (1966) pointed out that it is generally accepted that the young of many species learn to respond to situations by observing and copying their mothers' responses, although he did also note that this theory needed to be empirically documented.

The use of affective cues in social referencing requires the capability to discriminate appropriately among facial expressions, vocalizations, bodily postures, and motor behaviors that reflect emotional states. Several studies have indeed indicated that this skill is found in nonhuman primates (Boccia & Capitanio, 1983; Plimpton, Swartz, & Rosenblum, 1981; Sackett, 1965, 1966). This capability does not, in itself, demonstrate that affective social referencing occurs in monkeys and apes. But it does indicate that one skill needed for affective social referencing is part of the repertoire of some nonhuman primate species.

The most direct extant evidence concerning social referencing in non-human primates derives from Novak's (1973) study of *social monitoring.* In the monitoring process, an infant monkey who is confronted with a novel stimulus is likely to observe the attachment object's behavior and emotional expressions and to use that information to shape its own response to the situation. This sequence of events that Novak calls social monitoring bears a strong resemblance to social referencing. Novak investigated the responses to a potentially fear-provoking stimulus for infant rhesus monkeys reared under three conditions: (1) mother reared; (2) surrogate reared (with peer contact); and (3) together reared. Each infant encountered the stimulus while in the company of its respective attachment object. The highest level of distress was found in together-reared infants and the lowest level was found in surrogate-reared infants. The mother-reared infants displayed an intermediate reaction. If infants did monitor and were influenced by the behavior of their attachment objects, it is reasonable to expect very little fear from infants attached to an inanimate surrogate because the surrogate cannot respond to the stimulus. In contrast, peer attachment objects are likely to display a high level of distress which could serve to define the situation as a fearful one.

While the observed pattern of differences among the three rearing-condition groups is consistent with a social monitoring (referencing) hypothesis, it is also necessary to consider alternative explanations. Rather than be a product of the specific input (or lack of input) received from the surrogate during the experimental session, could the low level of distress exhibited by surrogate-reared infants derive from the atypical emotional development that may result from such rearing experiences? Furthermore, it is difficult to evaluate whether the differences between together-reared and mother-reared infants were due to variation in the information received from the attachment individuals during the experimental session or to differences in the relative effectiveness of the peer and the mother to serve as a base of security.

The prevalence of social learning and social attention in some non-human primates, and their apparent ability to recognize and respond appropriately to the expressive behavior of conspecifics suggest that social referencing may occur in these species. Novak's (1973) study of social monitoring provides additional and more direct evidence that this phenomenon may not be exclusively human. Clearly, the extant evidence is suggestive rather than demonstrative. But it should be noted that the initial research on social referencing in human infancy was stimulated, at least in part, by similar suggestive evidence in infants (Feinman, 1982; Klinnert, Campos, Sorce, Emde, & Svejda, 1983).

Summary

There is a growing body of evidence that indicates that social referencing plays a significant role in the socialization of emotional and instrumental response during infancy. By the end of the first year of life, infants appear to use other people as bases of information and to be influenced by others' affective interpretations of situations. Thus, human infants act as if they are engaging in social referencing, a process that has a major impact upon the behavior and the emotional expression of older humans, and perhaps on that of members of other primate species as well.

But there seem to be boundaries within which social referencing influences infant behavior and emotional expression. First of all, infants may err in their identification of the intended referent of the referee's message. Such mistakes may indicate that infants are especially prepared to learn about some components of their environments, for example, primary caregivers.

Second, infants may be more prepared to engage in social referencing when the situation does not provide cognitive clarity than when the situation is clear-cut. Furthermore, resistance to others' interpretations of unambiguous events may be, to some extent, a protective mechanism that contributes to the infant's survival. When faced with a mother who conveys positive emotional expressions about crossing an apparent visual cliff of 3½ feet or one who indicates strong fear with regard to a harmless and pleasurable toy, it may be beneficial for an infant to act as if he or she does indeed know better.

Acknowledgments

Discussions with Michael Lewis and Debra Roberts were helpful in formulating and refining some of the ideas presented in this chapter. Gail Zivin's comments on an earlier version contributed both conceptually and stylistically. I would also like to thank Marcia Boccia for suggesting the importance of considering the role of social referencing in the behavior of nonhuman primates.

References

Ainsworth, M. D., Blehar, M. C., Waters, E., & Wall, S. *Patterns of attachment.* Hillsdale, NJ: Erlbaum, 1978.

Baron, R. A. *Human aggression.* New York: Plenum, 1977.

Bates, E., Benigni, L., Bretherton, I., Camaioni, L., & Volterra, V. *The emergence of symbols: Cognition and communication in infancy.* New York: Academic Press, 1979.

Benedict, H. Early lexical development: Comprehension and production. *Journal of Child Language,* 1979, *6,* 183–200.

Berger, P. L., & Luckmann, T. *The social construction of reality.* Garden City, NY: Doubleday, 1966.

Boccia, M. L., & Campos, J. J. *Maternal emotional signals and infants' reactions to strangers.* Paper presented at the Biennial Meeting of the Society for Research in Child Development, Detroit, April 1983.

Boccia, M. L., & Capitanio, J. P. *The role of social signals in the development of dominance relations between unfamiliar pigtail macaques.* Paper presented at the Fifth Annual Meeting of the American Society of Primatologists, East Lansing, MI, August 1983.

Breland, K., & Breland, M. The misbehavior of organisms. *American Psychologist,* 1961, *61,* 681–684.

Bretherton, I. Making friends with one-year-olds: An experimental study of infant–stranger interaction. *Merrill-Palmer Quarterly,* 1978, *24,* 29–51.

Bühler, C., & Hetzer, H. Das erste verständnis für ausdruck im ersten lebensjahr. [The first comprehension of emotional expression during the first year of life] *Zeitschrift für Psychologie, [Journal of Psychology],* 1928, *107,* 50–61.

Campos, J. J. The importance of affective communication in social referencing. *Merrill Palmer Quarterly,* 1983, *29,* 83–87.

Campos, J. J., & Stenberg, C. Perception, appraisal, and emotion: The onset of social referencing. In M. Lamb & L. Sherrod (Eds.), *Infant social cognition.* Hillsdale, NJ: Erlbaum, 1981.

Caron, A. J., Caron, R. F., Caldwell, R. C., & Weiss, S. J. Infant perception of the structural properties of the face. *Developmental Psychology,* 1973, *9,* 385–399.

Carr, S., Dabbs, J., & Carr, T. Mother–infant attachment: The importance of the mother's visual field. *Child Development,* 1975, *46,* 331–338.

Chance, M. R. A. Attention structure as the basis of primate rank orders. *Man,* 1967, *2,* 503–518.

Charlesworth, W. R., & Kreutzer, M. A. Facial expressions of infants and children. In P. Ekman (Ed.), *Darwin and facial expression.* New York: Academic Press, 1973.

Cooley, C. H. *Human nature and the social order.* New York: Schocken, 1964. (Originally published, 1902.)

Eisenberg, R. B., Griffin, E. J., Coursin, D. B., & Hunter, M. Auditory behavior in the human neonate: A preliminary report. *Journal of Speech and Hearing Research*, 1964, 7, 245–269.

Fein, G. G. Children's sensitivity to social contexts at 18 months of age. *Developmental Psychology*, 1975, 11, 853–854.

Feinman, S. Infant response to race, size, proximity, and movement of strangers. *Infant Behavior and Development*, 1980, 3, 187–204.

Feinman, S. Social referencing in infancy. *Merrill Palmer Quarterly*, 1982, 28, 445–470.

Feinman, S. How does baby socially refer? Two views of social referencing: A reply to Campos. *Merrill Palmer Quarterly*, 1983, 29, 467–471.

Feinman, S., & Lewis, M. Social referencing and second order effects in ten-month-old infants. In J. Rubenstein (Chair), *Conceptualizing Second Order Effects in Infancy*. Symposium presented at the Biennial Meeting of the Society for Research in Child Development, Boston, April 1981.

Feinman, S., & Lewis, M. *Infant temperament and social referencing*. Paper presented at the International Conference on Infant Studies, Austin, TX, March 1982.

Feinman, S., & Lewis, M. Social referencing at 10 months: A second order effect on infants' responses to strangers. *Child Development*, 1983, 54, 878–887.

Festinger, L. A theory of social comparison processes. *Human Relations*, 1954, 7, 17–40.

Friedrich, L. K., & Stein, A. H. Aggressive and prosocial television programs and the natural behavior of preschool children. *Monographs of the Society for Research in Child Development*, 1973, 38(No. 4).

Garland, J. B. *Social referencing and self-produced locomotion*. Paper presented at the International Conference on Infant Studies, Austin, TX, March 1982.

Garcia, J., & Koelling, R. A. Relation of cue to consequences in avoidance learning. *Psychonomic Science*, 1966, 4, 123–124.

Gunnar, M. R. Control, warning signals, and distress in infancy. *Developmental Psychology*, 1980, 16, 281–289.

Gunnar, M. R., & Stone, C. *The effects of maternal positive affect on one-year olds reactions to toys: Is it social referencing?* Paper presented at the Biennial Meeting of the Society for Research in Child Development, Detroit, April 1983.

Hainline, L. Developmental changes in visual scanning of faces and nonface patterns by infants. *Journal of Experimental Child Psychology*, 1978, 25, 90–115.

Hall, K. R. L. Social learning in monkeys. In P. C. Jay (Ed.), *Primates: Studies in adaptation and variability*. New York: Holt, 1968.

Haviland, J., & Lewis, M. *Infants' greeting patterns to strangers*. Paper presented at the Human Ethology Session of the Animal Behavior Society Meeting, Wilmington, NC, May 1975.

Hochschild, A. R. Emotion work, feeling rules, and social structure. *American Journal of Sociology*, 1979, 85, 551–575.

Itani, J. On the acquisition and propagation of a new food habit in the troop of Japanese monkeys at Takasakiyama. *Primates*, 1958, 1(2), 84–98.

Kawai, M. Newly-acquired pre-cultural behavior of the natural troop of Japanese monkeys on Koshima Islet. *Primates*, 1965, 6, 1–30.

King, D. L. A review and interpretation of some aspects of the infant–mother relationship in mammals and birds. *Psychological Bulletin*, 1966, 65, 143–155.

Klinnert, M. D. *The regulation of infant behavior by maternal facial expression*. Unpublished doctoral dissertation, University of Denver, 1981.

Klinnert, M. D., Campos, J. J., Sorce, J., Emde, R. N., & Svejda, M. J. Social referencing: An important appraisal process in human infancy. In R. Plutchik & H. Kellerman (Eds.), *The emotions* (Vol. 2). New York: Academic Press, 1983.

Klinnert, M. D., Emde, R. N., & Butterfield, P. *Social referencing: The infant's use of emotional signals from a friendly adult with mother present.* Paper presented at the Biennial Meeting of the Society for Research in Child Development, Detroit, April, 1983.

LaBarbera, J. D., Izard, C. E., Vietze, P., & Parisi, S. A. Four- and six-month-old infants' visual responses to joy, anger, and neutral expressions. *Child Development,* 1976, *47,* 535–538.

Lamb, M. E., Thompson, R. M., Gardner, W., Charnov, E. L., & Estes, D. Security of infantile attachment as assessed in the "Strange Situation": Its study and biological interpretation. *Behavioral and Brain Sciences,* 1984, *7,* 127–171.

Latané, B., & Rodin, J. A lady in distress: Inhibiting effects of friends and strangers on bystander intervention. *Journal of Experimental Social Psychology,* 1969, *5,* 189–202.

Lazarus, R. S. Emotions and adaptation: Conceptual and empirical relations. In W. J. Arnold (Ed.), *Nebraska Symposium on Motivation* (Vol. 16). Lincoln, NE: University of Nebraska Press, 1968.

Leung, E. H. L., & Rheingold, H. L. Development of pointing as a social gesture. *Developmental Psychology,* 1981, *17,* 215–220.

Lewis, M., & Feiring, C. Direct and indirect interactions in social relationships. In L. Lipsitt (Ed.), *Advances in infancy research.* New York: Ablex, 1981.

Lewis, M., & Michalson, L. *Children's emotions and moods: Developmental theory and measurement.* New York: Plenum, 1983.

Mead, G. H. *Mind, self, and society.* Chicago: University of Chicago Press, 1934.

Mech, L. D. *The wolf.* Garden City, NY: Natural History Press, 1970.

Merton, R. K., & Rossi, A. S. Contributions to the theory of reference group behavior. In R. K. Merton, *Social theory and social structure.* New York: Free Press, 1968.

Murphy, C. M., & Messer, D. J. Mothers, infants and pointing: A study of a gesture. In H. R. Schaffer (Ed.), *Studies in mother–infant interaction.* London: Academic Press, 1977.

Novak, M. A. *Fear-attachment relationships in infant and juvenile rhesus monkeys.* Unpublished doctoral dissertation, University of Wisconsin, 1973.

Phillips, D. P. The influence of suggestion on suicide: Substantive and theoretical implications of the Werther effect. *American Sociological Review,* 1974, *39,* 340–354.

Piaget, J. *The origins of intelligence in children.* New York: International Universities Press, 1952.

Pitcairn, T. K. Attention and social structure in Macaca fascicularis. In M. R. A. Chance & R. R. Larsen (Eds.), *The social structure of attention.* New York: Wiley, 1976.

Plimpton, E. H., Swartz, K. B., & Rosenblum, L. A. Responses of juvenile bonnet macaques to social stimuli presented through color videotapes. *Developmental Psychobiology,* 1981, *14,* 109–115.

Rheingold, H. L., & Eckerman, C. O. Fear of the stranger: A critical review. In H. W. Reese (Ed.), *Advances in child development and behavior* (Vol. 8). New York: Academic Press, 1973.

Rogoff, B., Gilbride, K., & Malkin, C. *Interaction with babies as guidance in development.* Paper presented at the Biennial Meeting of the Society for Research in Child Development, Detroit, April 1983.

Sackett, G. P. Response of rhesus monkeys to social stimulation presented by means of colored slides. *Perceptual and Motor Skills,* 1965, *20,* 1027–1028.

Sackett, G. P. Monkeys reared in isolation with pictures as visual input: Evidence for an innate releasing mechanism. *Science,* 1966, *154,* 1468–1473.

Salapatek, P. Pattern perception in early infancy. In L. B. Cohen & P. Salapatek (Eds.), *Infant perception: From sensation to cognition* (Vol. 1): *Basic visual processes.* New York: Academic Press, 1975.

Scaife, M., & Bruner, J. S. The capacity for joint visual attention in the infant. *Nature,* 1975, *253,* 265–266.

Schachter, S. *The psychology of affiliation.* Stanford: Stanford University Press, 1959.

Schachter, S. The interaction of cognitive and physiological determinants of emotional state. In L. Berkowitz (Ed.), *Advances in experimental social psychology* (Vol. 1). New York: Academic Press, 1964.

Schaffer, H. R. *The growth of sociability.* Baltimore: Penguin, 1971.

Schaffer, H. R., Greenwood, A., & Parry, M. H. The onset of wariness. *Child Development,* 1972, *43,* 165–175.

Seligman, M. E. P. On the generality of the laws of learning. *Psychological Bulletin,* 1970, *77,* 406–418.

Sherif, M. Group influences upon the formation of norms and attitudes. In E. Maccoby, T. Newcomb, & E. Hartley (Eds.), *Readings in social psychology.* New York: Holt, 1958.

Smith, W. J. Referents of animal communication. *Animal Behaviour,* 1981, *29,* 1273–1275.

Sorce, J. F., & Emde, R. N. Mother's presence is not enough: Effect of emotional availability on infant exploration. *Developmental Psychology,* 1981, *17,* 737–745.

Sorce, J. F., Emde, R. N., Klinnert, M. D., & Campos, J. J. *Maternal emotional signaling: Its effect on the visual cliff behavior of one-year-olds.* Paper presented at the Biennial Meeting of the Society for Research in Child Development, Boston, April 1981.

Sroufe, L. A., Waters, E., & Matas, L. Contextual determinants of infant affective response. In M. Lewis & L. A. Rosenblum (Eds.), *The origins of fear.* New York: Wiley, 1974.

Sullivan, H. S. *Conceptions of modern psychiatry.* Washington, DC: White Psychiatric Foundation, 1947.

Svejda, M. J., & Campos, J. J. *Mother's vocal expression of emotion as a behavior regulator.* Paper presented at the International Conference on Infant Studies, Austin, TX, March 1982.

Thomas, W. I. *The child in America.* New York: Knopf, 1928.

Walk, R. The development of depth perception in animals and human infants. *Monographs of the Society for Research in Child Development,* 1966, *31*(No. 5).

Weber, M. *The theory of social and economic organization.* (Edited by T. Parsons). New York: Free Press, 1964.

Webster, M. *Actions and actors: Principles of social psychology.* Cambridge, MA: Winthrop, 1975.

Wolff, P. Observations on the early development of smiling. In B. M. Foss (Ed.), *Determinants of Infant Behavior II.* London: Methuen, 1963.

Zarbatany, L., & Lamb, M. E. *Social referencing as a function of information source: Mothers versus strangers.* Paper presented at the Biennial Meeting of the Society for Research in Child Development, Detroit, April 1983.

Chapter 13

The Development of the Ability to Interpret Emotional Signals—What Is and Is Not Known

Kim G. Dolgin and Margarita Azmitia

Relationship to Other Chapters and to the Field

Relevant Issues in the Field

In contrast to the other chapters in this section that examine the production of bodily emotional signals, this chapter summarizes our small amount of knowledge about infants' abilities to interpret them. In being one chapter among five, it reflects how little attention the field has paid to interpretation, as compared to production, and notes methodological reasons that partially explain this paucity of research. It likewise reflects the field's relatively slight attention to vocal signals by being one of only two chapters, along with Cole's (Chapter 11, this volume) that reviews work on auditory signals.

Dolgin and Azmitia address the ontogenetic starting place of biology–environment interaction by focusing on the relative roles of learning and innate response propensity in infants' earliest emotional interpretive abilities (and their cognitive precursors). From their review of the literature and its weaknesses, they suggest research questions to more sharply delineate the roles of learning and propensity, and they suggest procedural revisions to allow greater sensitivity and ecological validity in evoking interpretive responses to find the age at which they appear.

THE DEVELOPMENT OF EXPRESSIVE BEHAVIOR:
BIOLOGY–ENVIRONMENT INTERACTIONS

319

Relationship to Other Chapters

While other chapters attend to the roles of relatively large scale environmental features, such as Mason's (Chapter 6) examination of general experiential effects or even Malatesta's (Chapter 8) attention to more fine grained reinforcement patterns, Dolgin and Azmitia think with the minute stimulus analysis of laboratory analyses of infant perception. In their explanation of why they expect to find emotional interpretive abilities below the age of attachment, they move to the larger scale needed to understand adaptive responses. Here in contrast with Fogel's (Chapter 10) argument that the timing of first responses in a subsystem is not necessarily adaptive, they assert the adaptiveness of inherited features as argument for the adaptiveness of the timing. They contrast also with Malatesta's conclusion that neonates have some categorical perception of facial expressions of emotion; they more conservatively conclude that although there is evidence that by age 4 months the human face seems to have special attractive status for the infant, there is not clear evidence that interpretive categories for emotional signals are used. —ED.

Introduction

The purpose of this chapter is to address the issue of biological and environmental interaction in the development of the human infant's ability to comprehend another's emotional signals. The chapter is conceptually divided into five sections. In the first section, we lay out the issues that need to be addressed if we are to ascertain the relative roles played by biology and environment in the development of the perception of emotions. The second section contains a review of current work and gives our present answers to the issues previously outlined. A critique of our current knowledge base follows, emphasizing its methodological problems. Next, we offer suggestions for methodological changes in future research. Finally, we present an argument as to why we expect to find the capacity to respond to both negative and positive emotions in preattachment-age infants, despite others' arguments to the contrary.

We concern ourselves only with infants' abilities to perceive emotional information from the visual and auditory channels, and in particular, their abilities to read emotions from facial expressions and tones of voice. Although it is very likely that infants also learn to recognize a caretaker's mood or intent from his or her body tension, interaction style, or other behavior patterns, space limitations prevent discussion of those sources of information.

The Important Issues and Questions

This section outlines those questions whose answers are most crucial to understanding biological and environmental interplay in the development of the ability to read emotional displays.

Because neonates have not yet had any significant opportunity to learn about the outside world, assessing their capacities would shed light on the relative roles played by biology and environment. It is crucial to understand the newborn's perceptual and cognitive skills: in order for environmental information to affect an individual, that individual must be able to sense this information. Furthermore, if any experience is to have more than a transitory impact, that individual must be capable of retaining it in memory. An infant is necessarily incapable of benefiting from experience until its perceptual and cognitive systems have both developed sufficiently.

Because human neonates are altricial and immature at birth and because they may not be able to comprehend emotional signals fully, we also need to examine the extent of older infants' capacities and to determine the approximate ages at which the ability to perceive different emotional signals fully develops. Of particular interest is the lag time between the age when the senses are sufficiently functional to allow for this learning and the subsequent emergence of this skill. Therefore, the first question to address involves the sensory and cognitive capacities of infants, whereas the second concerns the degree to which neonates and older infants respond to emotional displays. It is of special interest to determine the role of environmental input in the development of these precursor abilities.

A third important issue is to find those biologically required forms of environmental stimulation and experience that are necessary for the development of the ability to understand emotional signals. Two areas of research are particularly cogent. Studies involving social isolation perhaps most directly address this topic because they involve directly manipulating the kinds and the amount of exposure to emotional signals that the subjects experience. Studies of this sort cannot, of course, be performed with human infants, but relevant animal research can provide clues to the extent and scope of experience needed if the ability to read emotional signals is to develop. In addition, cross-cultural studies can help us assess the necessity of particular kinds of experience for acquiring the ability to perceive and comprehend emotions. Studies of these kinds can augment the information obtained by studying inexperienced human neonates.

A related issue—our fourth—concerns the opportunities that infants

raised in a normal environment have to learn about facial and vocal signals. In what social settings do they most often find themselves? Of
what signals are they typically the recipients? What reinforcements are
given for comprehension of or response to these signals, and which of
these signals are most reliably followed by strong reinforcement? A very
different picture emerges if infants are found to respond to some signals
at a certain age, even if they have had little opportunity to observe them,
than if responding begins only after lengthy exposure.

Moreover, a full understanding of biological and environmental interplay requires knowing whether or not the comprehension of facial
and auditory signals has a special status. One way in which biology and
environment interact involves innate tendencies predisposing individuals to behave in such a way that they are highly likely to attend to or
to quickly learn about important stimuli: biological biases might ease the
way of learning about emotional signals by ensuring that particular stimuli—in this case, emotional expressions and tones of voice—are salient.
The fifth issue, then, is whether infants are more interested in
faces/voices than they are in other complex stimuli. In addition to this,
are infants better at discriminating or understanding these signals than
they are other complex stimuli? If so, there are grounds for belief in an
innate preference that facilitates learning of emotional signals.

The Present State of Knowledge

Infants' Abilities

In this section, we concentrate almost exclusively upon studies using
human subjects. The infant literature that addresses basic perceptual
abilities and that which is concerned with the ability to perceive emotional signals is discussed separately. These reviews will be brief and
will convey only those points most central to our purpose.

Infants' Auditory Abilities

From the time of birth, an infant's hearing is sufficiently mature to
allow perception of the human voice (Walk, 1981). Furthermore, as is
subsequently shown, it appears well enough developed to allow discrimination of at least some aspects of the voice thought to convey emotional information. Structurally, both the inner and middle ear of the
neonate are well developed, and although trapped fluid and tissue in

the middle ear may impair hearing by increasing auditory threshold, most of this fluid is absorbed within the first few days of life (Werner & Lipsitt, 1981). Whatever the cause, the auditory threshold is somewhat higher for neonates than for children or young adults (Hecox, 1975).

The neonate's auditory abilities are impressive: many studies (e.g., Crassini & Broerse, 1980; Leventhal & Lipsitt, 1964; Muir & Field, 1979; Wertheimer, 1961) have demonstrated that 4-day-olds have the capacity to integrate visual and auditory information by showing that they will orient to a sound source. Infants are sensitive to the loudness or the intensity of sounds: for example, heart rate and motor activity increase in the presence of loud noises (Steinschneider, Lipton, & Richmond, 1966). The *rise time* of sound (the lag between initiation of a sound and attainment of full intensity) also affects infants: sounds exhibiting slow rises promote orienting responses whereas sounds with fast rises elicit defensive movements (Kearsley, 1973). Because different emotional tones may differ along these dimensions, these three sensitivities may contribute to ability to perceive auditory emotional signals.

Infants are most sensitive to sounds within the range of the human voice (Hutt, Hutt, Lenard, Bernuth, & Muntjewerff, 1966); furthermore, Eisenberg, Griffin, Coursin, and Hunter (1964) have demonstrated that newborns prefer the sound of the female human voice above other sounds. From the time of birth, infants can discriminate their mother's voice from the voices of other women (DeCasper & Fifer, 1980; Hammond, 1970; Mills & Melhuish, 1974). They are most attentive to complex, patterned sounds in this and other pitch ranges (Hutt *et al.*, 1966). Within the preferred frequency range, infants demonstrate a preference for lower-pitched sounds. These tones serve to soothe crying and stimulate motor activity in active babies, whereas higher-pitched sounds promote distress (Eisenberg, 1970). Again, these tonal differences may signal different emotional content.

Infants' Perception of Auditory Emotional Displays

Virtually no studies have directly addressed this question. The vast majority of research on infants' abilities to perceive emotional signals has been done by developmental, perceptual psychologists whose major interest lies in vision, not in audition; researchers who have studied infants' auditory abilities have largely been interested in the discrimination and comprehension of speech components (see, for example, Eimas, 1975). It is particularly unfortunate that there is this gap in our knowledge, because, as has been described, the human infants' hearing is well developed from the time of birth. There is every reason to believe that infants are in a position to respond to or to learn about meaningful, subtle vocal patterns well before their visual acuity allows frequent, accurate perception of subtly different facial expressions.

We are certain that emotional information is contained in the voice and that this information can be used by adult listeners (e.g., Kramer, 1963). It is not surprising that this is true, because being in an emotional state will in itself induce changes in the musculature surrounding the larynx and lungs and may affect coordination of the tongue and lips (Scherer, 1979). Information about an individual's emotional state can be gleaned both from speech proper and from interjected, nonspeech sounds, the presence of which usually indicates emotional arousal.

Studies have demonstrated that pitch, for example, rises as arousal increases (Ekman, Friesen, & Scherer, 1976), that judges can determine a speaker's emotional state even if the message is scrambled (Scherer, Koivumaki, & Rosenthal, 1972), and that voice synthesizers can be programmed to produce sounds that will be heard as having emotional overtones (Scherer, 1974). Because pitch, loudness, and other voice features are also integral to the conveying of semantic content, it is probable that complex patterns of featural changes must be relied upon to indicate emotions; studies have shown that different emotions can be described as having similar features (see Scherer, 1979, for a review).

The only research that we are aware of which is relevant to this issue concerns newborn's responses to the sounds produced by crying infants. Studies by Simner (1971) and Sagi and Hoffman (1976) have indicated that neonates become distressed when exposed to the cries of other infants, and that they are particularly sensitive to the sounds made by other newborns (rather than the cries of older babies). Furthermore, Sagi and Hoffman also showed that loud noises, per se, aroused but did not distress the infants. This seems to indicate that neonates selectively respond in a negative way only to sounds embodying particular features and that these features are conveyed by (at least some) distressed voices.

In a subsequent study, Martin and Clark (1982) not only replicated Sagi and Hoffman's results but also demonstrated that exposure to recordings of their own cries actually calmed neonates. Taken together, results from these studies suggest that newborns can not only differentiate their own cries from those of others, but, as Martin and Clark propose, that this differential responding indicates that precursors of empathic responding may be functional at or shortly after birth. The latter findings do seem to indicate that infants do not become distressed merely because they find the sound of crying irritating.

Infants' Ability to Perceive Visual Stimuli

Although there is a considerable body of information on the development of infants' visual abilities, due to space limitations the present discussion is brief (see Aslin, Alberts, & Peterson, 1981; Cohen & Salapatek, 1975, for comprehensive reviews of this topic). In the first month of life, infants' visual abilities are severely hampered by their poor acuity and accommodation as well as by limited contrast sensitivity and peripheral vision. However, although the 1-month-old infant's sight is far from approximating that of adults—especially when viewing distant stimuli—his or her vision is accurate at close distances. Newborns can, for example, discriminate the major facial features and expressions if they are presented within 50 centimeters (Atkinson & Braddick, 1981).

There is considerable improvement in visual abilities between the first and third months of life, as acuity, consistent muscle control for accommodating to stimuli, and sensitivity to contrast develop. It is also around this time that infants become able to recognize features within a contour (Milewski, 1976)—although initially they do not attend to them, preferring instead to look at peripheral features such as the hairline surrounding a face (Bushnell, 1982), at least when presented with static stimuli. It is important to note that despite its poor resolution, infants' vision is functional from birth, because most of the objects with which they interact (e.g., their mothers) are usually well within the range of their visual capacities (Atkinson & Braddick, 1981). Although infants' vision continues to improve after the third month of life, the most dramatic improvements occur during this time.

Subsequent to Fantz's (1958) demonstration that infants prefer to look at patterned stimuli, researchers have attempted to determine which patterns are most attractive to them. The results of such studies suggest that during the first 2 months of life, infants prefer to look at the outer contours of complex patterns (Maurer & Salapatek, 1976; Milewski, 1976). At around 5 months of age, infants begin to focus on internal features of stimuli, and show preference for increased complexity and intensity in patterns (Acredolo & Hake, 1982). However, it may be that these early preferences for external pattern characteristics may have been an artifact of the type of stimuli employed, because Girton (1979) has shown that when infants are presented with pictures of faces in which the eyes are in motion, they will preferentially scan the interior of the face. It is not surprising that scanning patterns are different when the stimulus has motion: motion is particularly salient to infants because their visual system is highly sensitive to movement whereas it is less able to discriminate fine patterns (von Hofsten, 1982).

Infants' Perception of Visual Emotional Signals

Considerable research effort has been expended on assessing visual perception of emotional displays. Three questions are addressed here. First, at what age are infants capable of perceiving facial expressions? Second, do infants use their visual skills to perceive emotion early in life? Third, are some emotional displays perceived earlier than others?

Faces have several properties that make them attractive to newborns. Specifically, faces have movement, solidity, contrast, contour, curvature, and symmetry, features which naturally attract infants' attention (Gibson, 1969). Fantz and Miranda (1975), for example, have shown that under appropriate conditions, neonates prefer curvature to straight lines. The presence of this early bias makes sense from an adaptive standpoint, because an infant can use this skill to detect his or her mother's breast or face (Walk, 1981).

Even though faces have characteristics that make them attractive to infants, given newborns' poor visual resolution and scanning preferences, one must address the question of whether infants are capable of and in fact do distinguish facial features at birth. Meltzoff and Moore's (1977) study indicates that this ability must be operative from that time, at least under certain circumstances and within limited distances, as the study demonstrated that neonates are able to imitate at least some facial expressions (i.e., tongue protrusion). It is clear that accurate perception of the facial expression is logically necessary for correct imitation. The question of how commonly and under what circumstances infants naturally discriminate facial features, however, has not yet been answered.

Although infants have the ability to discriminate facial features from birth, they do not establish eye contact until 3½ weeks of age (Walk, 1981). In addition to this, Mauer and Salapatek (1976) showed that infants initially scan only the perimeter of faces. Given infants' poor peripheral vision, this suggests that the newborn is not looking at his mother's face—or is at least not looking at the features of his mother's face that convey emotional information—but is instead looking at her outer edges (Salapatek, 1975).

Finally, Caron, Caron, Caldwell, and Weiss (1973) have shown that infants first start focusing on both the eyes and the mouth of a face at around 5 months of age. This is an important finding, because the emotional information conveyed by facial expressions is most heavily concentrated in the mouth and eye regions (Peiper, 1963, cited in Izard, 1971). These data suggest that, prior to this time, infants may not be sensitive to the meaning of facial expressions. Further support for this conclusion comes from a study conducted by Walker (1982). In her study, Walker showed that infants begin to integrate visual and acoustic emotional information at between 4 and 5 months of age, indicating that at this age infants have at least a rudimentary understanding of the meaning of invariance in auditory and in visual emotional information.

At what age do infants begin to discriminate between faces and facial expressions? Several studies have demonstrated that neonates can discriminate normal faces from scrambled (Goren, Sarety, & Wu, 1975) and distorted faces (Jirari, 1970, cited in Freedman, 1974). (These findings contradict earlier reports, e.g., Kagan, 1967.) Melhuish (1981) has shown that 1-month-olds cannot discriminate their mother's from a stranger's face; this ability to recognize their caretaker does not emerge until the third month (Barrera & Maurer, 1979). Again, these studies used static images of faces as stimuli.

In addition to this, recent studies have shown that at about 3 to 5 months of age infants become able to discriminate among joy, surprise, anger, and sad expressions, at least when they are posed by the same model (Barrera & Maurer, 1979; LaBarbera et al., 1976; Oster & Ewy, 1980; Younge-Browne et al., 1977) (see Oster, 1981 for a more complete review of these and earlier studies). These studies also show that joy is the first expression to be discriminated, followed by surprise, fear, and sadness. Moreover, Nelson, Morse, and Leavitt (1979) have shown that by 7 months of age infants can discriminate among facial expressions posed by different (same-gender) models. Caron, Caron, and Myers (1982) have extended Nelson et al's findings to show that infants can abstract invariance from expressions posed by models of different ages, and in our lab, Nelson and Dolgin (in press) have recently shown that 7-month-olds can also abstract invariance across different-gender models. On the basis of these studies, it seems that the ability to discriminate between different facial expressions begins to emerge at around the fifth month of life. These studies, though, were not ideally designed to test for the lower-age limit of emotional recognition; the limitations of these studies will be discussed in The Problems with the Present Approach section.

Infants' Abilities to Learn

Numerous studies have left no doubt that infants have sophisticated learning and mnemonic skills (see Lipsitt, 1981, for a review of this literature). From birth, infants can be classically as well as instrumentally conditioned. Papousek (1967), for example, demonstrated that infants can be classically conditioned to grimace at the sound of a tone, whereas Lipsitt (1967) demonstrated that infants can learn to modify their sucking behavior in order to obtain sucrose. Similarly, both auditory (e.g., DeCasper & Fifer, 1980) and visual (e.g., Fantz & Miranda, 1975) stimuli have been shown to be effective reinforcers as well as effective stimuli. The fact that infants can recognize their mothers' voices from the time of birth indicates that they can prenatally learn about auditory stimuli (see Spence & DeCasper, 1982).

Within the context of the discrimination of facial expressions, it would be interesting to know if different facial expressions have different reinforcement values. If they do, this would provide evidence that infants interpret these signals as having different meanings. However, it is important to note that just because infants can be shown to be sensitive to classical or operant contingencies in the context of laboratory studies, this does not prove that these are typical, everyday learning mechanisms for human infants. Thus, despite these demonstrations of infant sensitivity to environmental contingencies, it still remains to be determined whether these represent the infants' usual learning mechanisms.

Finally, there is evidence that, beginning at the age of 10 weeks, infant boys are more sensitive to visual reinforcement and infant girls are more sensitive to auditory reinforcement (Watson, 1969). Although this is not direct evidence, it suggests that infant girls may be more receptive to auditory emotional signals than infant boys. Conversely, infant boys may be more responsive to visual displays. One study that used images of facial expressions as stimuli, however, found evidence that girls' perception was superior (Caron, Caron, & Myers, 1980). Consequently, any hypotheses as to sex differences in emotional signal comprehension must remain tentative at this time.

The Necessity of Experiences

One of the problems in determining the degree and ways in which emotional perception may be influenced by innate mechanisms is that human infants are so immature at birth. Many abilities ultimately attained first emerge only after several months of life, and one cannot immediately know whether their late appearance results from delayed maturation of a sensory or a cognitive function or if they could emerge only after sufficient experience with appropriate stimuli.

Although today nature or nurture is no longer seen as a viable issue, until recently considerable effort was expended on attempting to discover whether biology or learning was responsible for the emergence of particular behaviors (see Lehrman, 1970, for a historical account of this topic). Deprivation studies represented one attempt to isolate the relative importance of the two factors; the rationale behind these studies was that emergence of a particular behavior in spite of isolation (and lack of stimulation) indicates that the behavior must be largely under genetic control. Although deprivation studies are infeasible with humans, the results of research conducted with other, nonhuman primates may help shed light on the role of innate factors in the preception of facial expressions.

In a seminal study, Sackett (1966) presented slides of conspecifics to rhesus monkeys that had been raised in isolation. Some of the monkeys were allowed to control how long they viewed the slides whereas others viewed them for fixed intervals. At 14 days of age, the monkeys failed to show either differential emotional reactions or differential looking time to images of conspecifics shown displaying friendly or threatening expressions. However, after an additional 6 weeks of isolation, at the age of 2 months, the monkeys reacted with fear to the threatening monkeys and differentially increased their looking time to pictures of friendly and infant monkeys.

The results of this study led Sackett (1966) to propose that fearful reaction to conspecific threat is initially under the control of an innate releasing mechanism that begins to be effective at 2 months of age. Because the fear responses decreased after time, he further concluded that the role of experience is to maintain the behavior after it emerges.

Sackett's (1966) conclusions have been somewhat tempered by the result of a more recent study by Kenney, Mason, and Hill (1979). Using a stimulus-deprivation paradigm, these researchers showed that the stimuli that elicited fear were not as specific as Sackett had suggested: they found that various and diverse animate and inanimate objects elicited these reactions. (See Mason, Chapter 6, this volume, for a review of such general effects of experience.) It seems, then, that the fearful reaction is not a response uniquely released by exposure to threatening emotional displays but is instead broadly elicited. It is important to note, however, that Kenney et al.'s results do not question the importance of maturational factors in the perception of the meaning of facial expressions: their subjects showed the same developmental pattern of behavior toward the threatening monkey as Sackett's. Their results do suggest, though, a greater role for experience in the development of facial perception. Experience affected the age of onset of the fear response in their subjects, the general responsiveness of the individuals, and the types of objects that elicited fear (Kenney et al., 1979; see also McCulloch & Haslerod, 1939).

Cross-cultural studies are another source, albeit a more indirect one,

of evidence for the role of innate factors in facial and emotional perception. Eibl-Eibesfeldt (1979), Izard (1971), and Ekman (Ekman, 1972; Ekman & Friesen, 1971; Ekman, Sorenson, & Friesen, 1969) have found
support in both literate and preliterate societies for the universality of
particular facial expressions. Given the variety of experience afforded
by different cultures, it is unlikely that the convergence of these reactions is under the sole control of learning mechanisms. Thus, this suggests that these emotional signals may be partially mediated by biological
mechanisms.

The Infant's Opportunities for Experiences

Most of the research that has jointly addressed emotions and infants
has focused upon the *expression* of emotions by the infant (e.g., Izard,
1979; Izard & Buechler, 1979; Sroufe & Wunsch, 1972; Wolff, 1963) rather
than on the infant's *response* to emotional displays; perhaps it is that
focus which is responsible for the lack of interest in cataloging the emotional climate surrounding the infant. As has been previously mentioned, infants have the opportunity to experience emotional signals for
many months prior to the age at which we have conclusive evidence
that they can respond to these signals.

Although cross-cultural studies have led to the assumption that no
specific set of experiences, or at least no unusual set of experiences, is
essential for the development of emotional behavior, the observed wide
cultural variations in child rearing practices may be more apparent than
real. All infants, for example, independent of culture, are born helpless
and develop an attachment relationship with their caregiver during the
first year of life (Bowlby, 1969). It may be because of this, at least in the
early years, there are more or more important similarities than differences between the experiences of infants. Although exceptional cases
can be found (e.g., the Ik; infants raised in understaffed institutions),
virtually all infants frequently experience positive affect from their first
days of life. If this is the case, there may in fact be some specific set of
experiences needed to foster the development of the ability to perceive
emotion. This necessity provides an opportunity for the evolution of
adaptive mechanisms to ensure both the provision of and the recep-
tiveness to those experiences.

We are aware of no study that specifically examined the day-to-day
emotional signaling between caretaker and infant over an extended
length of time. Although Malatesta and Haviland (1982; Malatesta,
Chapter 8, this volume) examined emotional signals between caretakers
and their 3- and 6-month-old infants during a brief interaction, it is dif-

ficult to generalize from these brief sessions to infants' day to day experiences. There are no data, therefore, concerning which signals are most frequently given, which signals are predictively followed (or not predictively followed) by positive or negative consequence, and the frequency with which infants are the recipients of the different emotional signals. We do not know, for example, how frequently or at what age infants are typically first in the presence of angry or fearful adults. Similarly, there is no research describing the emotional signals available to infants because of sibling interaction or because of interaction between parents and siblings.

Common sense would suggest that the majority of infants are exposed with greater frequency to smiling faces and friendly sounding and soothing voices than they are to other emotional signals. The results of Malatesta and Haviland's study (1982) support this position: mothers tended to express positive emotions whereas avoiding negative displays. It is not so immediately apparent, however, that these signals are reliable indicators of concurrent interaction quality. Many caretakers sometimes smile at or speak in singsong to an infant even if they are rushed, tired, or angry, perhaps because they believe that these signals will reassure and soothe the infant. Forced smiles and false hearty tones of voice might very well differ from true versions of these signals, but we cannot be sure that infants can discriminate among those subtle differences. Each infant will of course be raised in a relatively unique environment in so far as available emotional signals are concerned, but without studies directed towards discovering what the typical patterns as well as what the effects of different signalling styles are, we can only make guesses as to the learning opportunities afforded to infants.

Do Faces and Other Emotional Signals Enjoy a Special Status?

Humans' great skill in face perception has led to the speculation that perhaps faces and facial expressions have a special status and are attended to and learned about more quickly than other comparably complex stimuli. One of the problems with deciding the status of facial expressions is that they do not occur in isolation, but rather are part of a larger social network of interactions. Thus, if an infant reacts differently to the human face than he or she reacts to other objects in the environment, it is impossible to determine whether this preferential response is rooted in the face per se or is instead subordinate to the social interaction.

One avenue for addressing the special status issue is to assess infants' reactions to facial expressions in settings that minimize the contribution of social factors such as interactions. In particular, many researchers (e.g., Nelson, Morse, & Leavitt, 1979) have examined infants' abilities to discriminate among static slides or pictures of individuals producing different facial expressions. This solution is inadequate by itself, however, because it will tell us little about the impact of facial expressions in natural contexts; the very fact that presentation of a static face is atypical and aberant may account for any lack of reaction, or lack of adaptive reaction, on the infant's part. At best, then, all one can hope to obtain from studies that address infants' perception of static facial expressions in isolation is indirect evidence of the role that facial perception plays in human behavior.

Numerous studies (e.g., Hainline, 1978; Spitz & Wolf, 1946) have shown that, even at birth, infants prefer to look at faces when they are simultaneously presented with other visual stimuli. However, despite this early preference, one cannot conclude that the attractiveness that faces have for infants resides in the concept of *faceness*. Instead this early bias seems to reflect a more general preference for oval shapes (Fagan, 1982). Of course, it seems reasonable to conclude that in the infants' typical environment, the oval shape most likely to be encountered is a human face or head. Similarly, Maurer and Salapatek (1976) found that before this age, infants' scanning patterns for (static) faces were no different than the scanning patterns exhibited when they were presented with other two-dimensional objects. In addition to this, Haaf (1974) has shown that complexity, not realism, mediates infants' early preference for facial as well as nonfacial stimuli. Finally, Caron et al. (1973) have shown that it is only after 4 months of age that the eyes acquire special meaning and that only at 5 months is the face first perceived as a cohesive gestalt. As it is also around this period that the previously discussed discrimination studies first demonstrated discrimination of different facial expressions by infants (e.g., Keane & Schwartz, 1981; Younge-Browne et al., 1977), it is possible that during the first 4 to 5 months of life the infant is actively engaged in the construction of a face schema that is then used to process and to interpret faces and facial expressions. The evidence from these and the other perceptual studies discussed earlier suggests that, at least before 4 months, faces do not have a special status. Again, it must be mentioned that these studies employed severely impoverished stimuli; it is uncertain whether comparable results would have been obtained had mobile stimuli been provided.

Another facet of the special status issue concerns whether discrimination of facial expressions proceeds at a faster rate or is more sophisticated than perception of other equally abstract concepts. We do know that by 5 months of age, infants can distinguish faces from other abstract, nonsocial patterns and can categorize faces on the basis of feature differences as well (Fagan, 1981). Infants are not only progressively capable of making finer and finer discriminations, but by 10 months their patterns of face categorization resemble those of adults (Cohen & Strauss, 1979; Strauss, 1979).

For a while, it was impossible to determine whether this categorization process was specific to faces or if it was a reflection of a more general cognitive skill. Part of the problem was that because the majority of categorization studies had employed facial stimuli—it was assumed that using faces would make a study more ecologically valid—there were no data available on the infant's ability to classify other complex stimuli. However, researchers have since demonstrated that infants are capable of abstracting invariance from nonfaces when changes involve constituent elements and orientation (Cornell, 1975) as well as form and color (Fagan, 1977). The evidence has led Fagan (1981) to conclude that the ability to detect invariance in faces does not reflect a special status but rather reflects the infant's more general emerging conceptual skill.

In sum, the results of infant facial perception and categorization studies suggest that the perception of faces does not merit special status. Even though by 4 months of age the infant has formed a face schema (Kagan, 1967) and becomes progressively able to abstract more and more complex invariances (Fagan, 1981; Strauss, 1979), the processes involved are not specific to faces. Instead, they represent only one manifestation of the infant's emerging cognitive abilities. What biologically based bias there is seems to concern preference for looking at faces, not in learning to categorize them. (But see Malatesta, Chapter 8, in this volume for an argument that neonates perceive and match categorical emotional expressions.)

Problems with the Present Approach

The results of the studies described in The Present State of Knowledge section suggest the conclusion, which has been often drawn by others, that infants are not capable of perceiving emotional signals until they are 5 to 7 months of age. (See, for example, Klinnert, Campos, Sorce, Emde, & Svedja, in press). Although the evidence is, in fact, in accord with this assumption, we believe that the strength that this unanimity lends to that conclusion is misleading: there have been several studies conducted, but they have by and large used the same two paradigms. We believe, given the sophistication of the infant's sensory capacities as well as the value of having a capacity to read another's emotions, that more powerful techniques should be used to assess the infant's abilities before this negative conclusion is drawn. We submit that the limitations of these paradigms has prevented us from adequately assessing infants' skills.

There are two paradigms commonly used to study infants' responses to facial expressions. The first, the *visual preference* paradigm, involves presenting infants with two or more different stimuli and determining which they prefer, usually as indicated by longer visual fixations. The second paradigm, *habituation*, assesses whether infants will dishabituate (become reinterested) to a new expression after being familiarized with a different one; this is also usually measured by increased visual fixation.

Although earlier researchers (e.g., Ahrens, 1954; Spitz and Wolf, 1946) presented live models, the stimuli most commonly used in later studies are static slides (e.g., LaBarbera *et al.*, 1976). A notable exception to this is the study by Kreutzer and Charlesworth (1973), who also presented their subjects with live models. Although two benefits are gained by using slides or photographs—(1) subjects are exposed to identical stimulus presentations and (2) it is easier to specify the properties of an unchanging stimulus—this approach is far from ideal. Negative data are at best difficult to interpret, and given that these stimuli are so impoverished, the problems compound and make it impossible to draw conclusions as to the cause of the infants' lack of response. In virtually all the studies discussed in The Present State of Knowledge section, emotion was presented via only one sensory modality and in a context-free situation. The dependent measure was almost always one that merely tested for ability to discriminate.

Selection of these paradigms is natural for one trained in the reductionist tradition of perceptual psychology. Within that tradition, the emphasis is strongly upon microanalyses of stimuli so as to find the bases of differentiated responses. The studies previously described do provide useful information—for example, dishabituation elegantly demonstrates perception of a difference between stimuli—but by themselves they cannot provide all of the answers needed if we are to discover the developmental course of the ability to comprehend emotional signals. Researchers with our different perspective and emphases and the belief that function and ecological validity are overridingly important could and should devise alternate paradigms.

We believe that six criticisms can be levied against studying infants' comprehension of emotions solely from this reductionistic perspective. We describe each one and then give suggestions for new paradigms that might be used and for issues that should be addressed in later research.

First, it is very unusual for infants to be presented with static faces; infants normally view faces that are constantly changing both in position and in featural configuration. Infants may find the experience so bizarre that they might not behave as they would towards a real person. Evidence for this can be found in a study by Tronick, Als, Wise, and Brazelton (1978): they demonstrated that 3-month-olds became upset if their mothers remained still faced (see Cairns, 1976; Cohen & Tronick, 1981). In addition, Girton (1979) showed that scanning patterns differed for moving faces and for stationary faces. Furthermore, in marked contrast to the studies in which slides were presented, Field, Woodson, Greenberg, and Cohen (1982) found evidence that newborns reacted differentially to different facial expressions when they were performed live. Films (e.g., Walker, 1982) or videotapes seem an ideal compromise because they provide movement yet still allow for rigorous stimulus control.

Second, it is important to determine whether infants can discriminate/comprehend an emotional signal itself, not merely whether they can detect that a given face has changed. Several of the discrimination studies required only that the infant note a change in one face. Demonstrating recognition of a facial expression per se, however, entails demonstrating discrimination across several individuals who differ in regards to age, gender, and appearance.

Third, the stimuli must be placed in a context. The fact that young infants fail to react to quiescent, two-dimensional pictures does not necessarily imply that they could not react to emotional signals under other circumstances. For example, preliminary findings in a study we are conducting (Dolgin & Azmitia, in preparation) indicate that 7-month-olds respond differently to images of an approaching individual depending upon whether those images look and/or sound neutral, friendly, or angry. Approaching angry-sounding voices seem particularly potent. Without context, stimuli that are sometimes attended to or understood often become meaningless.

Next, these visual paradigms do not provide information about infants' sensitivity to auditory emotional signals. As has been demonstrated, there is every reason to believe that infants have the capacity to extract affective information from voices. (For example, consider the plausibility of calming a distressed infant by shouting at him in an angry voice.)

Fifth, the studies that have been conducted have not addressed the variability of emotional signals: smiles, for example, can be wan or broad, toothy or close lipped, and can convey emotions ranging from slight satisfaction to intense bliss. Although we as adults might qualify our descriptions of these smiles (e.g., a crooked smile), we nevertheless perceive them as smiles—members of the same broad signaling category. If we wish to conclude that infants perceive emotional signals in an adultlike manner, then we should categorize them similarly to adults and generalize over intensity and extraneous feature.

We are at present testing infant perception of emotional categories in our laboratory by determining whether they treat physically-different exemplars drawn from the same category—such as slight smiles and broad, open-mouthed grins—more similarly than they treat physically more similar exemplars chosen from two different emotional categories—slight smiles and slight frowns. Although slight smiles and slight frowns differ primarily by small differences in the angle of the mouth, that difference is criterial for determining category membership; open-mouthed grins and slight smiles differ in many configurational aspects but each communicates that the signaller is in some way satisfied.

Six, although it is true that one cannot make a differentiated response if one cannot perceive a difference between stimuli, it is also true that studying dishabituation per se, even if a wide range of stimuli are used, cannot tell us whether infants are taking meaning, or at least behaving as if they are taking meaning, from the stimuli to which they have been exposed. More powerful, multiple-response measures are needed. Functionally tied dependent variables that might be measured include changes in the infants' facial expressions, reaching behavior (used, for example, by Yonas, Cleves, and Petterson, 1978), and body postures (for example, leaning forward, or turning towards the mother). Measurements of this sort would better justify the inference that infants can or cannot comprehend the meaning of affective displays.

Suggestions for Research

In light of our criticisms of current approaches, we deem it necessary to make specific, positive suggestions in regard to future research. We have already mentioned several directions in which such research might go. In particular, we have suggested that richer, more natural stimuli be employed. This is particularly important if we are to set the lower-age limit for infants' comprehension of emotional signals. If impoverished stimuli are used, it is impossible to determine the cause of a failure to respond appropriately. Thus, films, videotapes, and carefully controlled live performances in which both visual and auditory information are available are needed. An additional method of enriching stimuli would involve presenting signals as they appear when used by a variety of individuals: both the signalers and the intensity and form of the signal must be varied if we are to assess whether infants have a concept of the particular emotion studied.

Tests of Learning Factors

According to learning theory, three factors are important in predicting the order with which emotional signals, or any other stimuli, are learned. The three factors are: (1) the discriminability of the signal; (2) the frequency with which the signal–outcome pairs are presented; (3) the salience and intensity of the outcome. Signals that differ greatly from other signals, from frequency occurring signals, and from signals followed by severe or intensely gratifying outcomes should be most readily learned. Research can be devised to test directly the importance and roles of these factors in interaction with biological predispositions to them.

For example, the studies that have addressed infants' reactions to different facial expressions, as previously discussed, have shown that infants are able to discriminate and to interpret positive emotions before they can interpret negative emotions, that they prefer to look at smiling over nonsmiling faces, and that they habituate to happy faces more quickly than to displays with a negative hedonic quality. According to a learning theory model, these behaviors can be accounted for by the fact that infants are more frequently exposed to positive than to negative affective displays.

A test of this hypothesis would involve recording both the frequencies of, and the consequences associated with, positive and negative signals in a variety of home environments. This would involve ethological observation of day-to-day interactions between infants and caretakers. Infants' and toddlers' responses to emotional signals could then be compared: if the predicted difference in the emergence of response to negative and positive signals is found in these homes, then a prevalent learning component would be supported and we would know the relative values of frequency and of intensity for learning to respond to emotions. Conversely, if there were no differences in the infants' responses in these differing situations, then other and more general factors—biological and experiential—need to be sought to explain the emergence of emotional signal comprehension.

Alternatively, very young infants could be placed in a learning situation in which different emotional signals were paired with different outcomes. If there is an innate bias for learning/interpreting certain of the emotional signals (perhaps, as will be discussed, those signals for which the infant possesses an adaptive response), then infants should learn about these signals more quickly than they learn about other signals. Furthermore, if there are no biases, then signals indicating different emotional states should be equally effective as positive or negative reinforcers.

In addition to this, studies directly testing infants' reactions to different tones of voice are needed and at present are sorely lacking. After it has been established that infants of a given age can differentially respond to voices conveying different emotions, then particular features of the voices should be manipulated. In this way, we can determine what aspects of the voice are responded to by infants. Discovering the features of voices that are important for the perception of emotion would be interesting, especially to perceptual psychologists. This approach is important in so far as it allows the separation of particular features of voices that are confounded under natural conditions.

Observational Studies

We have primarily been discussing new directions for laboratory research. In addition, we believe that ethological studies of the phenomenon should be undertaken. It is only in natural environments that responses to the full richness of signaling can be observed. Infants' affective reactions to adults' emotional signaling can be observed, as can more indirect indexes of comprehension. For example, exploratory behavior or motor activity might vary with the mother's emotional signaling. (For a review of this social referencing literature, see Klinert et al., in press, plus Feinman, Chapter 12, Malatesta, Chapter 8, and Cole, Chapter 11, this volume). These indirect measures would provide information as to the multiple-behavior correlates that accompany the perception of emotions. They could, of course, be further studied in the laboratory.

When Should Response Capacity Appear?

Any explanation having adaptation at its core needs to provide a functional account of the pattern and order by which infants come to comprehend emotional signals. It is generally accepted that behavior becomes fixed in a repertoire because it serves an adaptive function for the individual performing it. Conversely, behaviors are selected against if they interfere with the individual's fitness. Because young infants are helpless and cannot act in diverse ways, reasonable questions to ask are, Why should infants be able to comprehend emotional signals?, What benefit might it serve them?, and When would this appear?

In our view, a functional account would hold that infants should first react to those emotional signals for which they can make some appropriate, adaptive response. (See, however, Fogel, Chapter 10, in this volume, who argues that response system start-up time need not be adaptive so long as it is not maladaptive and later coordinates with other systems.) Although human infants are altricial, despite their limited behavior patterns, there are certain circumstances for which they have adaptive responses. Although there is little an infant can appropriately do in response to another's boredom, disgust, or sadness, they are capable of responding in an adaptive way to other emotional signals. In particular, they can cry (and thus alert their caretakers) when in an aversive situation or when confronted by an aggressive or fearful individual, and they can smile when in the presence of a neutral, or positive-seeming, stranger.

It seems certain that infants can communicate their own positive or negative state to others, even if it is unclear when they can first read those emotional signals in others. For example, it is common knowledge that infants' cries are treated as indicators of distress. In addition, Oster and Ekman (1978) have found that almost all of the facial muscle movements performable by adults are also performable by neonates, and after providing neonates with both pleasant and unpleasant tastes and odors, Steiner (1979) found that judges could reliably assess to which the infants had been exposed.

Given that they can so communicate, it seems to us that an early ability to read the emotional signals provided by others would be adaptive for infants. Oster (1981) has suggested otherwise: she has proposed that it might be maladaptive for infants to perceive accurately emotional signals until after the attachment bond has been formed. She believes that an infant capable of reading the negative signals emitted by its caretaker may have a greater difficulty in forming a strong attachment bond than one who fails to comprehend signals or one who interprets all signals positively. In her view, then, only after the attachment bond has been formed does it become adaptive for the infant to be able to read signals appropriately (about 7 months in the case of human infants, Maccabee, 1980). Oster (1981) cites only one piece of evidence in support of her hypothesis. Kaufmann (1966), when conducting a field study of rhesus monkeys on Cayo Santiago, observed that infants (age unspecified) ignored threatening displays made by adult males. Oster (1981) herself admits that attacks by males on infants are a rare occurrence.

Although Oster's (1981) hypothesis is appealing, it rests upon scanty data. Moreover, even if it were adaptive for infants to ignore any negative signals given off by their caretakers, they could still benefit from being able to read the negative affect in noncaretakers' expressions. Because infants can discriminate their mother's face from a stranger's face by the age of 3 months and their mother's voice from a stranger's voice from the time of birth, it is certainly conceivable that there is an evolved capacity to respond differently to a signal produced by the mother versus a signal produced by a stranger. This could readily be tested by having strangers (of both genders) and the mother and the father perform various emotional signals.

Other data are not in accord with Kaufmann's (1966) findings: it has been shown that human infants of 4 or more months habituate more slowly to—that is, are more attentive to—threatening faces than they are to smiling faces (Nelson et al., 1979). This interest might be accounted for by novelty, or as Field and Walden (1981) have suggested, by an adaptive defense mechanism. It does seem to indicate that infants are not oblivious to negative affective displays. Because the attachment bond has not yet formed by this age, this attention is not in accord with Oster's (1981) hypothesis. As stated before, differences in response to the mother and to other adults is readily subject to, and requires, empirical verification.

Our adaptive perspective leads us to a second hypothesis. Infants might differentially be attentive to, or differentially respond to, negative signals depending upon their proximity to their mothers. No mother attends to her infant constantly (e.g., she must sleep); this is true for humans and for other primates as well (see Hardy, 1976, for a review of *aunting* behavior—caretaking of another's offspring—within the primate order). Because infants can distinguish between their mothers and other individuals from an early age and because infants are sometimes cared for by individuals not their parents, selection forces might have pressured the evolution of response to fear or to aggressive expressions on the part of nonprimary caretaker adults even if negative emotions by caretakers are ignored. If, for example, the infant is being held, then it is not so necessary for it to cry out and alert its caretaker: in fact, infants frequently cease crying when picked up by their mothers. If the mother is not holding the infant, or is not near it, then crying often serves to bring the mother closer. This hypothesis too awaits direct empirical test.

For the many reasons treated in this chapter, it is clear that early infant emotional recognition has probably been underestimated. Not only have test paradigms used impoverished and unnatural stimuli and ignored natural context, they have been done in an atmosphere in which early capacity for response has not particularly been expected on theoretical grounds. This can lead researchers to accept negative findings before fully sharpening their instruments of investigation.

Summary

In this chapter we attempt to set forth the issues that need to be resolved if we are to understand the relative roles played by biology and learning in the development of the infant's ability to comprehend emotional signals. It appears that infants have the necessary perceptual and cognitive capacities to allow comprehension of these signals from birth or shortly thereafter; a different question is whether they use their capacities to process emotional signals. Although the most cogent studies have found little support for infants' meaningful perception of emotions, as indicated earlier, these studies have not been very powerful. When the few studies that have used live models are compared (i.e., Field et al., 1982; Kreutzer & Charlesworth, 1973; Watson et al., 1979), are more equivocal. Although Kreutzer and Charlesworth found no evidence of infants' comprehension of emotional information prior to 6 months of age, Field et al.'s results suggest that, at least under some circumstances, this ability is present at birth. Thus, additional studies in which auditory and visual emotional information is presented in relatively common contexts are needed before we can determine at what age infants begin to comprehend emotional signals.

The evidence suggests that there are biological biases that contribute to the learning of the meaning of visual and auditory affective signals: comparative (e.g., Bolwig, 1964; Chevalier-Skolnikoff, 1973), cross-cultural (e.g., Izard, 1971), deprivation (e.g., Sackett, 1966), and developmental (Hainline, 1978) research converges on the same conclusion. From early in life, for example, infants prefer to look at oval shapes (faces) and to listen to women's voices. The role of learning cannot be overstressed, however; the majority of the existing research suggests that infants must actively construct schemas (representations) for the emotional signals. Unfortunately, much critical information is needed before strong characterizations of the interactions of biology and environment can be drawn. As outlined previously, this information would include a better assessment of the infant's ability to interpret emotional signals.

References

Acredolo, C. P., & Hake, J. L. Infant perception. In B. B. Wolman (Ed.), *Handbook of developmental psychology*. Englewood Cliffs, NJ: Prentice-Hall, 1982.

Ahrens, R. Beitrag zur Entwicklung des Physiognomie und Mimikerkennens. *Zeitschrift fur experimentielle und angewandte Psychologie*, 1954, *2*, 412-454.

Aslin, R. N., Alberts, J. R., & Peterson, M. R. *Development of perception: Psychobiological perspectives* (Vol. 2). New York: Academic Press, 1981.

Atkinson, J., & Braddick, O. Acuity, contrast, sensativity, and accommodation in infancy. In R. Aslin, J. Alberts, & M. Peterson (Eds.), *Development of perception: Psychobiological perspectives* (Vol. 2). London: Academic Press, 1981.

Barrera, M. E., & Maurer, D. The perception of facial expressions by the three-month-old. *Child Development*, 1979, *52*, 203-206.

Bolwig, N. Facial expression in primates with remarks on a parallel development in certain carnivores. *Behaviour*, 1964, *22*, 167-192.

Bowlby, J. *Attachment and loss* (Vol. 1). New York: Basic Books, 1969.

Bushnell, I. W. R. Discrimination of faces by young infants. *Journal of Experimental Child Psychology*, 1982, *33*, 298-308.

Cairns, R. B. The ontogeny and phylogeny of social interactions. In M. Hahn & E. Simmel (Eds.), *Communicative behavior and evolution*. New York: Academic Press, 1976.

Caron, A. J., Caron, R. F., Caldwell, R. C., & Weiss, S. J. Infant perception of the structural properties of the face. *Development Psychology*, 1973, *9*, 385-399.

Caron, R. F., Caron, A. J., & Myers, R. S. Abstraction of invariant face expressions in infancy. *Child Development*, 1982, *53*, 1008-1015.

Chevalier-Skolnikoff, S. Facial expression of emotion in non-human primates. In P. Ekman (Ed.), *Darwin and facial expressions*. New York: Academic Press, 1973.

Cohen, J. F., & Tronick, E. Z. Communicative rules and the sequential structure of infant behavior during normal and depressed interaction. In E. Tronick (Ed.), *The development of human communication and the joint regulation of behavior*. University Park, MD: University Park Press, 1981.

Cohen, L. B., & Salapatek, P. *Infant perception: From sensation to cognition* (Vol. 1). New York: Academic Press, 1975.

Cohen, L. B., & Strauss, M. S. Concept acquisition in the human infant. *Child Development*, 1979, *50*, 419-424.

Cornell, E. Infants visual attention to pattern arrangement and orientation. *Child Development*, 1975, *46*, 229-232.

Crassini, B., & Broerse, J. Auditory-visual integration in neonates: A signal detection analysis. *Journal of Experimental Child Psychology*, 1980, *29*, 144-155.

DeCasper, A. J., & Fifer, W. P. Of human bonding: Newborns prefer their mothers' voices. *Science*, 1980, *208*, 1174-1176.

Eibl-Eibesfeldt, I. Human ethology: Concepts and implications for the science of man. *The Behavioral and Brain Sciences*, 1979, *2*, 1-57.

Eimas, P. D. Speech perception in early infancy. In L. B. Cohen & P. Salapatek (Eds.), *Infant perception: From sensation to cognition* (Vol. 2). New York: Academic Press, 1975.

Eisenberg, R. B. The organization of auditory behavior. *Journal of Speech and Hearing Research*, 1970, *13*, 461–464.

Eisenberg, R. B., Griffin, E. J., Coursin, D. B., & Hunter, M. Auditory behavior in the human neonate: A preliminary report. *Journal of Speech and Hearing Research*, 1964, *7*, 245–269.

Ekman, P. Universals and cultural differences in facial expressions of emotion. *Nebraska Symposium on Motivation*. Lincoln, NB: University of Nebraska Press, 1972.

Ekman, P., & Friesen, N. V. Constants across cultures in the face and emotion. *Journal of Personality and Social Psychology*, 1971, *17*, 124–129.

Ekman, P., Friesen, N. V., & Scherer, K. R. Body movement and voice pitch in deceptive interaction. *Semiotica*, 1976, *16*, 23–27.

Ekman, P., Sorenson, E., & Friesen, N. V. Pan-cultural elements in facial displays of emotion. *Science*, 1969, *164*, 86–88.

Fagan, J. An attentional model of infant recognition. *Child Development*, 1977, *48*, 345–359.

Fagan, J. The origins of facial pattern recognition. In M. Bornstein & W. Kressen (Eds.), *Psychological development from infancy*. Hillsdale, NJ: Erlbaum, 1981.

Fagen, J. *Infant memory*. Paper presented at the Erindale Conference on Infant Memory, University of Toronto, May 14, 1982.

Fantz, R. C. Pattern vision of young infants. *Psychological Record*, 1958, *8*, 43–47.

Fantz, R. C., & Miranda, S. B. Newborn infant attention to form and contour. *Child Development*, 1975, *46*, 224–228.

Field, T. M., & Walden, T. A. Production and perception of facial expressions in infancy and early childhood. *Advances in Child Development and Behavior*, 1981, *16*, 169–211.

Field, T., Woodson, R., Greenberg, R., & Cohen, D. Discrimination and imitation of facial expressions by neonates. *Science*, 1982, *218*, 179–181.

Freedman, D. G. *Human infancy: An evolutionary perspective*. New York: Wiley, 1974.

Gibson, E. J. *Principles of perceptual learning and development*. New York: Appleton, 1969.

Girton, M. Infants' attention to intrastimulus motion. *Journal of Experimental Child Psychology*, 1979, *28*, 416–423.

Goren, C. C., Sarty, M., & Wu, P. Y. K. Visual patterning and pattern discrimination of face-like stimuli by newborn infants. *Pediatrics*, 1975, *56*, 544–549.

Haaf, R. Visual response to complex facelike patterns by 15- and 20-week-old infants. *Developmental Psychology*, 1974, *13*, 77–78.

Hainline, L. Developmental changes in visual scanning of faces and nonface patterns by infants. *Journal of Experimental Child Psychology*, 1978, *25*, 90–115.

Hammond, J. Hearing and response in the newborn. *Developmental Medicine and Child Neurology*, 1970, *12*, 3–5.

Hecox, K. Electrophysiological correlates of human auditory development. In L. B. Cohen & P. Salapatek (Eds.), *Infant perception: From sensation to cognition*. New York: Academic Press, 1975.

Hrdy, S. Care and exploitation of nonhuman primate infants by conspecifics other than the mothers. *Advances in the Study of Behavior*, 1976, *6*, 101–158.

Hutt, S. J., Hutt, C., Lenard, H. G., Bernuth, H. V., & Muntjewerff, W. J. Auditory responsivity in the human neonate. *Nature*, 1966, *218*, 888–890.

Izard, C. E. *The face of emotion*. New York: Appleton, 1971.

Izard, C. E., & Buechler, S. Emotional expressions and personality integration in infancy. In C. E. Izard (Ed.), *Emotions in personality and psychopathology*. New York: Plenum, 1979.

Jirari, C. *Form perception, innate form preferences and visually-mediated head-turning in human neonates*. Unpublished doctoral dissertation, 1970. (Cited in Freedman, 1974).

Kagan, J. The growth of the ''face'' schema: Theoretical significance and methodological issues. In J. Hellmuth (Ed.), *Exceptional infant* (Vol. 1). Seattle: Special Child Publications, 1967.

Kaufmann, J. H. Behavior of infant rhesus monkeys and their mothers in a free-ranging band. *Zoologica*, 1966, *51*, 17–27.

Keane, T., & Schwartz, K. B. *Visual habituation to sad and happy facial expressions in 3- and 6-month-olds*. Paper presented at the Biennial Meeting of the Society for Research in Child Development, Boston, MA, 1981.

Kearsley, R. B. The newborn's response to auditory stimulation: A demonstration of orienting and defensive behaviors. *Child Development*, 1973, *44*, 582–590.

Kenney, M., Mason, W., & Hill, S. Effects of age, objects, and visual experience on affective responses of rhesus monkeys to strangers. *Developmental Psychology*, 1979, *15*, 176–184.

Klinnert, M. D., Campos, J. J., Sorce, J. F., Emde, R. N., & Svejda, M. Emotions as behavior regulators: Social referencing in infancy. In R. Plutchik and H. Kellerman (Eds.), *Emotions in early development* (Vol. II): *The emotions*. New York: Academic Press, in press.

Kramer, E. Judgment of personal characteristics and emotions from nonverbal properties of speech. *Psychological Bulletin*, 1963, *60*, 408–420.

Kreutzer, M. A., & Charlesworth, W. R. *Infant's reactions to different expressions of emotions*. Paper presented at the Biennial Meeting of the Society for Research in Child Development, Philadelphia, PA, 1973.

LaBarbera, J. D., Izard, C. E., Vietze, P., & Parisi, S. A. Four- and six-month-old infants' visual responses to joy, anger, and neutral expressions. *Child Development*, 1976, *47*, 535–538.

Lehrman, D. S. Semantic and conceptual issues in the nature–nurture problem. In L. R. Aronson, E. Tobach, D. S. Lehrman, & J. S. Rosenblatt (Eds.), *Development and the evolution of behavior*. San Francisco: Freeman, 1970.

Leventhal, A. S., & Lipsitt, L. P. Adaptation, pitch discrimination, and sound localization in the neonate. *Child Development*, 1964, *35*, 759–767.

Lipsitt, L. P. Learning in the human infant. In H. W. Stevenson, E. H. Hess, & H. L. Rheingold (Eds.), *Early behavior: Comparative-developmental approaches*. New York: Wiley, 1967.

Lipsitt, L. P. *Advances in infancy research* (Vol. 1). Norwood, NJ: Ablex, 1981.

Maccoby, E. E. *Social development*. New York: Harcourt Brace Jovanovich, 1980.

McCulloch, T., & Haslerod, G. M. Affective responses of an infant chimpanzee reared in isolation from his kind. *Journal of Comparative Psychology*, 1939, *28*, 437–445.

Maletesta, C. Z., & Haviland, J. M. Learning display rules: the socialization of emotion and expression in infancy. *Child Development*, 1982, *53*, 991–1003.

Martin, G. B., & Clark, R. D. Distress crying in neonates: Species and peer specificity. *Developmental Psychology*, 1982, *18*, 3–9.

Maurer, D., & Salapatek, P. Developmental changes in the scanning of faces by young infants. *Child Development*, 1976, *47*, 523–527.

Melhuish, E. Visual attention to mothers' and strangers' faces and facial contrast in 1-month-old infants. *Developmental Psychology*, 1982, *18*, 229–232.

Meltzoff, A. N., & Moore, M. K. Imitation of facial and manual gestures by human neonates. *Science*, 1977, *198*, 75–78.

Milewski, D. E. Infant's discrimination of internal and external pattern elements. *Journal of Experimental Child Psychology*, *22*, 229–246.

Mills, M., & Melhuish, E. Recognition of mother's voice in early infancy. *Nature*, 1974, *252*, 123–124.

Muir, D., & Field, J. Newborn infants orient to sounds. *Child Development*, 1979, *50*, 431–436.

Nelson, C. A. & Dolgin, K. G. The generalized discrimination of facial expressions by 7-month-olds *Child Development*, in press.

Nelson, C. A., Morse, P. A., & Leavitt, L. A. Recognition of facial expressions by seven-month-old infants. *Child Development*, 1979, *56*, 1239–1242.

Oster, H. "Recognition" of emotional expressions in infancy? In M. E. Lamb & L. R. Sherrod (Eds.), *Infant social cognition: Empirical and theoretical considerations*. Hillsdale, NJ: Erlbaum, 1981.

Oster, H., & Ekman, P. Facial behavior in child development. In A. Collins (Ed.), *Minnesota Symposium on Child Psychology* (Vol. 11). Hillsdale, NJ: Erlbaum, 1978.

Oster, H., & Ewy, R. *Discrimination of sad vs. happy faces by 4-month-olds: When is a smile seen as a smile?* Unpublished manuscript, 1980. (Cited in Oster, 1981.)

Papousek, H. Conditioning during early postnatal development. In Y. Brackbill & G. Thompson (Eds.), *Behavior in infancy and early childhood*. New York: Free Press, 1967.

Peiper, A. *Cerebral function in infancy and childhood*. New York: Consultants Bureau, 1963.

Sackett, G. P. Monkeys reared in isolation with pictures as visual input: Evidence for an innate releasing mechanism. *Science*, 1966, *154*, 1468–1472.

Sagi, A., & Hoffman, M. L. Empathic distress in the newborn. *Developmental Psychology*, 1976, *12*, 175–176.

Salapatek, P. Pattern perception in early infancy. In L. B. Cohen & P. Salapatek (Eds.), *Infant perception: From sensation to cognition* (Vol. 1). New York: Academic Press, 1975.

Scherer, K. R. Acoustic concomitants of emotional dimensions: Judging affect from synthesized tone sequences. In S. Weitz (Ed.), *Non-verbal communication*. New York: Oxford University Press, 1974.

Scherer, K. R. Nonlinguistic vocal indicators of emotion and psychopathology. In C. E. Izard (Ed.), *Emotions in personality and psychopathology*. New York: Plenum, 1979.

Scherer, K. R., Koivumaki, J., & Rosenthal, R. Minimal cues in the vocal communication of affect: Judging emotions from content masked speech. *Journal of Psycholinguistic Research*, 1972, *1*, 269–285.

Simner, M. L. Newborn's response to the cry of another infant. *Developmental Psychology*, 1971, *5*, 136–150.

Spence, M. J., & DeCasper, A. J. *Human fetuses perceive maternal speech*. Paper presented at the International Conference on Infant Studies, Austin, TX, March 1982.

Spitz, R. A., & Wolf, K. M. The smiling response: A contribution to the orthogenesis of social relations. *Genetic Psychology Monographs*, 1946, *34*, 57–125.

Sroufe, L. A., & Wunsch, J. P. The development of laughter in the first year of life. *Child Development*, 1972, *43*, 1326–1344.

Steiner, J. E. Human facial expressions in response to taste and smell stimulation. *Advances in Child Development*, 1979, *13*, 257–295.

Steinschneider, A., Lipton, C. L., & Richmond, B. Auditory sensitivity in the infant: Effect of intensity on cardiac-motor activity. *Child Development*, 1966, *37*, 233–252.

Strauss, M. S. Abstraction of prototypical information by adults and 10-month-old infants. *Journal of Experimental Psychology, Human Learning and Memory*, 1979, *5*, 618–632.

Tronick, E., Als, H., Wise, S., & Brazelton, T. The infant's response to entrapment between contradictory messages in face-to-face interaction. *Journal of the American Academy of Child Psychiatry*, 1978, *17*, 1–13.

von Hofsten, C. Foundations for perceptual development. *Advances in Infancy Research*, 1982, *2*, 239–262.

Walk, R. *Perceptual development*. Monterey, CA: Brooks/Cole.

Walker, A. Intermodal perception of expressive behaviors in infants. *Journal of Experimental Child Psychology*, 1982, *33*, 514–535.

Watson, J. S. Operant conditioning of visual fixation in infants under visual and auditory reinforcements. *Developmental Psychology*, 1969, *1*, 508–516.

Watson, J., Hayes, L., Vietze, P., & Becker, J. Discrimination of infant smiling to orientations of talking faces of mothers and strangers. *Journal of Experimental Child Psychology*, 1979, *28*, 92–99.

Werner, J. S., & Lipsitt, L. P. The infancy of human sensory systems. In E. S. Gollin (Ed.), *Developmental plasticity: Behavioral and biological aspects of variation in development*. New York: Academic Press, 1981.

Wertheimer, M. Psychomotor coordination of auditory and visual space at birth. *Science*, 1961, *134*, 1692.

Wolff, P. H. Observations on the early development of smiling. In B. M. Foss (Ed.), *Determinants of infant behavior* (Vol. 2). New York: Wiley, 1963.

Yonas, A., Cleves, W., & Petterson, L. Infants' sensitivity to pictorial depth. *Science*, 1978, *200*, 77–79.

Younge-Browne, G., Rosenfeld, H. M., & Horowitz, F. D. Infant discrimination of facial expressions. *Child Development*, 1977, *48*, 555–567.

Author Index

Numbers in italics refer to the pages on which the complete references are cited.

A

Aboud, F., 283, *289*
Abramovitch, R., 282, *287*
Acredolo, C. P., 325, *342*
Adamson, L., 18, *22*, 193, 210, *219*
Ahrens, R., 193, 197, *213*, 334, *342*
Ainsworth, M. D., 309, *315*
Alberts, J. R., 325, *342*
Albon, S. D., 112, *115*
Allen, V. L., 278, 279, *287*, *288*
Als, H., 193, 208, 210, *213*, *219*, 335, *345*
Altmann, S. A., 79, *100*
Anderson, C. O., 135, 136, *149*
Andrew, R. J., 120, *149*
Anokhin, P. K., 227, *246*, 262, *266*
Apple, W., 177, *180*
Aron, M., 236, 239, *247*
Aslin, R. N., 325, *342*
Atkinson, J., 325, *342*
Atkinson, M. L., 279, *287*

B

Baerends, G. P., 105, 107, 108, *115*
Bain, A., 30, *48*
Bakeman, R., 18, *22*
Baken, R. J., 209, *219*
Baldwin, J. M., 17, *22*, 67, *74*
Barden, R. C., 283, *287*
Barlow, G., 64, *74*
Baron, R. A., 296, *315*
Barrera, M. E., 327, *342*
Barrett, P. H., 38, 39, 40, 41, 42, 47, *48*
Bates, E., 299, 301, *315*
Bateson, G., 15, 16, *22*
Bauermeister, R., 20, *22*
Beach, F. A., 200, *213*
Beatty, W. W., 199, *213*
Becker, J. D., 133, 137, *149*, 341, *346*

Bell, C., 30, 32, 33, 37, *49*
Benedict, H., 301, *315*
Benedict, R., 177, *178*
Benigni, L., 299, 301, *315*
Berger, P. L., 295, *315*
Berkson, G., 129, 133, 137, 138, *149*, *151*
Bernstein, N., 225, *246*
Bernstein, S., 121, 122, 123, 124, 129, 130, 145, *149*
Bernuth, H. V., 323, *343*
Bertrand, J., 200, *215*
Biscoe, B. M., 197, *215*
Blehar, M. C., 309, *315*
Blest, A. D., 108, *115*
Blurton-Jones, N., 282, *287*
Boal, L. M., 82, *100*
Boccia, M. L., 305, 307, 308, 309, 313, *315*
Bolwig, N., 341, *342*
Borchert, M., 82, *101*
Borke, H., 173, *178*
Bossema, I., 109, 112, *115*
Bourgeoise, J., *215*
Bowlby, J., 33, 251, *266*, 330, *342*
Bowman, R. E., 140, *151*
Boysen, S., 12, *24*
Braddick, O., 324, *342*
Bradshaw, G., 229, 232, 237, 238, 240, *248*
Brazelton, T. B., 208, 210, *213*, *214*, 235, *246*
Breland, K., 310, *315*
Bretherton, I., 299, 300, 301, *315*
Bridges, K. M. B., 165, *178*, 251, *266*
Brody, N., 200, *215*
Broerse, J., 323, *342*
Brooks, J., 168, *179*
Brooks-Gunn, J., 166, 170, *178*, 275, *287*
Brown, R., 56, *74*
Bruner, J. S., 21, *22*, 302, *318*
Brzelton, T., 335, *345*

347

Subject Index

A

Adaptation, *see* Evolution; Natural selection

Adrenocorticotropic hormone (ACTH), 201, 202

Affect, *see* Display; Emotion; State

Affect system, nature, of, 186, 187

Affective signaling, *see also* Signal
and external reference, 77–99
roles of, 93, 94, 185–213, 293, *see also* Emotional expression; Emotional state; Facial expression

Affective suppression, 271

Age and facial expression, 156–158, 162–166

Animal signal, *see* Signal, nonverbal

Animals
apes, 34, 43, 96, 97, 313
baboons, 72, 90
birds, 19, 43, 44, 66, 72, 87, 108, 142
blue tits (*Parus caeruleus*), 62, 106, 109
Burmese red junglefowl, 107
eagle, 62, 64, 85, 86, 94
hawks, 82
herring gulls (*Larus argentatus*), 66
jay (*Garrulus glandarius*), 109, 110
cattle, 44
chimpanzees, 11, 12, 45, 70, 97, 129
dogs, 35, 41, 44, 136, 139
foxes, 82
goats, 44
honeybee, 9, 77, 79, 97
horses, 32, 44
leopard, 81, 85, 86, 94, 95
lions, 32
mammals, 66

monkeys, 12, 34, 43, 78, 112, 312, 313
Japanese macques (*Macaca fuscata*), 83, 137, 143
Old World, 84, 86
raised in social isolation versus wild-born, 132–137, 140, 148
Rhesus macque, 19, 52, 55, 65, 78, 89–93, 95, 98, 117–149, 313, 329, 339, 340
neonatal Rhesus macaque, 141, 142, 147
toque macaque (*Macaca sinica*), 86–88, 93, 98
vervet monkeys (*Cercopithecus aethiops*), 62, 64, 81, 84–86, 88–90, 93, 95, 96, 98
wild-and laboratory-born, 138, 139
raccoon, 310
sheep, 44
snakes, 85, 86, 139, 140
squirrel
California ground (*Spermophilus beecheyi*), 82–86, 88, 89, 93, 98
ground (*Spermophilus beldingii*), 72
wolves, 313

Anthropomorphism, 32, 43

Appraisal mechanism, 141–145

Arousal state, 253

Arousal-plus-emotion attribution, 5

Associative naming versus representational symbolism, 96, 97

Asynchrony, 164, 165

Attachment, *see* Caregivers; Bonding

Auditory
abilities, 322, 323
emotional displays, 323–325

Automatic display rules, 20